Communications
in Computer and Information Science   1405

More information about this series at http://www.springer.com/series/7899

Hieyong Jeong · Kazuhiko Sumi (Eds.)

Frontiers of Computer Vision

27th International Workshop, IW-FCV 2021
Daegu, South Korea, February 22–23, 2021
Revised Selected Papers

Editors
Hieyong Jeong 🆔
Chonnam National University
Gwangju, Korea (Republic of)

Kazuhiko Sumi 🆔
Aoyama Gakuin University
Kanagawa, Japan

ISSN 1865-0929 ISSN 1865-0937 (electronic)
Communications in Computer and Information Science
ISBN 978-3-030-81637-7 ISBN 978-3-030-81638-4 (eBook)
https://doi.org/10.1007/978-3-030-81638-4

This Springer imprint is published by the registered company Springer Nature Switzerland AG
The registered company address is: Gewerbestrasse 11, 6330 Cham, Switzerland

Preface

The International Workshop on Frontiers of Computer Vision (IW-FCV) alternates annually between the Republic of Korea and Japan, and IW-FCV 2021 was hosted in Daegu, Republic of Korea. Although the workshop is hosted by a different country each year, the basic policy and format is determined by the Steering Committee to ensure continuous operation. This year was so particular because of COVID-19 pandemic situation. Although many international conferences or workshops were postponed or cancelled, our Steering Committee decided to hold the workshop virtually, to promote the exchange of research regardless of COVID-19 restrictions.

There were many technical problems to address to host and access IW-FCV 2021 online; however, researchers from seven different countries were still able to meet during February 22–23, 2021. It was such a pity not to be able to have some demo sessions, but IW-FCV 2021 still offered a rich program of informative talks and presentations. In total, 44 paper submissions were received despite the impacts of COVID-19. Each paper was reviewed by three reviewers from the Program Committee in a single-blind manner. After presentation at the workshop, 16 full papers and 8 short papers were selected for the post-workshop proceedings.

Thank you to all the committee members who made a great effort in planning and holding the event. We are grateful to the members of the Program Committee and the publication chair who were dedicated in creating a wonderful program and high-quality post-proceedings.

August 2021   Hieyong Jeong

Organization

Organizing Committee

General Chairs

Soon Ki Jung   Kyungpook National University, South Korea
Takio Kurita   Hiroshima University, Japan

Program Chairs

Hieyong Jeong   Chonnam National University, South Korea
Kazuhiko Sumi   Aoyama Gakuin University, Japan

Publication Chairs

Hieyong Jeong   Chonnam National University, South Korea
Kazuhiko Sumi   Aoyama Gakuin University, Japan

Publicity Chair

Hyeyoung Park   Kyungpook National University, South Korea

Local Arrangements Chair

Jaeil Kim   Kyungpook National University, South Korea

Financial Chair

Sang-hyo Park   Kyungpook National University, South Korea

Web Chair

Maryam Sultana   Kyungpook National University, South Korea

Steering Committee

Yoshimitsu Aoki	Keio University, Japan
Hiroyasu Koshimizu	YYC-Solution, Japan
Takio Kurita	Hiroshima University, Japan
Chikahito Nakajima	CRIEPI, Japan
Makoto Niwakawa	Meidensha, Japan
Rin-ichiro Tanaguchi	Kyushu University, Japan
Kazuhiko Yamamoto	Gifu University, Japan
Jun-ichiro Hayashi	Kagawa University, Japan
Kazuhiko Sumi	Aoyama Gakuin University, Japan
Kanghyun Jo	University of Ulsan, South Korea
Soon Ki Jung	Kyungpook National University, South Korea
Chilwoo Lee	Chonnam National University, South Korea
Weon-Geun Oh	ETRI, South Korea
Jong-Il Park	Hanyang University, South Korea

Main Sponsors

| Korean Computer Vision Society | Daegu Convention & Visitors Bureau | Kyungpook National University | Virtual Conference Host Microsoft Teams |

Contents

Human Behaviour

Algorithm/Application

Segmentation/Object Tracking

Robust Foreground Segmentation in RGBD Data from Complex Scenes Using Adversarial Networks

Maryam Sultana[1] , Thierry Bouwmans[2] , Jhony H. Giraldo[2] ,
and Soon Ki Jung[1(✉)]

[1] School of Computer Science and Engineering, Kyungpook National University,
Daegu, South Korea
{maryam,skjung}@knu.ac.kr
[2] Laboratoire MIA, La Rochelle Université, La Rochelle, France
{thierry.bouwmans,jgiral01}@univ-lr.fr

Abstract. Foreground segmentation is a fundamental problem in many artificial intelligence and computer vision based applications. However, robust foreground segmentation with high precision is still a challenging problem in complex scenes. Currently, many of the existing algorithms process the input data in RGB space only, where the foreground segmentation performance is most likely degraded by various challenges like shadows, color camouflage, illumination changes, out of range camera sensors and bootstrapping. Cameras capturing RGBD data are highly active visual sensors as they provide depth information along with RGB of the given input images. Therefore, to address the challenging problem we propose a foreground segmentation algorithm based on conditional generative adversarial networks using RGB and depth data. The goal of our proposed model is to perform robust foreground segmentation in the presence of various complex scenes with high accuracy. For this purpose, we trained our GAN based CNN model with RGBD input data conditioned on ground-truth information in an adversarial fashion. During training, our proposed model aims to learn the foreground segmentation on the basis of cross-entropy loss and euclidean distance loss to identify between real vs fake samples. While during testing the model is given RGBD input to the trained generator network that performs robust foreground segmentation. Our proposed method is evaluated using two RGBD benchmark datasets that are SBM-RGBD and MULTIVISION kinect. Various experimental evaluations and comparative analysis of our proposed model with eleven existing methods confirm its superior performance.

Keywords: Foreground segmentation · Generative adversarial networks · Supervised learning

1 Introduction

One of the major step in many applications of artificial intelligence and computer vision includes foreground segmentation in tasks like image in painting [26], object

© Springer Nature Switzerland AG 2021
H. Jeong and K. Sumi (Eds.): IW-FCV 2021, CCIS 1405, pp. 3–16, 2021.
https://doi.org/10.1007/978-3-030-81638-4_1

detection [10,29], video surveillance [2], visual object tracking [31] and salient motion detection [5]. Foreground segmentation is a result of dynamic background subtraction. In practice, robust foreground segmentation becomes very challenging in the presence of complex scenes containing illumination changes, color camouflage, shadows, or bootstrapping [17]. Many existing algorithms use only RGB information from video frames to address the problem of foreground segmentation in complex scenes. The reason to use RGB information is that it provides a lot of useful information to segment foregrounds [1,9,20,21,25]. But the recent availability of the depth information captured from the stereo vision to off-the-shelf RGBD camera sensors has presented a new domain to deal with the foreground segmentation problem in complex scenes. Moreover, the dense depth information captured by the RGBD cameras is very useful for foreground segmentation in indoor complex scenes as it does not suffer from the aforementioned challenges that affect color-based algorithms [17]. The existing set of algorithms train two different models for RGB and depth information then obtain foreground segmentation masks and post-processed the final results by combining both of the outputs [14,27]. However, noisy depth information causes performance degradation in these algorithms.

In this work we proposed an algorithm based on conditional generative adversarial network (CGAN) [11] using combined RGBD data to address the challenging problem of robust foreground segmentation in complex scenes. The basic objective of our proposed model named 'CGAN-RGBD' is to obtain foreground segmentation masks with high accuracy from various complex scenes. We perform training of our GAN based CNN model with RGBD input data conditioned on ground-truth (foreground segmentation masks) in an adversarial fashion. In the training module, our proposed CGAN-RGBD model aims to learn foreground segmentation using cross-entropy loss and euclidean distance loss for the identification of real vs fake samples. Whereas during testing the model is given input with RGBD frames information to the generator network that performs robust foreground segmentation with high precision. The main contributions of this study are summarized as follows:

- Our proposed model is novel in terms of the application using CGANs.
- CGAN-RGBD is free from the limitation of training separate models using RGB and Depth as done by existing methods [14,27] rather it processed the input in a combined way and thus achieving high accuracy.
- The experimental evaluation of our proposed CGAN-RGBD model on benchmark SBM-RGBD and MULTIVISION kinect datasets achieving high accuracy in comparison to various existing methods shows the strength of our model.

The rest of the paper is organized as follows: Sect. 2 explains the details of existing methods addressing the problem of foreground segmentation in complex scenes.

Section 3 provides a brief description of our proposed CGAN-RGBD model. In Sect. 4 we explained the details of the implementation settings of CGAN-RGBD, while Sect. 5 discusses the experimental evaluations on two benchmark datasets SBM-RGBD and MULTIVISION kinect. We present the conclusion of this study in Sect. 6.

2   Related Work

Over the past two decades for the challenging problem of robust foreground objects segmentation in complex scenes many algorithms have been proposed that exploit RGB as well as depth information [4, 6, 8, 12, 14, 16, 23, 24, 28, 30, 32]. Javed *et al.* [14] proposed a Robust Principal Component Analysis (RPCA) based method for foreground segmentation in complex scenes. The model is called 'Spatiotemporal Robust Principal Component Analysis' (SRPCA) is a hybrid RPCA based approach with Spatio-temporal constraints. SRPCA is a graph-regularized algorithm that preserves the Spatio-temporal information of the low-rank background in the form of dual spectral graphs. SRPCA performs foreground object segmentation with two separate models RGB and Depth and then it combines the outputs from each model for final results. Another existing model called SOBS [18] is based on self-organizing neural networks that show improved performance using RGB and depth features. Xiaowei Zhou *et al.* [32] proposed an algorithm named 'Moving Object Detection by Detecting Contiguous Outliers in the Low-Rank Representation' (DECOLOR). This method works with Markov random field approach to reconstruct the missing context of foreground segmentation. Furthermore, Bo Xin *et al.* [30] proposed a technique named 'Background Subtraction via Generalized Fused Lasso Foreground Modeling' (BS-GFL). The main objective of this model is to address the challenging problem of missing information in foreground segmentation caused by challenges of illumination changes and dynamic background information. In this method, generalized fused lasso regularization is considered for searching the intact structured foreground objects in order to recover the missing context during the segmentation process. Massimo De Gregorio *et al.* [6] proposed a method called 'cwisardH+' that works by decoupling the RGB information from the depth information of the pixels. The two input videos run synchronously but independently for this algorithm and are modeled by the weightless neural network at the pixel level.

3   Proposed Methodology

CGAN-RGBD is a conditional generative adversarial network working with two deep neural networks, a discriminator network and a generator network as shown in the Fig. 1. The discriminator network (D) aims to distinguish between real (training images) vs fake (generated images) samples. However, the generator network (G) aims to create realistic fake image samples to fool the discriminator network. Given a probability distribution $z \sim p_z$, the generator network defines a

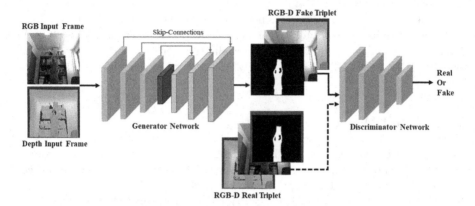

Fig. 1. CGAN-RGBD systematic training framework. The images shown in this figure are from challenging category 'Color Camouflage', video sequence 'Cespatx_ds', SBM-RGBD dataset [3].

probability distribution refereed as p_g to be the distribution of the samples $G(z)$. The main goal of a GAN model is to learn the generator network's distribution p_g that approximates the real input data distribution p_{data}. Both of the models are simultaneously optimized using the following objective function:

$$\max_D \min_G \ \mathcal{L}_1(D, G) = \mathbb{E}_{x,y\sim p_{data}(x,y)}[log(D(x,y))]$$
$$+ \mathbb{E}_{z\sim p_z(z),x\sim p_{data}(x)}[log(1 - D(x, G(z,x)))]. \tag{1}$$

Another loss we have exploited besides the above mentioned adversarial loss is Euclidean distance loss term between real vs fake training samples [13]. This classical euclidean distance data loss is used because it encourages the straight and accurate regression of the target input samples during training. Euclidean distance loss is formulated as follows

$$\mathcal{L}_2(G) = \mathbb{E}_{x,y,z}[||y - G(z,x)||], \tag{2}$$

where x is RGBD input frame as shown in the Fig. 1, z is random noise vector, y is the target or ground-truth (foreground segmentation mask) and $G(z, x)$ is the generated output by the generator network. Both of the networks, discriminator and generator are simultaneously optimized by the final training objective given as follows:

$$arg \ \max_D \min_G \ (\mathcal{L}_1(D, G) + \lambda \mathcal{L}_2(G)). \tag{3}$$

3.1 Unet Generator Network

The generator network in our proposed CGAN-RGBD model is a Unet based encoder-decoder with skip connections [22]. The input is downsampled using five convolutional layers as shown in the Fig. 2. Each convolutional operation is

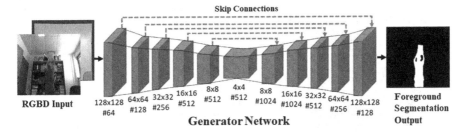

Fig. 2. Unet based generator network architecture of our proposed CGAN-RGBD method [19]. The images shown in this figure as from challenging category 'Color Camouflage', video sequence 'Cespatx_ds', SBM-RGBD dataset [3]

applied with stride 2 for downsampling the input feature maps. While in the decoding part the feature maps of downsampling part are concatenated with the upsampling part in the form of skip connections. The idea of skip connections helps the encoder-decoder CNN model to fuse the localization (information captured from the downsampling part) and the context (information captured from the upsampling part) of the deep features. All weights in Unet are randomly initialized and LeakyReLU activations are exploited in all the layers except in the last layer that uses `Tanh` activation function to generate foreground segmentation outputs. Furthermore, the noise z in Unet model only exists is in the form of dropouts and is applied on various decoding layers at training as well as testing time.

3.2 PatchGAN Discriminator Network

The discriminator in our proposed CGAN-RGBD model works on the idea of PatchGANs [13]. Its basic goal is to perform real vs fake classification on the $N \times N$ overlapping patches on the input as shown in the Fig. 3. The PatchGAN discriminator network is very beneficial as it has fewer parameters in contrast to a full image discriminator formulation. Moreover, it also has the potential to process arbitrarily sized input images as it is a Fully Convolutional Network (FCN) [13]. PatchGAN penalizes the structures in input images only at the scale of over lapping patches. It runs convolutional operations in the given input image and average the responses to provide the final output. The last convolutional output consisting of single channel is of size 30×30 where each element corresponds to the classification of one patch in the given input image [13] as shown in the Fig. 3. All weights in PatchGAN discriminator are also randomly initialized with 3×3 spatial kernels. The activation function exploited in this network is also leakyReLU.

RGBD Input

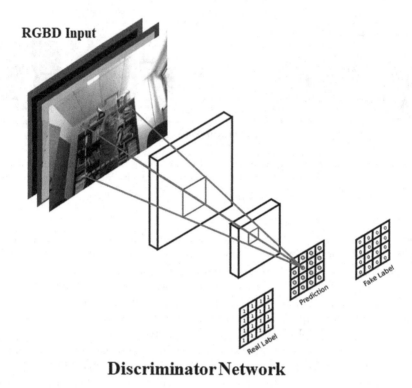

Discriminator Network

Fig. 3. PatchGAN based discriminator network architecture of our proposed CGAN-RGBD method [7]. The images shown in this figure are from challenging category 'Color Camouflage', video sequence 'Cespatx_ds', SBM-RGBD dataset [3].

4   Implementation

Our proposed method CGAN-RGBD model is a conditional GAN with a discriminator network and a generator network architectures described in sub Sects. 3.2 and 3.1. Both of the networks use the systematic formulation of convolution-BatchNorm-LReLu [13]. We trained our model on the fixed input size ($256 \times 256 \times 4$) conditioned with respect to its ground-truth information. CGAN-RGBD is optimized using Adam [15] with parameters, momentum $\beta = 0.5$ and learning rate $= 0.0002$ for 300 epochs. The training is done on augmented input RGBD data by random flipping of the samples. While for the case of testing on the given input RGBD frame the generator will perform foreground segmentation.

5   Experiments

We performed extensive experimental analysis on two benchmark datasets 'Scene Background Modeling RGBD' (SBM-RGBD) [3] and 'MULTIVISION kinect' [8]. We compared our proposed CGAN-RGBD model with several existing methods including SRPCA [14], BS-GFL [30], cwisardH+ [6], DECOLOR [32], RGB-SOBS [16], CB [8], KDE [28], DECB [8], CB4D [8], RSBS [12] and SAFBS [4]. For the quantitative evaluation of our proposed CGAN-RGBD model we exploited the following metrics:

Percentage of Wrong Classifications (PWC):

$$PWC = 100 \times \frac{(F_p + F_n)}{(F_p + F_n + T_p + T_n)}, \tag{4}$$

False Positive Rate (FPR):

$$FPR = \frac{F_p}{F_p + T_n}, \tag{5}$$

Jaccard Similarity (JS):

$$JS = \frac{T_p}{T_p + F_n + F_p}, \tag{6}$$

Recall (Re):

$$Re = \frac{T_p}{T_p + F_n}, \tag{7}$$

Precision (Pre):

$$Pre = \frac{T_p}{T_p + F_p}, \tag{8}$$

F1 Score:

$$F1 = 2\frac{Pre \times Re}{Pre + Re}, \tag{9}$$

where T_n is True negatives, T_p is True positives, F_p is False positives, F_n is False negatives.

5.1   Evaluation of CGAN-RGBD on SBM-RGBD Dataset

The SBM-RGBD [3] is a benchmark dataset specifically designed for the evaluation and comparison of various methods for foreground segmentation on RGBD videos. SBM-RGBD is the most extensive dataset for RGBD videos in complex scenes that is ever made for this specific task. We performed experiments on six challenging categories of this dataset. The detailed discussion is as follows:

Intermittent Motion challenging category contains six videos including dynamic foregrounds that either stop moving (e.g. abandoned objects) or they were initially static and then start moving again. On average of all videos in this category our proposed CGAN-RGBD model achieved best scores for all the evaluation metrics as shown in the Table 1. The best F1 score achieved by our

Table 1. Quantitative results of our proposed CGAN-RGBD method for each category of the on six metrics using SBM-RGBD dataset. The best results are highlighted with red color for each metric in each challenging category. Where IM* is 'Intermittent Motion'.

Categories	PWC ↓	FPR ↓	JS ↑	Re ↑	Pre ↑	F1 ↑
IM*	1.222	0.022	0.960	0.977	0.981	0.979
Out of Range	0.242	0.017	0.975	0.982	0.992	0.987
Shadows	0.143	0.559	0.982	0.994	0.998	0.991
Bootstrapping	0.863	0.011	0.977	0.988	0.988	0.988
Color Camouflage	0.612	0.009	0.954	0.992	0.962	0.976
Depth Camouflage	0.062	0.065	0.895	0.935	0.949	0.942
Average	0.524	0.113	0.957	0.978	0.978	0.977

Table 2. CGAN-RGBD quantitative performance comparison with five existing approaches on the basis of F1 score. The best results are highlighted with red color for each challenging category. Where IM* is 'Intermittent Motion'

Categories	CGAN-RGBD	SRPCA	cwisardH+	BS-GFL	RGB-SOBS	DECOLOR
IM*	0.979	0.773	0.663	0.400	0.539	0.460
Out of Range	0.987	0.801	0.898	0.718	0.852	0.587
Shadows	0.991	0.759	0.926	0.586	0.921	0.905
Bootstrapping	0.988	0.809	0.566	0.571	0.800	0.760
Color Camouflage	0.976	0.832	0.951	0.733	0.486	0.703
Depth Camouflage	0.942	0.808	0.764	0.754	0.893	0.725
Average	0.977	0.746	0.746	0.580	0.706	0.660

proposed CGAN-RGBD model is 0.979 while the second best score is achieved by SRPCA method of 0.773 as shown in Table 2. The visual results of our proposed CGAN-RGBD model as compared to ground-truth and other existing methods are shown in the Fig. 4. The reason of best performance of our proposed model is that it does not work on the assumption that the background should be static and foreground should be dynamic.

Out of Range challenging category contains five videos with foreground and background objects that are either too close from the camera (sensor) or too far from it. Our proposed CGAN-RGBD model has again achieved best results for this category too with an average F1 score of 0.987 while cwisardH+ method has obtained second best score of 0.898. The visual results are shown in the Fig. 4 as compared to existing methods and ground truth information.

Shadows challenging category also contains five videos with shadows mainly caused by foregrounds. All the videos have either visible-light shadows in the RGB channels or there could be IR shadows in the depth channel [3]. Once again our proposed CGAN-RGBD model has achieved best results as shown in Table 1 and 2 with an average F1 score of 0.991 while again cwisardH+ method has obtained second best score of 0.926. The qualitative results are shown in the Fig. 4 as compared to two existing methods and ground truth.

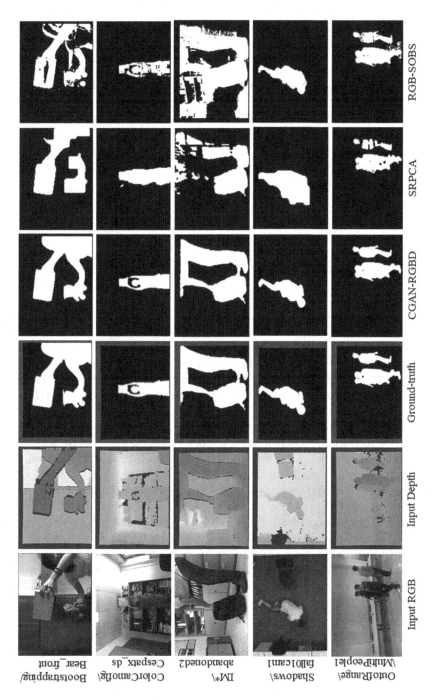

Fig. 4. Visual performance comparison of our proposed CGAN-RGBD model with two existing methods and ground-truth on SBM-RGBD dataset.

Table 3. CGAN-RGBD quantitative performance comparison on MULTIVISION kinect [8] dataset with five existing approaches on the basis of F1 score. The best results are highlighted with red color for each challenging category. Where IM* is 'Intermittent Motion'.

Methods /Video Sequences	ChairBox	Hallway	Shelves	Wall	Average
CGAN-RGBD	0.987	0.983	0.970	0.967	0.976
CB	0.847	0.555	0.699	0.843	0.736
RGB-KDE	0.881	0.632	0.885	0.918	0.829
CB-D	0.854	0.770	0.835	0.595	0.763
D-KDE	0.933	0.923	0.709	0.665	0.807
DECB	0.914	0.783	0.848	0.938	0.870
CB4D	0.886	0.617	0.711	0.868	0.770
RSBS	0.895	0.843	0.900	N/A	0.879
RGBD-KDE	0.962	0.873	0.921	0.886	0.910
SAFBS	0.910	0.745	0.894	0.930	0.869

Bootstrapping challenging category also has five videos with foreground in all the frames that means no pure background information is available. It can be seen in Table 2 that our proposed method has achieved highest F1 score of 0.988 and SRPCA has achieved second best score of 0.809. The main reason behind the best performance of our proposed CGAN-RGBD model is that it is not dependent on pure background information as input to segment foregrounds. Therefore, this challenging complex scene situation does not effect the performance of our proposed model.

Color Camouflage challenging category contains four videos with foregrounds that have similar color statistics as the background information. On average our proposed model obtained the best F1 score of 0.976 while cwisardH+ method has obtained the second best score of 0.951 as shown in the Table 2.

Depth Camouflage challenging category also contains four videos with foregrounds that are very close in depth with the background information. Our proposed CGAN-RGBD method has outperformed all the existing methods with a F1 score of 0.942. While RGB-SOBS method has performed second best in this challenging category with a F1 score of 0.893. The quantitative results of all the evaluation metrics are presented in Table 1 and 2.

On the average of all the six challenging categories our proposed CGAN-RGBD model has achieved best score F1 score of 0.977 while SRPCA has performed second best with a F1 score of 0.746.

5.2   Evaluation of CGAN-RGBD on MULTIVISION Kinect Dataset

Another dataset we have exploited to evaluate our proposed CGAN-RGBD model is MULTIVISION kinect dataset [8]. This dataset has four video sequences

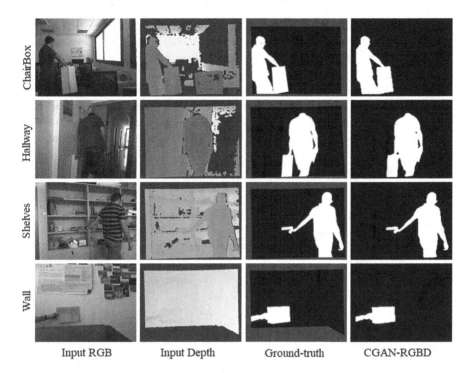

Fig. 5. Qualitative performance comparison of CGAN-RGBD with ground-truth for foreground segmentation on MULTIVISION kinect [8] dataset.

('ChairBox', 'Hallway', 'Shelves' and 'Wall') captured by a Kinect camera. It contains various complex scenes like flickering lights causing sudden illumination changes, color and depth camouflage and out of range sensor range depth data. Table 3 shows the quantitative results of our proposed CGAN-RGBD model with five existing methods on the basis of F1 score. On average of all the four video sequences our proposed CGAN-RGBD model has achieved the best F1 score of 0.976 while RGBD-KDE method has achieved the second best score of 0.910. The visual results presented in Fig. 5 shows that our proposed CGAN-RGBD model has the strength to segment foreground objects with high precision in various complex scenes.

6   Conclusion

In this study, we presented a robust foreground segmentation algorithm in various complex scenes based on conditional generative adversarial networks using RGB and depth information. The primary aim of our proposed model 'CGAN-RGBD' is to perform foreground segmentation in the presence of complex scenes with challenges like illumination changes, bootstrapping, shadows and color camouflage. In order to address this problem we trained our model with RGB as well as depth channels conditioned on ground-truth information using an adversarial fashion. During training our proposed CGAN-RGBD model learns to perform foreground segmentation on the basis of cross-entropy loss that is classification between real vs fake samples and also euclidean distance loss that is the visual difference between the real input and the generated data. Furthermore, in testing the model is given RGBD input and the trained U-net based generator performs robust foreground segmentation. The quantitative and qualitative performance comparison of our proposed CGAN-RGBD method on two benchmark datasets (SBM-RGBD and MULTIVISION kinect) with eleven existing methods shows the strength of our proposed algorithm for foreground segmentation in various complex scenes.

Acknowledgment. This study was supported by the BK21 FOUR project (AI-driven Convergence Software Education Research Program) funded by the Ministry of Education, School of Computer Science and Engineering, Kyungpook National University, Korea (4199990214394).

References

1. Bouwmans, T., Javed, S., Sultana, M., Jung, S.K.: Deep neural network concepts for background subtraction: a systematic review and comparative evaluation. Neural Netw. **117**, 8–66 (2019)
2. Bouwmans, T., Zahzah, E.H.: Robust PCA via principal component pursuit: a review for a comparative evaluation in video surveillance. Comput. Vis. Image Underst. **122**, 22–34 (2014)
3. Camplani, M., Maddalena, L., Gabriel, M., Petrosino, A., Salgado, L.: RGB-D dataset: background learning for detection and tracking from RGBD videos. In: IEEE ICIAP-Workshops (2017)
4. Chacon-Murguia, M.I., Orozco-Rodriguez, H.E., Ramirez-Quintana, J.A.: Self-adapting fuzzy model for dynamic object detection using RGB-D information. IEEE Sens. J. **17**(23), 7961–7970 (2017)
5. Chen, Y., Zou, W., Tang, Y., Li, X., Xu, C., Komodakis, N.: SCOM: spatiotemporal constrained optimization for salient object detection. IEEE Trans. Image Process. **27**(7), 3345–3357 (2018)
6. De Gregorio, M., Giordano, M.: Cwisardh+: background detection in RGBD videos by learning of weightless neural networks. In: Battiato, S., Farinella, G., Leo, M., Gallo, G. (eds.) International Conference on Image Analysis and Processing, vol. 10590, pp. 242–253. Springer, Heidelberg (2017). https://doi.org/10.1007/978-3-319-70742-6_23
7. Demir, U., Unal, G.: Patch-based image inpainting with generative adversarial networks. arXiv preprint arXiv:1803.07422 (2018)
8. Fernandez-Sanchez, E.J., Diaz, J., Ros, E.: Background subtraction based on color and depth using active sensors. Sensors **13**(7), 8895–8915 (2013)
9. Garcia-Garcia, B., Bouwmans, T., Silva, A.J.R.: Background subtraction in real applications: challenges, current models and future directions. Comput. Sci. Rev. **35**, 100204 (2020)
10. Giraldo, J.H., Javed, S., Bouwmans, T.: Graph moving object segmentation. IEEE Trans. Pattern Anal. Mach. Intell. (2020)

11. Goodfellow, I., et al.: Generative adversarial nets. In: Advances in Neural Information Processing Systems, pp. 2672–2680 (2014)
12. Huang, J., Wu, H., Gong, Y., Gao, D.: Random sampling-based background subtraction with adaptive multi-cue fusion in RGBD videos. In: 2016 9th International Congress on Image and Signal Processing, Biomedical Engineering and Informatics (CISP-BMEI), pp. 30–35. IEEE (2016)
13. Isola, P., Zhu, J.Y., Zhou, T., Efros, A.A.: Image-to-image translation with conditional adversarial networks. In: Proceedings of the IEEE Conference on Computer Vision and Pattern Recognition, pp. 1125–1134 (2017)
14. Javed, S., Bouwmans, T., Sultana, M., Jung, S.K.: Moving object detection on RGB-D videos using graph regularized spatiotemporal RPCA. In: Battiato, S., Farinella, G., Leo, M., Gallo, G. (eds.) International Conference on Image Analysis and Processing, vol. 10590, pp. 230–241. Springer, Heidelberg (2017). https://doi.org/10.1007/978-3-319-70742-6_22
15. Kingma, D.P., Ba, J.: Adam: a method for stochastic optimization. In: 3rd International Conference on Learning Representations, ICLR 2015, San Diego, CA, USA, 7–9 May 2015, Conference Track Proceedings (2015)
16. Maddalena, L., Petrosino, A.: The sobs algorithm: what are the limits? In: 2012 IEEE Computer Society Conference on Computer Vision and Pattern Recognition Workshops (CVPRW), pp. 21–26. IEEE (2012)
17. Maddalena, L., Petrosino, A.: Background subtraction for moving object detection in RGBD data: a survey. J. Imaging 4(5), 71 (2018)
18. Maddalena, L., Petrosino, A., et al.: A self-organizing approach to background subtraction for visual surveillance applications. IEEE Trans. Image Process. 17(7), 1168 (2008)
19. Midoh, Y., Nakamae, K.: Image quality enhancement of a cd-sem image using conditional generative adversarial networks. In: Metrology, Inspection, and Process Control for Microlithography XXXIII, vol. 10959, p. 109590B. International Society for Optics and Photonics (2019)
20. Minematsu, T., Shimada, A., Taniguchi, R.: Rethinking background and foreground in deep neural network-based background subtraction. In: 2020 IEEE International Conference on Image Processing (ICIP), pp. 3229–3233. IEEE (2020)
21. Minematsu, T., Shimada, A., Uchiyama, H., Taniguchi, R.: Analytics of deep neural network-based background subtraction. J. Imaging 4(6), 78 (2018)
22. Ronneberger, O., Fischer, P., Brox, T.: U-net: convolutional networks for biomedical image segmentation. In: Navab, N., Hornegger, J., Wells, W., Frangi, A. (eds.) International Conference on Medical image computing and computer-assisted intervention, vol. 9351, pp. 234–241. Springer, Heidelberg (2015). https://doi.org/10.1007/978-3-319-24574-4_28
23. Sultana, M., Mahmood, A., Bouwmans, T., Jung, S.K.: Dynamic background subtraction using least square adversarial learning. In: 2020 IEEE International Conference on Image Processing (ICIP), pp. 3204–3208. IEEE (2020)
24. Sultana, M., Mahmood, A., Bouwmans, T., Ki Jung, S.: Complete moving object detection in the context of robust subspace learning. In: Proceedings of the IEEE International Conference on Computer Vision Workshops (2019)
25. Sultana, M., Mahmood, A., Javed, S., Jung, S.K.: Unsupervised deep context prediction for background estimation and foreground segmentation. Mach. Vis. Appl. (2018). https://doi.org/10.1007/s00138-018-0993-0
26. Sultana, M., Mahmood, A., Javed, S., Jung, S.K.: Unsupervised deep context prediction for background foreground separation. arXiv preprint arXiv:1805.07903 (2018)

27. Sultana, M., Mahmood, A., Javed, S., Jung, S.K.: Unsupervised RGBD video object segmentation using GANs. In: Asian Conference on Computer Vision (2018)
28. Trabelsi, R., Jabri, I., Smach, F., Bouallegue, A.: Efficient and fast multi-modal foreground-background segmentation using RGBD data. Pattern Recogn. Lett. **97**, 13–20 (2017)
29. Wu, Y., He, X., Nguyen, T.Q.: Moving object detection with a freely moving camera via background motion subtraction. IEEE Trans. Circuits Syst. Video Technol. **27**(2), 236–248 (2017)
30. Xin, B., Tian, Y., Wang, Y., Gao, W.: Background subtraction via generalized fused lasso foreground modeling. In: Proceedings of the IEEE Conference on Computer Vision and Pattern Recognition, pp. 4676–4684 (2015)
31. Zhang, T., Liu, S., Ahuja, N., Yang, M.H., Ghanem, B.: Robust visual tracking via consistent low-rank sparse learning. Int. J. Comput. Vision **111**(2), 171–190 (2015)
32. Zhou, X., Yang, C., Yu, W.: Moving object detection by detecting contiguous outliers in the low-rank representation. IEEE T-PAMI **35**(3), 597–610 (2013)

Robust Tracking via Feature Enrichment and Overlap Maximization

Mustansar Fiaz[1] , Kamran Ali[2], Sang Bin Yun[1], Ki Yeol Baek[1], Hye Jin Lee[1],
In Su Kim[1], Arif Mahmood[3], Sehar Shahzad Farooq[1], and Soon Ki Jung[1(✉)]

[1] School of Computer Science and Engineering, Kyungpook National University,
Daegu, Republic of Korea
{mustansar,skjung}@knu.ac.kr
[2] Department of Computer Science, University of Central Florida, Orland, USA
kamran@nights.ucf.edu
[3] Department of Computer Science, Information Technology University,
Lahore, Pakistan
arif.mahmood@itu.edu.pk

Abstract. Recently, Convolutional Neural Networks (CNNs) based approaches have demonstrated an impressive gain over conventional approaches which resulted in rapid development of various visual object tracker. However, these advancements are limited in terms of accuracy due to the distractors available in the videos. Moreover, most of the deep trackers operate on low-resolution features, such as template matching, which are semantically reliable but are spatially less accurate. We propose an efficient feature enrichment module within tracking framework to learn the contextual reliable information and spatially accurate feature representation. Proposed feature enrichment combines enriched feature sets by exploiting contextual information from multiple scales as well as preserving the spatial information details. We integrate proposed feature enrichment module within baseline ATOM which solves the tracking problem by target estimation and classification components. The former component estimates the target based on IoU-predictor, while the later component is trained online to enforce high discrimination power. Experimental study over three benchmarks including VOT2015, VOT2016, and VOT2017 revealed that proposed feature enrichment module boosts the tracker accuracy.

Keywords: Feature enrichment · Convolutional Neural Networks · Visual Object Tracking · Dual attention

1 Introduction

Visual Object Tracking (VOT) is a primary computer vision research problem, which aims to identify the location of the target object in videos. VOT has become popular among researchers owing to wide range of applications such as robotics, intelligent surveillance, activity recognition, scene understanding, and

© Springer Nature Switzerland AG 2021
H. Jeong and K. Sumi (Eds.): IW-FCV 2021, CCIS 1405, pp. 17–30, 2021.
https://doi.org/10.1007/978-3-030-81638-4_2

autonomous vehicles. In VOT, initial target information is given in the bounding box at the first frame of a video and objective is to estimate the new target position in the incoming frames. In the past few decade, many VOT algorithms have been proposed, but it is still an open challenge due to complex and challenging scenarios such as occlusion, motion blur, deformation, background clutter, scale changes, illumination variations, and many more.

There exists two types of tracking approaches i.e., generative and discriminative tracking methods. In the former case, a target appearance representation is build based on minimum reconstruction error and model finds the best candidate for the next frames [30,40,44], while in the later case, tracking problem is solved as regression or classification problem [1,35,45]. Discriminative trackers requires a lot of training data to train and update the model parameters, which increases the computational complexity. Various Correlation Filter based discriminative Trackers (CFTs) have been proposed which exploit large training samples using circular samples. In the current times, Convolutional Neural Networks (CNNs) have demonstrated an astonishing performance gain in many applications such as video object segmentation [18], object detection [21], and scene understanding [47]. Fiaz et al. [14,15] performed an extensive study and their findings shows that deep feature based trackers exhibit better performance compared to other handcrafted feature based trackers. However, training deep trackers is a tedious job, due to data hungry property, to get better results. There exists many deep trackers [8,9,36] that operate with pretrained models to get better target representation but they are incapable to tackle different target variations. In order to tackle this issue, online model update is utilized [12,37,49]. Nevertheless, the model may incur overfitting problem owing to noisy updates. In addition, this process will also add computational burden due to feature extraction and update steps.

While recent years, we have witnessed that Siamese-based trackers have attained much attention because of balanced robustness and accuracy [3,11,13,16,17,22,23]. Siamese trackers perform tracking based on template matching from the first frame. Siamese trackers have demonstrated outstanding performance but still incur performance degradation under various challenging scenarios. Attention networks [17,19,39,43] have been integrated within the Siamese tracking frameworks to achieve efficient features but yet it is an open challenge as target may undergo many appearance variations. Moreover. Existing CNN-based deep trackers have shown remarkable performance and can learn strong generalization over large scale of datasets especially in Siamese tracking frameworks. Deep trackers operates over the low resolution features from the pre-trained models which are more semantic features. The downside of these features is that they may lose the detailed spatial information for better tracking. In addition, these low resolution features which encodes contextual information are less effective due to limited receptive fields.

In this article, we propose a feature enrichment module which encodes crucial contextual information such that it not only removes the undesired degraded information but also preserves the fine detailed spatial information to get powerful discriminative features for better tracking. To do so, we develop a multi-scale feature enrichment model that processes the low-resolution features to generates contextually enriched features as well as spatially more reliable features representation. The proposed module dynamically selects the most important feature kernels using semantic feature selection module based on self-attention technique. In other words, the proposed module fuses features from different receptive fields, while preserving their complementary discriminative information. We utilized ATOM [7] as our baseline tracker, and integrated our proposed feature enrichment module within it, which is composed of two-stage tracking framework including target estimation network and target classification network. The target is coarsely located based on IoU-Net [26] which is offline trained in the former network, while the later stage is based on regression online network to get the fine target location. We preformed extensive experiments over three publicly available datasets such as VOT2015 [28], VOT2016 [29], and VOT2017 [27]. Experimental resulted demonstrates that our feature enrichment module boosts the performance compared to other state-of-the-art trackers.

We summarize our contributions in this article as:

- We propose a feature enrichment module which operates over low-resolution features to generate contextually enriched more precise feature representation.
- We validate the effectiveness of our module by integrating in ATOM tracker. The experimental results were computed over VOT2015, VOT2016, and VOT2017 datasets.

The rest of the article is organized as: Sect. 2 presents the related study, while Sect. 3 explains the details of the proposed tracking framework. Section 4 has our experimental details and finally Sect. 5 has the summary of this paper.

2   Related Work

In recent times, though machine learning approaches including deep learning has been performing tracking at its best. Still, visual tracking is facing several shortcomings. Using deep learning features and its ability to achieve higher performance using limited training data, several deep features are merged using correlation filter tracking for performance boost. As an example, pretrained models (AlexNet, ResNet etc.) have been benefited from deep learning extracting feature capabilities in at multiple layers for accuracy and robustness of tracking [9,36,38]. However, it is been explained in [4] that the incompatible resolutions and unknown target objects along with increasing dimensions are restraints for fetching performance boost. There has been several applications of deep learning in the literature for classification and regression [24,37,41]. A combination of Support Vector machines (SVM) in Convolution Neural network (CNN) is employed with saliency map to perform classification [24]. In [37] Multi-domain dependent online deep tracker employed classification task using a practical filter framework. In comparison to deep networks, these trackers use powerful feature representations but lacks in performance with noisy updates during an online learning and require an additional computation upon updating networks.

Recently, several Siamese networks are used in tracking problem to handle accuracy and speed [3,6,13,16,42]. Moreover, attention networks are widely used owing to better feature discrimination within Siamese tracking framework [17, 19,39,43]. Although, these methods have increased the tracking performance by generating discriminative features. We argue that there is still space to generate more robust and efficient features. In addition, most of the trackers proceed with low level features which are spatially less accurate. Therefore, we propose a feature enrichment module to generate spatially more precise and contextually more reliable features.

3   Proposed Method

In this section, first we present an overview of our baseline tracker, as shown in Fig. 1, and then provide a detailed explanation of our proposed feature enrichment module.

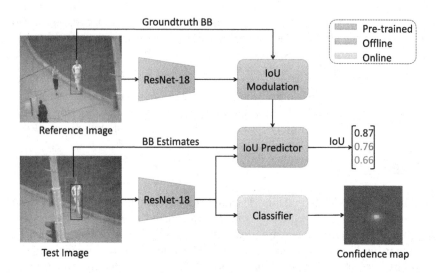

Fig. 1. The pipeline of ATOM tracker [7]. IoU Modulation and Predictors are part of target estimation networks and are trained offline, while classifier is trained online

3.1   Overview of ATOM

In these days, Discriminative Correlation Filter-based (DCF) and Region Proposal Network (RPN)-based techniques are popular in the field of single object tracking. Existing DCF and RPN based trackers lack in flexible scale adaptability and sufficient discriminative feature power respectively. Danelljan et al.

[7] proposed ATOM tracking framework, as illustrated in Fig. 1, to efficiently handle the trade-off between aforementioned trackers' characteristics. ATOM is composed of two subnetworks (1) target estimation network and (2) target classification network and are explained below.

Target Estimation Network: ATOM tracker utilizes IoU-Net within the target estimation network as displayed in Fig. 2, which is trained such that it estimates the IoU score between the groundtruth and predicted Bounding Boxes (BB) for the input images. ATOM uses PrPool [26] to pool the region of interest within the bounding box information. For a given input image, the features are extracted from backbone network, represented as $x \in \mathcal{R}^{C \times H \times W}$, and forwarded to PrPool along with BB of the object. ATOM predicts the IoU score for given input image and BB estimates.

Target Classification Network: ATOM uses two fully convolutional layers as classification network during the test time, and is defined as.

$$f(x; w) = \psi_2(w_2 * \psi_1(w_1 * x)), \tag{1}$$

where w_1, w_2 represents the convolutional filter applied over input features x, while ψ_1 and ψ_2 indicates the activation functions. The standard convolution

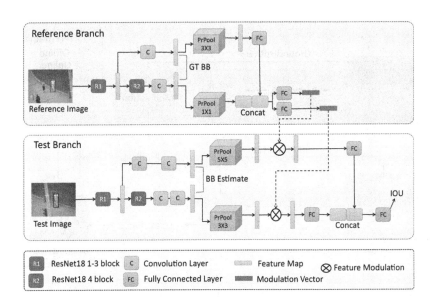

Fig. 2. The illustration of the target estimation network in ATOM tracker.

operator is presented by $*$. The network is trained online to minimize the loss function defined as:

$$l(w) = \sum_{i=1}^{n} \alpha_i \left\| f(x_i; w) - y_i \right\|^2 + \sum_j \beta_j \left\| w_j \right\|^2, \qquad (2)$$

where w_j denotes the regularization and its weight is represented by β_j, α_i presents the training sample weight, and label for each sample is presented by y_i which is set to Guassian function at the center of target location. ATOM adopted applied Conjugate-Gradient-based methodology to optimize this classification network.

3.2   Feature Enrichment Module

In general, most of the deep trackers employ low-resolution features to proceed with the tracking which are semantically more precise but reduced in spatial details and receptive field. We propose an efficient feature enrichment module which is capable to encode rich contextual information while preserving the spatial information from the low resolution features. The proposed framework is shown in Fig. 3. We integrated our proposed module after the backbone feature extractor (ResNet-18). The details of the proposed module is explained in the section below.

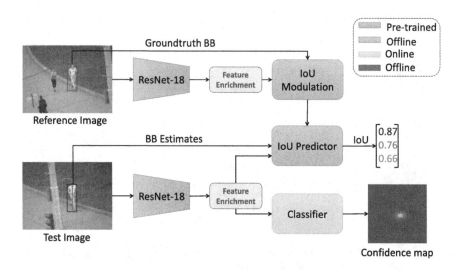

Fig. 3. The proposed tracking framework.

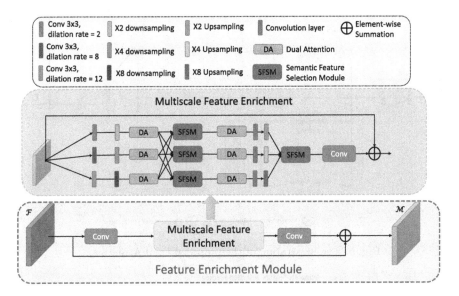

Fig. 4. The pipeline of the proposed feature enrichment module.

Feature Enrichment Module: The proposed feature enrichment module is shown in Fig. 4. The objective is to generate spatially accurate and contextually more reliable features. Given the input features $\mathcal{F}$ from backbone network (ResNet-18) are forwarded to multiscale feature enrichment network followed by convolution layer, and this output is forwarded to convolution layer and added with $\mathcal{F}$ to get the final output $\mathcal{M}$.

Proposed multi-scale feature enrichment module is composed of multiple subnetworks including pyramid pooling, dual attention, and semantic feature selection module. Pyramid pooling network is inspired by Chen et al. [5], which exploits the features at different dilation rates to access features at different receptive fields, as shown in Fig. 4. The features at different dilation rates are downsampled and forwarded to Dual Attention (DA) networks. The DA network is inspired by Woo et al. [46], which exploits the input features across channel as well as spatial domain. Modified DA network is illustrated in Fig. 5. Downsampled features are attended using DA network and passed to Semantic Feature Selection Module (SFSM). This modules selects the most reliable features as shown in Fig. 6, which is motivated by Selective Kernel Network (SKNet) [33]. These semantically selective features are again passed to DA to get attention across channel and spatial dimensions, and then upsampled to get the same resolution features. These upsampled features are again passed to SFSM and convolution layer. The output is fused using element-wise summation with the input of multiscale feature enrichment module to get the final fined and discriminative features as shown in Fig. 4.

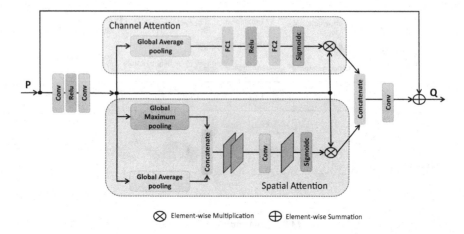

Fig. 5. The illustration of the proposed Dual Attention.

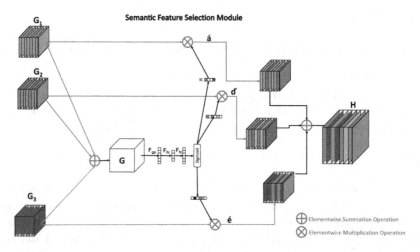

Fig. 6. The pipeline of semantic feature selection module. G_1, G_2, and G_3 are the input features while H is the output of the SFSM. The brightness indicates the weights of the feature channel i.e., the brighter the shade of the channel, more is the feature weight.

4   Experiments

We trained our method over GOT10K and COCO2017 datasets. The experimental results are shown below. The performance can be increased if more data is provided such as LaSOT, and TrackingNet etc. We trained and tested our algorithm on a machine having Intel i7 3.6 GHz processor, 32 GB of RAM, and an NVIDIA TITAN XP GPU card.

4.1 Comparison with State-of-the-Art Trackers

We performed an extensive experimental evaluation over VOT2015, VOT2016, and VOT2017 datasets. We used Expected Average Overlap (EAO), Accuracy (A), and Robustness (R) measure to evaluate aforementioned datasets. We compared our method with 18 SOTA methods including DeepSRDCF [9], Staple [2], MDNet [37], CCOT [10], SiameseRPN [31], SiameseFC [3], TADT [34], SA-Siam [23], SiamFCRes22 [50], MemDTC [48], SCSAtt [39], CMKCF [25], IRCA-Siam [13], SCS-Siam [17], SATIN [20], SiamDCF [6], GradNet [32], and AFS-Siam [19].

4.2 Experiments on VOT2015

In Table 1, we compared our method over VOT2015 dataset. Top ranking, TADT [34] and SA-Siam [23] exhibited the same accuracy of 59.0%, while MDNet [37] achieved 60.0% accuracy. However, our method secured highest accuracy 62.7%. On the other hand, CCOT [10] and SiamFCRes22 [50] obtained 0.238 and 0.322 robustness while our method achieved lowest which is 0.21. MDNet [37] and SiameseRPN [31] showed more then 0.350 EAO score while our approached exhibited 0.425 EAO score. We note that our tracker should outstanding performance in terms of EAO, A, and R compared to other state-of-the-art trackers.

Table 1. Performance evaluation over VOT2015. The top three results are shown in red, green and blue colors, respectively.

Trackers	Overlap (↑)	Robustness (↓)	EAO (↑)
DeepSRDCF [9]	0.556	1.050	0.318
Staple [2]	0.570	1.390	0.300
MDNet [37]	0.600	0.690	0.380
CCOT [10]	0.529	0.238	0.331
SiameseRPN [31]	0.580	0.930	0.358
SiameseFC [3]	0.540	0.930	0.292
TADT [34]	0.590	1.090	0.327
SA-Siam [23]	0.590	1.260	0.310
SiamFCRes22 [50]	0.587	0.322	0.318
Ours	0.627	0.21	0.425

4.3 Experiments on VOT2016

In Table 2, we compared our method over VOT2016 dataset with other SOTA such as MemDTC [48], CCOT [10], SCSAtt [39], SiameseFC [3], CMKCF [25], SiamFCRes22 [50], IRCA-Siam [13], and SCS-Siam [17]. We observe that SCSAtt

[39], SCS-Siam [17], and IRCA-Siam [13] achieved more than 0.54 accuracy score but our method gained best accuracy score of 0.61. It can be observed that our method ranked 3rd in terms of robustness, while CMKCF [25], IRCA-Siam [13] and SCSAtt [39] obtained less robustness score compared to our algorithm. Meanwhile our method attained rank first using overlap and EAO scores. Overall, our tracker showed best performance.

Table 2. Performance evaluation over VOT2016. The top three results are shown in red, green and blue colors, respectively.

Trackers	Overlap (↑)	Robustness (↓)	EAO (↑)
MemDTC [48]	0.51	1.82	0.27
CCOT [10]	0.54	0.24	0.33
SCSAtt [39]	0.55	0.19	0.30
SiameseFC [3]	0.53	0.46	0.23
CMKCF [25]	0.53	0.18	0.30
SiamFCRes22 [50]	0.54	0.38	0.30
IRCA-Siam [13]	0.56	0.19	0.30
SCS-Siam [17]	0.55	0.21	0.28
Ours	0.61	0.20	0.41

4.4 Experiments on VOT2017

We also evaluate proposed tracker our VOT2017 and results are shown in Table 3. SCSAtt [39], IRCA-Siam [13], AFS-Siam [19], and SCS-Siam [17] obtained more than 0.50 accuracy while our method surpassed them and obtained best score 0.59. In case of robustness, although other method showed better robustness, our method achieved the lowest value i.e., 0.21. Moreover, our method also surpassed the other SOTA methods in terms of EAO and obtained 0.40. In addition, we also performed speed analysis. We note that SiameseRPN showed the best speed, while our method performs tracking at 36 fps which is a realtime tracker. In short, our method showed outstanding performance and showed best results compared to other trackers.

4.5 Ablation Study

We performed an ablation study over VOT2015 dataset. For a fair comparison, similar to our network, we retrained ATOM [7] using GOT10K and COCO2017 datasets. We report the results in Table 4. We note that integrating feature enrichment module within the ATOM [7] increases the performance accuracy as well as improve the robustness against distractors.

Table 3. Performance evaluation over VOT2017 dataset. The top three results are shown in red, green and blue colors, respectively.

Trackers	Overlap (↑)	Robustness (↓)	EAO (↑)	FPS
MemDTC [48]	0.49	1.77	0.25	40
SATIN [20]	0.49	1.34	0.25	24
SiamDCF [6]	0.50	0.47	0.25	60
SiameseFC [3]	0.50	0.59	0.19	86
GradNet [32]	0.50	0.37	0.24	80
SCSAtt [39]	0.52	0.39	0.19	61
SiameseRPN [31]	0.49	0.46	0.24	200
SiamFCRes22 [50]	0.50	0.49	0.23	70
AFS-Siam [19]	0.53	0.20	0.25	66
IRCA-Siam [13]	0.52	0.29	0.25	77
SCS-Siam [17]	0.52	0.29	0.24	73
Ours	0.59	0.21	0.40	36

Table 4. Ablation study over VOT2015.

Trackers	Overlap (↑)	Robustness (↓)	EAO (↑	FPS)
ATOM [7]	0.59	0.322	0.410	45
Ours	0.627	0.210	0.425	36

5   Conclusion

In this paper, we propose a feature enrichment module to generate spatially more precise and contextually more informative features. We integrated the proposed module within ATOM tracking framework. Generally, deep trackers operate on low resolution features are semantically more accurate but spatially less precise with limited receptive field. Our proposed module generates more informative features while preserving contextual and spatial information. Experimental study over VOT2015, VOT2016, and VOT2017 showed that our tracker achieved better tracking performance compared to other state-of-the-art trackers.

Acknowledgment. This study was supported by the BK21 FOUR project (AI-driven Convergence Software Education Research Program) funded by the Ministry of Education, School of Computer Science and Engineering, Kyungpook National University, Korea (4199990214394).

References

1. Avidan, S.: Support vector tracking. IEEE Trans. Pattern Anal. Mach. Intell. **26**(8), 1064–1072 (2004)

2. Bertinetto, L., Valmadre, J., Golodetz, S., Miksik, O., Torr, P.H.: Staple: complementary learners for real-time tracking. In: IEEE CVPR, pp. 1401–1409 (2016)
3. Bertinetto, L., Valmadre, J., Henriques, J.F., Vedaldi, A., Torr, P.H.: Fully-convolutional Siamese networks for object tracking. In: Hua, G., Jégou, H. (eds.) ECCV 2016. LNCS, vol. 9914, pp. 850–865. Springer, Cham (2016). https://doi.org/10.1007/978-3-319-48881-3_56
4. Bhat, G., Johnander, J., Danelljan, M., Shahbaz Khan, F., Felsberg, M.: Unveiling the power of deep tracking. In: Ferrari, V., Hebert, M., Sminchisescu, C., Weiss, Y. (eds.) ECCV 2018. LNCS, vol. 11206, pp. 483–498. Springer, Cham (2018). https://doi.org/10.1007/978-3-030-01216-8_30
5. Chen, L.C., Papandreou, G., Schroff, F., Adam, H.: Rethinking atrous convolution for semantic image segmentation. arXiv preprint arXiv:1706.05587 (2017)
6. Chen, S., Qiu, D., Huo, Q.: Siamese networks with discriminant correlation filters and channel attention. In: 2018 14th International Conference on Computational Intelligence and Security (CIS), pp. 110–114. IEEE (2018)
7. Danelljan, M., Bhat, G., Khan, F.S., Felsberg, M.: Atom: accurate tracking by overlap maximization. In: Proceedings of the IEEE Conference on Computer Vision and Pattern Recognition, pp. 4660–4669 (2019)
8. Danelljan, M., Bhat, G., Shahbaz Khan, F., Felsberg, M.: Eco: efficient convolution operators for tracking. In: Proceedings of the IEEE Conference on Computer Vision and Pattern Recognition, pp. 6638–6646 (2017)
9. Danelljan, M., Hager, G., Shahbaz Khan, F., Felsberg, M.: Convolutional features for correlation filter based visual tracking. In: Proceedings of the IEEE International Conference on Computer Vision Workshops, pp. 58–66 (2015)
10. Danelljan, M., Robinson, A., Khan, F.S., Felsberg, M.: Beyond correlation filters: learning continuous convolution operators for visual tracking. In: Leibe, B., Matas, J., Sebe, N., Welling, M. (eds.) ECCV 2016. LNCS, pp. 472–488. Springer, Cham (2016). https://doi.org/10.1007/978-3-319-46454-1_29
11. Dong, X., Shen, J.: Triplet loss in siamese network for object tracking. In: Ferrari, V., Hebert, M., Sminchisescu, C., Weiss, Y. (eds.) ECCV 2018. LNCS, vol. 11217, pp. 459–474. Springer, Cham (2018). https://doi.org/10.1007/978-3-030-01261-8_28
12. Fan, H., Ling, H.: Sanet: structure-aware network for visual tracking. In: Proceedings of the IEEE Conference on Computer Vision and Pattern Recognition Workshops, pp. 42–49 (2017)
13. Fiaz, M., Mahmood, A., Baek, K.Y., Farooq, S.S., Jung, S.K.: Improving object tracking by added noise and channel attention. Sensors 20(13), 3780 (2020)
14. Fiaz, M., Mahmood, A., Javed, S., Jung, S.K.: Handcrafted and deep trackers: recent visual object tracking approaches and trends. ACM Comput. Surv. (CSUR) 52(2), 43 (2019)
15. Fiaz, M., Mahmood, A., Jung, S.K.: Tracking noisy targets: a review of recent object tracking approaches. arXiv preprint arXiv:1802.03098 (2018)
16. Fiaz, M., Mahmood, A., Jung, S.K.: Convolutional neural network with structural input for visual object tracking. In: Proceedings of the 34th ACM/SIGAPP Symposium on Applied Computing, pp. 1345–1352. ACM (2019)
17. Fiaz, M., Mahmood, A., Jung, S.K.: Learning soft mask based feature fusion with channel and spatial attention for robust visual object tracking. Sensors 20(14), 4021 (2020)

18. Fiaz, M., Mahmood, A., Jung, S.K.: Video object segmentation using guided feature and directional deep appearance learning. In: Proceedings of the 2020 DAVIS Challenge on Video Object Segmentation-CVPR, Workshops, Seattle, WA, USA, vol. 19 (2020)

19. Fiaz, M., Rahman, M.M., Mahmood, A., Farooq, S.S., Baek, K.Y., Jung, S.K.: Adaptive feature selection Siamese networks for visual tracking. In: Ohyama, W., Jung, S. (eds.) IW-FCV 2020. CCIS, vol. 1212, pp. 167–179. Springer, Singapore (2020). https://doi.org/10.1007/978-981-15-4818-5_13

20. Gao, P., Yuan, R., Wang, F., Xiao, L., Fujita, H., Zhang, Y.: Siamese attentional keypoint network for high performance visual tracking. Knowl.-Based Syst. **193**, 105448 (2019)

21. Girshick, R., Donahue, J., Darrell, T., Malik, J.: Rich feature hierarchies for accurate object detection and semantic segmentation. In: Proceedings of the IEEE Conference on Computer Vision and Pattern Recognition, pp. 580–587 (2014)

22. Guo, Q., Feng, W., Zhou, C., Huang, R., Wan, L., Wang, S.: Learning dynamic Siamese network for visual object tracking. In: IEEE CVPR, pp. 1763–1771 (2017)

23. He, A., Luo, C., Tian, X., Zeng, W.: A twofold Siamese network for real-time object tracking. In: IEEE CVPR, pp. 4834–4843 (2018)

24. Hong, S., You, T., Kwak, S., Han, B.: Online tracking by learning discriminative saliency map with convolutional neural network. In: International Conference on Machine Learning, pp. 597–606 (2015)

25. Huang, B., Xu, T., Jiang, S., Chen, Y., Bai, Y.: Robust visual tracking via constrained multi-kernel correlation filters. IEEE Trans. Multimed. **22**, 2820–2832 (2020)

26. Jiang, B., Luo, R., Mao, J., Xiao, T., Jiang, Y.: Acquisition of localization confidence for accurate object detection. In: Ferrari, V., Hebert, M., Sminchisescu, C., Weiss, Y. (eds.) ECCV 2018. LNCS, vol. 11218, pp. 784–799. Springer, Cham (2018). https://doi.org/10.1007/978-3-030-01264-9_48

27. Kristan, M., Leonardis, A., Matas, J., Felsberg, M., et al.: The visual object tracking vot2017 challenge results. In: Proceedings of the IEEE International Conference on Computer Vision, pp. 1949–1972 (2017)

28. Kristan, M., et al.: The visual object tracking vot2015 challenge results. In: Proceedings of the IEEE International Conference on Computer Vision Workshops, pp. 1–23 (2015)

29. Kristan, M., et al.: The visual object tracking vot2016 challenge results. In: Hua, G., Jégou, H. (eds.) ECCV 2016. LNCS, vol. 9914, pp. 777–823. Springer, Cham (2016). https://doi.org/10.1007/978-3-319-48881-3_54

30. Kwak, S., Nam, W., Han, B., Han, J.H.: Learning occlusion with likelihoods for visual tracking. In: 2011 IEEE International Conference on Computer Vision (ICCV), pp. 1551–1558. IEEE (2011)

31. Li, B., Yan, J., Wu, W., Zhu, Z., Hu, X.: High performance visual tracking with Siamese region proposal network. In: Proceedings of the IEEE Conference on Computer Vision and Pattern Recognition, pp. 8971–8980 (2018)

32. Li, P., Chen, B., Ouyang, W., Wang, D., Yang, X., Lu, H.: GradNet: gradient-guided network for visual object tracking. In: Proceedings of the IEEE International Conference on Computer Vision, pp. 6162–6171 (2019)

33. Li, X., Wang, W., Hu, X., Yang, J.: Selective kernel networks. In: Proceedings of the IEEE Conference on Computer Vision and Pattern Recognition, pp. 510–519 (2019)

34. Li, X., Ma, C., Wu, B., He, Z., Yang, M.H.: Target-aware deep tracking. In: Proceedings of the IEEE Conference on Computer Vision and Pattern Recognition, pp. 1369–1378 (2019)

35. Ma, B., Hu, H., Shen, J., Liu, Y., Shao, L.: Generalized pooling for robust object tracking. IEEE Trans. Image Process. **25**(9), 4199–4208 (2016)

36. Ma, C., Huang, J.B., Yang, X., Yang, M.H.: Hierarchical convolutional features for visual tracking. In: IEEE CVPR, pp. 3074–3082 (2015)

37. Nam, H., Han, B.: Learning multi-domain convolutional neural networks for visual tracking. In: Proceedings of the IEEE Conference on Computer Vision and Pattern Recognition, pp. 4293–4302 (2016)

38. Qi, Y., et al.: Hedged deep tracking. In: IEEE CVPR, pp. 4303–4311 (2016)

39. Rahman, M.M., Fiaz, M., Jung, S.K.: Efficient visual tracking with stacked channel-spatial attention learning. IEEE Access **8**, 100857–100869 (2020)

40. Sevilla-Lara, L., Learned-Miller, E.: Distribution fields for tracking. In: 2012 IEEE Conference on Computer Vision and Pattern Recognition (CVPR), pp. 1910–1917. IEEE (2012)

41. Song, Y., et al.: Vital: visual tracking via adversarial learning. In: Proceedings of the IEEE Conference on Computer Vision and Pattern Recognition, pp. 8990–8999 (2018)

42. Tao, R., Gavves, E., Smeulders, A.W.: Siamese instance search for tracking. In: Proceedings of the IEEE Conference on Computer Vision and Pattern Recognition, pp. 1420–1429 (2016)

43. Valmadre, J., Bertinetto, L., Henriques, J., Vedaldi, A., Torr, P.H.: End-to-end representation learning for correlation filter based tracking. In: Proceedings of the IEEE Conference on Computer Vision and Pattern Recognition, pp. 2805–2813 (2017)

44. Wang, D., Lu, H., Xiao, Z., Yang, M.H.: Inverse sparse tracker with a locally weighted distance metric. IEEE Trans. Image Process. **24**(9), 2646–2657 (2015)

45. Wen, L., Cai, Z., Lei, Z., Yi, D., Li, S.Z.: Online spatio-temporal structural context learning for visual tracking. In: Fitzgibbon, A., Lazebnik, S., Perona, P., Sato, Y., Schmid, C. (eds.) ECCV 2012. LNCS, vol. 7575, pp. 716–729. Springer, Cham (2012). https://doi.org/10.1007/978-3-642-33765-9_51

46. Woo, S., Park, J., Lee, J.Y., So Kweon, I.: CBAM: convolutional block attention module. In: Ferrari, V., Hebert, M., Sminchisescu, C., Weiss, Y. (eds.) ECCV 2018. LNCS, vol. 11211, pp. 3–19. Springer, Cham (2018). https://doi.org/10.1007/978-3-030-01234-2_1

47. Yang, S., Wang, W., Liu, C., Deng, W.: Scene understanding in deep learning-based end-to-end controllers for autonomous vehicles. IEEE Trans. Syst. Man. Cybern.: Syst. **49**(1), 53–63 (2018)

48. Yang, T., Chan, A.B.: Visual tracking via dynamic memory networks. IEEE Trans. Pattern Anal. Mach. Intell. **43**, 360–674 (2019)

49. Yun, S., Choi, J., Yoo, Y., Yun, K., Young Choi, J.: Action-decision networks for visual tracking with deep reinforcement learning. In: Proceedings of the IEEE Conference on Computer Vision and Pattern Recognition, pp. 2711–2720 (2017)

50. Zhang, Z., Peng, H.: Deeper and wider Siamese networks for real-time visual tracking. In: Proceedings of the IEEE Conference on Computer Vision and Pattern Recognition, pp. 4591–4600 (2019)

The Emerging Field of Graph Signal Processing for Moving Object Segmentation

Jhony H. Giraldo[1]([envelope]) [ID], Sajid Javed[2] [ID], Maryam Sultana[3] [ID], Soon Ki Jung[3] [ID], and Thierry Bouwmans[1] [ID]

[1] La Rochelle Université, 17000 La Rochelle, France
{jgiral01,tbouwman}@univ-lr.fr
[2] Khalifa University, Abu Dhabi 127788, United Arab Emirates
sajid.javed@ku.ac.ae
[3] Kyungpook National University, Daegu 41566, South Korea
{maryam,skjung}@knu.ac.kr

Abstract. Moving Object Segmentation (MOS) is an important topic in computer vision. MOS becomes a challenging problem in the presence of dynamic background and moving camera videos such as Pan–Tilt–Zoom cameras (PTZ). The MOS problem has been solved using unsupervised and supervised learning strategies. Recently, new ideas to solve MOS using semi-supervised learning have emerged inspired from the theory of Graph Signal Processing (GSP). These new algorithms are usually composed of several steps including: segmentation, background initialization, features extraction, graph construction, graph signal sampling, and a semi-supervised learning algorithm inspired from reconstruction of graph signals. In this work, we summarize and explain the theoretical foundations as well as the technical details of MOS using GPS. We also propose two architectures for MOS using semi-supervised learning and a new evaluation procedure for GSP-based MOS algorithms. GSP-based algorithms are evaluated in the Change Detection (CDNet2014) dataset for MOS, outperforming numerous State-Of-The-Art (SOTA) methods in several challenging conditions.

Keywords: Moving Object Segmentation · Graph Signal Processing · Semi-supervised learning

1 Introduction

Moving Object Segmentation (MOS) is a fundamental topic in computer vision. MOS has several applications [17], and it is also a fundamental step in numerous computer vision and image/video processing tasks such as video surveillance, security, visual object tracking, and human activity analysis, among others. The target of MOS is to separate the moving from the static objects in a scene [4]. MOS is also considered as a classification problem, where the objective is

© Springer Nature Switzerland AG 2021
H. Jeong and K. Sumi (Eds.): IW-FCV 2021, CCIS 1405, pp. 31–45, 2021.
https://doi.org/10.1007/978-3-030-81638-4_3

to classify between background and foreground each pixel in the videos, and therefore MOS is also known as background subtraction [7]. MOS becomes very challenging in the presence of undesirable variations in the background scene for static and moving camera sequences [21].

The approaches to solve MOS can be categorized as unsupervised, semi-supervised, and supervised learning methods. Unsupervised methods usually rely on a background model [25] of the video to segment the moving pixels (or foreground) [4–6, 28]. However, these unsupervised methods usually fail in dynamic background and moving camera sequences. On the other hand, supervised methods usually train very deep Convolutional Neural Networks (CNN) [31] to predict the foreground [8, 22, 35, 50]. Common CNNs in the literature contain millions of parameters [23], and thus several tricks such as dropout and data augmentation techniques [30] are required to avoid the overfitting problem. Furthermore, a general answer about the sample complexity required to guarantee performance in deep learning regimen does not exist in CNNs [15, 47, 53]. Recently, a new semi-supervised learning category for MOS has emerged [18, 20, 21]. These semi-supervised methods for MOS can achieve good performance in several challenges with a small amount of labeled information, and they are inspired from the Graph Signal Processing (GSP) community [37, 48].

GSP tries to extend the classical concepts of digital signal processing to signals supported on graphs. Graphs can model complex relationships among data, and therefore GSP has attracted a lot of interest in the last few years. Specifically, the problems of sampling and reconstruction of graph signals have been broadly studied [2, 13, 39, 40, 46]. In the same way, GSP has been used in numerous applications such as computer vision [18, 20, 21], image and 3D point cloud processing [38, 52, 57], sensor networks [16], and the estimation of new cases of Coronavirus Disease 2019 [19].

In this work, we explain the basic notions, as well as the mathematical and technical foundations of MOS using GSP, for simplicity we call Graph Signal Processing-Moving Object Segmentation (GSP-MOS) to this new approach. We propose two new architectures and a new evaluation procedure for GSP-MOS. This new evaluation scheme takes into account the amount of labeled information used in the GSP-MOS algorithms. The idea of GSP-MOS is to model regions of pixels in videos as nodes living in a high dimensional space, and thereafter a semi-supervised method classifies if each node is either a static or moving object. GSP-MOS algorithms are usually composed of: 1) a segmentation method, 2) feature extraction procedure for nodes representation, 3) a graph construction method, 4) graph signal representation, 5) a graph signal sampling strategy, and 6) a semi-supervised learning algorithm inspired from reconstruction methods of GSP. GSP-MOS has the advantage of having good performance for static and moving camera videos with small amounts of labeled information. Furthermore, Giraldo *et al.* [21] answered the question of the sample complexity in semi-supervised learning regimen for GSP-MOS using the concept of Paley-Wiener space in graphs [44].

The rest of the paper is organized as follows. Section 2 presents the related work in GSP-MOS. Section 3 explains the basic concepts and mathematical notions of GSP-MOS algorithms. Section 4 introduces the experimental framework that has been used for GSP-MOS, and the new evaluation procedure. Finally, Sects. 5 and 6 present a summary of results and the conclusions of this work, respectively.

2   Related Work

There are few GSP-MOS algorithms in the literature. The first GSP-MOS algorithm was proposed in [20] and coined as Graph BackGround Subtraction with Total Variation minimization (GraphBGS-TV), this method uses a Mask Region CNN (Mask R-CNN) [24] with a set of handcrafted features. GraphBGS-TV solves the semi-supervised learning problem using the Total Variation (TV) of graph signals [29]. Giraldo and Bouwmans [18] proposed the GraphBGS method, where the segmentation step uses a Cascade Mask R-CNN [10], and the semi-supervised learning problem is solved with the Sobolev norm of graph signals [19]. Finally, Giraldo *et al.* [21] proposed Graph Moving Object Segmentation (GraphMOS). This method uses superpixel segmentation with handcrafted plus deep features. GraphMOS solves the semi-supervised learning problem with the Sobolev norm or TV of graph signals. Additionally, Giraldo *et al.* [21] extended the GSP-MOS ideas to Video Object Segmentation (VOS) [41], and they coined their algorithm as GraphVOS. This work summarizes and discusses the results of the GSP-MOS algorithms. Similarly, we present potential future directions in the field of GSP-MOS.

3   Moving Object Segmentation and Graph Signal Processing

This section presents the basic concepts and mathematical foundations of GSP-MOS. Figure 1 shows the general pipeline for GSP-MOS. Most GSP-MOS algorithms follow the same pipeline with some modifications, in this work we refer to architecture as the pipeline of a certain GSP-MOS algorithm.

3.1   Graph Signals Preliminaries

A graph $G = (\mathcal{V}, \mathcal{E})$ is represented with a set of nodes $\mathcal{V} = \{1, \ldots, N\}$ and a set of edges $\mathcal{E} = \{(i, j)\}$, where (i, j) is the edge between the nodes i and j. $\mathbf{W} \in \mathbb{R}^{N \times N}$ is the adjacency matrix of the graph such that $\mathbf{W}(i, j) \in \mathbb{R}^+$ is the weight of the edge (i, j) and $\mathbf{W}(i, j) = 0 \ \forall \ (i, j) \notin \mathcal{E}$. Therefore, $\mathbf{W}$ is symmetric for undirected graphs. $\mathbf{D} \in \mathbb{R}^{N \times N}$ is a diagonal matrix called the degree matrix of G such that $\mathbf{D} = \text{diag}(\mathbf{W1})$, where $\mathbf{1} \in \mathbb{R}^N$ is a vector of ones. Similarly, $\mathbf{L} = \mathbf{D} - \mathbf{W}$ is the combinatorial Laplacian operator. $\mathbf{L}$ is positive semi-definite for undirected graphs, and thus $\mathbf{L}$ has eigenvalues $0 = \lambda_1 \leq \lambda_2 \leq \cdots \leq \lambda_N$ and

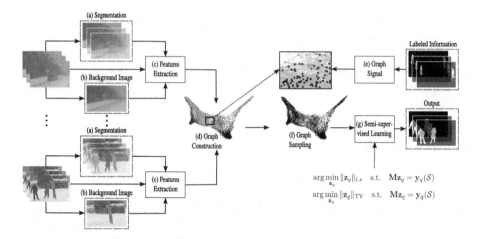

Fig. 1. General pipeline for GSP-MOS algorithms. These architectures use background initialization and segmentation. Each output of the segmentation algorithm represents a node in G, and therefore each node is represented with some features. The labeled information is used to classify if a node is a moving (green nodes) or a static object (blue nodes). Finally, some nodes are sampled and the semi-supervised algorithm classify all the non-sampled nodes in the graph. (Color figure online)

corresponding eigenvectors $\{\mathbf{u}_1, \mathbf{u}_2, \ldots, \mathbf{u}_N\}$. Finally, a graph signal is a function $y : \mathcal{V} \rightarrow \mathbb{R}$, and we can represent this signal as $\mathbf{y} \in \mathbb{R}^N$.

The graph Fourier basis of G is given by the eigenvalue decomposition of $\mathbf{L} = \mathbf{U}\boldsymbol{\Lambda}\mathbf{U}^{\mathsf{T}}$ [37], where $\mathbf{U} = [\mathbf{u}_1, \mathbf{u}_2, \ldots, \mathbf{u}_N]$ and $\boldsymbol{\Lambda} = \mathrm{diag}(\lambda_1, \lambda_2, \ldots, \lambda_N)$. The Graph Fourier Transform (GFT) $\hat{\mathbf{y}}$ of the graph signal is given by $\hat{\mathbf{y}} = \mathbf{U}^{\mathsf{T}}\mathbf{y}$, and similarly the inverse GFT is given by $\mathbf{y} = \mathbf{U}\hat{\mathbf{y}}$ [37]. A graph signal $\mathbf{y}$ is called bandlimited if $\exists\, \rho \in \{1, 2, \ldots, N-1\}$ such that its GFT satisfies $\hat{\mathbf{y}}(i) = 0 \,\forall\, i > \rho$. Similar to the classical digital signal processing theory, ρ is called the bandwidth of $\mathbf{y}$ in GSP, and λ_ρ is the frequency associated with that bandwidth. Pesenson [44] used these concepts of frequency to define the space of all ω-*bandlimited* graph signals such as $PW_\omega(G) = \mathrm{span}(\mathbf{U}_\rho : \lambda_\rho \leq \omega)$, where $\mathbf{U}_\rho$ is the first ρ eigenvectors of $\mathbf{L}$, and $PW_\omega(G)$ is called the Paley-Wiener space of the graph.

3.2   Nodes Representation in GSP-MOS

GSP-MOS requires a representation for the nodes $\mathcal{V}$ in the graph. A node of G is represented with a feature characterization of a group of pixels, where these regions are obtained with some segmentation algorithm. State-Of-The-Art (SOTA) GSP-MOS algorithms have mainly used superpixel [1], block-based [21], semantic [12], and instance segmentation [24] for the representation of nodes. Figure 2 shows an example of nodes representation with instance segmentation, where each instance is mapped to a node in the graph using certain feature representation. Figure 2 also shows the representation with the graph signals, where the green nodes are moving objects, the blue nodes are static objects, and the black nodes are unknown. Intuitively, the task of the semi-supervised learning algorithm is to color the graph signals (blue and green) as best as possible from the sampled graph (last graph to the right in Fig. 2).

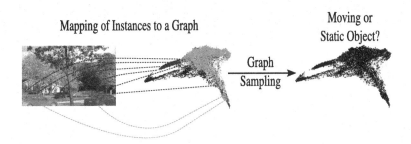

Fig. 2. Mapping of the segmented regions (moving or static objects) to G and graph signal sampling. (Color figure online)

Superpixel Segmentation. Giraldo *et al.* [21] used the Simple Linear Iterative Clustering (SLIC) method for superpixel segmentation [1]. SLIC is a well known classical method for superpixel segmentation. In the same way, more recent superpixel segmentation methods such as [56] can also be used. SLIC method outputs approximately ζ superpixels per image, where ζ is an important parameter for GSP-MOS algorithms. For example, bigger values of ζ allow the processing of more detailed regions, but at the same time these values increase the computational complexity of the GSP-MOS algorithm. Indeed, Giraldo *et al.* [21] used a powerful Nvidia DGX-2 server machine to execute the experiments related to superpixels.

Block-Based Segmentation. Giraldo *et al.* [21] also used block-based segmentation for the representation of nodes in G. This method divides each image in equally sized blocks for further processing. Block-based has the advantage of being faster than SLIC, but it also introduces degradation in performance as shown in [21].

Semantic Segmentation. Some GSP-MOS algorithms in the literature have used Fully CNN based segmentation methods. For instance, Giraldo *et al.* [21] used the DeepLab method [12] for the representation of nodes. Semantic-based GSP-MOS algorithms work well in several challenging conditions, however it fails when there is interception of static and moving objects of the same semantic class. Figure 3 shows the output of a semantic segmentation method in a scene where there are moving cars just in front of parked cars in the background. In such cases, semantic methods fail for GSP-MOS since the method cannot differentiate between the static and moving object.

Fig. 3. Segmentation outputs for semantic and instance segmentation.

Instance Segmentation. Several GSP-MOS algorithms have focused on instance segmentation methods such as Mask R-CNN [24] and Cascade Mask R-CNN [10]. For example, GraphBGS-TV [20] used a Mask R-CNN with a ResNeXt-101 [55] as backbone, while GraphBGS [18] used a Cascade Mask R-CNN with a ResNeSt-200 [58] as backbone. Unlike semantic segmentation, instance segmentation for GSP-MOS algorithms has the advantage of differentiating between intercepted static and moving objects of the same semantic class as shown in Fig. 3. Instance segmentation also dramatically reduces the computational complexity with respect to superpixel and block-based segmentation [21].

3.3   Feature Extraction

The feature representation plays a central role for GSP-MOS. SOTA GSP-MOS algorithms have used combinations of handcrafted and deep features. For example, GraphBGS [18] and GraphBGS-TV [18] uses a combination of optical flow [33], intensity, background, and texture [36] features. In the same way, Graph-MOS [21] uses the same combination of handcrafted features of GraphBGS and GraphBGS-TV, plus deep features inspired from the visual object tracking community [14,27]. The deep features of GraphMOS are extracted from a pre-trained VGG-m model [11]. Each node in $\mathcal{V}$ is represented by a M-dimensional vector $\mathbf{x}_v \in \mathbb{R}^M$, where $\mathbf{x}_v$ is the concatenation of all previously extracted features.

3.4   Graph Construction

GSP-MOS algorithms have little explored the construction of the graph, SOTA methods have used a k Nearest Neighborhood (k-NN) with a Gaussian kernel. Let $\mathbf{X} \in \mathbb{R}^{N \times M}$ be the matrix of features of the N nodes such that $\mathbf{X} = [\mathbf{x}_1, \mathbf{x}_2, \ldots, \mathbf{x}_N]^\mathsf{T}$. The construction of G is accomplished connecting the first k neighbors of each node, and thereafter the following kernel is applied to get the weight of each edge:

$$w_{ij} = \exp{-\frac{\|\mathbf{x}_i - \mathbf{x}_j\|_2^2}{\sigma^2}}, \tag{1}$$

where σ is the standard deviation of the Gaussian kernel. σ is computed as follows:

$$\sigma = \frac{1}{|\mathcal{E}| + N} \sum_{(i,j) \in \mathcal{E}} \|\mathbf{x}_i - \mathbf{x}_j\|_2. \tag{2}$$

Finally, we got the adjacency matrix $\mathbf{W}(i,j) = w_{ij} \ \forall \ (i,j) \in \mathcal{E}$ from this procedure.

3.5   Graph Signal

The graph signal is a matrix $\mathbf{Y} \in \{0,1\}^{N \times Q}$, where Q is the number of classes of the problem. For example, Q is equal to two corresponding to static and moving objects in MOS. In the same way, Q is equal to the number of different objects for each video in VOS. Each row of $\mathbf{Y}$ is a one-hot vector encoding the class of each node (static or moving object for MOS). Furthermore, the construction of $\mathbf{Y}$ depends on the segmentation algorithm. One can construct the graph signal using the Intersection over Union (IoU) and the Intersection over Node (IoN) metrics proposed in [21]. The decision of whether a node is a static or moving object has been done using empirical formulations based on IoU, IoN, and the specific segmentation method. For further details, the readers are referred to [21].

3.6   Sample Complexity for Semi-supervised Learning

An important question in GSP-MOS is: how many labeled nodes are required to get perfect classification in the semi-supervised learning algorithm? The answer can be found in the Paley-Wiener space of G. Let $\mathbf{y}$ be one of the columns of $\mathbf{Y}$, if $\mathbf{y} \in PW_\omega(G)$ then we can perfectly reconstruct the original graph signal $\mathbf{y}$ with at least ρ samples. Formally, let $\mathcal{S} \subset \mathcal{V}$ be a subset of nodes with $\mathcal{S} = \{s_1, s_2, \ldots, s_m\}$, where $m = |\mathcal{S}| \leq N$ is the number of sampled nodes. Let $\mathbf{y}(\mathcal{S}) = \mathbf{My}$ be the sampled graph signal such that $\mathbf{M}$ is a sampling matrix whose entries are given by $\mathbf{M} = [\boldsymbol{\delta}_{s_1}, \ldots, \boldsymbol{\delta}_{s_m}]^\top$ and $\boldsymbol{\delta}_v$ is the one-hot vector centered at v. Let $\tilde{\mathbf{y}} = \boldsymbol{\Phi}\mathbf{My}$ be the reconstructed graph signal where $\boldsymbol{\Phi} \in \mathbb{R}^{N \times m}$ is an interpolation operator. One can get perfect reconstruction if $\boldsymbol{\Phi}\mathbf{M} = \mathbf{I}$, i.e., $\tilde{\mathbf{y}} = \mathbf{Iy} = \mathbf{y}$. In general, perfect reconstruction is not possible because rank$(\boldsymbol{\Phi}\mathbf{M}) \leq m \leq N$. However, Chen et al. [13] proved that perfect reconstruction is possible when $|\mathcal{S}| \geq \rho$. Giraldo et al. [21] used this idea to compute the sample complexity in GSP-MOS with the following corollary:

Corollary 1 (Giraldo's corollary [21]). *Let $\mathbf{Y} \in \mathbb{R}^{N \times Q}$ be a graph signal matrix of a semi-supervised learning problem with Q classes. Let N_s be the sample complexity of the learning problem. $\mathbf{Y}$ has a set of cutoff frequencies $\{\omega_1, \ldots, \omega_Q\}$, with corresponding bandwidths $\{\rho_1, \ldots, \rho_Q\}$ for each column of the graph signal. As a consequence, N_s is bounded as follows:*

$$N_s \leq \max\{\rho_1, \ldots, \rho_Q\}. \tag{3}$$

Proof: see [21].

Corollary 1 provides an upper bound in the sample complexity for a semi-supervised learning problem. The upper bound is the maximum of the bandwidths $\{\rho_1, \ldots, \rho_Q\}$ of each column of $\mathbf{Y}$, *i.e.*, we are assuming that each column of $\mathbf{Y}$ is in the Paley-Wiener space of G.

3.7 Semi-supervised Learning Algorithms

GSP-MOS algorithms have mainly used semi-supervised learning algorithms inspired from reconstruction of graph signals. The objective functions of these semi-supervised learning problems usually involve a graph signal norm. For instance, GraphBGS [18] and GraphMOS [21] used the Sobolev norm, while GraphBGS-TV [20] used the TV norm.

Sobolev Norm. The Sobolev norm of graph signals was defined by Pesenson [45] as follows:

Definition 1. *For parameters $\epsilon \geq 0$ and $\alpha \in \mathbb{R}$, the Sobolev norm of graph signals is introduced as follows:*

$$\|\mathbf{f}\|_{\alpha,\epsilon} = \|(\mathbf{L} + \epsilon\mathbf{I})^{\alpha/2}\mathbf{f}\|_2^2, \alpha \in \mathbb{R}, \tag{4}$$

where $\mathbf{I}$ is the identity matrix.

The semi-supervised learning algorithm based on the Sobolev norm in Definition 1 can be expressed as follows:

$$\arg\min_{\mathbf{z}_q} \|\mathbf{z}_q\|_{\alpha,\epsilon} \quad \text{s.t.} \quad \mathbf{M}\mathbf{z}_q = \mathbf{y}_q(\mathcal{S}), \tag{5}$$

where we need to find $\mathbf{z}_q \; \forall \; 1 \leq q \leq Q$. Giraldo *et al.* [21] highlighted two valuable properties of Eqn. (5): 1) the optimization problem is convex, and 2) the Sobolev term $\mathbf{L} + \epsilon\mathbf{I}$ is always invertible for $\epsilon > 0$ in undirected graphs. For small values of N, the optimization function for all $1 \leq q \leq Q$ in Eqn. (5) can be solved as follows:

$$((\mathbf{L} + \epsilon\mathbf{I})^{-1})^{\alpha}\mathbf{M}^{\top}(\mathbf{M}((\mathbf{L} + \epsilon\mathbf{I})^{-1})^{\alpha}\mathbf{M}^{\top})^{-1}\mathbf{Y}(\mathcal{S}), \tag{6}$$

where $\mathbf{Y}(\mathcal{S})$ is the sub-matrix of $\mathbf{Y}$ with rows indexed by $\mathcal{S}$. For larger values of N, one can solve Eqn. (5) using the interior-point method from quadratic programming or the GSP toolbox [43].

Total Variation. The optimization problem for TV minimization is given as follows:

$$\arg\min_{\mathbf{z}_q} \|\mathbf{z}_q\|_{\text{TV}} \quad \text{s.t.} \quad \mathbf{M}\mathbf{z}_q = \mathbf{y}_q(\mathcal{S}), \tag{7}$$

where the TV norm is such that:

$$\|\mathbf{y}\|_{\mathrm{TV}} = \sum_{i \in \mathcal{V}} \sum_{j \in \mathcal{N}_i} \sqrt{\mathbf{W}(i,j)} \|\mathbf{y}(j) - \mathbf{y}(i)\|_1, \tag{8}$$

where $\mathcal{N}_i$ is the set of first neighbors of the ith node. The minimization of the TV is related to the cluster assumption [29] and leads to piecewise constant signals as the solution of the optimization problem. GraphBGS-TV [20] solved Eqn. (7) using the GSP [43] and the Unlocbox [42].

4   Experimental Framework

The evaluation of GSP-MOS algorithms in [18, 20, 21] have been adjusted to the classical evaluation of MOS method (such as in background subtraction and VOS) for comparing with previous SOTA methods. These comparisons have been conducted with the F-measure metric defined as follows:

$$\text{F-measure} = 2 \frac{\text{Precision} \times \text{Recall}}{\text{Precision} + \text{Recall}}, \text{ where} \tag{9}$$

$$\text{Recall} = \frac{\text{TP}}{\text{TP} + \text{FN}}, \text{ Precision} = \frac{\text{TP}}{\text{TP} + \text{FP}}, \tag{10}$$

where TP, FP, and FN are the number of true positives, false positives, and false negatives pixels, respectively. However, another interesting approach for evaluation is to compute the F-measure along a set of different sampling densities (percentage of training images). As a result, we can see what is the performance of each method for a small labeled data regimen. In this work, we adopt both evaluation approaches: the classical procedure and the evaluation of GSP-MOS algorithms for several sampling densities.

4.1   Dataset

GSP-MOS algorithms have been evaluated on several datasets for background subtraction and VOS. Arguably, The most popular dataset is the Change Detection (CDNet2014) [54]. CDNet2014 contains 11 challenging categories including: bad weather, low frame rate, night videos, turbulence, baseline, dynamic backgrounds, Pan–Tilt–Zoom cameras (PTZ), camera jitter, intermittent object motion, shadow, and thermal. Each challenge of CDNet2014 contains from four up to six videos, and each video has a certain amount of labeled ground truth images.

4.2   Resources for GSP-MOS

There are some important resources to study GSP-MOS. For GSP, the survey papers [37, 48] are fundamental sources of information. Moreover, the paper [21] contains detailed theoretical explanations and proofs for GSP-MOS along with a GitHub repository[1] with publicly available codes. The readers are also encouraged to visit the GSP Website[2].

5   Results and Discussion

Table 1 shows some visual results of the GSP-MOS algorithms GraphBGS-TV [19] and GraphBGS [18] on CDNet2014 against the deep learning method BSUV-Net [51]. Furthermore, Table 2 shows the numerical comparison of three GSP-MOS algorithms (GraphBGS [18], GraphBGS-TV [20], and GraphMOS [21]), two deep learning methods (FgSegNet v2 [32] and BSUV-Net [51]), and three unsupervised methods (SuBSENSE [49], IUTIS-5 [3], and SemanticBGS [9]). All methods in Table 2 have been evaluated with an agnostic video scheme [19,34,51] (unseen videos). One can see that GSP-MOS algorithms are good in almost all challenges except in intermittent object motion (I-O Motion) and in low frame rate (Low-F Rate). All GSP-MOS algorithms have used the median filter as the background initialization method, however more sophisticated methods such as [26] can be used to improve the performance of GSP-MOS in I-O Motion. Furthermore, the computation of the optical flow for the feature extraction can be affecting the performance of GSP-MOS algorithms due to the nature of Low-F Rate videos.

For the new evaluation strategy using several sampling densities, we adopt the following convention to name the architecture of a GSP-MOS algorithm: (semi-supervised learning method) - (segmentation method) - (k parameter for the k-NN method). Similarly, the following abbreviations are given: 1) SN means Sobolev norm with $\epsilon = 0.2$ and $\alpha = 1$, 2) TV means Total Variation, 3) M50 means instance segmentation with a Mask R-CNN with a ResNet-50, 4) X101 means instance segmentation with a Mask R-CNN with a ResNeXt-101, 5) C200 means instance segmentation with a Cascade Mask R-CNN and a ResNeSt-200, and 6) DL means semantic segmentation with DeepLab method. For example, SN-M50-30 is a GSP-MOS architecture that uses Sobolev norm minimization, a Mask R-CNN with ResNet-50, and k-NN with $k = 30$.

Figure 4 shows the results of several configurations of GSP-MOS algorithms. For example, TV-X101-20 corresponds to GraphBGS-TV [19], while SN-C200-30 corresponds to GraphBGS [18]. GraphMOS [21] was not evaluated using this procedure due to its high computational complexity. Similarly, we evaluate two new architectures namely SN-DL-30 and SN-X101-30. The design of an architecture for GSP-MOS should be focused on the specific challenges that we can have in our dataset. For instance, TV works better than Sobolev norm minimization in PTZ, camera jitter, and bad weather. Similarly, C200 works better than the others segmentation methods in almost all cases, however one should consider the high computational complexity of C200. Figure 4 also helps to evaluate certain algorithms given an amount of labeled information. For example, if one has a dataset with intermittent objects motions, and the percentage of labeled

---

[1] https://github.com/jhonygiraldo/GraphMOS.
[2] https://sites.google.com/view/gsp-website.

Table 1. Some visual results on CDNet2014 dataset for the GSP-MOS algorithms GraphBGS-TV [20] and GraphBGS [18] compared with BSUV-Net [51].

Categories	Original	Ground Truth	BSUV-Net	GraphBGS-TV	GraphBGS
Bad Weather Snow Fall in002776					
Baseline PETS2006 in000986					
Camera Jitter Badminton in000980					
Dynamic-B Fall in002795					
I-O Motion Sofa in000651					
PTZ Intermittent-P in001873					

Table 2. Comparisons of average F-measure over nine challenges of CDNet2014. GSP-MOS algorithms are compared with unsupervised and supervised methods in MOS. The best and second best performing method for each challenge are shown in red and **blue**, respectively.

Challenge	SuBSENSE	IUTIS-5	SemanticBGS	FgSegNet v2	BSUV-Net	GraphBGS	GraphBGS-TV	GraphMOS
Bad Weather	0.8619	0.8248	0.8260	0.7952	0.8713	**0.9085**	0.8072	0.9411
Baseline	0.9503	0.9567	0.9604	0.6926	**0.9693**	0.9535	0.9436	0.9710
Camera Jitter	0.8152	0.8332	0.8388	0.4266	0.7743	**0.8826**	0.7194	0.9233
Dynamic-B	0.8177	0.8902	0.9489	0.3634	0.7967	0.8353	0.7581	**0.8922**
I-O Motion	0.6569	0.7296	0.7878	0.2002	**0.7499**	0.5036	0.4376	0.6455
Low-F Rate	0.6445	**0.7743**	0.7888	0.2482	0.6797	0.6022	0.5191	0.6910
PTZ	0.3476	0.4282	0.5673	0.3503	0.6282	0.7993	**0.8031**	0.8511
Shadow	0.8986	0.9084	0.9478	0.5295	0.9233	**0.9712**	0.9660	0.9901
Thermal	0.8171	0.8303	0.8219	0.6038	0.8581	**0.8594**	0.7305	0.9010
Overall	0.7566	0.7923	**0.8320**	0.4158	0.8056	0.8128	0.7427	0.8674

images in the dataset is less than 2%, TV-X101-20 works better than the other architectures in that case.

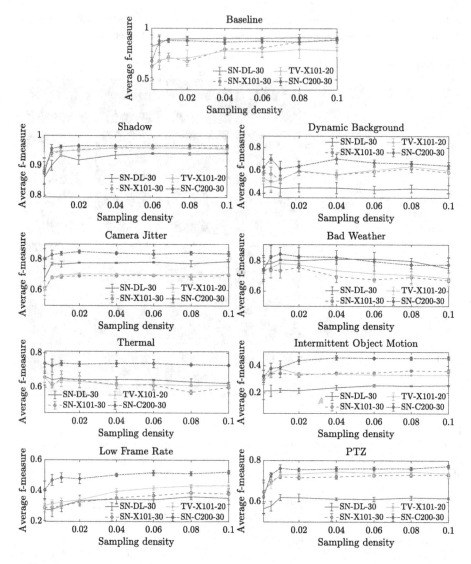

Fig. 4. Average F-measure vs sampling density for several architectures of GSP-MOS in nine challenges of CDNet2014. Each point in the plots is a Monte Carlo cross-validation experiment with 5 repetitions.

6 Conclusions

In this study, we summarized the ideas and theoretical developments of SOTA GSP-MOS algorithms. Similarly, we proposed two new architectures of GSP-MOS and a new evaluation procedure for taking into account the sampling density of labeled information (the amount of training images). GSP-MOS architectures are usually composed of: 1) a segmentation method, 2) a background model, 3) a feature extraction for nodes representation, 4) a graph construction, 5) graph signal representation, 6) a sampling method, and 7) a semi-supervised learning method. GSP-MOS algorithms have shown good results for static as well as moving camera sequences. Furthermore, GSP-MOS algorithms have important theoretical guarantees rooted from the rich theory of GSP.

GSP-MOS algorithms have several directions for future research. For example, one can try to use light CNN architectures to learn better movement features than using handcrafted and pre-trained CNN features. Similarly, one can try to improve the performance of GSP-MOS using other tools such as more sophisticated background initialization methods, or feature selection/dimensionality reduction after the feature extraction procedure.

References

1. Achanta, R., et al.: SLIC superpixels compared to state-of-the-art superpixel methods. IEEE Trans. Pattern Anal. Mach. Intell. **34**(11), 2274–2282 (2012)
2. Anis, A., Gadde, A., Ortega, A.: Efficient sampling set selection for bandlimited graph signals using graph spectral proxies. IEEE Trans. Signal Process. **64**(14), 3775–3789 (2016)
3. Bianco, S., Ciocca, G., Schettini, R.: Combination of video change detection algorithms by genetic programming. IEEE Trans. Evol. Comput. **21**(6), 914–928 (2017)
4. Bouwmans, T.: Traditional and recent approaches in background modeling for foreground detection: an overview. Comput. Sci. Rev. **11**, 31–66 (2014)
5. Bouwmans, T., El Baf, F., Vachon, B.: Background modeling using mixture of Gaussians for foreground detection-a survey. Recent Patents Comput. Sci. **1**(3), 219–237 (2008)
6. Bouwmans, T., Zahzah, E.H.: Robust PCA via principal component pursuit: a review for a comparative evaluation in video surveillance. Comput. Vis. Image Underst. **122**, 22–34 (2014)
7. Bouwmans, T., et al.: Decomposition into low-rank plus additive matrices for background/foreground separation: a review for a comparative evaluation with a large-scale dataset. Comput. Sci. Rev. **23**, 1–71 (2017)
8. Bouwmans, T., et al.: Deep neural network concepts for background subtraction: a systematic review and comparative evaluation. Neural Netw. **117**, 8–66 (2019)
9. Braham, M., Piérard, S., Van Droogenbroeck, M.: Semantic background subtraction. In: IEEE ICIP (2017)
10. Cai, Z., Vasconcelos, N.: Cascade R-CNN: high quality object detection and instance segmentation. IEEE Trans. Pattern Anal. Mach. Intell. **43**, 1483–1498 (2019)
11. Chatfield, K., et al.: Return of the devil in the details: delving deep into convolutional nets. In: BMVC (2014)
12. Chen, L.C., et al.: DeepLab: semantic image segmentation with deep convolutional nets, atrous convolution, and fully connected CRFs. IEEE Trans. Pattern Anal. Mach. Intell. **40**(4), 834–848 (2017)
13. Chen, S., et al.: Discrete signal processing on graphs: sampling theory. IEEE Trans. Signal Process. **63**(24), 6510–6523 (2015)
14. Danelljan, M., et al.: ECO: efficient convolution operators for tracking. In: IEEE CVPR (2017)

15. Du, S.S., et al.: How many samples are needed to estimate a convolutional neural network? In: NeurIPS (2018)
16. Egilmez, H.E., Ortega, A.: Spectral anomaly detection using graph-based filtering for wireless sensor networks. In: IEEE ICASSP (2014)
17. Garcia-Garcia, B., Bouwmans, T., Silva, A.J.: Background subtraction in real applications: challenges, current models and future directions. Comput. Sci. Rev. **35**, 100204 (2020)
18. Giraldo, J.H., Bouwmans, T.: GraphBGS: background subtraction via recovery of graph signals. In: ICPR (2021)
19. Giraldo, J.H., Bouwmans, T.: On the minimization of Sobolev norms of time-varying graph signals: estimation of new Coronavirus disease 2019 cases. In: IEEE MLSP (2020)
20. Giraldo, J.H., Bouwmans, T.: Semi-supervised background subtraction of unseen videos: minimization of the total variation of graph signals. In: IEEE ICIP (2020)
21. Giraldo, J.H., Javed, S., Bouwmans, T.: Graph moving object segmentation. IEEE Trans. Pattern Anal. Mach. Intell. (2020)
22. Giraldo, J.H., Le, H.T., Bouwmans, T.: Deep learning based background subtraction: a systematic survey. In: Handbook of Pattern Recognition and Computer Vision, p. 51 (2020)
23. He, K., et al.: Deep residual learning for image recognition. In: IEEE CVPR (2016)
24. He, K., et al.: Mask R-CNN. In: IEEE CVPR (2017)
25. Javed, S., et al.: Spatiotemporal low-rank modeling for complex scene background initialization. IEEE Trans. Circuit Syst. Video Technol. **28**(6), 1315–1329 (2016)
26. Javed, S., et al.: Background-foreground modeling based on spatiotemporal sparse subspace clustering. IEEE Trans. Image Process. **26**(12), 5840–5854 (2017)
27. Javed, S., et al.: Robust structural low-rank tracking. IEEE Trans. Image Process. **29**, 4390–4405 (2020)
28. Javed, S., et al.: Moving object detection in complex scene using spatiotemporal structured-sparse RPCA. IEEE Trans. Image Process. **28**(2), 1007–1022 (2018)
29. Jung, A., et al.: Semi-supervised learning in network-structured data via total variation minimization. IEEE Trans. Signal Process. **67**(24), 6256–6269 (2019)
30. Krizhevsky, A., Sutskever, I., Hinton, G.E.: ImageNet classification with deep convolutional neural networks. In: NeurIPS (2012)
31. LeCun, Y., Bengio, Y., Hinton, G.: Deep learning. Nature **521**(7553), 436–444 (2015)
32. Lim, L.A., Keles, H.Y.: Learning multi-scale features for foreground segmentation. Pattern Anal. Appl. **23**(3), 1369–1380 (2020)
33. Lucas, B.D., Kanade, T., et al.: An iterative image registration technique with an application to stereo vision (1981)
34. Mandal, M., Vipparthi, S.K.: Scene independency matters: an empirical study of scene dependent and scene independent evaluation for CNN-based change detection. IEEE Trans. Intell. Transp. Syst., 1–14 (2020)
35. Mandal, M., et al.: 3DCD: scene independent end-to-end spatiotemporal feature learning framework for change detection in unseen videos. IEEE Trans. Image Process. **30**, 546–558 (2020)
36. Ojala, T., Pietikäinen, M., Mäenpää, T.: Multiresolution gray-scale and rotation invariant texture classification with local binary patterns. IEEE Trans. Pattern Anal. Mach. Intell. **7**, 971–987 (2002)
37. Ortega, A., et al.: Graph signal processing: overview, challenges, and applications. Proc. IEEE **106**(5), 808–828 (2018)

38. Pang, J., et al.: Optimal graph Laplacian regularization for natural image denoising. In: IEEE ICASSP (2015)
39. Parada-Mayorga, A., et al.: Blue-noise sampling on graphs. IEEE Trans. Signal Inf. Process. Netw. **5**(3), 554–569 (2019)
40. Parada-Mayorga, A., et al.: Sampling of graph signals with blue noise dithering. In: IEEE DSW (2019)
41. Perazzi, F., et al.: A benchmark dataset and evaluation methodology for video object segmentation. In: IEEE CVPR (2016)
42. Perraudin, N., et al.: UNLocBoX a Matlab convex optimization toolbox using proximal splitting methods. arXiv preprint arXiv:1402.0779
43. Perraudin, N., et al.: GSPBOX: a toolbox for signal processing on graphs. arXiv preprint arXiv:1408.5781 (2014)
44. Pesenson, I.: Sampling in Paley-Wiener spaces on combinatorial graphs. Trans. Amer. Math. Soc. **360**(10), 5603–5627 (2008)
45. Pesenson, I.: Variational splines and Paley-Wiener spaces on combinatorial graphs. Constructive Approximation **29**(1), 1–21 (2009)
46. Romero, D., Ma, M., Giannakis, G.B.: Kernel-based reconstruction of graph signals. IEEE Trans. Signal Process. **65**(3), 764–778 (2016)
47. Shalev-Shwartz, S., Ben-David, S.: Understanding Machine Learning: From Theory to Algorithms. Cambridge University Press, Cambridge (2014)
48. Shuman, D.I., et al.: The emerging field of signal processing on graphs: extending high-dimensional data analysis to networks and other irregular domains. IEEE Signal Process. Mag. **30**(3), 83–98 (2013)
49. St-Charles, P.L., Bilodeau, G.A., Bergevin, R.: SuBSENSE: a universal change detection method with local adaptive sensitivity. IEEE Trans. Image Process. **24**(1), 359–373 (2014)
50. Sultana, M., et al.: Unsupervised deep context prediction for background estimation and foreground segmentation. Mach. Vis. Appl. **30**(3), 375–395 (2019)
51. Tezcan, O., Ishwar, P., Konrad, J.: BSUV-Net: a fully-convolutional neural network for background subtraction of unseen videos. In: IEEE WACV (2020)
52. Thanou, D., Chou, P.A., Frossard, P.: Graph-based compression of dynamic 3D point cloud sequences. IEEE Trans. Image Process. **25**(4), 1765–1778 (2016)
53. Vapnik, V.: The Nature of Statistical Learning Theory. Springer, New York (2013). https://doi.org/10.1007/978-1-4757-2440-0
54. Wang, Y., et al.: CDnet 2014: an expanded change detection benchmark dataset. In: IEEE CVPR-W (2014)
55. Xie, S., et al.: Aggregated residual transformations for deep neural networks. In: IEEE CVPR (2017)
56. Yang, F., et al.: Superpixel segmentation with fully convolutional networks. In: IEEE CVPR (2020)
57. Zhang, C., Florencio, D., Loop, C.: Point cloud attribute compression with graph transform. In: IEEE ICIP (2014)
58. Zhang, H., et al.: ResNeSt: split-attention networks. arXiv preprint arXiv:2004.08955 (2020)

Multi-scale Global Reasoning Unit for Semantic Segmentation

Yukihiro Domae[✉], Hiroaki Aizawa, and Kunihito Kato

Gifu University, 1-1 Yanagido, Gifu 501-1193, Japan
domae@cv.info.gifu-u.ac.jp

Abstract. Obtaining context information in a scene is an essential ability for semantic segmentation. GloRe [1] learns to infer the context from a graph-based feature constructed by the Global Reasoning unit. The graph nodes are features that are segmented into regions in image space, and the edges are relationships between nodes. Therefore, a failure to construct the graph results in poor performance. In this study, to resolve this problem, we propose a novel unit to construct the graph using multi-scale information. We call it Multi-scale Global Reasoning Unit. It considers the relationship between each region that retains detailed multi-scale spatial information. Specifically, the proposed unit consists of a Feature Aggregation Module and a Global Reasoning Module. The former selects the features required to construct the graph using the multi-scale features. The latter uses GloRe to infer the relationship from the features. The unit is trained in an end-to-end manner. In experiments, we evaluate the effectiveness of the proposed method on Cityscapes and Pascal-context datasets. As a result, we confirmed that the proposed method outperforms the original GloRe.

Keywords: Semantic segmentation · Graph convolution · Global reasoning

1 Introduction

Semantic segmentation is a fundamental task in computer vision. For the task to be successful, it is essential to obtain the context to understand the scene and spatial information. However, obtaining the context is difficult. To resolve this issue, graph-based semantic segmentation approaches have been proposed [1–7]. GloRe aggregates features from segmented regions as the node and then constructs a graph with the nodes. The regions are implicitly learned from the cross-entropy loss. To obtain the context from the graph, GloRe infers the relationships between the regions by graph convolution [8]. Finally, the graph is then transformed into the features in coordinate space in order to predict a segmentation map. Therefore, the performance depends on the construction of the graph. However, the feature maps to construct the graph do not retain detailed spatial information for semantic segmentation due to passing through the dilated convolution [9] and pooling over multiple times. Consequently, as shown in Fig. 1, this problem leads to the overlook of small objects and the confusion between objects.

© Springer Nature Switzerland AG 2021
H. Jeong and K. Sumi (Eds.): IW-FCV 2021, CCIS 1405, pp. 46–56, 2021.
https://doi.org/10.1007/978-3-030-81638-4_4

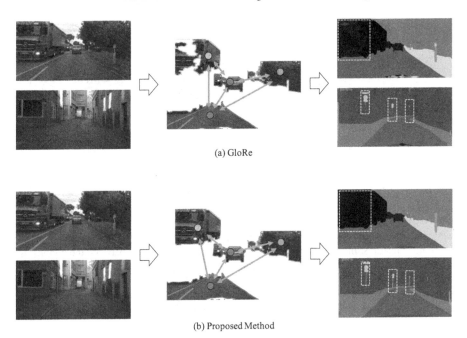

(a) GloRe

(b) Proposed Method

Fig. 1. Illustration of the difference between GloRe and the proposed method. GloRe (a) is a graph-based method to obtain global context information. However, GloRe uses features lacking spatial information to construct the graph, which leads to the overlook of small objects and the confusion between objects. On the other hand, the proposed method (b) construct the graph from the features that captures detailed spatial information using multi-scale feature maps.

In this work, we propose a novel unit to construct the graph using multi-scale information in order to reason the global context. We call it Multi-scale Global Reasoning Unit. Specifically, the proposed unit comprises two modules: a Feature Aggregation Module and a Global Reasoning Module. In the former module, we aggregate the feature from each layer of ResNet101 [10] that captures spatial and semantic information in detail. The aggregated features are used to construct the graph while preserving the detailed context. In the latter module, we extract a global context by considering the relationships between the regions of the multi-scale features using GloRe.

2   Related Work

Global context information is used to understand the relationships between objects, the layout of objects, and the scene in an input image. Repeated convolutional opertions generate large receptive fields and capture the dependence between distant features. However, increasing the convolutional layer is inefficient because the resulting receptive field would be smaller than the expected size [11]. Recent methods obtain global context information after feature extraction.

The major approaches to obtain global context information are the attention mechanism [12–15] and graph-based methods [1–7]. DANet [13] is a method that uses a

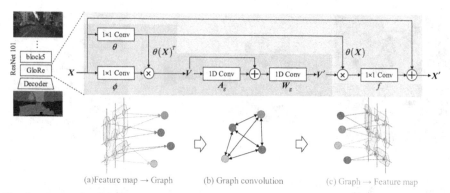

(a)Feature map → Graph   (b) Graph convolution   (c) Graph → Feature map

Fig. 2. The pipeline of GloRe. The above figure shows the detailed operation of GloRe, and the figure below shows the outline of the operation of GloRe. The operations of GloRe are mainly divided into three types of operations. In (a), it infers regions from the feature map and converts them to node features. In (b), a graph convolution infers the relationship between the regions. In (c), each node feature is transformed into a feature map to obtain global contextual information. X is the input feature of GloRe, θ is a function for generating the region information, ϕ is a function for dimensionality reduction, V is an input node feature GC, A_g and W_g are functions for realizing GC, V' is a node feature output by GC, and X' is the output of GloRe.

self-attention mechanism. This method computes the relationship between all elements by taking the inner product in the spatial and channel directions. The aggregation of features related to each element is based on the relationship. Therefore, each element obtains global context information.

GloRe is a method for obtaining global context information using a graph. It constructs a graph with the features included in the inferred regions as nodes. The regions are implicitly learned by segmentation loss for the final prediction. It then considers the relationship between each region by graph convolution (GC) [8]. GC learns filters and edge weights. Each node after GC has the features of strongly related nodes in addition to the features before GC. It provides global context information. Each node feature is broadcasted to the corresponding regions. GloRe can be added to existing models and obtain effective global context information for various recognition tasks.

In GloRe, the region directly affects the performance because it is used in constructing the graph and transforming from coordinate space to graph space. Thus, if the regions can capture objects in more detail, it is possible to consider the appropriate relationships between each region and transformations between the two spaces. The proposed method is based on GloRe and refines the region to build the nodes from multi-scale feature maps.

3   Global Reasoning Unit

The goal of the Global Reasoning Unit (GloRe) is to extract useful global contextual information for semantic segmentation and image classification. An overview of it is shown in Fig. 2. GloRe takes the output from ResNet101 as input and outputs a feature map $X \in \mathbb{R}^{C \times L}$ with global contextual information. First, It performs two pointwise convolutions ($\theta(\cdot)$ and $\phi(\cdot)$) to the input feature map. H, W, and C denote the height, width, and number of channels of the feature map, respectively. L is the number of spatial elements ($L = H \times W$). The goal of $\theta(\cdot)$ is to obtain the region where we want to consider the relationship and the goal of $\phi(\cdot)$ is to reduce the dimension of the feature map. The outputs from the two pointwise convolutions are $\theta(X) \in \mathbb{R}^{N \times L}$ and $\phi(X) \in \mathbb{R}^{C' \times L}$, respectively. C' is the number of channels in the feature map after dimensionality reduction. N is the number of nodes in the graph and is also the number of regions to consider in the relationship. The feature map is transformed into a node feature $V \in \mathbb{R}^{C' \times N}$ as shown in Eq. (1). It can be considered as a weighted global average pooling for $\phi(X)$, with $\theta(X)$ as the weight. Thus, as shown in Fig. 2(a), the N feature vectors of node feature V is built from each feature in the regions $\theta(X)$.

$$V = \frac{1}{N}\phi(X)\theta(X)^T, \tag{1}$$

The graph is built as a fully connected graph consisting of the adjacency matrix $A \in \mathbb{R}^{N \times N}$ and node features V. The relationship between the N features is learned by GC as in Eq. (2).

$$V = (I + A)VW, \tag{2}$$

$W \in \mathbb{R}^{N \times N}$ is a parameter of graph convolution (GC) [8] and $V' \in \mathbb{R}^{C' \times N}$ is a node feature after GC. The unit matrix I is a residual pass to facilitate optimization, and A and W are randomly initialized. The GC also learns the strength of the relationship between each node, since the adjacency matrix A is a learnable parameter. In other words, it means that GC learns the relationship between each region, as shown in Fig. 2(b). Equation (2) is implemented with 1D convolutions ($A_g(\cdot)$ and $W_g(\cdot)$) on the channel and node dimensions for node feature V. It results in Eq. (3). The output channels of $A_g(\cdot)$ and $W_g(\cdot)$ are $A_g(V) \in \mathbb{R}^{C' \times N}$ and $W_g(V) \in \mathbb{R}^{C' \times N}$ with the same number of input node channels.

$$V' = W_g\big(V + A_g(V)\big), \tag{3}$$

The input V and the output V' of the GC have the same number of nodes, and the node indices of the two graphs correspond to each other. As shown in Fig. 2(c) and Eq. (4), the node feature V' is transformed from graph space to coordinate space by weighted broadcasting with the region $\theta(X)$ as the weight. It means that features in each region have features of other regions that are strongly related. It allows GloRe to obtain global context information. After that, the output from pointwise convolution $f(\cdot)$ has the same dimension as the GloRe input.

$$X' = f\big(V'\theta(X)\big). \tag{4}$$

$f(\cdot)$ denotes a pointwise convolution. Finally, global contextual information X' is added to GloRe's input features X.

4 Multi-scale Global Reasoning Unit

In this study, we propose a Multi-scale Global Reasoning Unit that aggregates global context information while retaining detailed information, as shown in Fig. 3. Specifically, the Feature Aggregation Module selects features with regions that capture the object's scale and shape in detail. The Global Reasoning Module considers the relationship between the regions using GloRe. An additional loss function, Auxiliary Loss, ensures that the Feature Aggregation Module selects features with regions that capture scale and shape in detail.

4.1 Feature Aggregation Module

As shown in Fig. 4(a), the Feature Aggregation Module selects features with regions that capture the object's scale and shape in detail. This module takes as input the feature maps obtained from Blocks 3, 4, and 5 of ResNet101. We describe the Module taking Block 3 in Fig. 5 as an example. Firstly, the features in Block 3 are applied to the convolution and pooling operations while maintaining the number of channels. Then global average pooling and softmax layers allow us to obtain the importance by channel. The output size of the softmax layer is $1 \times 1 \times 512$, which corresponds to the number of channels in the module's input feature map. Then, in order of softmax value, N_3 features are selected from the input feature. N_3 is the number of features to select from the input feature and is also a hyperparameter. Each feature map in Blocks 4 and 5 of ResNet101 is selected in the same way as block3. The number of features to select from the feature map in Blocks 4 and 5 is N_4, N_5. The Auxiliary Loss described in Sect. 4.3 ensures this module select features with regions that are captured in the scale and shape of the object in detail.

4.2 Global Reasoning Module

The purpose of the Global Reasoning Module is to obtain global contextual information while maintaining detailed information. To achieve this, we make GloRe consider the relationships between the detailed regions selected in the Feature Aggregation Module. Original GloRe infers regions from the output in ResNet101 to construct nodes. Then, it considers those relationships. The output in ResNet101 lacks detailed spatial information due to Dilated convolution [9] and Pooling. It prevents proper transformation between coordinate and graph space and consideration of the relationships between regions. It causes overlooking of small objects and confusion of objects. As shown in Fig. 4(b), the proposed method replaces $\theta(X)$ in Fig. 2 with a feature with detailed regions selected in the Feature Aggregation Module. Constructing nodes from that region allows us to appropriately transform between coordinate and graph spaces and consider the relationship. Therefore, the proposed method is able to obtain global context information while retaining detailed region information.

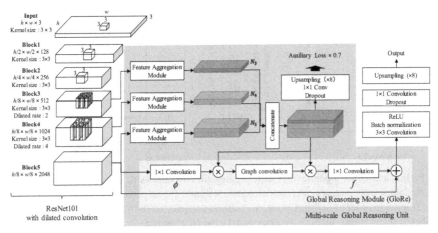

Fig. 3. Architecture of the proposed method. The Feature Aggregation Module selects from Block 3, 4, 5 features of ResNet101 to construct nodes. Then, Minimizing the Auxiliary loss ensures that the module selects features with region information that capture the shape and scale of the object in detail. The Global Reasoning Module is based on GloRe and construct a graph with the features contained in each selected region as node. Therefore, we obtain global context information while maintaining the detailed information. h and w are the height and width of the input images, and N_3, N_4 and N_5 are the number of features selected from the output of each block.

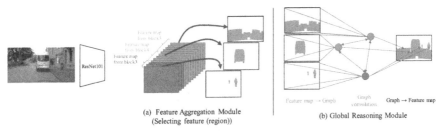

(a) Feature Aggregation Module
(Selecting feature (region))

(b) Global Reasoning Module

Fig. 4. Overview of Feature Aggregation Module and Global Reasoning Module. (a): In the Feature Module Aggregation, features with region information that capture the shape and scale of the objects in detail are selected from the features in Blocks 3, 4, and 5 of ResNet101. (b): In the Feature Aggregation Module, the detailed regions selected in the Feature Aggregation Module are used in GloRe. It allows for appropriate consideration of relationships between regions and transformations from coordinate to graph space.

4.3 Auxiliary Loss

The proposed method predicts and learns segmentation maps from selected features in the Feature Aggregation Module. Auxiliary loss is defined as a cross-entropy loss. The Loss allows the module to train the value of softmax to be larger for features that capture the more detailed scale and shape of the objects. The Loss function L_{opt} for optimizing the entire model is shown in Eq. (5).

$$L_{opt} = L + \alpha L_{aux}, \tag{5}$$

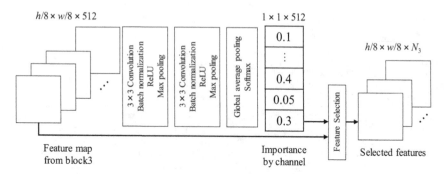

Fig. 5. Illustrating the pipeline of Feature Aggregation Module using a feature map in Block 3. The module selects features to construct nodes. We infer the importance of each channel from input feature. In order of Softmax value, N_3 features are selected from the input feature. N_3 is the number to select from a features in Block 3 and a hyperparameter.

L is the cross-entropy loss for the final prediction, L_{aux} is the auxiliary loss, and α is the penalty term of L_{aux} to focus more on L.

5 Evaluation

To evaluate the proposed method, we conduct experiments on cityscapes and the Pascal-context dataset. We compared the proposed method with the original GloRe.

5.1 Evaluation Settings

Cityscapes. The dataset [16] is an urban street scenes dataset. It has 5,000 imgaes including 50 cities and the image size is 2048 × 2048. It is divided into 2975 images for train, 500 images for validation, and 1525 images for test. This dataset has 30 classes, and we use 19 classes for evaluation. We only used fine annotations.

Pascal Context. This dataset [17] consists of 4998 training images and 5105 validation images. The Pascal-context is re-annotated for the entire image against PASCAL VOC 2010. Following the settings [18], we employed 59 classes except for background class.

Implementation Details. Following the architecture of GloRe[1], we use ResNet101 [10] as a backbone network, which is pre-trained in ImageNet [19] and employs a multi-grid dilated convolution [13] for the last two down-sampling phases. Thus, the output stride is 1/8. The number of features selected from Blocks 3, 4, and 5 in the Feature Aggregation Module is 10, 20, and 30, respectively. The optimization method is Stochastic gradient descent with momentum 0.9 and weight decay 1e-4. The initial learning rate was set to 0.006 for cityscapes and 0.001 for Pascal Context. The batch size was set to 8 for cityscapes and 16 for Pascal Context. For data argumentation, we apply random cropping, random scaling, and random flipping. The size of the random crop is set to 768 for cityscapes and 480 for Pascal Context. The range of the random scale is set to 0.5–2.0 and the probability of random flip is set to 0.5. Auxiliary Loss is set to

0.7 to emphasize the loss to the final prediction. We use Online Hard Example Mining (OHEM) [20] on Cityscapes to make the network focus its training on pixels with large errors.

Table 1. Results on cityscapes testing set.

	Road	Sidewalk	Building	Wall	Fence	Pole	Traffic light	Traffic sign	Vegetation	Terrain	Sky	Person	Rider	Car	Truck	Bus	Train	Motorcycle	Bicycle	Mean IoU
Original GloRe	98.4	85.9	92.5	53.8	58.5	68.7	77.8	80.2	93.6	72.3	95.3	86.8	72.8	96.3	74.1	86.4	78.1	71.2	78.1	80.1
Ours	98.6	86.3	92.8	52.6	61.5	70.2	79.2	82.4	93.7	72.1	94.9	87.6	73.4	96.4	72.5	86.6	80.6	73.5	79.4	80.8

Table 2. Results on Pascal-context validation set.

	pixAcc%	mIoU%
Original GloRe	80.26	53.33
Ours	80.78	54.07

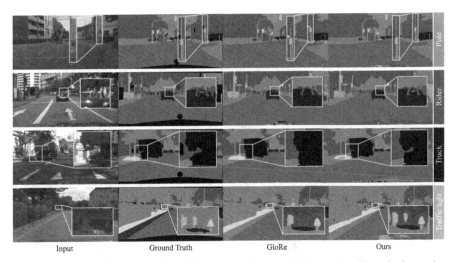

Fig. 6. Comparison between GloRe and the proposed method. It shows the effect of using regions that capture the shape and scale of the object in detail in the proposed method.

5.2 Quantitative Results

Table 1 shows our results for cityscapes. A mean IoU score of the original GloRe achieved 80.1. On the other hand, the score of our proposed method achieved 80.8, which is an improvement over the original GloRe. In particular, the Pole, traffic light, and traffic sign classes achieved higher scores in the proposed method. This shows the effect of using the detail regions that capture the shape and scale of the object by the proposed method. On the other hand, for the wall, terrain, sky, and truck classes, the original GloRe performed better than the proposed method. This will be analyzed in the next Sect. 5.3.

Table 2 shows our results for Pascal Context. The score of the original GloRe achieved 53.33. The score of our proposed method achieved 54.07. We confirmed that our proposed method outperforms the GloRe on two datasets.

5.3 Qualitative Results

In Figs. 6 and 7, we show the predictions of GloRe and the proposed method in the validation dataset of Cityscapes. In Fig. 6, GloRe overlooked the small rider's head, traffic lights, and pole in the yellow frame. On the other hand, we confirmed that the proposed method suppresses it by using the detail regions selected in the Feature Aggregation Module. In Fig. 7, there are objects with similar appearances in the yellow box (road vs. building, sidewalk vs. road, building vs. wall or fence, and pole vs. bus). In GloRe, ambiguous recognition occurred in the object region. On the other hand, the proposed method suppresses that misclassification by considering the relationship between detail regions selected by the Feature Aggregation Module.

other   hand,

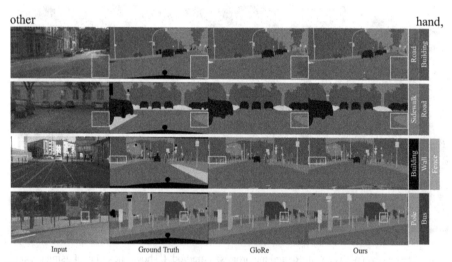

Input   Ground Truth   GloRe   Ours

Fig. 7. Comparison between GloRe and the proposed method. It shows the effect of using detailed region information to extract global features in the proposed method.

We investigate the classes for which GloRe performs better than the proposed method in Cityscapes. Figure 8 shows an input image, prediction results, and a part of the region inferred by the proposed method. The prediction result of the proposed method in the above figure shows that the confusion of classes occurs in the sky class. And we can see that the inferred region is affected by the change in texture pattern. Besides, the prediction results of the proposed method in the below figure show the same problem in the wall class. This factor is because the region information is obtained from the lower layer features. The features of the lower layer have detailed information about the shape and scale of the object. However, they are also sensitive to small changes in appearance. Some of the selected regions contain such changes, which negatively affects the accuracy.

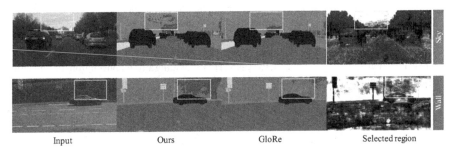

| Input | Ours | GloRe | Selected region |

Fig. 8. Visualization of segmentation results and a part of the selected regions in test data of cityscapes. The proposed method uses features in lower layer to obtain detailed region information. However, that feature is sensitive to small changes in the image, which affects the accuracy.

6   Conclusion

The use of global contextual information is useful in semantic segmentation and is necessary to understand the relationships between objects, layouts, and scenes in the input image. In this study, we proposed a Multi-scale Global Reasoning Unit based on GloRe. It learns relationships between regions that capture the shape and scale of the object in detail. As a result, the proposed method suppressed the small object's overlooking and confusion between objects in the original GloRe.

References

1. Chen, Y., Rohrbach, M., Yan, Z., Shuicheng, Y., Feng, J., Kalantidis, Y.: Graph-based global reasoning networks. In: The IEEE Conference on Computer Vision and Pattern Recognition, pp. 433–442 (2019)
2. Yin, L., Abhinav, G.: Beyond grids: learning graph representations for visual recognition. In: Advances in Neural Information Processing Systems, pp. 9225–9235 (2018)
3. Zhiheng, L., Wenxuan, B., Jiayang, Z., Chenliang, X.: Deep grouping model for unified perceptual parsing. In: Proceedings of the IEEE Conference on Computer Vision and Pattern Recognition, pp. 4053–4063 (2020)

4. Xia, L., Yibo, Y., Qijie, Z., Tiancheng, S., Zhouchen, L., Hong, L.: Spatial pyramid based graph reasoning for semantic segmentation. In: Proceedings of the IEEE Conference on Computer Vision and Pattern Recognition, pp. 8950–8959 (2020)

5. Yu, C., Liu, Y., Gao, C., Shen, C., Sang, N.: Representative graph neural network. In: Vedaldi, A., Bischof, H., Brox, T., Frahm, J.-M. (eds.) ECCV 2020. LNCS, vol. 12352, pp. 379–396. Springer, Cham (2020). https://doi.org/10.1007/978-3-030-58571-6_23

6. Wu, T., et al.: GINet: graph interaction network for scene parsing. In: Vedaldi, A., Bischof, H., Brox, T., Frahm, J.-M. (eds.) ECCV 2020. LNCS, vol. 12362, pp. 34–51. Springer, Cham (2020). https://doi.org/10.1007/978-3-030-58520-4_3

7. Hu, H., Ji, D., Gan, W., Bai, S., Wu, W., Yan, J.: Class-wise dynamic graph convolution for semantic segmentation. In: Vedaldi, A., Bischof, H., Brox, T., Frahm, J.-M. (eds.) ECCV 2020. LNCS, vol. 12362, pp. 1–17. Springer, Cham (2020). https://doi.org/10.1007/978-3-030-58520-4_1

8. Kipf, T.N., Welling, M.: Semi-supervised classification with graph convolutional networks. In: International Conference on Learning Representations, pp. 1–14 (2017)

9. Yu, F., Koltun, V.: Multi-scale context aggregation by dilated convolutions. In: International Conference on Learning Representations, pp. 1–14 (2016)

10. Chen, L.C., Papandreou, G., Schroff, F., Adam, H.: Rethinking atrous convolution for semantic image segmentation. arXiv:1706.05587 (2017)

11. Zhou, B., Khosla, A., Lapedriza, A., Oliva, A., Torralba, A.: Object detectors emerge in deep scene CNNs. In: International Conference on Learning Representations, pp. 1–14 (2015)

12. Vaswani, A., et al.: Attention is all you need. In: Advances in Neural Information Processing Systems, pp. 5998–6008 (2017)

13. Fu, J., et al.: Dual attention network for scene segmentation. In: The IEEE Conference on Computer Vision and Pattern Recognition, pp. 3146–3154 (2019)

14. Yuan, Y., Wang, J.: Ocnet: object context network for scene parsing. arXiv:1809.00916 (2018)

15. Huang, Z., Wang, X., Huang, L., Huang, C., Wei, Y., Liu, W.: Ccnet: Criss-cross attention for semantic segmentation. In Proceedings of the IEEE International Conference on Computer Vision, pp. 603–612 (2019)

16. Cordts, M., et al.: The cityscapes dataset for semantic urban scene understanding. In: The IEEE Conference on Computer Vision and Pattern Recognition, pp. 3213–3223 (2016)

17. Mottaghi, R., et al.: The role of context for object detection and semantic segmentation in the wild. In Proceedings of the IEEE Conference on Computer Vision and Pattern Recognition, pp. 891–898 (2014)

18. Sun, K., et al.: High-resolution representations for labeling pixels and regions. arXiv:1904.04514 (2019)

19. Krizhevsky, A., Sutskever, I., Hinton, G.E.: Imagenet classification with deep convolutional neural networks. In: Advances in Neural Information Processing Systems, pp. 1097–1105 (2012)

20. Wu, Z., Shen, C., Hengel, A.V.D.: High-performance semantic segmentation using very deep fully convolutional networks. arXiv preprint arXiv:1604.04339 (2016)

Recognition

Multi-modality Based Affective Video Summarization for Game Players

Sehar Shahzad Farooq[1] [ID], Abdullah Aziz[2] [ID], Hammad Mukhtar[3],
Mustansar Fiaz[1] [ID], Ki Yeol Baek[1] [ID], Naram Choi[1,2,3,4], Sang Bin Yun[1] [ID],
Kyung Joong Kim[3], and Soon Ki Jung[1(✉)] [ID]

[1] School of Computer Science and Engineering, Kyungpook National University,
Daegu, South Korea
skjung@knu.ac.kr
[2] Department of Computer Science, Electrical and Space Engineering,
Luleå University of Technology, 97187 Luleå, Sweden
[3] Department of Computer Science, National University of Computer and Emerging Sciences,
Lahore, Pakistan
[4] Institute of Integrated Technology, Gwangju Institute of Science and Technology, Gwangju,
South Korea

Abstract. Games has been considered as a benchmark for practicing computational models to analyze players interest as well as its involvement in the game. Though several aspects of game related research are carried out in different fields of research including development of game contents, avatar's control in games, artificial intelligent competitions, analysis of games using professional gamer's feedback, and advancements in different traditional and deep learning based computational models. However, affective video summarization of gamer's behavior and experience are also important to develop innovative features, in-game attractions, synthesizing experience and player's engagement in the game. Since it is difficult to review huge number of videos of experienced players for the affective analysis, this study is designed to generate video summarization for game players using multi-modal data analysis. Bedside's physiological and peripheral data analysis, summary of recorded videos of gamers is also generated using attention model-based framework. The analysis of the results has shown effective performance of proposed method.

Keywords: Video summarization · Affective analysis · Multi-modal data · Game player modeling

1 Introduction

Games has been widely used as a source of entertainment for every age of groups [1]. Among them, mostly young and child group of people have shown more interest in playing games to keep themselves engage in achieving artificially developed challenges and achievements in the game [2]. Beside this, on the other side, game developers have put their visionary and imaginary ideas to develop such an advanced and challenging games

© Springer Nature Switzerland AG 2021
H. Jeong and K. Sumi (Eds.): IW-FCV 2021, CCIS 1405, pp. 59–69, 2021.
https://doi.org/10.1007/978-3-030-81638-4_5

that it gives a hard time to players to achieve the goals [3, 4]. People invest time and money to cope up with the latest trends and techniques developed to deal the situations in the games [2]. Several video games have been developed in which the players have to control an avatar in the game and participate in a group of people who plays the game at the same time over the internet [5]. This not only gives the players an environment to express their personal behavior and emotions in the game but also help to develop themselves from experience of the other persons playing the game [6]. In recent times, these video games are been recorded and a huge volume of video data is generated [7, 8]. This data is then visualized to extract efficient and affective features. Based on these extractions, a feedback is shared to game developers and game industries to introduce new innovative features in the game [9, 10]. Along with these, this also help to develop in-game attractions to synthesize player's experience and escalate player's engagement in the game [11].

Previously computing was mainly focused to influence on text or numeric data, but as this digital system advanced, it come up with the introduction of several types of data including videos, audios, and images [2]. These heterogeneous types of data provide a platform for the development of huge numbers of applications. Some of the applications includes multimedia surveillance, content generation and analysis, dummy videos in medical experimental studies, advertisements, and games [12, 13]. To effectively manipulate a huge amount of such databases, it is the need of the hour to have a system to fulfil the requirements. It has been seen that traditional methods for data analysis and data management have deficient observations when requested for indexes and labeling. Video summarization techniques fulfil such deficiencies by effectively and efficiently generating and identifying pertinent contents [14, 15].

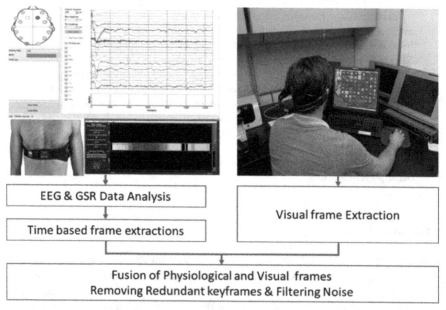

Fig. 1. Framework of proposed multi-modality based affective video summarization

Summary of affective videos can be generated in several forms, but most popular methodology is the combination of video skims, static storyboards, and affective content based keyframes [16, 17]. The final goal of video summarization is to develop highlights of the whole video of a particular event in humanly manners. The purpose of such highlights or short videos is to annotate contents and index long videos with-in database. It helps not only to save storage but also access time to find desired contents quickly. Although, such short videos can be generated manually but due to the long videos and limited manpower, it becomes impossible. A vital scenario is to develop an automated system to reduce manual processing.

Emotions play a crucial role for game players to develop their interest in the game [18]. These emotions are based on the physiological fluctuations caused by an object, a situation in the game as well as the surrounding environment [1, 19]. Emotions can be elicited in many situations within the games as well as the feelings of the players during the game [20, 21]. Such emotions represent behavior and experience of the gamers. Game player modeling refers to the descriptions of the players based on the framework of the data derived from the interaction of the player within the game as well as the association of the human player during the game [22]. In simple words what does a player do in the game is known as its behavior and how does a player feel during the game is its experience. Both behavior and experience of the gamers can be visualized in the game video analysis. To do this it is necessary to find out the most prominent and important events being happened in the videos. To figure it out, a framework is developed to extract smaller video skims with highly affective activities independently and combining them to a short summary. For the affective content analysis an attention-based summary in terms of time frames is generated from the analysis of physiological and peripheral data of the game players. Attention is a helpful mental procedure in cognition and permits humans to interrelate with the outer world in a more concentrated and specialized manner. The authors in [23] proposed the first attention-model based video summarization framework, which decomposes an original video sequence into the primary elements of its basic channels. Next, a set of features related to visual, aural, and linguistic attention is extracted to generate a comprehensive attention curve, which is used as an importance ranking, or to index the video content. On the other hand, a content-based summary is extracted from the recorded video of the players playing the game. These summaries then merge for affective video summarization. A framework of the proposed method is depicted in Fig. 1.

2 Proposed Methodology

2.1 Visual Frame Extraction

Due to the limited resources and time complexities, it is impracticable sometimes to analyze the long videos of games. However, parsing videos [24] is a suitable option in which we divide the lengthy videos into several chunks. In these chunks there are also many shots that have a considerable temporal component. The first step in video summarization is the detection of shots. These depends upon the changes in a scene or an activity from the previous one. These boundaries define a hierarchy to make short videos. A transition between these boundaries is analyzed to break the large videos in to small video chunks. Among these short chunks of videos, there are abrupt as well as gradual transitions [25]. An example of these transitions includes a totally different scene and a fade scene. The scenes are most importantly available in multiplayer video games where one person while performing its tasks is also dependent upon the other's performances. His progress is widely dependent upon his partners in a real time strategy game. Based on abrupt transition and multi-scene transitions, several methods have been developed in recent years. Though many considered low-level features to identify these transitions from successive frame including frame's intensity, edge detection, entropy and color histogram [25, 26]. In this research we utilized the approach developed in [27] to compute summaries based on the parsed videos. It is done by considering histogram difference of consecutive frames as can be seen in Fig. 2.

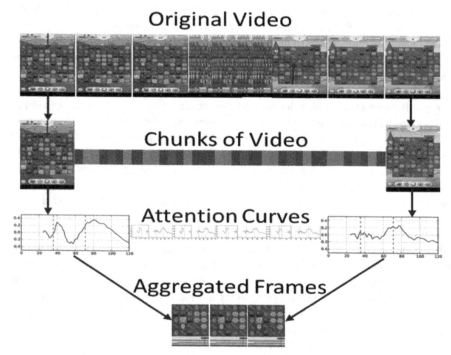

Fig. 2. Video summarization using attention curve modal

2.2 EEG and GSR Based Frame Extraction

Electroencephalogram (EEG) reveal an electrical activity of the brain through electrodes that are placed at specific locations of the human scalp [28]. It generates waves of different heights and frequencies. The height displays the strength and frequency displays number of cycles. These signals of different amplitude can be classified into several categories. These classifications represent different psychophysiological situations. Among them, beta-frequency band ranging from 12–30 Hz represent attentiveness. The up and down of human emotional arousal represents its attention or awakens/alertness and hence beta-band can be used to find the attention of the game players. Galvanic Skin Response (GSR) on the other hand reflect changes in our skin glands known as sweat glands and represent intensity of emotional state [29]. This is mostly dependent on the surrounding environment and basically related to the experience. Thus, EEG represents the in-human emotional activities and GSR represents the gamer's association while playing the game.

It is been evidenced by the neurobiologists that the attentiveness is regulated by arousal level known as the reactivity state in human. It can be panic, anger or excitement state. This is because of the beta-band in EEG signals. Hence, the attention features are measured by extracting the power spectral densities (PSDs) of beta-band of EEG Data [30]. Similarly experience based intensity of emotional state is also extracted using GSR's data. During pre-processing of raw data, the attention curve was normalized between 0 and 1. Careful synchronization of EEG data and player's video frames was the key element in this study which could give negative results if altered. So, at each particular time frame, a video frame is synchronized, and a specific frame is extracted from the video shots. The value close to 1 is considered as a high attention and values close to zero as lower or less attention (Fig. 3).

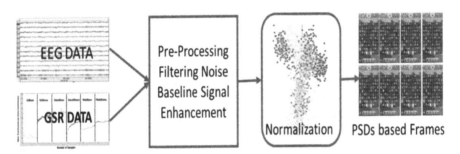

Fig. 3. EEG and GSR data-based frame extraction process

2.3 Inter-modality Attention Fusion

The visual frames synchronized with the same time frame of high attention curves of EEG and GSR data modal and visual frames extracted from the attention curve model of the parsing videos are than combined linearly to obtain the final video frames. This inter-modality fusion combines the strength of above individual modals and generate a non-redundant final summary. To reduce the duplicate scenes, we removed redundant frames.

3   Experiments and Results

The proposed method is evaluated based on the videos recorded during play time of the gamers in laboratory environment. The details are explained in the following section.

3.1 Data Collection

Devices

To access the potential response of the proposed methodology, the input data is generated by the subjects (game players) during their game play. For this purpose, we have set up an experimental environment where the EEG and GSR data is collected for the players during their game play. Along with it, we also set up a recording medium for the recording of the videos of the game screen during game play. This is done in such a way that each subject is wearing an EMOTIV EPOC headset[1] on its head with its electrodes at specific places of the scalp. The Bio Harness[2] device is worn around the chest of each game player. Both devices are controlled by a separate person to turn on and off the recordings of the game players. A mobile device is used to let the game players play the game. The game selected for this experiment is Candy Crush Saga[3]. It is freely available on the android platform. The recording capabilities of the Samsung Galaxy S7 mobile is used to record the screen of the game players during the game play. Windows 10 pro (64-Bit) operating system with Processor Intel® Core™ i7-4790 CPU@3.60 GHz (8 CPUs), RAM 32 Gigabyte and LG ULTRAWIDE (HDMI) MONITOR is used to monitor EEG and GSR signals and accurate video recordings for better synchronization of time at every device.

Data Types

Three types of data are collected in a way that the EEG signals of 14 channels is recorded by Emotive device with its real-time display on the monitor for every channel to work fine. The GSR signal display is connected to a computer and is manually recorded (start and end time). The video is recorded by itself from the mobile device. Before the experiment, each step of the experiment is explained to the subjects and upon their fully understanding, the experiment was conducted. The purpose of the experimental setup was to carefully synchronize the EEG and GSR data and video on the same time frame so that it become easy to extract the specific key frames from the videos based on the attention curve model response.

Game Levels and Subjects

Two Candy Crush Sage game levels were chosen for each player to play and its neuronal responses were recorded. These levels are number 8 and 343. Each subject is requested to play calmly and without extra stress to avoid depression-based alertness. After each level played by the subject, it is requested to each player to produce a summary of the game play by its own experience to maintain the ground truths for comparative analysis. A total of 10 subjects participated in this experiment and 10 videos were recorded. The subjects chosen for this experiment are the university students at graduate school. There was different type of players categorized as novice, intermediate and expert players. It

---

[1] https://www.emotiv.com.

[2] https://www.biopac.com/product-category/research/telemetry-and-data-logging/bioharness/#:
~:text=BioHarness%20with%20AcqKnowledge%20software%20is,respiration%2C%20post
ure%2C%20and%20acceleration.

[3] https://king.com/game/candycrush.

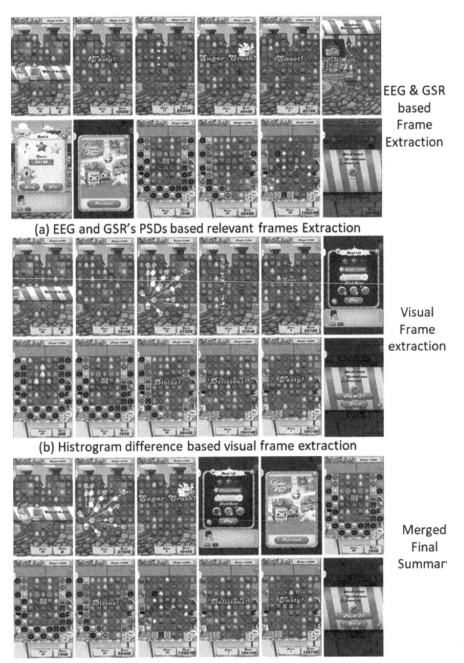

EEG & GSR
based
Frame
Extraction

(a) EEG and GSR's PSDs based relevant frames Extraction

Visual
Frame
extraction

(b) Histrogram difference based visual frame extraction

Merged
Final
Summar

(c) Merged above frames for combined video summary

Fig. 4. Comparison of affective video contents

took around 8–10 min for each player to play two levels whereas a 5-min gap is given between two levels. In this rest period, it is requested to manually define a summary. To synchronize the EEG and GSR data with the visual frames of the video, EEGLAB's toolbox was used. It acquires EEG data wirelessly from the EMOTIV device and stores it. MATLAB platform was used to extract the features from EEG Data as well as from the Videos.

3.2   Case Study: Extracting Keyframes from a Single Video

To demonstrate the effectiveness of the proposed model, one subject's data is presented in detail. It will help the reader to easily and correctly understand the proposed method and results acquired through it. The subject is a graduate student of one of the universities in South Korea, and is young, healthy, and intermediate game player. The video recorded for this subject consists of 2490 frames in which he plays two levels (easy and hard). The subject easily achieves the target in an easy level whereas it fails to complete hard level. However, the ground truth of the subject reveals that he felt emotional stimuli during the game play (Table 1).

Table 1. F-measure comparison of proposed method and STIMO

Video no	STIMO	Proposed
1	0.51	**0.60**
2	0.55	**0.70**
3	0.65	0.55
4	0.47	**0.48**
5	0.60	0.58
6	0.66	0.64
7	0.72	0.67
8	0.74	**0.77**
9	0.50	0.46
10	0.48	**0.48**

For the underlying video recording, the video frames extracted from the video are presented. The attention features are measured by extracting the power spectral densities (PSDs) of beta-band of EEG and GSR Data. Based on that the relevant frames synchronized with the same time frame are extracted and displayed in Fig. 4(a). For video frame extractions, we used histogram difference of consecutive frames. However, since the background and overall game display remains the same, we have multiplied the difference several times to measure major changes in the video frames. Hence the frames extracted using this method are shown in Fig. 4(b). Figure 4(c) merges the video frames extracted using video frame extraction method and EEG and GSR based frame extractions into a combined summary. To reduce the duplicate scenes, we removed redundant frames. Also, to keep the most interesting frames we combined the strengthened frames and removed the frames with weak features.

$$\text{Precision} = \frac{\text{TP}}{\text{TP} + \text{FP}} \tag{1}$$

$$\text{Recall} = \frac{\text{TP}}{\text{TP} + \text{FN}} \tag{2}$$

$$\text{F-measure} = 2 * \frac{\text{recall} * \text{precision}}{\text{recall} + \text{precision}} \tag{3}$$

3.3 Ground Truth Comparison-Based Summary Evaluation

To access the effectiveness of the proposed video summarization, we used evaluation matrices for ground truth comparison-based summary. In this research, we requested each subject to evaluate the summary of the video for the ground truth. Though it is a difficult task for each subject, but we evaluate based on their experience. Along with it, we also get help from the expert group of multimedia team members. The f-measure, recall and precision matrices are usually used to evaluate the effectiveness of the models. The ratio of relevant keyframes chosen and the total frames either relevant or irrelevant is known as precision. Whereas recall is ratio of chosen keyframes to the total number of keyframes available in ground truth summary. The average of precision and recall is known as the f-measure. Higher the f-measure represents higher precision and higher recall values. In this research we find out the f-measure after evaluating precision and recall from the given formulas in Eqs. 1, 2 and 3 respectively. According to the equations, TP represents true positive frames chosen and FP are false positive frames. To compare the proposed method with state-of-the-art techniques, the dataset is modified and facilitated to the previous known methods used in [17].

4 Conclusions and Future Work

In this research work, multi-modal based affective video summarization for game players is proposed. This research is based on a combination of extracting affective key frames for game players using two different models. The attention features are measured by extracting the power spectral densities (PSDs) of beta-band of EEG and GSR data. Based on that the relevant frames synchronized with the same time frame are extracted and combined to generate a short summary of the whole video. We also used histogram differences of consecutive frames from the whole video for video frame extractions. At last, we combined these two-attention based short summaries linearly into a single summary and removed redundant frames and less strengthened frames. The game player's attention is modeled based on several sensory perceptions. i.e., GSR signals, EEG, or neurological signals. In EEG attention model, we preferred beta-band frequency of the neuronal signals of the game player. It is found out that EEG based attention model reveal the emotional attachment of the game player within the game in terms of interest and focus. The f-measure of the proposed method is not ignorable. Comparing with previous method STIMO, though the proposed model does not perform well for every video, but the results are considerable. Since most of the background of the Candy Crush Saga game is similar in every scene. Hence, it becomes difficult to compare the change in each key-frame. Though it is a primarily study, in the future, it can be improved using other videos of the game players and results shall be comparable.

Acknowledgement. This study was supported by the BK21 FOUR project (AI-driven Convergence Software Education Research Program) funded by the Ministry of Education, School of Computer Science and Engineering, Kyungpook National University, Korea (4199990214394).

This work was also supported by Global University Project (GUP) grant funded by the GIST in 2020.

References

1. Farooq, S.S., Kim, K.-J.: Game player modeling. In: Lee, N. (ed.) Encyclopedia of Computer Graphics and Games, pp. 1–5. Springer, Cham (2015). https://doi.org/10.1007/978-3-319-08234-9_14-1
2. Hooshyar, D., Yousefi, M., Lim, H.: Data-driven approaches to game player modeling: a systematic literature review. ACM Comput. Surv. (CSUR) **50**, 90 (2018)
3. Bateman, C., Boon, R.: 21st Century Game Design (Game Development Series). Charles River Media Inc., Newton (2005)
4. Lamb, R., Annetta, L., Hoston, D., Shapiro, M., Matthews, B.: Examining human behavior in video games: the development of a computational model to measure aggression. Soc. Neurosci. **13**, 301–317 (2018)
5. Hsieh, J.-L., Sun, C.-T.: Building a player strategy model by analyzing replays of real-time strategy games. In: IEEE International Joint Conference on Neural Networks, IJCNN 2008. IEEE World Congress on Computational Intelligence, pp. 3106–3111 (2008)
6. Ahmad, M., Ab Rahim, L., Osman, K., Arshad, N.I.: Towards modelling effective educational games using multi-domain framework. In: Encyclopedia of Information Science and Technology, 4th edn, pp. 3337–3347. IGI Global (2018)
7. Bauckhage, C., Drachen, A., Sifa, R.: Clustering game behavior data. IEEE Trans. Comput. Intell. AI Games **7**, 266–278 (2015)
8. Yannakakis, G.N., Togelius, J.: Artificial Intelligence and Games. Springer, Cham (2018). https://doi.org/10.1007/978-3-319-63519-4
9. Newbery, R., Lean, J., Moizer, J., Haddoud, M.: Entrepreneurial identity formation during the initial entrepreneurial experience: the influence of simulation feedback and existing identity. J. Bus. Res. **85**, 51–59 (2018)
10. Ambinder, M.: Biofeedback in gameplay: how valve measures physiology to enhance gaming experience. In: Game Developers Conference (2011)
11. Arsenault, D.: Video game genre, evolution and innovation. Eludamos. J. Comput. Game Cult. **3**, 149–176 (2009)
12. Ekanayake, H.: CognitiveEmotional user correction for multimedia interactions using visual attention and psychophysiological signals (2009)
13. Mei, S., Ma, M., Wan, S., Hou, J., Wang, Z., Feng, D.D.: Patch based video summarization with block sparse representation. IEEE Trans. Multimedia **23**, 732–747 (2021). https://doi.org/10.1109/TMM.2020.2987683
14. Ejaz, N., Baik, S.W.: Video summarization using a network of radial basis functions. Multimedia Syst. **18**, 483–497 (2012)

15. Ji , Z., Zhao, Y., Pang, Y., Li, X., Han, J.: Deep attentive video summarization with distribution consistency learning. IEEE Trans. Neural Netw. Learn. Syst. **32**(4), 1765–1775 (2021). https://doi.org/10.1109/TNNLS.2020.2991083
16. Money, A.G., Agius, H.: Video summarisation: a conceptual framework and survey of the state of the art. J. Vis. Commun. Image Represent. **19**, 121–143 (2008)
17. Furini, M., Geraci, F., Montangero, M., Pellegrini, M.: STIMO: STIll and MOving video storyboard for the web scenario. Multimedia Tools Appl. **46**, 47 (2010)
18. Cowie, R., Pelachaud, C., Petta, P.: Emotion-Oriented Systems. Cognitive Technologies, pp. 9–30. Springer, Heidelberg (2011). https://doi.org/10.1007/978-3-642-15184-2
19. Loderer, K., Pekrun, R., Plass, J.L.: Emotional foundations of game-based learning. In: Handbook of Game-Based Learning, p. 111 (2020)
20. Du, G., Zhou, W., Li, C., Li, D., Liu, P.X.: An emotion recognition method for game evaluation based on electroencephalogram. IEEE Trans. Affect. Comput. (2020)
21. Miller, B.K.: Guess the emotion: a tablet game to support emotion regulation skills for children with autism (2020)
22. Farooq, S.S., Baek, J.-W., Kim, K.: Interpreting behaviors of mobile game players from in-game data and context logs. In: 2015 IEEE Conference on Computational Intelligence and Games (CIG), pp. 548–549 (2015)
23. Ma, Y.-F., Hua, X.-S., Lu, L., Zhang, H.-J.: A generic framework of user attention model and its application in video summarization. IEEE Trans. Multimedia **7**, 907–919 (2005)
24. Tsekeridou, S., Pitas, I.: Content-based video parsing and indexing based on audio-visual interaction. IEEE Trans. Circuits Syst. Video Technol. **11**, 522–535 (2001)
25. Hussain, T., Muhammad, K., Ding, W., Lloret, J., Baik, S.W., de Albuquerque, V.H.C.: A comprehensive survey of multi-view video summarization. Pattern Recognit. **109**, 107567 (2020)
26. Ma, M., Mei, S., Wan, S., Hou, J., Wang, Z., Feng, D.D.: Video summarization via block sparse dictionary selection. Neurocomputing **378**, 197–209 (2020)
27. Mehmood, I., Sajjad, M., Rho, S., Baik, S.W.: Divide-and-conquer based summarization framework for extracting affective video content. Neurocomputing **174**, 393–403 (2016)
28. Jirayucharoensak, S., Pan-Ngum, S., Israsena, P.: EEG-based emotion recognition using deep learning network with principal component based covariate shift adaptation. Sci. World J. **2014**, 1–10 (2014)
29. Val-Calvo, M., Álvarez-Sánchez, J.R., Ferrández-Vicente, J.M., Díaz-Morcillo, A., Fernández-Jover, E.: Real-time multi-modal estimation of dynamically evoked emotions using EEG, heart rate and galvanic skin response. Int. J. Neural Syst. **30**, 2050013 (2020)
30. Sanei, S., Chambers, J.A.: EEG Signal Processing. Wiley, Hoboken (2013)

Focusing on Discrimination Between Road Conditions and Weather in Driving Video Analysis

Hanwei Zhang[1(✉)], Hiroshi Kawasaki[2], Tsunenori Mine[2], and Shintaro Ono[3]

[1] Graduate School of Information Science and Electrical Engineering,
Kyushu University, Fukuoka, Japan
`zhang.hanwei.706@s.kyushu-u.ac.jp`
[2] Faculty of Information Science and Electrical Engineering, Kyushu University,
Fukuoka, Japan
[3] Institute of Industrial Science, The University of Tokyo, Tokyo, Japan

Abstract. We study an often ignored problem, the discrimination between road conditions and weather in driving videos, which may possibly lead to imperceptible errors on driving data analysis. We explore BDD100K, a common driving video database, and Kyushu Driving Data, a huge driving database created by ourselves. In our experiments, we use road condition labels and weather labels respectively to train several deep models on driving image sequences and demonstrate the difference between the two varieties of labels. The results indicate a significant difference between the two varieties, which leads to different performance of deep models.

Keywords: Driving video · Road condition · Weather classification · Deep learning

1 Introduction

With more and more driving data available since the era of big data began, analysis on driving data has attracted huge attentions. Typically, driving videos contain plentiful and comprehensive information, which can be extracted using modern computer vision approaches.

Usually, when performing analysis on driving, probe data which contains common information such as velocities, GPS positions is the first choice that researchers may consider. With the rapid development of computer vision technology, more and more works start to involve utilization of driving videos and public driving video datasets such as BDD100K [13], which contains various ground truth attributes have been released. Typically, road condition is an important factor which may have huge impact on driving behaviors. For example, a driver who is driving on a wet road may slow down the vehicle. In low visibility conditions such as heavy snow or fog, sudden braking may occur more than in usual clear conditions.

ⓒ Springer Nature Switzerland AG 2021
H. Jeong and K. Sumi (Eds.): IW-FCV 2021, CCIS 1405, pp. 70–80, 2021.
https://doi.org/10.1007/978-3-030-81638-4_6

Confusion of Road Condition and Weather. In fact, the concept of road condition is rarely seen in modern driving video datasets. Instead, "weather" is more commonly presented. Even from a normal person's intuition, it is believed that these two concepts are different, and road condition has more impact on driving behaviors rather than weather. In practical, these two concepts also may have discrimination. For example, after a heavy rain stops, the road may still keep being wet for a period of time. However, we observe that these two concepts are often been confused or the discrimination is often ignored in research. When we try to determine the "weather" from a driving video, we may use the clues of the road condition, the pedestrians who hold up umbrellas, etc., which may lead to confusion of the two concepts. Figure 1 shows an example from BDD100K [13] dataset. Both the images are labeled with weather attribute "rainy", but the left one is exactly the circumstance that the weather is clear but the road is wet.

Fig. 1. Two sample images from BDD100K test set. The left one has clear sky but wet road, while the right one is totally rainy. The ground truth weather attributes of the both are "rainy".

In this paper, we tend to raise the concern that when performing driving video analysis, a clear distinguish between "weather" and "road condition" should necessarily be made. To address this issue, we concretely design an application scene, which is performing image classification by a deep neural network. To switch between weather and road condition, we feed the network with differently labeled data. In the following, we first introduce related works (Sect. 2). Then we explain our research process in detailed, including our modified datasets (Sect. 3). In Sect. 4, we show our experimental results with proper analysis. Finally, we conclude our work (Sect. 5).

2   Related Works

In this section, we first introduce works on driving data analysis, followed by an introduction about weather classification from a single image.

2.1   Vehicle Probe Data Analysis

Many works have adopted data mining techniques to analyze vehicle data. He *et al.* [4] uses a mapping-to-cells method to construct a dynamic traffic diagram, and uses it to extract traffic congestion from the probe data. Park *et al.*

[10] proposes a Bayesian structure equation to recognize congestion patterns for road segments. Their work can predict secondary incident occurrences with new information available from the approach, which is significant to traffic accident prevention. As for the sudden braking estimation, Kawatani et al. [6] proposes an SVM-based feature selection model to estimate sudden braking.

2.2 Road Condition Analysis

Analysis on road conditions is actually not rare in researches related to transportation systems. Commonly, road conditions refer to whether the road is easy to drive. Several factors such as smoothness, incline may be considered. However, researchers usually use their own concrete aspects of road conditions depending on their different objectives in their works.

Tang et al. [11] proposes a new car-following model which considers road conditions. In their work, road conditions are defined as "good" or "bad" according to whether they are easy to drive. Bhoraskar et al. [1] develops a traffic and road condition estimation which can estimate road conditions (smooth, bumpy, inclined) and environment conditions (clear sky, covered with trees) with smartphone sensors. Jokela et al. [5] proposes a road condition monitoring system with stereo input. Their road conditions refer to ice, water, snow, dry and so on and utilize texture analysis to detect them.

2.3 Weather Classification

Weather classification on images has been widely studied since Convolutional Neural Networks (CNN) have achieved great success on image classifications. Lu et al.'s work [9] propose a 2-class classification method which extracts weather cues into features during the training process. They also provide a outdoor weather image dataset consisting of 10K sunny and cloudy images. Elhoseiny et al. [2] improves the previous work with a better-designed model, which reached an accuracy of 82.2%. However, in practical the categories of weather are relatively rich. Hence multi-class weather classification is essential for practical usage.

Zhang et al. [14] proposes a multi-class weather classification method which aims to 4 categories, sunny, rainy, snowy and haze by extracting corresponding features. They provide another weather classification dataset which contains 20K outdoor images called MWI dataset. Lin et al. [8] notice the regional differences of images between different weather. They leverage that information and propose a concurrency model which can classify among sunny, cloudy, rainy, snowy, haze and thunder. They provide a improved dataset called Multi-class Weather Dataset (MWD) which contains 65,000 images. Guerra et al. [12] adopt a novel data augmentation technique to improve the classification performance. Their classifier recognizes among sunny, cloudy, rainy, snowy and foggy. Similarly, they provide another dataset called RFS dataset.

The data used in above works usually has clear clues that can indicate the weather. However, driving videos are rarely used for weather classification, which are more difficult because the clues in driving images are not so apparent.

3   Image Classification

3.1   BDD100K Dataset

BDD100K [13] is a large-scale diverse driving video database by University of California, Berkeley, which contains 100k driving images with a variety of attributes such as weather, scene, time of day and 2D bounding boxes. The weather of images is clarified to 6 categories, which are clear, rainy, snowy, partly cloudy, overcast and foggy. We only adopt images during the day. Table 1 shows the quantities of each category.

Table 1. The quantities of each categories in BDD100K after selecting only daytime data.

Weather	Training set	Test set
Clear	12454	1764
Rainy	2522	396
Snowy	2862	422
Overcast	7551	1039
Partly cloudy	4262	638
Foggy	48	5
Total	29699	4264

Since a concrete annotation criteria of weather is not mentioned in [13], we believe that the "weather" in BDD100K may be annotated depending on annotators' judgment when they see the images due to our observation. We consider that the probability which they have referred to meteorological information is low and no strict criteria is made to define the "weather" attribute.

3.2   Kyushu Driving Data

Besides the public BDD100K data, we collect data from drive recorders among 45 vehicles from December 2017 to January 2018 in Kyushu region and Yamaguchi Prefecture, Japan. The total number of recorded hours is roughly 1493, and all the driving videos have a total size of 172 GB. Figure 2 shows some sample images from the driving videos.

Fig. 2. Some examples of our driving video data.

Meteorological Observatories. To leverage pure weather information without any confusion, we exploit weather-related information from 19 meteorological observatories with the frequency of 60 min. The weather categories of observatories are relatively abundant, including "overcast", "rainy", "clear", "sleet", "snowy", "foggy", "sunny", "precipitation", "light cloudy", "thunder", "hail", "drizzle", "smog". We associate weather observations to driving images by assigning the information from the nearest observatory according to the position information in probe data recorded by drive recorders. To unify the labels across different datasets, we remove "precipitation", "thunder", "hail", "drizzle", "smog", which have extremely low quantities and perform a mapping from the rest labels to BDD100K labels. Figure 3 summarizes the procedure.

Since the number of images is too large, we extract two sets from original driving videos according to the distance between the vehicle and the nearest observatory, which are "Kyushu 1 km" and "Kyushu 5 km" set. "x km" indicates that the distance is less or equal x km. The concrete number of images of each category can be viewed in Table 2.

Road Condition Labeling. To provide road condition labels, we label the test set of "Kyushu 1 km" manually for testing. During the labeling process, we prioritize the "road condition" information. Because we need to unify all the labels, and "partly cloudy", "overcast" as well as "foggy" don't have much connection with road conditions, we label "rainy" if the road is wet and "snowy" if the road has

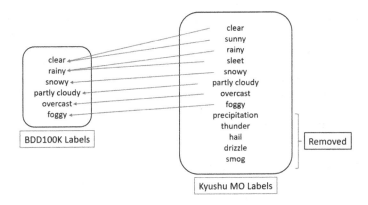

Fig. 3. The label mapping between the two datasets. "Clear" and "sunny" are merged to "clear". "Rainy" and "sleet" are merged to "rainy". "Precipitation", "thunder", "hail", "drizzle", "smog" are removed due to low quanlities.

snow accumulated. If the road condition doesn't belong to any of the 2 cases, we label the image by determining weather and choose a label from "clear", "partly cloudy", "overcast" and "foggy".

3.3 Deep Image Classification

Deep residual learning [3] have reached great success on various kinds of image recognition problems. With our prepared data, we train 3 deep models with ResNet50 with BDD100K training data, Kyushu 1 km training data and Kyushu 5 km training data and we evaluate the models with test/manual data.

Table 2. The quantities of each categories of BDD100K, Kyushu 1 km and Kyushu 5 km. Test data is selected from 10% of each categories of the original data. The rest 90% is used as training data. "Manual" means the manually labeled road conditions.

	BDD100K		Kyushu 1 km			Kyushu 5 km	
	Train	Test	Train	Test	Manual	Train	Test
Clear	12454	1764	1744	195	321	19522	2170
Rainy	2522	396	391	44	46	9655	1074
Snowy	2862	422	431	48	25	1865	208
Partly cloudy	4262	638	603	68	25	4325	481
Overcast	7551	1039	2665	297	235	20197	2245
Foggy	48	5	0	0	0	62	7
Total	29699	4264	5834	652	652	55626	6185

4 Experiments

4.1 Training Details

We train our networks with a single Nvidia GTX 2080Ti graphic card. The learning rate is 0.0001. We train each model 20 epochs with a batch size of 32. The loss function we use is the classical cross entropy loss [15] and the optimizer is set to be adam [7].

4.2 Test Accuracy

Table 3. The test results of the 3 models on 4 test datasets. Each row represents a test set and each column represents a model trained by the corresponding training set. "Kyushu 1 km manual" is the manually labeled road condition test set.

Training/Test set	BDD100K	Kyushu 1 km	Kyushu 5 km
BDD100K	**70.99%**	44.17%	44.85%
Kyushu 1 km	41.12%	**99.11%**	**96.58%**
Kyushu 1 km manual	39.34%	54.12%	53.22%
Kyushu 5 km	38.53%	49.94%	**95.33%**

Table 3 shows the evaluation results on each test dataset. From the result, we can observe the following points significantly.

1. Testing on corresponding datasets achieves relatively high performance. Especially for Kyushu data, weather estimation has good accuracy.
2. Testing on BDD100K with the model trained by BDD100K cannot achieve as much performance as testings on Kyushu data with models trained by corresponding Kyushu data.
3. All models trained weather information fail to perform well with manually labeled road condition test data.

4.3 Analysis

High Performance on Weather Estimation. From the above results, we can see a surprisingly high performance on weather estimation with models trained by meteorological observatory data. Usually, it is even hard for human to recognize the weather in a meteorological level from a single image taken by a drive recorder. This means that the deep network may have the ability to track small unaware features which can indicate meteorological information. Moreover, this high performance may also be related to the selection of training and test sets.

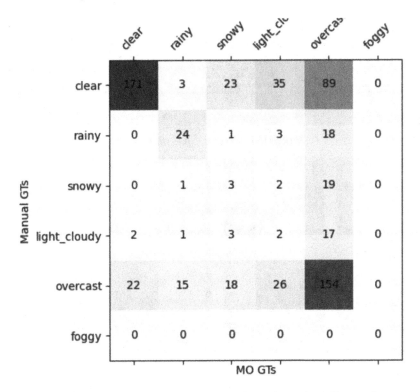

Fig. 4. A confusion matrix liked matrix that tends to show the difference between the meteorological test set and the manually labeled road condition test set of the Kyushu 1 km data. We manually labeled all images in the test set of Kyushu 1 km data with the same categories but a different idea. We first consider whether the road condition is "wet" or "snow", corresponding to "rainy" and "snowy", respectively. If the road condition is dry, we then consider the whole image and select a label from "clear", "light cloudy", "overcast" and "foggy" which can best describe the whole image.

Since we randomly select 10% of each categories, similar frames of a single sequence may be divided into both sets. Therefore, the test set of Kyushu data may not be distinguished from the training set clearly. However, even though the trained models may have bad extendable performance for other sequences, for "Kyushu 1 km manual", which has same data but different road condition labels, they cannot show a good performance, meaning that a model that can classify meteorological weather well cannot perform a good classification on road conditions.

Low Performance on Manually Labeled Set. As mentioned above, all models have bad performance on the manually labeled road condition dataset. We also explore the difference between this set and the original meteorological test set. Figure 4 displays a matrix that indicate the differences between the two sets. From the matrix, we can see that there are three kinds of main differences.

(a) Manual: clear. MO: rainy.

(b) Manual: clear. MO: snowy.

(c) Manual: overcast. MO: rainy.

(d) Manual: overcast. MO: snowy.

(e) Manual: rainy. MO: overcast.

(f) Manual: snowy. MO: overcast.

Fig. 5. Examples of images that produce difference between hand-labeled road conditions and meteorological weather attributes.

- Some non-clear images by MOs are labeled as clear.
- Some non-overcast images by MOs are labeled as overcast.
- Some overcast images by MOs are labeled by non-overcast.

We localize those images and show them in Fig. 5. Although because of the low resolution, a few mistakes can be seen for manual labeled images, (For example, the image in Fig. 5-a-2, we can see the reflection of the road, which indicates that the road is wet.) we can see that most images indicate that the actual road condition is different from the information from the nearest meteorological observatory, and the observatory makes the mistake. Typically as show in 5-e-4, we can see sunlight clearly, but the road is wet. In this situation, the most important factor that influence the driving behavior is the wet road condition, and the weather information here may lead to some certain misunderstandings.

5   Conclusions

In this work, we would like to raise the concern that the discrimination between road conditions and meteorological weather should be necessarily considered during the analysis of driving video data. We explore the public BDD100K data, and find out that the weather attributes in BDD100K are confused with road conditions. To provide pure weather information, we collect driving videos with probe data as well as weather information from meteorological observatories in Kyushu region. We train three deep neural networks using ResNet50 and test them on four test sets. As the result, meteorological weather estimation achieves a high performance, but fails to estimate road conditions. In addition, we localize concrete images find a significant discrimination between road conditions and weather.

5.1   Limitation and Future Work

Because of the training/test set selection strategy mentioned above, the models trained by Kyushu data in this work may be overfitting. Although a good accuracy is demonstrated, they may have bad extendable ability. Moreover, we haven't given a concrete definition of road conditions and only consider three aspects, which are dry, wet and snow.

As for the future work, we are going to first create a general dataset based on our Kyushu driving data. In the dataset, we are going to provide both the meteorological weather attributes and manually labeled road condition attributes. With this dataset, more supplement experiments of this work can be made and more precise driving data analysis can be done in the future. In addition, we will improve our weather estimation framework. Instead of trivial ResNet50, we plan to propose a new novel deep framework focusing on estimating various information such as weather, road conditions, wind from driving videos.

References

1. Bhoraskar, R., Vankadhara, N., Raman, B., Kulkarni, P.: Wolverine: traffic and road condition estimation using smartphone sensors. In: 2012 Fourth International Conference on Communication Systems and Networks (COMSNETS 2012), pp. 1–6. IEEE (2012)
2. Elhoseiny, M., Huang, S., Elgammal, A.: Weather classification with deep convolutional neural networks. In: 2015 IEEE International Conference on Image Processing (ICIP), pp. 3349–3353 (2015). https://doi.org/10.1109/ICIP.2015.7351424
3. He, K., Zhang, X., Ren, S., Sun, J.: Deep residual learning for image recognition. In: Proceedings of the IEEE Conference on Computer Vision and Pattern Recognition, pp. 770–778 (2016)
4. He, Z., Zheng, L., Chen, P., Guan, W.: Mapping to cells: a simple method to extract traffic dynamics from probe vehicle data. Comput. Aid. Civ. Infrastruct. Eng. **32**, 252–267 (2017)
5. Jokela, M., Kutila, M., Le, L.: Road condition monitoring system based on a stereo camera. In: 2009 IEEE 5th International Conference on Intelligent Computer Communication and Processing, pp. 423–428. IEEE (2009)
6. Kawatani, T., Itoh, E., Hirokawa, S., Mine, T.: Machine learning and visualization of sudden braking using probe data. In: 2019 8th International Congress on Advanced Applied Informatics (IIAI-AAI), pp. 67–72 (2019). https://doi.org/10.1109/IIAI-AAI.2019.00024
7. Kingma, D.P., Ba, J.: Adam: a method for stochastic optimization. arXiv preprint arXiv:1412.6980 (2014)
8. Lin, D., Lu, C., Huang, H., Jia, J.: RSCM: region selection and concurrency model for multi-class weather recognition. IEEE Trans. Image Process. **26**(9), 4154–4167 (2017). https://doi.org/10.1109/TIP.2017.2695883
9. Lu, C., Lin, D., Jia, J., Tang, C.K.: Two-class weather classification. In: Proceedings of the IEEE Conference on Computer Vision and Pattern Recognition (CVPR), June 2014
10. Park, H., Haghani, A.: Real-time prediction of secondary incident occurrences using vehicle probe data. Transp. Res. Part C Emerg. Technol. **70**, 69–85 (2016)
11. Tang, T., Wang, Y., Yang, X., Wu, Y.: A new car-following model accounting for varying road condition. Nonlinear Dyn. **70**(2), 1397–1405 (2012)
12. Villarreal Guerra, J.C., Khanam, Z., Ehsan, S., Stolkin, R., McDonald-Maier, K.: Weather classification: a new multi-class dataset, data augmentation approach and comprehensive evaluations of convolutional neural networks. In: 2018 NASA/ESA Conference on Adaptive Hardware and Systems (AHS), pp. 305–310 (2018). https://doi.org/10.1109/AHS.2018.8541482
13. Yu, F., et al.: Bdd100k: a diverse driving dataset for heterogeneous multitask learning. In: The IEEE Conference on Computer Vision and Pattern Recognition (CVPR), June 2020
14. Zhang, Z., Ma, H.: Multi-class weather classification on single images. In: 2015 IEEE International Conference on Image Processing (ICIP), pp. 4396–4400 (2015).https://doi.org/10.1109/ICIP.2015.7351637
15. Zhang, Z., Sabuncu, M.: Generalized cross entropy loss for training deep neural networks with noisy labels. In: Bengio, S., Wallach, H., Larochelle, H., Grauman, K., Cesa-Bianchi, N., Garnett, R. (eds.) Advances in Neural Information Processing Systems, vol. 31, pp. 8778–8788. Curran Associates, Inc. (2018). https://proceedings.neurips.cc/paper/2018/file/f2925f97bc13ad2852a7a551802feea0-Paper.pdf

Age Estimation from the Age Period by Using Triplet Network

Gaojian Zhang[1] and Takio Kurita[2(✉)]

[1] Department of Information Engineering, Hiroshima University,
1-7-1, Higashi-Hiroshima, Japan
[2] Graduate School of Advanced Science and Engineering, Hiroshima University,
1-7-1, Higashi-Hiroshima, Japan
tkurita@hiroshima-u.ac.jp

Abstract. This paper proposes an age estimation method from the age period using Triplet Network. Age estimation is still an active research topic in machine learning, and it can be formulated as a regression problem. Usually, a specific age value to each of the training face images is assigned as a correct label, and the model to estimate the age value of an unknown face image is trained from the training samples. In this paper, we consider the age estimation problem from the age period in which only the label of each of the training samples is the age period, such as teens or twenties. In this setting, the model has to interpolate the age values from the age period based on the similarity between the samples in the same age period. To achieve this functionality, we use Triplet Network to capture the age relationship between the face images. Then the age of each image is estimated by the linear regression. The effectiveness of the proposed approach is experimentally confirmed by using MegaAge-Asian, UTKFace, and MegaAge.

Keywords: Age estimation · Deep learning · Regression

1 Introduction

Age estimation from a single face image is a hot topic in the fields of computer vision and machine learning. There are many related studies so far. The appearance of our face changes with age. The color of the face, the hair color, the wrinkles in the corners of the eyes are different when he/she becomes old. In general, this is known as the aging process of the face. Some studies have taken advantage of this and proposed the ranking method [2]. DEX [3] used the expectation method in statistics. They divided the age range into 101 kinds of consecutive possibilities, and then calculate expectations to achieve the purpose of age prediction. After this work, there are some ways to improve the loss function [4].

In these studies of age estimation, the authors assumed the principle in which the facial appearance changes linearly with age. For example, we have photos

© Springer Nature Switzerland AG 2021
H. Jeong and K. Sumi (Eds.): IW-FCV 2021, CCIS 1405, pp. 81–92, 2021.
https://doi.org/10.1007/978-3-030-81638-4_7

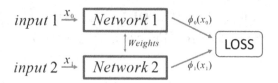

Fig. 1. Architecture of Siamese Network.

of the same person at the age of 40, then when we compare the photos of this person at the age of 50 and 60, the changes in the facial features can be used as the clue of the estimation. The feature quantity of a 50-year-old photo should be closer to the person of 40-year-old than the person of 60 years old, which is also in line with our sensory perception.

However, in some cases, not all problems can be solved smoothly. The problem is that the number of data sets that can be used for age prediction is limited, and producing them requires many resources, namely training samples with correct age labels. Therefore, how to effectively expand the data set for training is key for age estimation. On the other hand, although it is difficult to get accurate age labels, it is relatively easy to determine the age period, such as teens or twenties, of the people in the image. Therefore, if we can use age periods instead of specific age labels to train the network, the available resources can be increased.

In this paper, we consider the age estimation problem from the training samples with labels of age period, namely the label of each of the training face images is given as the age period. In this setting, the model has to interpolate the age values from the age period based on the similarity between the samples in the same age period. To achieve this functionality, we use Siamese Network and Triplet Network to capture the age relationship between face images. Then the age of each image is estimated by the linear regression. The effectiveness of the proposed approach is experimentally evaluated by using MegaAge-Asian, UTKFace, and MegaAge dataset.

2   Related Works

2.1   Siamese Network

Siamese Network was introduced by [5]. Figure 1 shows the architecture of Siamese Network. The structure of Siamese Network is two parallel neural networks with shared weights. It has two inputs and two outputs. We can think that one network is trained because the parameters of the two networks are the same. Siamese Network can not only apply the teacher signal to the output but also use the relationship between the two outputs. As shown in [5], for two signature verification inputs at the same time, Siamese Network can judge the similarity to identify whether the owner of the fingerprint is the same person.

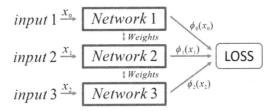

Fig. 2. Architecture of Triplet Network.

Therefore, we can use a structure similar to Siamese Network for extracting a feature vector from an input sample when we want to compare the input samples depending on whether they are the same and different from each other, or the similarity between different them. The similarity can be a simple Euclidean distance or be defined according to the task.

Siamese Network has been used in many applications, such as handwritten checks recognition, automatic detection of faces, and matching queries with indexed documents. The most practical application is face recognition. Vinod Nair and Geoffrey E. Hinton [6] used Siamese Network for face verification, and got excellent results. Its principle is very simple. They feed two face images into a convolutional neural network and get the output that can be the same or different. For example, in an automatic door system, the face information of the owner is pre-stored and compared whether the face in the camera and the pre-stored face are the same person each time he enters or leaves, then determine whether to unlock.

2.2   Triplet Network

Triplet Network was proposed as an extension of Siamese Network. The difference between Triplet Network and Siamese Network is that Triplet Network has three networks with shared weights in its architecture, as shown in Fig. 2. E Hoffer and N Ailon [7] compared them in the problem to learn useful variables by comparing distances, and it showed that Triplet Network was better than Siamese Network in multiple different dataset. The drawback of Siamese Network is that, when using a dataset randomly, one data may be considered similar to another. But when we only want to distinguish two samples in a group of data, it may be considered not similar to another sample of the same. When selecting features, it is not enough to judge the relationship between the two. In the case of simple classification problems with a small number of training samples, errors may occur. However, Triplet Network can solve this drawback of Siamese Network. Because three samples are used in each iteration in the training process as a training group, and the fitting function is constructed from the relationship of three samples.

The traditional Siamese Network uses constrictive loss. There are more choices for the loss function. The original intention of Siamese Network is to calculate the similarity between two inputs. For the case of Siamese Network, the two neural networks convert the two inputs into the two output feature vectors, and the similarity can be calculated as the distance between the two output vectors. We can also choose the Exponential function to convert the distance to the similarity. In the case of Triplet Network, three output vectors are obtained. Then the goal of training is to make the distance between two similar inputs as small as possible and the distance between two different classes as large as possible.

2.3   Facial Expression Intensity Estimation by Siamese Network and Triplet Network

M. Sabri et al. proposed a method to estimate facial expression intensity by using the ranking information of the expression intensities of the extracted face images in videos [1]. The authors verified the ability of Siamese Network and Triplet Network for facial expression intensity estimation and Micro-Expressions tasks. In the experiments of facial expression intensity estimation in [1], the authors used three datasets Cohn-Kanade, MUG, and MMI to do experiments on Siamese Network and Triplet Network respectively. Face images were extracted frame by frame from the videos in these datasets in which facial expressions were gradually changing. Due to the continuity of the frames in the video, the ranking information of the expression intensity can be obtained by extracting the frames in the videos in order. For example, in a video where the facial expression is getting stronger, we can easily know the expression intensity of the current frame is higher than the previous frame.

Siamese Network and Triplet Network were used to train the neural network by using the ranking information to estimate the facial expression intensity from an input face image. According to the author's definition, the expression intensity of the first frame of the video is set to 0, and the last frame is set to 1. Then the trained network can estimate the expression intensity of an unknown face image. From the results of the experiments using Cohn-Kanade, MUG, and MMI dataset, it is noticed that Siamese Network and Triplet Network perform better than traditional methods, and Triplet Network gives higher accuracy than Siamese Network.

3   Age Estimation from the Age Period

3.1   Problem of Age Estimation from the Age Period

In this paper, we propose an age estimation method from the age period using Siamese Network and Triplet Network. Here we assume that age periods are divided into units of 10 years. If only the age period is given as teacher signal, the estimation model have to interpolate the age values in the age period. When the two face images belong to different age periods, the network can easily determine the age period of the two face images. For example, when the two input images belong to the period from 10 to 19 years old and the period from 40 to 49 years old, it is easy to judge that the former is younger than the latter. On the other hand, when the ages of the input images belong to the same age period, no clue is obtained from the training samples. This makes the problem of age estimation from the age period challenging.

But there are some ranking information. Assume we have face images of 32 and 38 years old. It is easy to know that the face image in the age period from 20 to 29 years old is younger than the age period from 40 to 49 years old. Because of the linear relationship of the age features of the face, the network can also know that the 32-year-old face is similar to the 20-to-29-year-old face, and the 38-year-old face is similar to the 40-to-49-year-old face. Thereby, as a result, the network can determine that the 32-year-old face is younger than the 38-year-old face.

3.2   Proposed Method

As introduced by [1], the task of facial expression intensity estimation from videos can be achieved by using Siamese Network and Triplet network. Although this is not an age estimation task, the intensity of the expression gradually changes as the facial expression changes. This change is linear and will be reflected in the changes of the facial features. Just like a person's aging process from 35 to 37 years old. Taking this as inspiration, we use Siamese Network and Triplet Network that can construct the representation which reflects the relationship between the two inputs. We train Siamese Network or Triplet Network by only relying on the comparison of the age bands of the two input face images as a teacher signal for training, rather than using specific age values. After a certain amount of training, Siamese Network and Triplet network can correctly predict the relationship. Further, we use the linear regression method to predict approximate age values.

Let $X^N = \{x^{(0)}, x^{(1)}, ...x^{(N-1)}\}$ be a set of face images in the training samples with age period as labels, where N is the number of face images in the training datasets. The age period of each face image in the training samples are denoted as $Y^N = \{R^{(0)}, R^{(1)}, ...R^{(N-1)}\}$.

To train the parameters of Siamese Network shown in Fig. 1, we extract the pairs of the training samples as $\{x^{(0)}, x^{(1)}\}$, $\{x^{(1)}, x^{(2)}\}$,...$\{x^{(N-2)}, x^{(N-1)}\}$, $\{x^{(N-1)}, x^{(0)}\}$ (N pairs in total). The age period labels are used to arrange the order of the paired data. For each pairs $\{x^{(k)}, x^{(k+1)}\}$, we let $x_0 = x^{(k)}, x_1 = x^{(k+1)}$ if $R^{(k)} \leq R^{(k+1)}$. Similarly, we let $x_0 = x^{(k+1)}, x_1 = x^{(k)}$ if $R^{(k)} > R^{(k+1)}$. This means that we can guarantee that the image given to the upper network (its output is ϕ_0) will be younger than the one given to the lower network (its output is ϕ_1) at any time. At a certain epoch in the training process, we randomly arrange the data and extract the pairs from beginning to end for training. Before the start of the next epoch, the order of the dataset will be shuffled.

In this paper, we use the loss function for Siamese Network

$$L_S = \sum_{x_0, x_1 \in X^N} e^{\phi_0(x_0) - \phi_1(x_1)} \tag{1}$$

In this function, the difference $\phi_0(x_0) - \phi_1(x_1)$ is minimized to make the output of younger people's face images smaller values, while the older ones output larger values.

Similarly, to train the parameters of Triplet Network as shown in Fig. 2, we have to select triplets from the training face images $X^N = \{x^{(0)}, x^{(1)}, ...x^{(N-1)}\}$ and the age periods of each face images $Y^N = \{R^{(0)}, R^{(1)}, ...R^{(N-1)}\}$. They are denoted as $\{x^{(0)}, x^{(1)}, x^{(2)}\}$, $\{x^{(1)}, x^{(2)}, x^{(3)}\}$,... $\{x^{(N-3)}, x^{(N-2)}, x^{(N-1)}\}$, $\{x^{(N-2)}, x^{(N-1)}, x^{(0)}\}$, $\{x^{(N-1)}, x^{(0)}, x^{(1)}\}$ (N is the total number of selected triplets). We also use the age period labels to arrange the order of the samples in each triplet. As a result, we can guarantee that the face image given to the upper network (its output is ϕ_0) will be younger than the one given to the middle network (its output is ϕ_1). Also, the face image given to the middle network will be younger than the one given to the lower network (its output is ϕ_2) at any time.

The loss function of Triplet Network is given as

$$L_T = \sum_{x_0, x_1, x_2 \in X^N} \left(e^{\phi_0(x_0) - \phi_1(x_1)} + e^{\phi_1(x_1) - \phi_2(x_2)} \right) \qquad (2)$$

In this function, we minimize the differences $\phi_0(x_0) - \phi_1(x_1)$ and $\phi_1(x_1) - \phi_2(x_2)$ to make the output value of network according to the order of ages of face images.

Since the outputs of the trained network reflect the order of the ages of the face image but the scale of the outputs is not correct, we have to convert them to the age values. We use the linear regression to construct this transformation.

Let $\{\phi(x^{(0)}), \phi(x^{(1)}), ...\phi(x^{(N_1-1)})\}$ be the set of outputs of the trained network for the training samples $X^{N_1} = \{x^{(0)}, x^{(1)}, ...x^{(N_1-1)}\}$. Here N_1 is the number of training samples. Then, we apply the linear regression for the outputs of the trained network as independent variable and the average value of age period $Y^{N_1} = \{R^{(0)}, R^{(1)}, ...R^{(N_1-1)}\}$ as dependent variable.

4   Experiments and Results

4.1   Dataset in Experiment

There are lots of datasets for age estimation. In this paper, **MegaAge/MegaAge-Asian** and **UTKFace** were used in the experiments.

The MegaAge dataset has a total of 41,941 face images with age labels [10]. The MegaAge-Asian contains 40,000 pictures of Asians (most of them are East Asians). Both data sets are from 0 to 70 years old. The authors in [10] mentions that the performance for MegaAge-Asian data sets by the same age estimation algorithm is generally better than that of the MegaAge dataset because MegaAge-Asian's race is relatively single.

The UTKFace is a large face dataset with a long age period (ranging from 0 to 116 years old) [11] dataset. The dataset contains more than 20,000 facial images with annotations for age, gender, and ethnicity. The image covers large changes in posture, facial expressions, lighting, occlusion, resolution, etc. The dataset

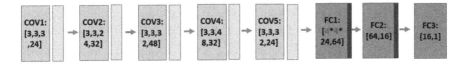

Fig. 3. Parameters of one network.

can be used for various tasks, for example, face detection, age estimation, age progression or regression, landmark positioning, etc.

In this paper, the age value labels of MegaAge, MegaAge-Asian, and UTK-Face datasets were converted to the age period labels for. For example, the age value 3 is converted to the age period from 0 to 9, and the age value 25 is the age period from 20 to 29, and so on.

4.2   Architecture of Neural Network in Experiment

Figure 3 shows the network architecture used in the following experiments. The each network in Siamese Network or Triplet Network is composed by 5 convolutional layers and 3 fully connected layers. In each convolutional layer, the size of the filter is 3×3 with padding of 1, and the max-pooling layer with padding of 2 is added after each of the convolution layers. The size of the input is $128 \times 128 \times 3$. The number of output channels in the first layer is 24. The number of output channels of the second layer is 32, the third layer is 48, the fourth layer is 32, the fifth layer is 24. Before the first layer of the fully connected layer, the dimension of the features is compressed to $4 \times 4 \times 24$. The output sizes of each three fully connected layers are 64, 16, and 1, respectively.

The network was implemented using the TensorFlow [12] and trained with GPU (NVIDIA GTX1080).

It should be noted that when we use TensorFlow to complete the creation of the basic network, we use the "reuse" parameter in TensorFlow to add an input interface to the network in the experiment using Siamese Network. In this way, we can achieve the goal of increasing the network only by activating "reuse" without using other operations, because all the parameters of the "new network" are exactly the same as the basic network we created first. Similarly, when we use the Triplet Network to do experiments, we use "reuse" again to add an input on the basis of the Siamese Network.

4.3   Training of Siamese Network and Triplet Network

Siamese Network and Triplet Network were trained by using 3 datasets (MegaAge-Asian, UTKFace, and MegaAge).

The range of age's distribution of MegaAge-Asian is 0 to 70 years old. This dataset has a total of 43945 face images with age labels. Among them, 40,000 images are used as the training samples, and the remaining 3945 images are used as the test samples. The proposed loss for Siamese Network and Triplet

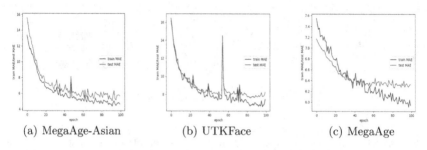

(a) MegaAge-Asian   (b) UTKFace   (c) MegaAge

Fig. 4. MAE for each dataset in the training by Siamese Network. (Color figure online)

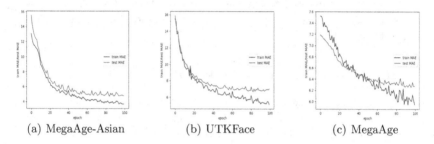

(a) MegaAge-Asian   (b) UTKFace   (c) MegaAge

Fig. 5. MAE for each dataset in the training by Triplet Network. (Color figure online)

Network was minimized by using Momentum-SGD as the optimizer with the momentum 0.9. The batch size and the learning rate were set to 40 and 0.0005 for this dataset. The training is stopped at 100 epochs.

The range of age's distribution of UTKFace is 0 to 116 years old. This dataset has a total of 23708 face images. Among them, 22,000 are used as the training samples, and the other 1708 images are for test samples. Momentum-SGD was also used for training. The parameters were set to the same as the MegaAge-Asian dataset expect the batch size and the learning rate. The batch size was set to 44 and the learning rate was set to 0.0004. The training process is stopped at 100.

The range of age's distribution MegaAge dataset is 0 to 70 years old. This dataset has a total of 41941 face images with age labels. Among them, 33411 are training dataset, and the other 8530 images are testing dataset. Momentum-SGD was used with the momentum to 0.9. The batch size and the learning rate were set to 37 and 0.0008. The training process is stopped at 100.

Figure 4 and Fig. 5 show the mean absolute error (MAE) during the training process. The results of Siamese Network and Triplet Network are shown in Fig. 4 and Fig. 5, respectively. For each figure, (a), (b), and (c) show the results for MagaAge-Asian, UTKFace, and MagaAge detasets. The blue lines show the MAEs for the training samples and the red lines show for the test samples. It is noticed that the error gradually decreases and tends to be stable.

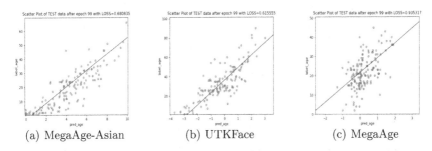

(a) MegaAge-Asian   (b) UTKFace   (c) MegaAge

Fig. 6. Scatter plot of the outputs of Siamese Network for test samples. (Color figure online)

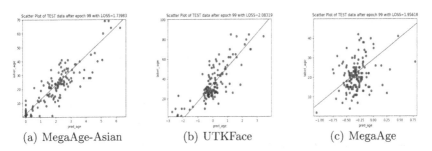

(a) MegaAge-Asian   (b) UTKFace   (c) MegaAge

Fig. 7. Scatter plot of the outputs of Triplet Network for test samples. (Color figure online)

4.4   Estimation of Age Values

Figure 6 and Fig. 7 show the results of the age value estimation by using linear regression of the outputs of the network. The x axis shows the outputs of the network and the y axis is for the age values. The estimated regression line is shown in the green line. The scatter plot of test samples are also shown. It can be seen that the distribution of and test samples tends to be diagonal. This means that the network can extract the age features of the data so that it tends to be linearly distributed.

Table 1. MAE of testing data for each dataset.

Method	MegaAge-Asian	UTKFace	MegaAge
Siamese	6.22404	7.79368	6.31552
Triplet	4.73246	6.67299	6.22340

Table 1 shows the MAEs achieved by Siamese Network and Triplet Network for test samples for each dataset. It can be concluded that we can still obtain relatively satisfactory age estimation results by using the proposed method even if the specific age values are not given for the training samples. From Table 1 we can conclude that the Triplet Network performs better than Siamese Network.

4.5   Comparison Experiment

For the MegaAge-Asian dataset, we also conducted experiments for usual regression experiments, including the experiments that using specific age labels and average age for each age periods. We used L1 loss function for these experiments and Momentum-SGD was still used with the momentum to 0.9. The batch size and the learning rate were set to 40 and 0.0008 for this dataset. The training was stopped at 50 epochs.

Table 2. MAE for each cases.

Method	Regression (True age)	Regression (Average age)	Triplet
MAE	4.162325	6.19267	4.73246

Table 2 shows the MAEs achieved by each methods. We can conclude that when we use Triplet Network with age period, the performance is closer to the case that using true age in regression experiment.

In research using Siamese Network, Contrastive Loss is a loss function that is often used. We have also tried to experiment with Contrastive Loss. In our experiment, the Contrastive Loss is given as

$$L_C = \frac{1}{2}Yd^2 + \frac{1}{2}(1-Y)max(0, m-d)^2 \qquad (3)$$

In this loss function, when two input data are from the same age period, Y is 1. When they are from different age periods, Y is 0. $d = \phi_0(x_0) - \phi_1(x_1)$ is the distance between the two outputs from Siamese Network. m stands for the margin in Contrastive Loss. In the experiment, we used different margins to try to improve the performance of the function. The results are shown in Table 3.

Table 3. MAE for each margins.

Margin	10	30	60	90	150	300
MAE	16.264	16.5644	15.7264	16.4011	16.1821	16.2009

From Table 3 we can see that even if we change the margin in Contrastive Loss to improve the accuracy of the model, the result does not change, it only has a poor performance (the value of MAE is much higher than the previous experiment, and it is not in a satisfactory interval for us) for the age estimation task.

We analyze the reasons why traditional Contrastive Loss cannot succeed as follows.

The goal of our research is to achieve age prediction without specific age label by using Siamese network or Triplet network which have the ability to obtain ranking features. This goal is achieved by controlling the distance of the output value from the data mapping in the model. The distance defined in traditional Contrastive Loss is usually a square distance (sometimes an absolute value), which is effective in a multi-dimensional feature space. However, its defect is also obvious, that is, it does not consider the order relationship between two or more inputs. Therefore, when it is used for such tasks, its effectiveness cannot be well reflected. On the other hand, in the loss function we proposed, because of the precise definition of the positive and negative of the distance, we have made it have a better ability to acquire ranking features, which is reflected in tasks such as age estimation.

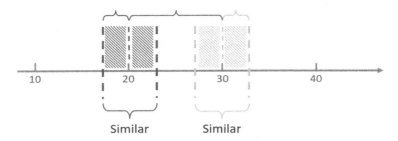

Fig. 8. The data are more similar to each other in their respective parts. (Color figure online)

As shown in Fig. 8, for example, as we mentioned earlier, in the period from 20 to 30, since the front part is similar to the rear part of 10 to 20 (they are all shown in blue), and the rear part is similar to the front part of 30 to 40 (they are all shown in yellow). So, our method can use this ranking relationship to make the data in the same period be correctly predicted. But for the Contrastive Loss, it is difficult to achieve this, as we know from Table 3.

5   Conclusion and Future Work

In this paper, we proposed age estimation methods from the age period by using Siamese Network and Triplet Network. The ability of Siamese Network and Triplet Network for age estimation from the age period labels were confirmed by experiments using three datasets MegaAge-Asian, UTKFace, and MegaAge. This means that Siamese Network and Triplet Network can train the mapping to estimate the age values from face images even if there is no specific age label and only the age period.

The results for the MegaAge-Asian dataset are satisfactory, but it has a larger errors for UTKFace which has a wider age range. When MegaAge was used as the dataset, although the error was small, the linear regression does not fit well. To fix these problems is the focus of our future works.

References

1. Sabri, M., Kurita, T.: Facial expression intensity estimation using Siamese and triplet networks. Neurocomputing **313**, 143–154 (2018)
2. Chen, S., Zhang, C., Dong, M., Le, J., Rao, M.: Using ranking-CNN for age estimation. In: CVPR, pp. 742–751 (2017)
3. Rothe, R., Timofte, R., Gool, L.V.: DEX: Deep expectation of apparent age from a single image. In: ICCVW, December 2015
4. Pan, H., Han, H., Shan, S., Chen, X.: Mean-variance loss for deep age estimation from a face. In: CVPR, June 2018
5. Bromley, J., Guyon, I., LeCun, Y., Sickinger, E., Shah, R.: Signature verification using a "Siamese" time delay neural network. Int. J. Pattern Recogn. Artif. Intell. **7**(4), 669–688 (1993)
6. Nair, V., Hinton, G.E.: Rectified linear units improve restricted Boltzmann machines. In: ICML (2010)
7. Hoffer, E., Ailon, N.: Deep metric learning using triplet network. In: Feragen, A., Pelillo, M., Loog, M., (eds.) Similarity-Based Pattern Recognition. LNCS, vol. 9370, pp. 84–92. Springer, Heidelberg (2015). https://doi.org/10.1007/978-3-319-24261-3_7
8. Panis, G., Lanitis, A., Tsapatsoulis, N., Cootes, T.F.: Overview of research on facial ageing using the FG-NET ageing database. Iet Biom. **5**(2), 37–46 (2016)
9. Ricanek, K., Tesafaye, T.: Morph: a longitudinal image database of normal adult age-progression. In: FG, pp. 341–345 (2006)
10. Zhang, Y., Liu, L., Li, C., Loy, C.C.: Quantifying facial age by posterior of age comparisons. In: Proceedings of British Machine Vision Conference (BMVC) (2017)
11. Zhang, Z., Song, Y., Qi, H.: Age: progression/regression by conditional adversarial autoencoder. In: IEEE Conference on Computer Vision and Pattern Recognition (CVPR) (2017)
12. Abadi, M.: Tensorflow: large-scale machine learning on heterogeneous distributed systems (2016)

Development of an Algae Counting Application to Support Vegetation Surveys in Fishing Grounds

Junsei Idegomori[1]($\boxtimes$), Masahiro Migita[2], Masashi Toda[2], and Hideki Akino[3]

[1] Kumamoto University, 2-39-1 Kurokami, Chuo-ku,
Kumamoto-shi 860-8555, Kumamoto, Japan
c7957@st.cs.kumamoto-u.jp
[2] Center for Management of Information Technologies, Kumamoto University,
Kurokami 2-39-1, Kumamoto City 860-8555, Kumamoto, Japan
{migita,toda}@cc.kumamoto-u.ac.jp
[3] Local Independent Administrative Agency Hokkaido Research Organization (HRO),
Kita 19 Nishi 11, Kita-ku, Sapporo 060-0819, Hokkaido, Japan
akino-hideki@hro.or.jp

Abstract. In the kelp and sea urchin fisheries, fishery surveys are required to select kelp and juvenile sea urchin release sites. In the fishery survey, underwater images obtained from cameras installed in the water are mainly used. Underwater images are used to read algae information and create an algae distribution map, which makes it possible to understand the fishing grounds. This process is expected to simplify the fishery survey and promote the conservation and utilization of fishing grounds. In this paper, we develop an Algae counting application that derives and records algae cover from underwater images using user instructions to simplify the fishing grounds survey process.

Keywords: Fishery surveys · Algae · Algae counting applications · Coverage

1 Introduction

1.1 Background

According to the Guidelines for Measures to Prevent the Extinction of Seagrass Bed Resources published by the Fisheries Agency, seagrass beds have been recognized as a food source or habitat for major coastal marine resource organisms. However, except for kelp, which has been positioned as a useful resource, quantitative understanding from the viewpoint of fishery resources has not been promoted. Currently, the number of seagrass beds in the coastal areas of Japan is decreasing, and the causes of this trend include direct geomorphological changes such as land reclamation, rock scorching, and changes in sea conditions. Therefore, it is necessary to survey the kelp and sea urchin fishing grounds in order to select the fishing grounds for kelp and the release site of young sea urchins. Since it is difficult to obtain information on seaweeds by aerial photography using drones

© Springer Nature Switzerland AG 2021
H. Jeong and K. Sumi (Eds.): IW-FCV 2021, CCIS 1405, pp. 93–105, 2021.
https://doi.org/10.1007/978-3-030-81638-4_8

or satellites due to halos and waves, it is effective to obtain underwater images using cameras installed underwater. Using the information obtained from these underwater images, it is possible to create algae distribution maps to understand the fishing grounds. In the conventional method of creating algae distribution maps, the person in charge at the experimental station looks at the underwater images on the image viewer one by one, judges the type of seaweed, reads the degree of cover, and converts the data. The percent cover is a percentage or a grade of how much of the ground surface is covered by each plant in a plant community. However, it is difficult to extract the data with high accuracy. It is necessary to enter the obtained data in a separate ledger or in a separate software program, and the processing is complicated. By simplifying this process, it will be possible to speed up the creation of algae distribution maps, which in turn will promote fisheries surveys and the advancement of fisheries conservation and utilization.

1.2 Purpose of Study

In this paper, we develop an algae counting application (Fig. 1) that derives and records the algae cover from underwater images using user instructions, thereby simplifying the fishery survey process.

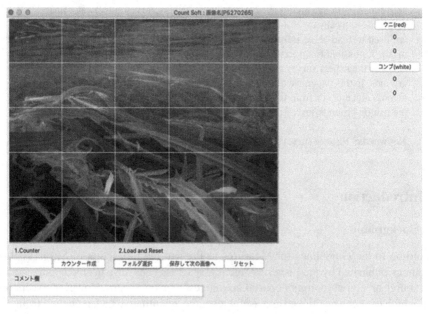

Fig. 1. Algae counting application

Fig. 2. Conceptual diagram of the application

2 Algae Counting Application

2.1 Design Philosophy

Originally, when creating algae distribution maps using underwater images, it is desirable to extract the area of each algae and obtain the percent cover.

In the conventional method, the measurer looks at the underwater images on the image viewer one by one, judges the type of seaweed, reads the percent cover, and converts the data. However, this method is prone to errors depending on the measurer.

In light of these problems, in this application, we propose a simple method for obtaining data in which the user specifies the type of algae growing in each subregion to be surveyed and the percent cover is considered to be equally divided among the algae growing in the subregion. The conceptual diagram is shown in Fig. 2.

2.2 Proposed Method

The data that can approximate the algae extraction in this application is derived as follows:

1. divide the underwater image into subregions.
2. the presence or absence of algae in each partial area is indicated by clicking.
3. the area A occupied by each algae in each subregion is divided equally by the algae species.
4. the data obtained in step 3 is summed over the entire underwater image and output as algae coverage B (%).

$$A = (\text{algae/number of algae species}) \times 100 \tag{1}$$

$$B = (\text{sum of A/number of area divisions}) \times 100 \tag{2}$$

2.3 Comparison with Conventional Methods

The conventional method and the proposed method are shown in Fig. 3. Three types of algae information are used: sea urchin (red), kelp (white) and others (yellow). The accuracy of the proposed method is confirmed by assuming that the cover (%) obtained by the conventional method is the correct data.

Table 1 shows the percentages obtained in Fig. 3. From Table 1, it can be seen that the proposed method provides data that can approximate the algae extraction.

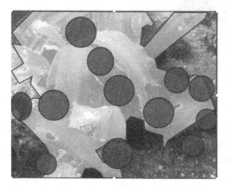 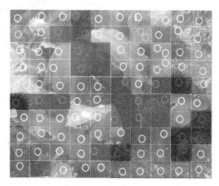

Fig. 3. Conventional and proposed methods

Table 1. Comparison of conventional and proposed methods

	Sea urchin (red)	Kelp (white)	Other (yellow)
Conventional methods	15	60	25
Proposed methods	18.5	58	23.5

Table 2. Development environment

CPU	2.2 GHz dual core Intel Core i7
OS	macOS
Memory	8 GB 1600 MHz DDR3
Tool	Anaconda Jupyter Notebook
Language	Python

2.4 Development Environment

Table 2 shows the development environment we used to develop this application.

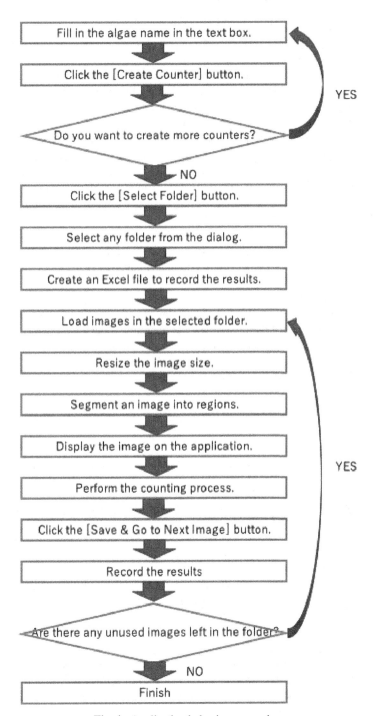

Fig. 4. Application behavior processing

2.5   Operation Process of Algae Counting Application

The operational process of this application is shown in the flowchart in Fig. 4.

2.5.1 Counter Creation Function

This function allows you to create a counter by entering any algae name you wish to count in the text box on this application and clicking the [Create Counter] button. By repeating this process, you can create multiple counters. The text box and the [Create Counter] button on the application are shown in Fig. 5. The created counter dis-plays the algae switching button with the algae name, the number of algae counted, and the algae cover (%), respectively. The counter is shown in Fig. 6. The maximum number of counters that can be created by this application is 8, and the count markers are given in the following order: red, white, yellow, magenta, cyan, green, purple, and peach.

2.5.2 Folder Selection Function

This function opens a dialog box by clicking the [Select Folder] button on the application, and by selecting a folder containing arbitrary image data, the image data in the folder can be handled. The [Select Folder] button on this application is shown in Fig. 7.

2.5.3 Resize Function

In this application, if images are loaded and displayed as they are, various problems may occur due to the influence of the image size. For example, if the image size is too small, it may be difficult to click on an arbitrary small area to be selected. In this application, we deal with this problem by resizing the loaded image and standardizing the image size. The size of the resized image is set to 640×480.

Fig. 5. Text box and [Create Counter] button application behavior processing

2.5.4 Grid Function

This function can divide a loaded underwater image into arbitrary small areas. The default setting is to divide the image into small areas of 5×5. Figure 8 shows the original image and the post-grid image.

2.5.5 Count Function

This function allows the user to count algae by clicking on the underwater image dis-played on the application. A hollow circle is displayed at the clicked point, and the obtained count results are displayed as the number of algae counted and the algae cover (%) on the counter, respectively. The counting procedure is as follows.

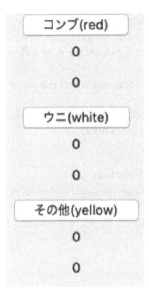

Fig. 6. Counter

Fig. 7. [Select Folder] button

Fig. 8. Images (left: original image, right: image after region segmentation)

1. Select the algae you want to count by clicking on the algae switching button.
2. lick on the small area of the underwater image where the selected algae exist.
3. Repeat steps 1 and 2 for other algae.

2.5.6 Count Cancellation Function

This function allows the user to cancel the count when a mistake is made during the counting process. The procedure for counting is as follows.

1. Click the "Switch Algae" button and select the algae for which you want to cancel the count.
2. Right-click on the count marker of the algae that you want to cancel the count.
3. Repeat steps 1 and 2 for the other algae.

2.5.7 Algae Cover Recording Function

This function allows you to record the algal cover B(%) obtained by this application in an Excel file by clicking the [Save and Go to Next Image] button. The procedure to record the algal cover is as follows. Figure 9 shows the [Save and Go to Next Image] button on this application.

Fig. 9. [Save and go to next image] button

1. Create an Excel table in which the vertical axis is the name of the underwater image and the horizontal axis is the name of the algae, using the same name as the file containing the referenced underwater image. The created Excel table is shown in Fig. 10.

	A	B	C	D
1		コンブ(red)	ヨレモク(white)	コメント欄
2	ファイル名	0	0	
3				

Fig. 10. Excel file for recording the degree of exposure

2. Record the algal cover B (%) in the Excel file created in step 1 by clicking the [Save and Go to Next Image] button on the application.
3. The algal cover obtained in the next image is recorded by appending it to the table in which the algal cover of the previous image was recorded. Instead of creating an Excel table for each underwater image from which the algal cover is derived, the algal cover is recorded by appending it to the created table, so that the results can be saved in each referenced folder, which facilitates statistical processing.

2.5.8 Image Switching Function

This function allows you to switch to the next image in the folder selected in 2.5.2

and display it on this application by clicking the [Save and Go to Next] button on this application. This function eliminates the need to specify and load underwater images every time when loading them, and allows for quick processing of the images in the folder.

2.5.9 Reset Function
This function allows the user to reset the underwater images displayed on the application, the counters, and the algae cover by clicking the [Reset] button on the application. The [Reset] button on this application is shown in Fig. 11.

Fig. 11. [Reset] button.

2.5.10 Memo Function
A memo function is implemented in this application to record explanations and supplementary information when inadequate underwater images or additional information are found during the counting process. In the memo function, the contents entered in the comment column in this application can be saved in the comment column in the table. The memo is recorded in the location corresponding to the name of the target underwater image for easy use when reviewing the data later. The comment field in the application is shown in Fig. 12.

Fig. 12. Comment box

2.5.11 Result Image Saving Function
In this function, the underwater image showing the hollow circle after the counting operation displayed on the application is saved as a result image. The result image to be saved is shown in Fig. 13. The name of the result image is the name of the referenced underwater image and the date when the image was saved.

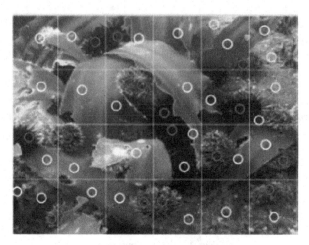

Fig. 13. Result image

2.5.12 Image Name Display Function

In this function, the name of the underwater image corresponding to the image displayed on the application is displayed at the top of the application. By implementing this function, users can know the name of the underwater image they are working on. When no image is loaded, the application is designed to display the message "Please select an image".

2.5.13 Image Datasets Creation Function

This function creates image data sets for U-net based on the coordinate information used to derive the algae cover. U-net is one of the FCN (fully convolution network), which is a network for estimating image segmentation. The image datasets to be created is a partial region image of the clicked underwater image and Monochrome image (Fig. 14). The advantage of this feature is that a large number of image datasets can be created while using this application. The method of creating image data sets is as follows

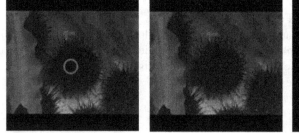

Fig. 14. Image datasets (left: Click image, center: Partial region image, right: Monochrome image).

1. Partial region image

   (1) Trim the partial area of the clicked underwater image and output it.

2. Monochrome image

   (1) Obtain the RGB value of the clicked coordinate.
   (2) The clicked coordinate is set as the origin, and the RGB values of the origin coordinate and the surrounding coordinates are compared; if the RGB difference is less than a threshold value, the origin coordinate and the surrounding coordinates are considered to have a high possibility of being the same algae. This process is carried out using the region expansion method to gradually expand the algae region from the origin to obtain the algae region. The threshold value is set to 25. The formula shows how to calculate the RGB values of click coordinates and surrounding coordinates.
   (3) Based on the result obtained in (2), output a black and white image of the obtained algae expressed in white.

Click coordinates (R_1, G_1, B_1), Surrounding coordinates (R_n, G_n, B_n)

$$threshold <= |R_1 - R_n| + |G_1 - G_n| + |B_1 - B_n|$$

3 Verification

3.1 Verification Method

With the local independent administrative agency Hokkaido Research Organization (HRO), this software was actually used and verified.

Using the conventional and proposed methods, the percent cover of 1-year-old kelp, 2 year-old kelp, Yoremoku, and Sugamo was derived and compared. Fifty underwater images were used, and the number of area divisions was 4 × 5. The validation results are shown in Fig. 15.

3.2 Result

Figure 15 shows that while there is a correlation between the percent cover (%) obtained by this software and the percent cover (%) of algae obtained by the conventional method, the overall percent cover (%) of algae is larger than that of the conventional method.

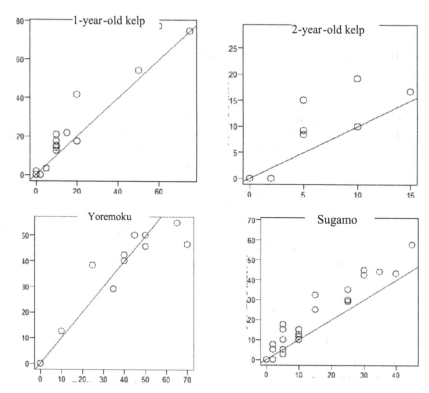

Fig. 15. Result (Conventional(horizontal axis) and proposed(vertical axis) methods[%])

4 Consideration

The reason why the proposed method shows a larger algae cover (%) than the conventional method is thought to be that the formula for deriving the algae cover (%) is affected by the number of area divisions of the underwater image. As an example, consider the situation as shown in Fig. 16. In Fig. 16, sea urchin (red) and kelp (white) are counted in

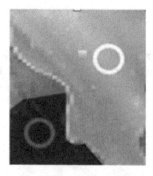

Fig. 16. Sea urchin (red) and kelp (white) in a partial area

a subregion of an underwater image. In this case, the area A occupied by each algae in the subregion is 50% respectively according to Eq. 1. However, when the percent cover (%) is read from Fig. 16 using the conventional method, sea urchin and kelp account for about 20% and 80%, respectively, which are different from the area A occupied by each algae in the subregion. This problem can be solved by increasing the number of subdivisions, and it is thought that the values obtained by the conventional method and the area A occupied by each alga in the subregion can be brought closer together. On the other hand, increasing the number of domain divisions may increase the workload. In other words, it is thought that there is a trade-off relationship between the accuracy of the software and the increase in the workload.

5   Conclusion

Through this research, we have developed an algae counting application.

With the developed application, it is possible to view images, determine the type of seaweed, derive the cover of seaweed, and output the aggregate results in a single application, simplifying the fishery survey process that has been performed with conventional methods.

In addition, we proposed a method to improve the problems of difficulty in extracting algae areas on underwater images and the problem of operator error caused by deriving algae cover by visual inspection, and implemented it in this application. As a result, we were able to derive data that can be regarded as algal cover using the proposed method.

Reference

1. Guidelines for measures to prevent the disappearance of seaweed bed resources, Fisheries Agency (2009, March)

ISHIGAKI Region Extraction Using Grabcut Algorithm for Support of Kumamoto Castle Reconstruction

Yuuki Yamasaki[1(✉)], Masahiro Migita[1(✉)], Go Koutaki[1(✉)],
Masashi Toda[1(✉)], and Tsuyoshi Kishigami[2(✉)]

[1] Kumamoto University, 2-39-1 Kurokami, Chuo-ku, Kumamoto, Japan
`yamasaki@st.cs.kumamoto-u.ac.jp`, {`migita,toda`}`@cc.kumamoto-u.ac.jp`,
`koutaki@cs.kumamoto-u.ac.jp`
[2] Toppan Printing CO., LTD., 1, KandaIzumi-cho, Chiyoda-ku, Tokyo, Japan
`tsuyoshi.kishigami@toppan.co.jp`
`https://www.kumamoto-u.ac.jp`, `https://www.toppan.co.jp`

Abstract. In April 2016, a severe earthquake occurred in Kumamoto, Japan. That damaged ISHIGAKI of Kumamoto castle and caused a large amount of stone to fall. We have developed support systems that use ICT and we have also investigated a method of extracting stone contour information. In our previous research, we have been improving GrabCut to try to automate stone contour extraction. However, in some cases, over-segmentation or under-segmentation occurred. In the paper, we dealt with this problem. From the observation results, it is considered that the stone shape has a convex polygonal shape to some extent. We set restrict regions for background-likely characteristics using a convex hull of a pre-extraction result by GrabCut close to the original iteratively. Convex hull fitness is a criterion to evaluate whether it is a convex polygon. In addition, the error with GT is calculated. From the results, the following can be considered. That with a small convex hull fitness value tended to have a small error with GT.

Keywords: Restoration assistance · Region extraction · Convex hull · GrabCut

1 Introduction

In April 2016, a severe earthquake occurred in Kumamoto, Japan, which damaged the stone walls of Kumamoto castle and caused a large amount of stone to fall and caused a large amount of stone to fall (Fig. 1).

The castle is an important tourist attraction and serves as spiritual support for the people of Kumamoto. Hence, it is necessary to restore them with as much as the original fallen stone as possible, as this stone is the tangible cultural

The A-STEP from Japan Science and Technology Agency, JST.

H. Jeong and K. Sumi (Eds.): IW-FCV 2021, CCIS 1405, pp. 106–116, 2021.
https://doi.org/10.1007/978-3-030-81638-4_9

property of Kumamoto. Currently, the restoration of stone walls costs significant time and money because craftsmen must visually determine the position of each stone, one by one. If this process could be automated, significant time and money would be saved in restoring these stone walls.

Based on this, we have developed support systems that use ICT(Information and Communication Technology) as part of a project aimed at facilitating recovery from earthquake disasters. Specifically, we have used image processing techniques and developed a system that compares each stone of a stone wall before a disaster to each stone after and identifies the locations in the wall previously filled by the fallen stones [1]. We have also investigated a method of extracting stone contour information, as this is important in the matching process [2] (Fig. 2). In [3], we proposed the method based on GrabCut [4] used in [2] by performing GrabCut, which adds the linear edges and low-brightness regions(following "background characteristics"), which are considered to be effective in contour extraction in images, as background labels. Further, in order to deal with over-segmentation and under-segmentation, we performed the method that their characteristics are used from the part located outside the stone by setting the square restriction range.

Fig. 1. Collapsed ISHIGAKI (left) and collapsed stone (right)

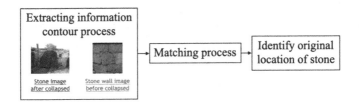

Fig. 2. Flow of retrieval system for stones

2   Previous Research

2.1   Area Extraction of Kumamoto Castle Stone Wall Stone Using GrabCut

In GrabCut, which is the foreground extraction method used in [2], the foreground and background area are roughly specified manually, each pixels are judged whether the foreground or background, misjudged area is fixed by user. High-precision extraction is achieved by making corrections by adding labels and determining the foreground and background again. However, the extraction of the stone region performed in this study is premised on automatic extraction. GrabCut user does not modify. In [3], linear edges in the image, which are considered to be effective as a characteristics of the stone contour, were detected by Canny Edge Detector and Hough Transform, and used as the background label for GrabCut. In addition, the depressions between the stones, which tend to be less bright than the stones, were detected by binarization of Otsu and used as a background label.

Unfortunately, depending on stone texture, over-segmentation or under-segmentation may occur due to the detection of linear edges and low-luminance areas on the texture of the stone surface (Fig. 3), and high-precision extraction may not be possible.

2.2   Characteristics Range Limitation Using Squares of Extraction Result

To address the challenge of over-segmentation with traditional stone textures, characteristics which are input to GrabCut are limited by position. Here, the stone wall 2D data used in this research was cut out so that it was located near the center of the image for each stone to be extracted. We assumed that background characteristics located far from the center of the image should be used, and conversely, ones close to the center should be not. In [3], a square area was set as the boundary to determine whether the characteristics were should be used or not. However, depending on the arrangement and shape of the stone, it was not possible to properly specify the "background characteristics", and over-segmentation and under-segmentation still occurred (Fig. 4).

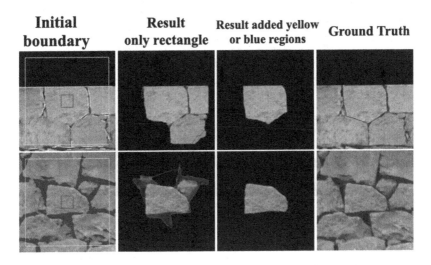

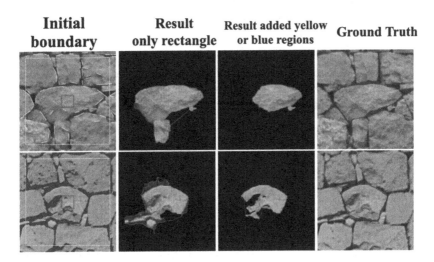

Fig. 3. A good result (above), A not good result (bottom). Inside of red is an initial foreground region, outside of green is an initial background region (Color figure online)

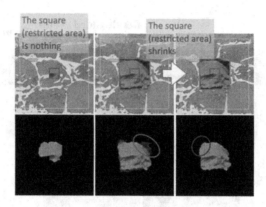

Fig. 4. Characteristics limitation by square

3   Proposed Method

3.1   Feature Range Specification Using Convex Hull of Extraction Result

In [4], in addition to the spectrum-based evaluation, highly accurate stone extraction was achieved by introducing an index called convex hull fitness, which evaluated convex polygonality as a stone-like shape. If the convex hull fitness is Fconv, it is expressed by Eq. 1. This value is greater than or equal to 0, and becomes smaller as the original region and its convex hull are equal, and 0 when they are exactly equal.

$$F_{conv} = \frac{l}{\sqrt{n}} \cdot (\frac{c}{n} - 1) \cdot \frac{l}{m} \qquad (1)$$

Where
n = number of pixels in an object l = boundary length of an object c = number of pixels in the convex hull of an object m = boundary length of the convex hull of an object

In our study as well, we evaluated the convex hull fitness for the region extracted by GrabCut using Eq. 1. As shown in Fig. 5, the extraction result including the extra region due to insufficient segmentation and the distorted shape due to over-segmentation. It shows that the value of convex hull fitness tends to be clearly smaller in the region to be extracted than in the extraction result.

In addition, it has been found from previous studies that the stone extraction results obtained by roughly specifying the area with the original rectangle of GrabCut are insufficiently divided, and the areas around the stone of interest tend to be partially combined. Therefore, as shown in Fig. 6, we consider using the convex hull region of the extraction result obtained by roughly specifying the region with a rectangle as the boundary for restricting the use of "background

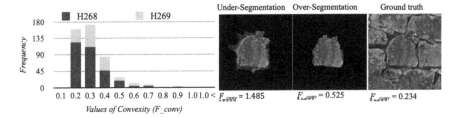

Fig. 5. Comparison of ground truth's convex hull suitability value (left) with over-segmentation, under-segmentation, and ground truth's Fconv (right). H268 and H269 in the graph are 2D data of the east side and the south side of the Kumamoto castle is ishigakiiidamaru – gokaiyagura, respectively.

Characteristics". We set convex hull the area of previous result by GrabCut as the restrict range along the target stone more than the boundary by the square. Furthermore, by eroding this convex hull region, the range is changed, and multiple contour candidates can be obtained for each stone, and we verified whether the best contour can be obtained among these in the experiment. Also, the erosion process erodes the entire area by 1 pixel.

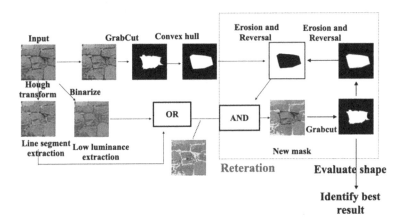

Fig. 6. Flow of "background Characteristics" restrictions.

3.2   Error Calculation with Ground Truth

We calculated the discrepancy between a manually extracted contour (the "ground truth", GT) and the contour extracted in this study. To calculate the error between the GT and the contour obtained by the proposed method, both of these must have the same scale (in this study, the image size is 800 pixels × 800 pixels and 100 points define the contour after processing is completed).

The error L is then calculated with the following formula. (The contour obtained by the proposed method is denoted P and the GT contour Q.)

$$L = \sum_{k=1}^{n} \sqrt{(P_{kx} - Q_{kx,nearest})^2 + (P_{ky} - Q_{ky,nearest})^2} \qquad (2)$$

Where
n is the number of contour points, 100 in this experiment.
P represents the coordinates of a point on the extracted contour P.
Q represents the coordinates of one point on the contour Q that becomes the GT.

The suffix *nearest* specifies the point on contour Q with the smallest Euclidean distance to a given point on contour P. The point on contour Q with the smallest Euclidean distance to a given point on contour P is recorded, and this calculation is repeated for all the points on P. L is then defined as the sum of these Euclidean distances, for each recorded P-Q pair. The points on both contours are interpolated to give 100 equally spaced points (Fig. 7).

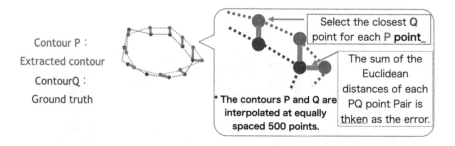

Fig. 7. Results by proposed method

4   Experiment

4.1   Application to Stone Wall Images Before Collapsed

The method described in Chap. 3 is applied to the stone wall image. Here, the convex hull of the extraction result of the previous result is contracted, GrabCut is performed as the next characteristics limiting range, and the shape evaluation called convex hull fitness (1) is performed. In addition, the error (2) from GT is calculated. We repeat the above 100 times. Also, the input image is 800×800, and the number of contour points is 100 points. The margin of error is 800 pixels.

Figures 8 and 9 shows results. In the case of the result shown in Fig. 8, the error with GT was the smallest at the 12th, and the margin of error of 800 pixels was cut. On the other hand, the 16th has the smallest convex hull fitness value, which is also less than 800 pixels. It is considered that the point where the

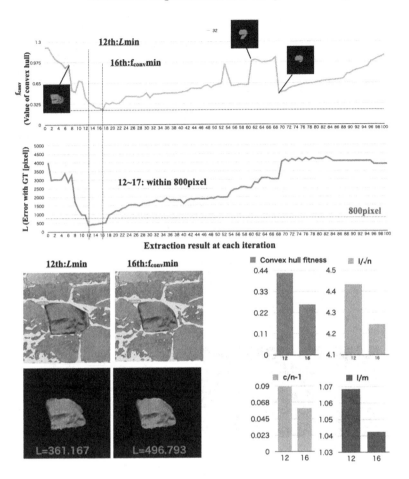

Fig. 8. Results by proposed method (Color figure online)

following red frame part has a large dent contributed to the area increase and the contour decrease at the time of convex hull as the reason why the convex hull fitness of 12 is larger.

In the results of Fig. 9, the value of convex hull fitness was the smallest at the 39th position, but the error with GT exceeded 800 pixels. On the other hand, the 41st had the smallest error with GT, and although it was less than 800 pixels, the convex hull fitness value was larger than the 39th. This is also thought to be due to the dent.

From the results, the following can be considered. The one with the minimum convex hull fitness tends to have a smaller error with GT than the other parts in both graphs. This is because the value of convex hull fitness becomes smaller when there are few extra areas or large recessed areas, and at the same time, the correct contour is also a shape close to a convex polygon.

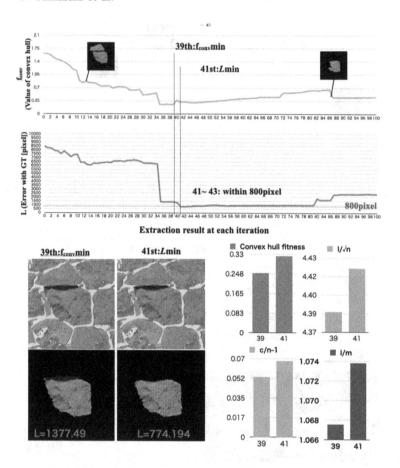

Fig. 9. Results by proposed method (Color figure online)

4.2   Application to Collapsed Stone Images

Consider using this method for images of collapsed stones. Figure 10 shows a case where over-division occurs due to the background features detected as in the case of the stone wall before the collapse. In the following, in addition to the line segment, the light blue and white areas are input with the area as the background. Over-segmentation occurs because the features detected by the texture inside the stone are specified as the background. Next, the result of applying the proposed method is shown in Fig. 11. From the figure, it can be seen that good results are obtained in the 0th to 3rd results, and the value of convex fitness is also small.

Fig. 10. Results by previous method

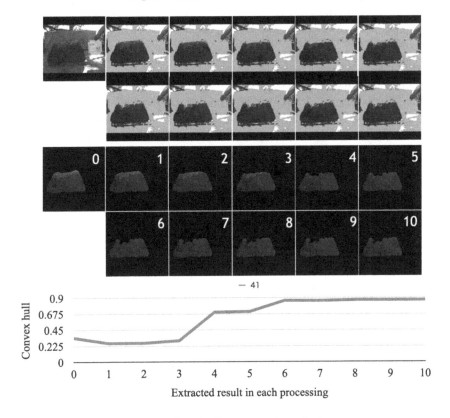

Fig. 11. Results by proposed method

5   Conclusion

In the paper, in order to make the restriction range specification method more suitable for stone regions, we considered the method introducing the convex hull of the region obtained by ordinary GrabCut as a new restriction range. We aimed to improve the extraction accuracy. As a result, depending on stones, it was possible to specify the label with background characteristics that were effectively restricted by the region obtained by the erosion of the convex hull, and good results were obtained. Also, extracted results with a small convex hull fitness value tended to have a small error with GT. It is necessary to perform a more suitable shape evaluation for stones with dents.

References

1. Miyazawa, A., Koutaki, G.: Retrieval system for stones of Kumamoto Castle using ISHIGAKI marker. In: The 62nd Annual Conference of the Institute of Systems Proceedings (2018)
2. Toda, M., Inoue, K., Koutaki, G., Kishigami, T.: Extraction method of stone contour for support of ISHIGAKI retrieval on Kumamoto Castle. IEEJ Trans. Electron. Inf. Syst. (2018)
3. Yamasaki, Y., Masahiro, M., Koutaki, G., Toda, M., Kishigami, T.: A research on Kumamoto Castle ISHIGAKI region extraction using stone features and shape evaluation. In: PRMU2020 (2020)
4. Rother, C., Kolmogorv, V., Blake, A.: GrabCut: Interactive foreground extraction using iterated graph cuts. ACM Trans. Graph. **23**(3), 309–314 (2004)

Study on 3D Extraction and Analysis of Blood Vessels and Cardiomyocytes on Neonatal Murine

Asuma Takematsu[1](✉), Masahiro Migita[2], Masashi Toda[2], and Yuichiro Arima[3]

[1] Department of Computer Science and Electrical Engineering, Kumamoto University, Kumamoto 860-8555, Japan
takematsu@st.cs.kumamoto-u.ac.jp

[2] Center for Management of Information Technologies, Kumamoto University, Kumamoto 860- 8555, Japan

[3] Department of Cardiovascular Medicine, Kumamoto University, Kumamoto 860-0811, Japan

Abstract. In order to elucidate the mechanism of heart disease, there is an urgent need for three-dimensional analysis of cardiomyocytes using a computer. However, microscopic images contain cells other than cardiomyocytes, so the cells must be classified before analysis. Cardiomyocytes are characterized by a relatively low volume fraction of cell nuclei in the cytoplasm compared to other cells. In this study, these features will be used to extract cell nuclei, cytoplasm and vascular regions from fluorescence microscopy images of the heart of newborn mice and classify cardiomyocytes and other cells based on volume ratio. The extracted blood vessels and cardiomyocytes were analyzed in normal mice and genetically modified mice. As a result of the experiment, a difference was observed between the two, and it was found that the genetically modified mouse had a larger number of blood vessel branches and a larger area of blood vessels in contact with cells. This result is consistent with the expected tendency and is considered to be valid in the analysis. We believe that this research will be part of the research to elucidate the mechanisms of blood vessels and cells in the myocardium by improving the accuracy in the future.

Keywords: 3D Image processing · Medical imaging · Cell classification

1 Introduction

In Japan, where the population is aging, the number of deaths due to heart disease accounts for about 15% of the total, and is still on the rise [1]. In addition, the number of donors is smaller than that of transplant-adapted patients, and it is unlikely that they will become widespread in the future. Therefore, elucidation of the mechanism of heart disease is urgently needed. In recent years, the development of computer technology is expected to elucidate the pathophysiology at the cellular level, and cardiomyocytes, which are the main constituents of the heart, are used as targets for analysis. Studies using mouse cardiomyocytes, which are the same mammals as humans, are being actively conducted, and as a typical study, there is a report that a mouse model was created

© Springer Nature Switzerland AG 2021
H. Jeong and K. Sumi (Eds.): IW-FCV 2021, CCIS 1405, pp. 117–130, 2021.
https://doi.org/10.1007/978-3-030-81638-4_10

so that the state would be similar to heart failure and the cross-sectional area of the cardiomyocytes was measured. There is [2]. However, many studies so far have discussed cardiomyocytes, which are three-dimensional bodies, in two dimensions. It is possible to obtain more information by performing three-dimensional analysis of minute cells such as cardiomyocytes. However, since cardiomyocytes and other cells coexist in the heart, it is desirable to classify each cell and analyze three-dimensional information such as the volume and positional relationship of each cell. Single cell analysis [3] is a method for acquiring three-dimensional information of cells. However, in single-cell analysis, cells are isolated and analyzed by focusing on one cell, so information such as the shape of cells in the tissue and the positional relationship between cells cannot be obtained. In this study, we classify cardiomyocytes and non-cardiomyocytes mixed in the fluorescence microscope image of the heart. Figure 1 shows one frame of the fluorescence microscope image and a three-dimensional visualization of a fluorescence microscope image. In this figure, the one that fluoresces red is the cell nucleus, the one that fluoresces green is the cell membrane, and the one that fluoresces white is the cell nucleus of cardiomyocytes.

Furthermore, not only cells but also blood vessels located around them are important factors in elucidating the mechanism of heart disease. Blood vessels carry oxygen and nutrients by contact with cells, and it is thought that there is a relationship between the growth rate of cells and blood vessels. Therefore, in this experiment, the relationship with blood vessels was analyzed after classifying cardiomyocytes. To do.

In this study, we extracted cell and blood vessel regions from fluorescence microscopic images of myocardium and analyzed the differences between normal mice and genetically modified mice. The figure on the left in Fig. 1 is a frame of the fluorescence microscope image, and the figure on the right is a three-dimensional visualization of the fluorescence microscope image using the 3D Viewer [4], which is a plug-in of the free software ImageJ [5]. In this figure, three objects are photographed at the same time, and each can be referred to individually. The three imaging targets are the cell nucleus, cell membrane, and vascular endothelial cells shown in Fig. 2, and the mechanism of myocardium is analyzed by observing the relationship between them.

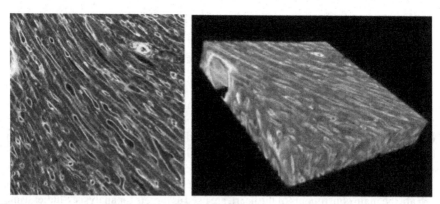

Fig. 1. Fluorescence microscope image (left) and three-dimensional visualization of fluorescence microscope images (right) (Color figure online)

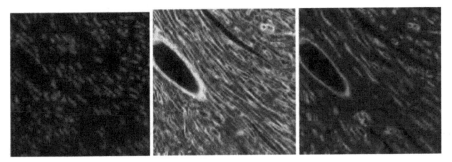

Fig. 2. Image taken, cell nucleus (left), cell membrane (center), vascular non-cell (right) (Color figure online)

2 Related Work

Many image processing methods have been proposed for analyzing cells from fluorescence microscopy images. In recent years, research on methods using deep learning has been actively conducted. It has various uses such as extraction of cell regions and classification of cells. U-net [6] is especially famous for domain extraction. This method was developed as an area extraction method for medical images, and is attracting attention with high accuracy, and it also supports 3D images [7]. Currently, many methods derived from the structure of U-net have been proposed. One of them is Cellpose [8]. This method has been proposed as a method for various cell images, and cells can be extracted without the need to train or adjust the model. Many systems have been developed that can be used without a deep understanding of deep learning because they do not place a heavy burden on medical personnel like this method. Machine learning is also used for blood vessels, and many methods for extracting blood vessel regions from MRI and CT images have been proposed. It is common to use images taken by fluorescing the entire blood vessel region using a contrast medium, such as MRI and CT, and there are few studies using images in which only the blood vessel surface is fluoresced. Bates et al. Extracted vascular networks from images in which only the endothelium was fluoresced by learning skeletons rather than vascular regions using Convolutional Recurrent Networks [9]. In this experiment, in order to utilize the vascular region, the vascular endothelial region was extracted and then filled in to extract the vascular region. Since the blood vessel region extraction of an image in which only the blood vessel surface is fluorescent has different characteristics from images such as CT, it is necessary to improve the accuracy by utilizing machine learning.

In addition to analyzing cell populations from microscopic images of tissue, there is also single-cell analysis, where cells are separated from the tissue and then individual cells are analyzed. A single analysis of cardiomyocytes is also being performed, and the molecular mechanism of cardiomyocytes is gradually being elucidated. Nomura et al. [3] obtained information on the expression of all genes in cardiomyocytes by singlecell analysis and used machine learning to clarify the behavior of molecular profiles in the process of cardiomyocyte remodeling for the first time in the world. I made it.Single-cell analysis requires the costly and time-consuming separation of cardiomyocytes, and if the cardiomyocytes exist as the muscle tissue of the heart, information such as their original shape and positional relationship cannot be obtained. In this study, we analyze cells and blood vessels from microscopic images using machine learning.

3   Method

3.1   Extraction of Vascular Area

The blood vessel region and cell region are extracted for analysis.

First, the blood vessel region is extracted (Sect. 3.1.1). Next, the extracted blood vessel region is thinned and divided into branches (Sect. 3.1.2). Next, noise is removed from the split branches (Sect. 3.1.3).

3.1.1   Extraction of Vascular Area

Figure 3 shows an image of the stained vascular endothelium. It shows the surface of blood vessels present in the imaged tissue. After smoothing this image with a Gaussian filter, Otsu is binarized to extract the blood vessel surface [10]. Then fill the surrounding area of each slice in each of the three directions. These processes extract the vascular area. The extracted area is shown in Fig. 4. This time, the blood vessels that were cut off at the edge of the screen were not taken into consideration during the filling process, so the extremely large blood vessels in the upper left were not filled. The cell nuclei existing in the vascular region were judged to be vascular endothelial cells, and were classified as non-cardiomyocytes at the time of cell classification in Sect. 3.2.4.

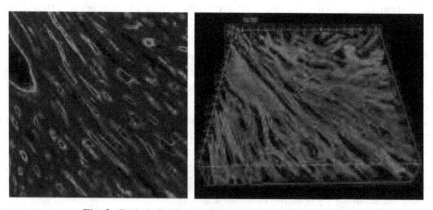

Fig. 3. Endothelial image (left) and extracted area (right)

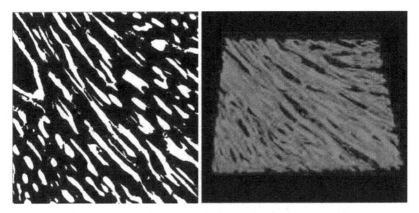

Fig. 4. Extracted blood vessel region (left) and 3D visualization image (right)

3.1.2 Creating Branches and Branch Points

Skeletonize the vascular region extracted in Sect. 3.1.1. In this way, a skeleton showing the connection status of blood vessels is created. Furthermore, a branch of the skeleton is created by dividing the skeleton by a branch point. Removed branches that are in contact with the other branch only at one end, as it can be noisy.The skeleton after thinning is shown on the left side of the figure, and the divided branches are shown on the right side of the figure. In this figure, the colors are colored so that different adjacent branches can be seen. Since it is likely to be noise, the branch at the end is removed (Fig. 5).

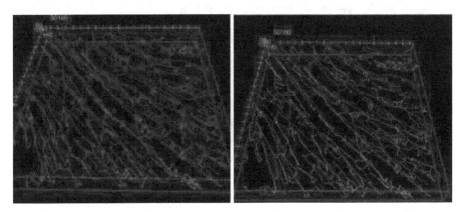

Fig. 5. Extracted skeleton image (left) and branched image (right) (Color figure online)

3.2 Extraction of Cell Regions and Identification of Cardiomyocytes

Next, the cell region is extracted. First, each region is extracted from the image in which the cell nucleus fluoresces and the image in which the cell membrane fluoresces (Sect. 3.2.1). The extracted cell nuclei are then identified as having multiple nuclei

(Sect. 3.2.2). The cytoplasmic region is separated from the nuclear and membrane regions using the marked watershed method (Sect. 3.2.3). Finally, each cell is categorized based on the relationship between the extracted cell and cytoplasmic regions (Sect. 3.2.4).

3.2.1 Extraction of Cell Nucleus and Cell Membrane Region

Each region is extracted from the image in which the cell nucleus is fluorescent and the image in which the cell membrane is fluorescent. For the cell nucleus region, individual cell nucleus regions were extracted from the cell nucleus image using Cellpose [8]. Some of the cell nucleus regions extracted at this time were over-divided, and some were partially erased as if they were blurred. Therefore, the overdivision was corrected using the result of dividing the binary image of the cell nucleus image by the watershed method [11]. In the cell membrane region, the difference in brightness value is large even in the same membrane region, and the membrane region cannot be extracted by simple binarization. Therefore, adaptive binarization is performed to determine the threshold value by limiting the image range to reduce noise. It was allowed and extracted in a form close to the current image. The cytoplasmic mask is obtained by inverting the cell membrane mask (Fig. 6).

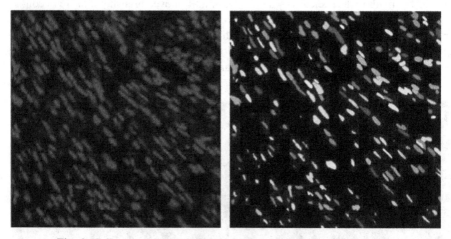

Fig. 6. Cell nucleus image (left) and extracted cell nucleus region (right)

3.2.2 Multi-nuclear Support

A multinucleate cell is a cell in which multiple cell nuclei exist in one cell, and is caused by cell nuclear division without cell division. Since this experiment is used as a marker for region division of cell nuclei, it is necessary to estimate multinuclei before dividing cells. From the cell nucleus mask created in Sect. 3.2.1, identify the combination of multinucleated cells contained in the cell. Multinucleated cells can be seen in the fluorescence microscope images used in this experiment. Figure 7 shows an image containing multiple nuclei. The cells circled in yellow are multinucleated cells.

For each cell nucleus, the multinucleus candidate was judged to be multinucleated by any value of the distance between the cell nucleus and the main axis direction, and the direction connecting the two cell nuclei and the main axis direction of the cell nucleus.

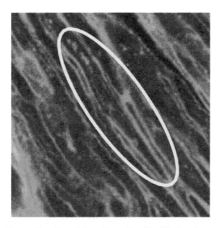

Fig. 7. Example of multinucleated cells (Color figure online)

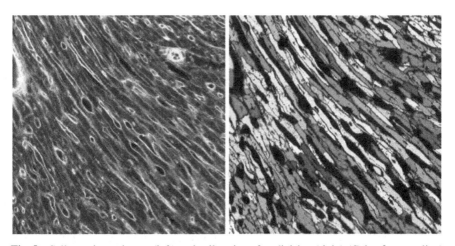

Fig. 8. Cell membrane image (left) and cell region after division (right) (Color figure online)

3.2.3 Cell Region Segmentation

The cytoplasmic mask is divided using the cell nucleus on the premise that there is always one cell nucleus in the cell region. The cytoplasmic region is divided by the watershed method using each center of gravity of the cell nucleus mask as a marker, and the cytoplasmic region of each cell is extracted. At this time, the corresponding nucleus as a multinucleus uses the midpoint of the center of gravity as a marker. Figure 8 shows the cytoplasmic region divided into regions. After labeling the cytoplasmic regions, the colors are randomly changed according to the label number so that the adjacent regions can be seen as different cytoplasms.

3.3 Cell Classification

Cardiomyocytes are characterized by a smaller ratio of cell nucleus volume to cytoplasm than non-cardiomyocytes. Therefore, the filling rate is determined as follows, and if the filling rate calculated from the extracted cell nucleus region and cytoplasm is smaller than the threshold value, it is judged as a cardiomyocyte. The threshold is calculated by discriminant analysis.

$$\text{filling rate } (\%) = \frac{\text{cell nucleus volume}}{\text{cytoplasmic volume}} \times 100.$$

4 Experiment

The specifications of this experiment are shown in Table 1.

Table 1. Experimental specifications

Target	Neonatal murine
Shooting location	Myocardium of the free wall of the left atrium
Shooting equipment	Multiphoton laser scanning microscope
Analysis software	MATLAB 2020

4.1 Target Image

In this study, we will analyze fluorescence microscopy images of the heart of a mouse. Target images were taken by staining mouse cell nuclei, cell membranes, and vascular endothelial cells with a confocal laser scanning microscope. This is an image of $1024 \times 1024 \times 109$ size, and each target can be referenced separately. In this experiment, we use images of the myocardium of normal mice and genetically modified mice of the same age. Genetically modified mice are mice that have been modified so that they cannot be metabolized, and it is assumed that their growth is immature because they cannot be metabolized. As a result, it is expected that there are more blood vessels and cells and smaller cells than normal mice. Furthermore, the histogram of the filling rate for cells in each image calculated in Sect. 3.2 was calculated as shown in the figure. The blue bar represents cardiomyocytes, the red bar represents non-cardiomyocytes, and the yellow bar represents vascular endothelial cells. Since the purpose of this experiment is to analyze the relationship between cardiomyocytes and blood vessels, the cell region classified as cardiomyocytes in each image is used for analysis (Figs. 9, 10 and 11).

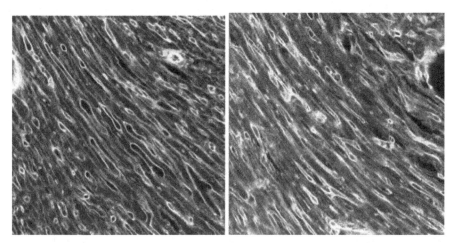

Fig. 9. Fluorescence microscope image of normal mouse (left), fluorescence microscope image of genetically modified mouse (right) (Color figure onine)

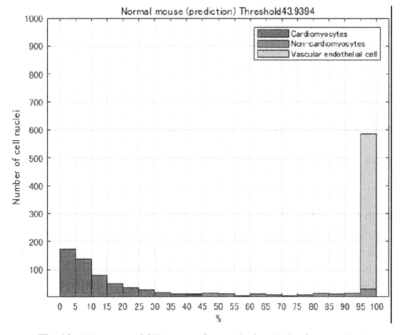

Fig. 10. Histogram of filling rate of normal mice (Color figure online)

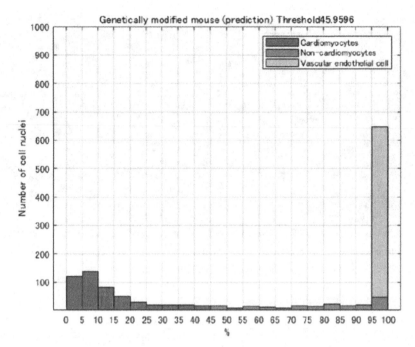

Fig. 11. Histogram of filling rate of genetically modified mice (right) (Color figure online)

4.2 Experiment Contents

In this experiment, the cell nucleus region, cell region, and blood vessel region are extracted from the target image, and the relationship between the region classified as cardiomyocytes and the blood vessels divided into each branch is analyzed. At that time, the values of normal mice and genetically modified mice are calculated and the data are compared. The following items are evaluated.

4.2.1 Degree of Contact of Blood Vessels with Each Cardiomyocyte

For each cell determined to be a cardiomyocyte from the image of each mouse, the contact area of the blood vessel in contact with the cell is examined. The right figure of Fig. 12 shows the extracted cells and the blood vessel region, and the left figure shows the surface of the extracted cells. If the voxels on this surface match the blood vessel region, it is judged to be in contact.

Compared to normal mice, genetically modified mice are considered to have under-developed cells and blood vessels, so it is expected that more blood vessels will be stretched. Therefore, the area of blood vessels in contact with each cell is considered to be large. Figure 13 is an image of one cell and the blood vessels in contact with it.

The results are shown below. Figure 14 shows a skeletonized version of each image. Table 2 shows the data of the branches after being divided into branches by the branch point.

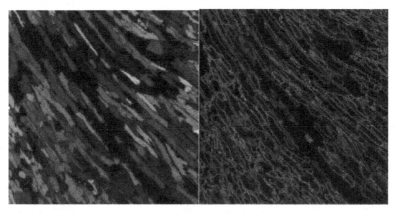

Fig. 12. Extracted blood vessel area and cell area (left), surrounding cell area (right)

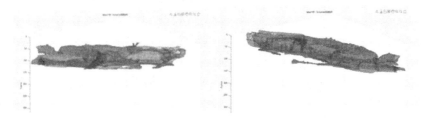

Fig. 13. Examples of cells and blood vessels around them

Table 2. Number and length of branches

	Number of branches	Average branch length
Normal mouse	2346	23.0
Genetically modified mouse	5195	21.2

From these data, it was found that genetically modified mice have more blood vessels and branches than normal mice, both visually and quantitatively. Histograms of the contact area between each cell nucleus and blood vessel are shown in Figs. 15 and 16.

These histograms show how much blood vessels are in contact with one cell, and the blue bar shows the distribution of cardiomyocytes in normal mice and the red bar shows the distribution of cardiomyocytes in genetically modified mice. The larger the value on the histogram, the larger the contact area and ratio. Comparing the two histograms, the genetically modified mouse occupies a larger proportion of the larger value than the normal mouse. Therefore, it can be interpreted that the genetically modified mouse has a larger contact area between cells and blood vessels as a whole.

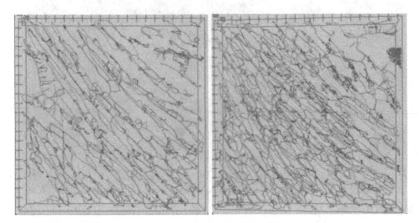

Fig. 14. Normal mouse skeleton (left), modified mouse skeleton (right)

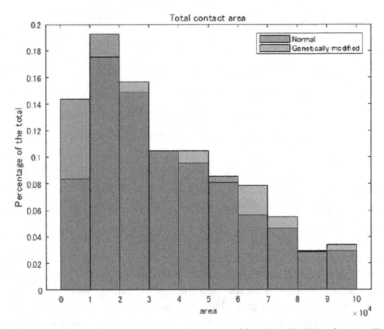

Fig. 15. Histogram of total contact area in contact with each cell (Color figure online)

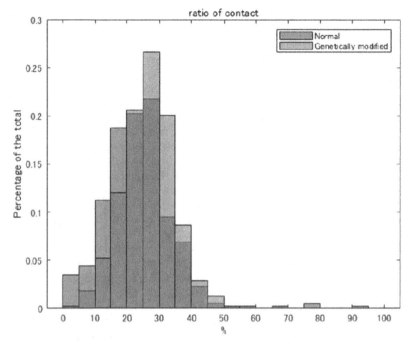

Fig. 16. Histogram of contact rate of blood vessels in contact with each cell (Color figure onine)

5 Conclusions

From the experimental results, there was a difference between the data of normal mice and genetically modified mice. In addition, as expected, data was obtained that the genetically modified mice had a larger contact area. From this, it can be said that cells and blood vessels can be extracted by this method and their relationships can be investigated. However, since it is possible that genetic modification is not the cause of the difference but merely the individual difference, we plan to increase the number of data to be examined and analyze multiple mice in the future. In addition, since we are using simple methods for blood vessel extraction, skeletonization, and branching this time, we are considering methods that utilize machine learning in the future. By using these methods, we would like to perform more accurate domain extraction and analyze highly reliable information. The future task is to solve the above problems and implement an improvement plan.

References

1. Ministry of Health, Labor and Welfare: Trends in leading causes of death (2020). https://www.mhlw.go.jp/english/database/db-hw/populate/dl/E03.pdf
2. Puente, B.N., et al.: The oxygen-rich postnatal environment induces cardiomycyte cell- cycle arrest through DNA damage response. Cell **157**, 565–579 (2014)

3. Nomura, S., Satoh, M., Fujita, T., et al.: Cardiomyocyte gene programs encoding morphological and functional signatures in cardiac hypertrophy and failure. Nat. Commun. **9**, 4435 (2018)
4. Schmid, B., Schindelin, J., Cardona, A. et al.: A high-level 3D visualization API for Java and ImageJ. BMC Bioinf. 11(1), PMID 20492697 (2010). https://doi.org/10.1038/nmeth.3392
5. Schneider, C.A., Rasband, W.S., Eliceiri, K.W.: NIH Image to ImageJ: 25 years of image analysis. Nat. Methods **9**, 671–675 (2012)
6. Ronneberger, O., Fischer, P., Brox, T.: U-Net: Convolutional networks for biomedical image segmentation. In: Navab, N., Hornegger, J., Wells, W., Frangi, A. (eds.) Medical Image Computing and Computer-Assisted Intervention. LNCS, vol. 9351, pp. 234–241. Springer, Heidelberg (2015). https://doi.org/10.1007/978-3-319-24574-4_28
7. Çiçek, O., Abdulkadir, A., Lienkamp, S., Brox, T., Ronneberger, O.: 3D U- Net: Learning dense volumetric segmentation from sparse annotation. In: Ourselin, S., Joskowicz, L., Sabuncu, M., Unal, G., Wells, W. (eds.) Medical Image Computing and Computer-Assisted Intervention. LNCS, vol. 9901, pp. 424–432. Springer, Heidelberg (2016). https://doi.org/10.1007/978-3-319-46723-8_49
8. Stringer, C., Michaelos, M., Pachitariu, M: Cellpose: a generalist algorithm for cellular segmentation. bioRxiv (2020). https://doi.org/10.1101/2020.02.02.931238
9. Bate, R., et al.: Extracting 3D vascular structures from microscopy images using convolutional recurrent networks. arXiv preprint arXiv:1705.09597 (2017)
10. Otsu, N.: Automatic threshold selection method based on discrimination and least squares criteria. IEICE Trans. Fundam. Electron. Commun. Comput. Sci. 349–356 (1980)
11. Meyer, F.: Topographic distance and watershed lines. Sig. Process. **38**, 113–125 (1994)

Challenges and Applications of Face Deepfake

Lamyanba Laishram⑩, Md. Maklachur Rahman⑩, and Soon Ki Jung⁽✉⁾⑩

School of Computer Science and Engineering, Kyungpook National University,
Daegu, Republic of Korea
{yanbalaishram,maklachur,skjung}@knu.ac.kr

Abstract. With the development of Generative deep learning algorithms in the last decade, it has become increasingly difficult to differentiate between what is real and what is fake. With the easily available "Deepfake" applications, even a person with less computing knowledge can also produce realistic Deepfake data. These fake data have many benefits while on the other hand, it can also be used for unethical and malicious purposes. Deepfake can be anything fake data generated by using deep learning methods. In this study, we focus on Deepfake with respect to face manipulation. We represent the currently used algorithms and datasets are represented for creating Deepfake. We also study the challenges and the real-world applications in which the benefits, as well as the drawbacks of using Deepfake, are being pointed out.

Keywords: Deepfake · DeepFake creation · Faceswap · Face attribute editing · Deepfake dataset

1 Introduction and Motivation

Face manipulation and editing have been used in film industry for many years. The editing of facial expression of the actor is done with the changes in the dialogues of the film actors, which are sometimes hard for the actors to perform and also swapping faces between the stunt performer and the real actors of the film. However, the face manipulation is not limited to the film industry, it is also used in many other areas.

With the introduction of Generative Adversarial Network (GAN) [34] in 2014, the hype or fake vs original data is on the top. Deepfake is a powerful computer vision technique which is used to manipulate or generate fake content. The term "Deepfake" obtained from the words "deep learning" and "fake" uses the techniques of machine learning and artificial intelligence to create new and fake contents but realistic looking and difficult to distinguished whether it is fake or real. 'Deepfake with face manipulation' is a part of Deepfake where it mainly focus on the manipulation and editing of the facial part of an individual. The method superimpose faces of a target on the faces of the source and create an image or a video of the target person doing things that they actually do not do.

© Springer Nature Switzerland AG 2021
H. Jeong and K. Sumi (Eds.): IW-FCV 2021, CCIS 1405, pp. 131–156, 2021.
https://doi.org/10.1007/978-3-030-81638-4_11

The common benefits of this technology are their creative and productive applications in areas of education, marketing, art and multimedia [3,8,20,22,23]. With all the positive applications of this technology, the potential of malicious use is of a great concern, as the technology becomes more refine over time. The term 'Deepfake' is first used by an anonymous user of Redditor in late 2017 by posting videos of celebrity in porn videos, which is a combination of a celebrities face and body of a porn actor fused together [25]. The vulnerable victims of these malicious activities are the celebrities and political figures as their face data can be easily collected for creating of the Deepfake videos.

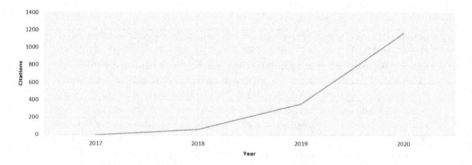

Fig. 1. Number of cited papers related to keyword "Deepfake" from [12]. The graph represents the number of papers from 2017 till the end of 2020.

Since 2017, the Deepfake technique became popular and skyrocketed in the academic community too. The technology has been advancing very rapidly and the Deepfake videos are becoming very realistic and difficult to be identified as fake videos. From the data obtained [12], the number of research papers increased from 3 to over 1000 during 2017 to 2020 as shown in Fig. 1. With the creation of realistic Deepfake contents, there is a need for the detection also. The growing interest of fake face detection is observed through the increasing number of workshops in top conferences [7,27] and in recent competition NIST's MFC2018 [21] and Facebook's DFDC [13]. At the same time the publicly available tools are also on the rise which is represented in the Table 1.

To understand the trending threats from Deepfake and in order to reduce them, we need to have a brief overview of what deepfake is. In this paper, we focus on the Deepfake with respect to the human face manipulation and edition. The main goals are (1) to identify current Deepfake creation techniques, (2) the types of database used in Deepfake creation (3) recent Deepfake approaches and the challenges, (3) discussing the future area of Deepfake.

2 Database Collection and Analysis

In this section we first reviewed the publicly available data collection in the Deepfake community used in training and testing of Deepfake creation and detection

Table 1. List of publicly available Deepfake tools.

Tools	Link	Type
DeepFaceLab	https://github.com/iperov/DeepFaceLab/	Open source
faceswap	https://github.com/deepfakes/faceswap/	Open source
FaceSwap	https://github.com/MarekKowalski/FaceSwap/	Open source
faceswap-GAN	https://github.com/shaoanlu/faceswap-GAN/	Open source
Fake	https://www.fakeapp.com/	App
FakeApp	https://fakeapp.softonic.com/	App
DeepFake_tf	https://github.com/StromWine/DeepFake_tf	Open source
Faceswap web	https://faceswapweb.com/	Website
dfaker	https://github.com/dfaker/df	Open source
fewshot-face-translation-GAN	https://github.com/shaoanlu/fewshot-face-translation-GAN	Open source
Reflect	https://reflect.tech/	Website
FaceSwap online	https://faceswaponline.com/	Website
Face Swap Live	http://faceswaplive.com/	Website
FakeApp 2.2.0.	https://www.malavida.com/en/soft/fakeapp/	App

methods and followed by the discussion on the characteristics of each set with the advantages and disadvantages thereof.

2.1 Data Collection

With the rise in the creation of manipulated faces in recent years, the key aspect of developing a good Deepfake system is the data collection used in training. However, Data collections are mostly overlooked, but they are extremely important. Based on the type of method, Data collection can be divided into three sections: only real database, real and fake database and only fake database. Table 2 shows all the Deepfake face database and their respective links.

Only Real Face Database. This database is made by the collection of only real faces found in internet. This data collection is used either in training or testing of different methods with respect to Deepfake. Currently, the main training set available are CelebFaces Attributes Dataset (celebA) [56], Radboud face database (RaFD) [49], Flickr-Faces-HQ (FFHQ) [17], CelebA-HQ [41] and CelebAMask-HQ [50].

celebA is a large-scale face attributes dataset with more than 200K celebrity images, each with 40 attribute annotations. The images in this dataset cover large pose variations and background clutter. CelebA has large diversities, large quantities, and rich annotations. This database contains 10177 number of identities with 5 landmark location and 40 binary attributes annotations for each images.

RaFD is a high quality face database which contains an image set of 8 emotional expression. This 8 expressions were collected from 67 individuals including Caucasian males and females, Caucasian children, both boys and girls, and

Moroccan Dutch males. Anger, disgust, fear, happiness, sadness, surprise, contempt, and neutral are the expressions. This database also provides 3 gaze directions: looking left, front and right.

FFHQ dataset consists of 70,000 high-quality PNG images at 1024 × 1024 resolution and contains considerable variation in terms of age, ethnicity and image background. It also has good coverage of accessories such as eyeglasses, sunglasses, hats, etc.

CelebA-HQ is a high quality facial image dataset that consists of 30000 images picked from CelebA dataset. These images are processed with quality improvement to the size of 1024 × 1024.

CelebAMask-HQ is a large scale face semantic label dataset consisting of 30,000 high resolution face images from CelebA. The size of the images are 512 × 512 and 19 classes of all facial components such as skin, nose, eyes, eyebrows, ears, mouth, lip, hair, hat, eyeglass, earring, necklace, neck, and cloth.

Real and Fake Face Database. This data collections consist of both pristine and fake images. There are fake images with the corresponding real images in this collection. Currently, the main database available are UADFV [52], DeepfakeTIMIT (DF TIMIT) [46], FaceForensics ++ [69], Deepfake detection (DFD) [31], Celeb-DF [53], Deepfake detection challenge (DFDC) [31], Deeper forensics 1.0 [40], Wild deepfake [85]. Table 3 show the camparison between the different dataset for real and deefake dataset.

UADFV database consist of 49 real YouTube and 49 Deepfake videos. All the swapped faces are created with the face of actor Nicolas Cage by using FakeAPP mobile application [16]. The data provided are of resolution 294 × 500 pixels with an average of 11.14 s.

DeepfakeTIMIT is generated from the original VidTIMIT database [26]. DeepfakeTIMIT database [10] consists of 620 fake videos generated using open source GAN based approach Faceswap application [14]. The database is provided with two different qualities (i) a lower quality (LQ) with 64 × 64 size (ii) higher quality (HQ) with 128 × 128 size. Each version is generated using 10 videos from the vidTIMIT with 32 subjects which provides 320 videos for corresponding LQ and HQ.

Faceforensics++ database was introduced in 2019. It is the extension of the original Faceforensics [68] which focuses on swapping facial expressions. This database contains 1000 pristine videos downloaded from the internet (YouTube) and 1000 fake videos. The manipulated dataset is generated using two computer graphics-based approaches: Face2Face [75] and FaceSwap [15] and two learning based approaches DeepFakes [14] and NeuralTextures [74].

Deepfake detection is Google and Jigsaw DeepFake detection dataset which has 3068 DeepFake videos generated based on 363 original videos of 28 consented individuals of various genders, ages and ethnic groups. The details of the synthesis algorithm are not disclosed, but it is likely to be an implementation of the basic DeepFake maker algorithm.

Table 2. The list of all the Deepfake face database with their respective links.

Type	Database	Link	Size/type
Real database	celebA	http://mmlab.ie.cuhk.edu.hk/projects/CelebA.html	202k/Images
	RaFD	http://www.socsci.ru.nl:8180/RaFD2/RaFD	201/Images
	FFHQ	https://github.com/NVlabs/ffhq-dataset	70k /Images
	CelebA-HQ	https://github.com/NVlabs/stylegan	30k/Images
	CelebAMask-HQ	https://github.com/switchablenorms/CelebAMask-HQ	30k /Images
Both real and fake database	UADFV	https://github.com/yuezunli/WIFS2018.In.Ictu.Oculi	90/Videos
	DeepfakeTIMIT	https://www.idiap.ch/dataset/deepfaketimit	620/Videos
	Faceforensics++	https://github.com/ondyari/FaceForensics	5k/Videos
	DFD	https://ai.googleblog.com/2019/09/contributing-data-to-deepfake-detection.html	3.3k/Videos
	Celeb-DF	https://github.com/yuezunli/celeb-deepfakeforensics	6.2k/videos
	DFDC	https://ai.facebook.com/datasets/dfdc/	5.2k/Videos
	Deeper Forensics-1.0	https://github.com/EndlessSora/DeeperForensics-1.0	60k/videos
	WildDeepfake	https://github.com/deepfakeinthewild/deepfake-in-the-wild	7.2k/Videos
Only fake database	100k generated images	https://drive.google.com/drive/folders/100DJ0QXyG89HZzB4w2Cbyf4xjNK54cQ1	100k/Images
	100k faces	https://generated.photos/	100k/Images
	DFFD	http://cvlab.cse.msu.edu/dffd-dataset.html	300k/Images
	FSRemovalDB	https://github.com/socialabubi/iFakeFaceDB	150k/Images

Celeb-DF is created with the goal to generate a better visual quality as compared to their previous work UADFV database. This database consists of 408 real youtube videos corresponding to interviews of 59 celebrities with a diverse distribution in terms of gender, age, and ethnic group. In addition, these videos exhibit a large range of variations in aspects such as the face sizes (in pixels), orientations, lighting conditions, and backgrounds. Regarding fake videos, a total of 795 videos were created using DeepFake technology, swapping faces for each pair of the 59 subjects. The final videos are in MPEG4.0 format.

DFDC dataset is by far the largest currently and publicly-available face swap video dataset, with over 100,000 total clips sourced from 3,426 paid actors, produced with several Deepfake, GAN-based, and non-learned methods. This database was released by Facebook in collaboration with other companies and academic institutions such as Microsoft, Amazon, and the MIT for the Kaggle contest. The DFDC database considers different acquisition scenarios (i.e., indoors and outdoors), light conditions (i.e., day, night, etc.), distances from the person to the camera, and pose variations, among others.

Deeper Forensics-1.0 dataset represents a large face forgery detection dataset, with 60,000 videos constituted by a total of 17.6 million frames. The database consists of 50000 real videos and 10000 fake videos. The source videos were recorded with 100 paid actors with different genders, ages, skin colors, and nationalities. Data are recorded in a controlled indoor environment. Seven different distortions were also provided in the database.

WildDeepfake contains both real and fake videos which are collected from the internet. The video contents are diverse: variety of activities, scenes, lighting condition, compression rates, backgrounds, formats and resolution. It is a collection of 7,314 face sequences from 707 videos with annotation.

Only Fake Face Database. This data collection consists of only synthetic images, not real images. These images are generated using deep learning methods, mixing different attributes from different people to generate a new face. Currently, the main database available are 100k generated images [2], 100k faces [1], Diverse Fake Face Dataset (DFFD) [72], iFakeFaceDB [61].

100k generated images is a set of 100,000 synthetic face images. This database was generated using StyleGAN architecture [42], which was trained using the FFHQ dataset. StyleGAN [42] is an improved version of the previous popular approach ProGAN [41], which introduced a new training methodology based on improving both generator and discriminator progressively. StyleGAN proposes an alternative generator architecture that leads to an automatically different learning style corresponding to different spacial resolution.

100k faces is another face synthetic public database. This database contains 100,000 synthetic images generated using StyleGAN as well. In this database, contrary to the 100K-Generated- Images database, the StyleGAN network was trained using around 29,000 photos from 69 different models, considering face images from a more controlled scenario (e.g., with a flat background). Thus, no strange artifacts created by the StyleGAN are included in the background of the images.

DFFD is a new database comprised of publicly available datasets and images that are synthesized/manipulated using publicly available methods. Regarding the entire face synthesis manipulation, the authors created 100,000 and 200,000 fake images through the pre-trained ProGAN and Style-GAN models, respectively.

iFakeFaceDB which is the Face Synthetic Removal database (FSRemovalDB). This database comprises of a total 150,000 synthetic face images originally created through StyleGAN. Contrary to the other databases, in this database the GAN "fingerprints" produced by the StyleGAN were removed from the original synthetic fake images through the use of autoencoders, while keeping the visual quality of the resulting images. Therefore, this database presents a higher level of manipulation for the detection systems.

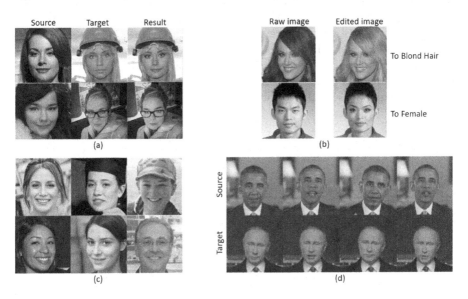

Fig. 2. Different DeepFake creation techniques; (a) face swap (b) attribute editing (c) face synthesis (d) reenactment.

2.2 Analysis

Deepfake database can be categorized into different generations as the methods for producing fake videos are continuously improved with time. More and more realistic dataset are produced and made available for the community. Some of the factors based on which the generations can be categorized are size of the database, variation and diversity of the data, pose and illumination, and quality of the image.

First Generation: Datasets which contain less then 1000 videos and the quality of the Deepfake videos are usually of low quality. The database included here are UADFV [52], DeepfakeTIMIT (DF TIMIT) [46], FaceForensics ++ [69].

These datasets contain videos from internet as source and swap face faces between the individuals. Additionally, there is no underlying consent or agreement with the individuals in the dataset.

Second Generation: The quality of the deepfake videos is much better as compared to the first generation. This category includes Deepfake detection (DFD) [31], Celeb-DF [53],WildDeepfake [85]. The consent of the individual in the database was publicly raised [71]. Some of the dataset include paid actors but are not enough for proper detection.

Third Generation: These dataset are very realistic and more diverse as compared to the previous generations. Deepfake detection challenge (DFDC) [31] and Deeper forensics 1.0 [40] are in this generation. DFDC dataset contains individuals in real world lighting conditions while Deeper forensics 1.0 contains videos taken in a control environment. Deeper forensics 1.0 provides different poses, expression and perturbations but has only 1000 real videos. DFDC has a lot of Deepfake videos produced by target/source swap.

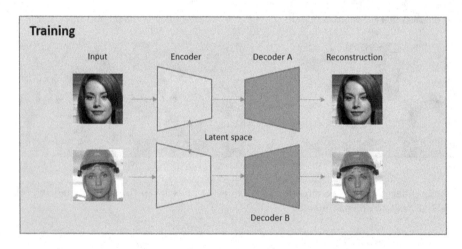

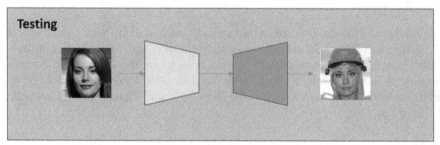

Fig. 3. Basic face swap technique using two encoder-decoder pair. Top presents the training process while other represents testing.

3   Deepfake

Deepfake is generally defined as the manipulated media which are difficult to distinguish between being pristine and being fake. The Deepfake domain is vast but in this article, we focus on the fake human faces. In the context of visual and technique, four categories are made: face replacement, facial attribute editing, face reenactment and face synthesis. Figure 2 shows the creation techniques. Considering that we have a source and a target person, the categories are discussed in the following sections.

3.1   Face Replacement

Face replacement is commonly known as "face swap". Face swap is the process of swapping a face of a person by another person's face and was first created by a Reddit user [14]. Let's consider two person, A and B. For the basic face swap creation, two autoencoder-decoder pair structure is required. The latent features from the face image are extracted using an autoencoder and then a decoder is used to reconstruct the original input face image from the latent features. One pair is first trained using a set of images for person A and another pair using the set of images for person B but the encoder's parameters are shared between the two network pairs. Both pairs have the same encoder and two different decoders. The target identity replaces the source identify while preserving headpose, exact facial expression and lighting condition. This approach replaces eyes, eyebrow, nose, mouth and sometime the contour of the face. Figure 3 show the basic face swap method.

Trending Approaches

Preprocessing: The first step is to get a collection of the face dataset. The dataset can be categoriesd into two types of input images, the source and the target images. The source image provides identity or content and a target image provides attributes, e.g., pose, expression, scene lighting and background. The goal is to render the semantic content of one face image to the style of another image. First, we need to locate the face area in an image or each frame if it is a video using a face detector. Then, the facial landmarks which carries important structural information such as eyes, noses, mouth and contours of the face area are to be located. The change of the head movement and change in the face orientation should be addressed as these changes produce artifacts in the generated face swapping. We must align the face region in a proper coordinate space by face alignment algorithm based on the landmarks obtained. The algorithm MTCNN [81] is a face detector commonly used to identify the face regions in each image or video frame. Facial keypoint or landmarks are extracted using dlib [44] but it is sometimes difficult for partial occluded face region.

Another face alignment technique is to fit a 3D shape on to the target face and modify the 3D faces to account for facial expression represented in [76].

Some of the popular 3D shapes are Basel Face Model (BFM) [63] to represent faces and the 3DDFA Morphable Model [84] for expression. Face segmentation can also be done by fitting 3D shape and it can also address the problem of partial occlusion on the face region [62]. The drawback of 3DMM swap method is that manual alignment is required for accurate fitting.

Different segmentations process are required for different methods. Some methods require face segmentation for processing [47], some use hair, face and background segmentation [60] and some use mask of the face [59]. The creation of a smooth and precise face mask based on the landmarks on eyebrow and points on cheeks and between lower lip and chin is critical in the final blending [53]. Improper mask generation can includes a part of the eyebrow region which may lead to wraping artifacts and a "double eyebrow" can appear in the final image or video.

Methodology: A 19-layer VGG network [70] is implemented in [46] which is simple yet yields realistic fake results. The goal is to render the semantic content [32] of face image in the style [51] of another face image. Sometime the lighting contents of the images are not preserved in the generated images. In order to obtain the desired lighting condition of the target face, a small siamese convolutional network [30] can be constructed, which are trained using Extended Yale Face Database B [33]. This dataset contains grayscale portraits of subjects under 9 poses and 64 lighting conditions.

RSGAN [60] extracts the latent-space representation of face and hair of the input image separately using two conditional variational auto-encoder networks [45]. A GAN network called composer is used to reconstruct the face from the two latent space representations. A new conditional variational auto-encoder called DF-VAE [40] is developed to generate high quality and scalable videos. It addressed the problem of face style mismatch caused by appearance variations by introducing MAdaIN based on the original AdaIN [36]. It also addressed the temporal continuity of generated videos by using FlowNet 2.0 [37].

As the number of layers in the encoder-decoder increases, the visual quality of the synthesize faces increases but it did cost some computational time [53]. Applying a color transfer algorithm [67] during the training process drastically increases the matching of color between the source and target faces which partially solve the problem of mismatching face color. Some Deepfake techniques also use attention mask to fuse the target face into the source face [85]. Using attention mask helps in handling occlusion, eliminating artifacts, and producing natural skin tone.

Postprocessing: The postprocessing concerned on fixing the imperfect parts in the Deepfake generation process. Kalman filter [79] and Gaussian blur [39] are the most commonly used post processing methods. These filters smoothen the boundary contour of the swap face and eliminates the inconsistency and flickering of the swapped face. Using a sharpening filter on the blended faces also greatly increases the quality of the final video with no extra computational cost. Some methods use poisson image blending [65] which also helps in the final blending image but it should not be applied on the entire mask as it would blend both faces and create an "average" face rather than a face that looks like the source face. Poisson blending should only be done in a small region along the edge of the mask. Finally, the blended face images can all be combined together with audio to produce the Deepfake video using ffmpeg [18].

To Blond Hair + Add Beard   To Blond Hair + Remove Beard

To Blond Hair

Fig. 4. Visual result of hair color manipulation for single and multiple attribute [35].

3.2   Facial Attribute Editing

Facial attribute editing is the manipulation of facial attributes (like hair color, age, gender, etc.) while preserving the identity of the person. The manipulation is performed in the attribute space. Given a face image with its corresponding attributes annotation, the editing method will give an image with altered attributes while keeping the unwanted attributes same as the original image. For developing this type of attribute editing method, celebA [56], CelebAHQ [41] and CelebAMask-HQ [50] datasets are required since the dataset are diverse with different attributes and well label annotations. Some of the examples includes changing of hair color (black, brown and blond) in Fig. 4, attribute transfer for smiling face in Fig. 5, style transfer in Fig. 6 and interactive mask modification in Fig. 7 (Table 4).

Current Editing Methods. The Invertible Conditional GANs (IcGANs) [64] are developed for complex facial image modification. This approachconsists of

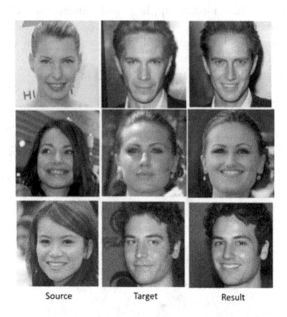

Source   Target   Result

Fig. 5. Visual result of smile transfer [50].

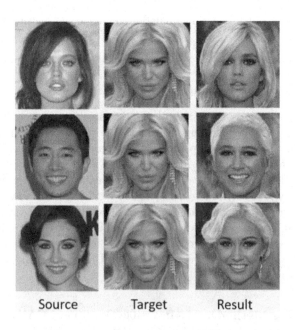

Source   Target   Result

Fig. 6. Visual result of style transfer [50].

Table 3. Different real and fake dataset comparison.

Generation	Database	Year	Real data #videos	Real data #frames	Origin	DeepFake data #Fake #videos	DeepFake data #frames	Generation technique	Frame/video quality	Temporal constraint	Control environment
1st	UADFV	2018	49	17.3k	Internet	49	17.3k	Fakeapp	64 × 64, 128 × 128	-	-
	DF TIMIT- LQ DF TIMIT- HQ	2018	320	34.0k 34.0k	Internet	320	34.0k 34.0k faceSwap-GAN faceSwap-GAN	faceSwap-GAN	64 × 64, 128 × 128	-	-
	Face forensics++	2019	1000	509.9k	Internet	1000	509.9k	Faceswap	480p, 720p, 1080p	-	-
2nd	DFD	2019	363	315.4k	Actors	3068	2242.7k	Deep fake	1080p	-	-
	CelebDF	2019	590	225.4k	Internet	5639	2116.8k	Deepfake	various	-	-
	WildDeepfake	2020	3.8k	620k	Internet	3.5k	560k	Unknown	HQ	-	-
3rd	DFDC	2019	1131	488.4k	28 Actors	4119	1783.3k	Unknown	240p-2160p	-	-
	DeeperForensics 1.0	2020	50k	12.6M	100 Actors	10k	5M	Faceswap	1080p	✓	✓

Table 4. Comparation between different face attribute editing methods.

Method	Year	Dataset Training	Dataset Testing	Total	# of Attributes /classes	Image scale	Architecture	Evaluation/quality assessment
IcGAN	2016	MNIST - 60k CelebA - 182k	MNIST - 10k CelebA - 20k	MNIST - 60K CelebA - 202k	0-9 (Digit) 18 (CelebA)	28 X 28 (MNIST) 64 x 64 (CelebA)	Encoder with a cGAN generator	Root mean square deviation Mean F1 score
Fader Network	2017	CelebA - 182k	CelebA - 20k	CelebA - 202k	18 (CelebA)	256 x 256	Encoder-decoder with adversarial component	Amazon Mechanical Turk (AMT) root-mean-square deviation
starGAN	2018	RaFD - 4.3k celebA - 200k	RaFD - 0.5k CelebA - 2k	RaFD - 4.8k CelebA - 202k	7 (RaFD) 3 (CelebA)	128 x 128	GAN with conditional domain information	Amazon Mechanical Turk (AMT)
AttGAN	2019	CelebA - 182k	CelebA - 20k	CelebA - 202k	13 (CelebA)	384 x 384	Encoder and decoded with attribute classifier and a discriminator	Facial Attribute Editing Accuracy/Error
STGAN	2019	CelebA - 201k	CelebA -1k	CelebA - 202k	13 (CelebA)	128 x 128 384 x 384	Encoder decoder with selective transfer unit	Facial Attribute Editing Accuracy/Error SSIM
RelGAN	2019	celebA - 200k CelebA-HQ - 27k	CelebA-HQ - 3k CelebA-HQ - 30k FFHQ - 70k	CelebA - 202k CelebA-HQ - 70k	9 (CelebA) 9 (CelebA-HQ) 17 (CelebA-HQ)	256 x 256	A generator and three discriminator	Frechet Inception Distance (FID) SSIM user study
ResAttr GAN	2019	CelebA - 182k	CelebA - 20k	CelebA - 202k	11 (CelebA)	128 x 128 256 256	Encoder decoder generator and a Siamese network discriminator	FID SSIM Attribute editing accuracy
ClsGAN	2020	celebA - 200k	celebA -2k	CelebA - 202k	13 (CelebA)	128 x 128	A generator (two encoders and a Tr-resnet) and a discriminator	FID SSIM

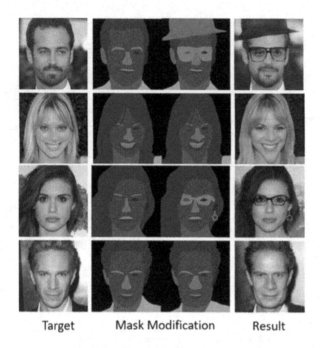

Target   Mask Modification   Result

Fig. 7. Visual results of interactive face editing [50].

an encoder and followed by a conditional GAN (cGAN) [58] generator. The real image is encoded into a latent representation with the attribute information and apply variations on it to generate a new modified image. Manipulation of 18 facial attributes are chosen for this approach. The result of this approach provides face attribute changes in complex face dataset which are satisfactory. It in fact changes the identity of the person.

Fader network [48] is a new encoder-decoder architecture which is trained to reconstruct an image by disentangling the salient information of the image and the values of attributes directly in the latent space. The approach performs adversarial training for the latent space instead of the output and adversarial training aims at learning invariance to attributes. This approach makes subtle changes to portraits that sufficiently alter the perceived value of attributes while preserving the natural aspect of the image and the identity of the person. It also provides the ability to swap multiple attributes at once.

Along with development of image-to-image translation [38,82], a novel and scalable approach that can perform image-to-image translations for multiple domains using only a single model called StarGAN [29] is introduced. This architecture allows training of multiple dataset with different domains using a single network. A flexible modification of facial attributes as well as synthesizing different expressions is also observed. The attribute translations network is trained via domain classification loss and cycle consistency. This model is scalable in terms of the number of parameters required. The visual results are good and provide multiple attribute transfers. It also provides the visual comparison of the model trained in a single dataset and combination of two datasets.

AttGAN [35] is another novel approach of face attribute editing. This method removes the strict attribute independent constraint from the latent representation which was used in the previous methods, and applies the attribute-classification constraint to the generated image to guarantee the correct change of the attributes. Imposing constraints on the latent space may result in the loss of information which eventually affects the attribute editing for the worst. This approach allows only the attribute desired to change in the portrait while preserving the attribute excluding details. The results are much better for single and multiple attribute editing with higher resolutions as compared to the previous approaches.

Ming Liu et al. proposed STGAN [54] which addresses the bottleneck layers of encoder-decoder in the end giving blurry and low quality editing results observed in starGAN [29] and attGAN [35]. The selective transfer units (STUs) are integrated with encoder-decoder to adaptively select and modify encoder feature for enhanced attribute editing. This approach preserves more information of the source image as only the attributes are to be changed instead of full target attribute vector. It also proves that the difference in the attributes of the source and the target provides valuable information. The Experimental results show that STGAN simultaneously improves single and multiple attribute manipulation accuracy with higher image quality as well as perception quality. It preserves fine details and identity of source image while performing against previous methods in arbitrary facial attribute editing translation.

With an increase in the popularity of multi domain image to image translation, many limitations are being identified and fixed. The previous methods assume binary valued attributes and required to specify the entire set of target attributes, even if most of the attributes would not be changed which eventually affects the result of the manipulation. Po Wei Wu et al. introduced relative-attribute-based method, dubbed RelGAN [80] to address these limitations. The key idea is to use relative attributes which specifies the desired changes in the selective attributes. The authors proposed a matching-aware discriminator that determines whether an input-output pair matches the relative attributes and also an interpolation discriminator for improving interpolation quality. This model achieves superior performance over the state-of-the-art methods in terms of both visual quality and interpolation for the single and multi-attribute editing.

Rentuo Tao et al. proposed ResAttr-GAN [73]. Compared to existing models that perform attributes editing based on an attributes classifier, he proposed deep residual attributes learning model utilized relatively weaker information of attribute differences for face image translation. The authors proposed a Siamese-Network based residual attributes learning model to learn the attributes difference in the high-level latent space. Several facial attributes edit experiments were conducted including comparative single-attribute editing, multiple attributes editing, attributes editing on higher resolution face images, to evaluate the effectiveness of the proposed model qualitatively and quantitatively. It also demonstrated that when the training data was reduced, the proposed deep residual learning model can improve the data utilization efficiency and thus boosting the editing performance. They showed the accuracy of the attribute editing results with five different data usage. The experimental results demonstrated the effectiveness of the proposed method in both single and multiple attributes editing.

The novel ClsGAN [55] shows significant improvement in realistic image generation with accurate attribute transfer. The method introduced two approaches: Upper convolution residual network (Tr-resnet) and an attribute adversarial classifier (Atta-cls). Tr-resnet is used to extract selective information from the source image and target label. The information is acquired for combining the input and output of upper convolution residual blocks, leading to high-quality image generation with accurate attribute editing. Atta-cls is developed to improve the attribute transfer accuracy by learning the transfer defects in the generator. The comparative result shows that this method outperforms the other state-of-the-art approaches.

The previous face attribute editing is done on a predefined set of face attributes and provides very less interactive manipulation for the user. These problem are addressed in this study with the introduction of MaskGAN [50] provides a diverse and interactive face manipulation. There are two main components: Dense Mapping Network (DMN) and Editing Behavior Simulated Training (EBST). DMN learns the style mapping between the interactive mask and the target image. The architectural backbone of DMN adopts pix2pixHD [38]. Spatial-Aware Style Encoder Network inside DMN receives the style information for target image and its corresponding spacial information from the target mask at the same time. Spatial Feature Transform (SFT) from SFT-GAN [77] is used for fusing the two domains. EBST models the user editing behavior on the source mask. EBST is the overall framework composing of DMN, MaskVAE and Alpha blender, all trained together. MaskVAE is responsible for modeling the manifold of structure priors and Alpha Blender is responsible for maintaining manipulation consistency.

3.3   Face Reenactment

A Deepfake reenactment is where the source is used to manipulate the expression of the target face. It can be the manipulation of mouth, head pose, gaze, and eye blinks. Manipulation expression can provide a wide range of flexibility. Mouth reenactment, also known as "dubbing", is when the target mouth is moved according to the movement of the source mouth. Another type is the mouth reenactment based on the audio input containing speech. Gaze reenactment is the change in the direction of target eyelids according to the movement of source eyelids. Head pose reenactment is changing of target head pose according to the source head pose. Figure 8 shows some of the reenactment approaches.

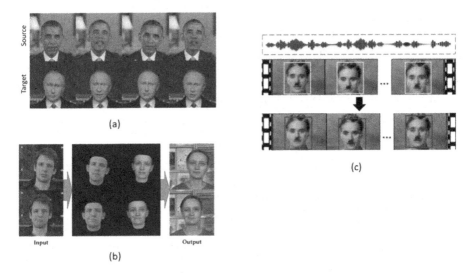

Fig. 8. Different types of face reenactment. (a) and (b) shows the full facial expression, head pose and eye motion transfer from the source to the target face with high level of photorealism [43]. (c) shows the lip-synchronization with a source and a audio segment resulting to a realistic video dubbing [66].

Current Methods. Face2Face [75] is a computer graphics based facial reenactment system that transfers the expression of a source video to a target video while maintaining the identity of the target person. This method is fully automated creating while performing face reenactment. The first frames of each video were used to obtain a temporary face identity (i.e., a 3D model), and track the expression over the remaining frames. The reenactment is done by transferring the source expression parameters of each frames of the target video.

Hyeongwoo kim et al. [43] introduced a novel approach that enables photorealistic re-animation of portrait videos using only an input video. The first implementation to transfer full head which includes 3d head position, head rotation, face expression, eye gaze and eye blinking. This is all made possible by designing a novel GAN based space-time architecture. The network takes as input synthetic renderings of a parametric face model, based on which it predicts photo-realistic video frames for a given target actor. In order to enable source-to-target video re-animation, a synthetic target video with the reconstructed head animation parameters from a source video is rendered, and feed it into the trained network thus taking full control of the target. The author also show how we can rewrite application by combining source and target parameters. The method provides high-fidelity visual dubbing.

Wav2lip [66] is the method of lip-syncing unconstrained videos. This method produces a talking face video of an identity to match with the target speech segment. The result produces a realistic lip movement on a static image or video of an arbitrary identity. Given a short audio segment and a random reference of face image or video, the proposed model task is to generate a lip-synced version of the input that coordinates with the given audio. A quantity evaluation on the challenging benchmarks shows this method produces accurate lip-sync video which is good as real synced videos. Many application areas for this method were also discussed such as dubbing movies, translated lectures and press conferences, generation of missing video call segments, and lip-sync animations.

3.4   Face Synthesis

Face synthesis is when a new Deepfake face is created by mixing styles from different faces. It is used to produce fake persona online. Style is generally, not manually designed by a user, but extracted from reference images. Figure 9 shows the visual result of synthetic face. Two sets of image (source A and B) were generated from their latent space and the rest of the images were generated by copying a specific style from source B and taking the rest from source A. The example result shows the copying of different style corresponding to different spacial resolutions. The first row corresponds the higher level of aspect such as pose, face shape whereas the second row shows the middle level such as facial features, eye open/close, hair color and finally the last row corresponds the fine level such as eye, lighting conditions.

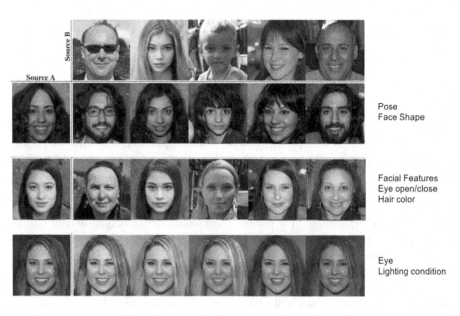

Fig. 9. Visual result of synthetic face [42]

Current Methods. A new progressive training of GAN, call PGAN [41] is introduced. The key insight is that both the generator and discriminator progressively, starting from easier low-resolution images, add new layers that introduce higher-resolution details as the training progresses. The training starts with having as low as 4×4 pixels and incrementally adds layer throughout the process till 1024×1024 pixels. The model not only generate new realistic synthetic images but also generates high quality CelebA-HQ dataset with resolution of 1024×1024.

A style based generator architecture, styleGAN [42] is also introduced. The architecture is designed to learn the style constant instead of just a feed forward network. This method has better interpolation properties, and also better disentangles the latent factors of variation. They also produces a high quality dataset called FFHQ dataset [17] which is better than the previous CelebA-HQ dataset. From two source images, set of synthesis images are generated from their latent codes. The style corresponding to coarse spatial resolution is responsible for high level aspect such as pose, hair, face shape whereas the style with middle level corresponds to facial features, eye open/close, hair style and finally with fine spacial correspond to eye, hair, lighting condition.

Semantic region-adaptive normalization, SEAN [83] is introduced. SEAN is constructed on SPADE with a generator SEAN ResNET blocks. These blocks describes the semantic regions of the segmented mask. Using SEAN normalization, a network architecture can be built that can control the style of each semantic region individually, e.g., we can specify one style reference image per region. Addition to style interpolation (bottom row), one style can be changed by selecting different styles per ResBlk.

3.5   Evaluation Methods

Root Mean Square Error (RMSE). The RMSE represents the cumulative squared error between the manipulated image and the original image.it is calculated in the pixel level. The result is better when RMSE is low.

Amazon Mechanical Turk (MTurk) [4]**.** Amazon Mechanical Turk (MTurk) is a crowdsourcing marketplace that makes it easier for individuals and businesses to outsource their processes and jobs to a distributed workforce who can perform these tasks virtually. Even when the computing technology continues to improve, there are many things that people do much more effectively than computers. Every day workers on Amazon Mechanical Turk (MTurk) help requester solve a range of data processing, analysis, and content moderation challenges. The range of includes Image and video processing, Data Verification and Cleanup, Information Gathering Data Processing. There are two ways for evaluating Deepfake: (i) one way where two images are provided in which one is fake and the other real and the user has to identify the real and the fake images and (ii) one image is provided, and user has to tell whether it is real or fake.

Structural Similarity (SSIM [78]**).** SSIM is an image quality assessment method based on the degradation of the structural information. It provides the similarity measurement between two images. The value ranges from 0 to 1 where higher value represents more similarities between the two images. The SSIM index can be viewed as a quality measure of one of the images being compared, provided that the other image is regarded as one of perfect quality.

Frechet Inception Distance (FID [57]**).** The 'Fréchet Inception Distance' (FID) captures the similarity of generated images to real ones better than the Inception Score. FID is supposed to improve the Inception Score [28] by comparing the statistics of generated samples to real samples, instead of evaluating generated samples in a vacuum. Lower FID is better, corresponding to closer distance between the generated and real data distributions.

User Study. User study is mainly the visual analysis on both real and fake images. The users are instructed to choose the best result which (i) which changes the attribute more successfully, (ii) which is of higher image quality and (iii) which one preserves the identity better with fine details of source image.

3.6 Real World Scenario

Advantages. The common benefits of Deepfake technology is their creative and productive applications in areas of education, marketing, art and multimedia [3]. Realistic video dubbing in different languages, is the next phase of dubbing. It provides the viewer an immersive experience and will think as if the person is actually speaking another language. [23] shows David Beckham lips movement with respect to the recorded audio. Digital de-aging makes a person look more younger or older digitally. It can be applied to movies, photographs, etc. In the movie "The Irishram", Robert De Niro is made to look younger [20]. Digital resurrection of a dead family member, a close friend or even a historical figure is another Deepfake application. Reanimation will bring memories or digitally interaction of a dead person. Reanimation of Salvador Dalí in the museum while taking selfies with the visitors [8]. A whole new online shopping with virtual trying on clothes or accessories [22]. Anyone can become a super model just by changing faces with your preferred body type [19]. It can also help in finding of missing children by generating faces of the appropriate age using childhood photos [6].

Drawbacks. The creation of fake porn videos, which can be used for blackmailing and taking revenge [11]. The abused of the technology can be seen when the researchers at the University of Washington posted Deepfake of President Barack Obama and spread on the internet [5]. They were able to make President Obama say whatever they want him to say. Similarly, Jordan Peele ventriloquizes Obama [24]. The fake video of Facebook CEO Mark Zuckerberg declaring "whoever controls the data, controls the future" went viral [9]. It could be a threat to the world security, increase xenophobia, violation of privacy, conspiracy theories, scams and frauds.

4   Discussion

It is becoming difficult to trust social media content as it can be fake content. With the advancement of Artificial Intelligence, realistic forensic data can be easily made. This information is misleading and it can cause distress to a lot of people in the form of hate speech, disinformation and could also stimulate political tension, public violence, or war. Deepfake can cover a large domain such as face swap and reenactment, fake news, fake photographs, fake voice, fake satellite images, and many more. Even though there are a lot of misused or unethical approaches, there is also the good side of Deepfake as was discussed before. As Artificial Intelligence can be scary sometimes, it can also be used to overcome the drawbacks brought by it. AI will be beaten by AI.

Challenges: There is always a challenge during the production of manipulated face images. The following are some of the challenges face during the production of the creation and detection process of Deepfake.

Data Necessity: For creating face Deepfake, a huge amount of data is required for the GAN to train their network. In the early stage, the number of fake datasets was in thousands but with time more fake datasets are being produced in hundreds of thousands in just a span of just 2 years. More realistic fake images are being produced in high quality but it still is not enough. A large amount of high quality real and fake images are required in the making of a good Deepfake detector system.

Data Variation: The variations in the available data are limited. There is less Deepfake dataset with eye blink or which mimics blink because nobody shares images with closing eyes. It's challenging but possible when Deepfake is generated from video extracted images where natural blinks occur. It is time-consuming when we don't get the desired images which we required for the dataset. Diverse data with distortions and noise is also needed to simulate real-world scenarios. Some of the distortion or noise can be compression techniques, blurring, and contrast change. Another diversity is how different people look and there is a need for diverse manipulated faces in terms of skin color, hair color and style, face shape, facial features, and lighting conditions. The diversity on the manipulated images or videos makes sure the data will be useful for developing a robust face forgery detection and more face related research.

Cost: Training a generative adversarial network for Deepfake is costly as it requires a lot of time to produce realistic manipulated images. There is a lot of preprocessing required before the training starts and a lot of post processing needed after. It usually takes weeks to do produce a Deepfake that looks authentic to human eyes. In order to produce fast manipulated images, high-end graphics cards are needed for training and swapping. Most of the generated manipulated image resolutions are low, so to get high-quality images, a stronger computer system will be needed.

Mandatory Post-processing: Current neural network technologies are great while producing manipulated or swapped faces but the resulting outputs are not flawless. When there is a face-swapping process, there are still some artifacts produce in the manipulated regions or on the edges. There is also a color mismatch between the swapped face and the target original face skin tone. For the current technologies, post-processing is needed to produce a final realistic manipulated face image.

5   Conclusion

This study provides the trending technology of Deepfake face manipulation especially the creation of the Deepfake. We focus on the swapping of face, editing facial attributes, face reenactment, and synthesizing a face. We also discussed the available database used in the creation of Deepfake. Some real-world scenarios were also discussed, with respect to the benefits and drawbacks of Deepfake, so not all Deepfakes are malicious.

Acknowledgment. This study was supported by the BK21 FOUR project (AI-driven Convergence Software Education Research Program) funded by the Ministry of Education, School of Computer Science and Engineering, Kyungpook National University, Korea (4199990214394).

References

1. 100k faces. https://generated.photos/. Accessed 14 Jan 2021
2. 100k generated faces. https://github.com/NVlabs/stylegan. Accessed 14 Jan 2021
3. AI enable deepfake. https://www.forbes.com/sites/bernardmarr/2019/07/22/the-best-and-scariest-examples-of-ai-enabled-deepfakes/?sh=86672662eaf1. Accessed 14 Jan 2021
4. Amazon Mechanical Turk. https://www.mturk.com/. Accessed 14 Jan 2021
5. BBC Obama. https://www.bbc.com/news/av/technology-40598465. Accessed 15 Jan 2021
6. Computer-generated age progression photos. https://www.reddit.com/r/interestingasfuck/comments/kxf12x/the_accuracy_of_computergenerated_age_progression/. Accessed 15 Jan 2021
7. Deep learning for detecting audiovisual fakes. https://sites.google.com/view/audiovisualfakes-icml2019/. Accessed 14 Jan 2021
8. Deepfake Salvador the Verge. https://www.theverge.com/2019/5/10/18540953/salvador-dali-lives-deepfake-museum. Accessed 14 Jan 2021

9. Deepfake video of Mark Zuckerberg. https://finance.yahoo.com/news/deepfake-video-mark-zuckerberg-goes-163128674.html?guccounter=1. Accessed 15 Jan 2021
10. Deepfaketimit. https://www.idiap.ch/dataset/deepfaketimit. Accessed 14 Jan 2021
11. Deepnude. https://www.vox.com/2019/6/27/18761639/ai-deepfake-deepnude-app-nude-women-porn. Accessed 15 Jan 2021
12. Dimentions. https://app.dimensions.ai/. Accessed 15 Jan 2021
13. Facebook AI deepFake detection challenge dataset. https://ai.facebook.com/datasets/dfdc/. Accessed 14 Jan 2021
14. Faceswap. https://github.com/deepfakes/faceswap. Accessed 14 Jan 2021
15. Faceswap. https://github.com/MarekKowalski/FaceSwap/. Accessed 14 Jan 2021
16. Fakeapp. https://fakeapp.softonic.com/. Accessed 14 Jan 2021
17. FFHQ dataset. https://github.com/NVlabs/ffhq-dataset. Accessed 14 Jan 2021
18. FFmpeg. https://ffmpeg.org/. Accessed 14 Jan 2021
19. Forbes digital doubles. https://www.forbes.com/sites/katiebaron/2019/07/29/digital-doubles-the-deepfake-tech-nourishing-new-wave-retail/?sh=4e656bac4cc7/. Accessed 14 Jan 2021
20. Making Robert de Niro in "the Irishman". https://www.businessinsider.com/deepfake-netflix-correcting-the-irishman-de-ageing-tech-2020-1. Accessed 14 Jan 2021
21. NIST media forensics challenge 2018. https://www.nist.gov/itl/iad/mig/media-forensics-challenge-2018. Accessed 14 Jan 2021
22. Retailwire. https://retailwire.com/discussion/can-deepfake-technology-reduce-retail-returns-without-rattling-reality/. Accessed 14 Jan 2021
23. Reuters David Beckham's 'deep fake' malaria awareness video. https://mobile.reuters.com/video/watch/david-beckhams-deep-fake-malaria-awarene-id536254167?chan=c1tal5kh. Accessed 15 Jan 2021
24. The Verge Barack Obama. https://www.theverge.com/tldr/2018/4/17/17247334/ai-fake-news-video-barack-obama-jordan-peele-buzzfeed. Accessed 15 Jan 2021
25. Vice. https://www.vice.com/en/article/gydydm/gal-gadot-fake-ai-porn. Accessed 15 Jan 2021
26. Vidtimit. https://conradsanderson.id.au/vidtimit/. Accessed 14 Jan 2021
27. Workshop on media forensics. https://sites.google.com/view/mediaforensics2019. Accessed 14 Jan 2021
28. Barratt, S., Sharma, R.: A note on the inception score. arXiv preprint arXiv:1801.01973 (2018)
29. Choi, Y., Choi, M., Kim, M., Ha, J.W., Kim, S., Choo, J.: StarGAN: unified generative adversarial networks for multi-domain image-to-image translation. In: Proceedings of the IEEE Conference on Computer Vision and Pattern Recognition, pp. 8789–8797 (2018)
30. Chopra, S., Hadsell, R., LeCun, Y.: Learning a similarity metric discriminatively, with application to face verification. In: 2005 IEEE Computer Society Conference on Computer Vision and Pattern Recognition (CVPR 2005), vol. 1, pp. 539–546. IEEE (2005)
31. Dolhansky, B., et al.: The deepfake detection challenge dataset. arXiv preprint arXiv:2006.07397 (2020)
32. Gatys, L.A., Ecker, A.S., Bethge, M.: Image style transfer using convolutional neural networks. In: Proceedings of the IEEE Conference on Computer Vision and Pattern Recognition, pp. 2414–2423 (2016)

33. Georghiades, A.S., Belhumeur, P.N., Kriegman, D.J.: From few to many: illumination cone models for face recognition under variable lighting and pose. IEEE Trans. Pattern Anal. Mach. Intell. **23**(6), 643–660 (2001)

34. Goodfellow, I., et al.: Generative adversarial nets. Adv. Neural Inf. Process. Syst. **27**, 2672–2680 (2014)

35. He, Z., Zuo, W., Kan, M., Shan, S., Chen, X.: AttGAN: facial attribute editing by only changing what you want. IEEE Trans. Image Process. **28**(11), 5464–5478 (2019)

36. Huang, X., Belongie, S.: Arbitrary style transfer in real-time with adaptive instance normalization. In: Proceedings of the IEEE International Conference on Computer Vision, pp. 1501–1510 (2017)

37. Ilg, E., Mayer, N., Saikia, T., Keuper, M., Dosovitskiy, A., Brox, T.: FlowNet 2.0: evolution of optical flow estimation with deep networks. In: Proceedings of the IEEE Conference on Computer Vision and Pattern Recognition, pp. 2462–2470 (2017)

38. Isola, P., Zhu, J.Y., Zhou, T., Efros, A.A.: Image-to-image translation with conditional adversarial networks. In: Proceedings of the IEEE Conference on Computer Vision and Pattern Recognition, pp. 1125–1134 (2017)

39. Ito, K., Xiong, K.: Gaussian filters for nonlinear filtering problems. IEEE Trans. Autom. Control **45**(5), 910–927 (2000)

40. Jiang, L., Li, R., Wu, W., Qian, C., Loy, C.C.: Deeperforensics-1.0: a large-scale dataset for real-world face forgery detection. In: 2020 IEEE/CVF Conference on Computer Vision and Pattern Recognition (CVPR), pp. 2886–2895. IEEE (2020)

41. Karras, T., Aila, T., Laine, S., Lehtinen, J.: Progressive growing of GANs for improved quality, stability, and variation. arXiv preprint arXiv:1710.10196 (2017)

42. Karras, T., Laine, S., Aila, T.: A style-based generator architecture for generative adversarial networks. In: Proceedings of the IEEE Conference on Computer Vision and Pattern Recognition, pp. 4401–4410 (2019)

43. Kim, H., et al.: Deep video portraits. ACM Trans. Graph. (TOG) **37**(4), 1–14 (2018)

44. King, D.E.: Dlib-ml: a machine learning toolkit. J. Mach. Learn. Res. **10**, 1755–1758 (2009)

45. Kingma, D.P., Mohamed, S., Jimenez Rezende, D., Welling, M.: Semi-supervised learning with deep generative models. Adv. Neural Inf. Process. Syst. **27**, 3581–3589 (2014)

46. Korshunov, P., Marcel, S.: Deepfakes: a new threat to face recognition? Assessment and detection. arXiv preprint arXiv:1812.08685 (2018)

47. Korshunova, I., Shi, W., Dambre, J., Theis, L.: Fast face-swap using convolutional neural networks. In: Proceedings of the IEEE International Conference on Computer Vision, pp. 3677–3685 (2017)

48. Lample, G., Zeghidour, N., Usunier, N., Bordes, A., Denoyer, L., Ranzato, M.: Fader networks: manipulating images by sliding attributes. In: Advances in Neural Information Processing Systems, pp. 5967–5976 (2017)

49. Langner, O., Dotsch, R., Bijlstra, G., Wigboldus, D.H., Hawk, S.T., Van Knippenberg, A.: Presentation and validation of the Radboud faces database. Cogn. Emot. **24**(8), 1377–1388 (2010)

50. Lee, C.H., Liu, Z., Wu, L., Luo, P.: Maskgan: towards diverse and interactive facial image manipulation. In: Proceedings of the IEEE/CVF Conference on Computer Vision and Pattern Recognition, pp. 5549–5558 (2020)

51. Li, C., Wand, M.: Combining Markov random fields and convolutional neural networks for image synthesis. In: Proceedings of the IEEE Conference on Computer Vision and Pattern Recognition, pp. 2479–2486 (2016)

52. Li, Y., Chang, M.C., Lyu, S.: In Ictu Oculi: exposing AI generated fake face videos by detecting eye blinking. arXiv preprint arXiv:1806.02877 (2018)

53. Li, Y., Yang, X., Sun, P., Qi, H., Lyu, S.: Celeb-DF: a large-scale challenging dataset for deepfake forensics. In: Proceedings of the IEEE/CVF Conference on Computer Vision and Pattern Recognition, pp. 3207–3216 (2020)

54. Liu, M., et al.: StGAN: a unified selective transfer network for arbitrary image attribute editing. In: Proceedings of the IEEE Conference on Computer Vision and Pattern Recognition, pp. 3673–3682 (2019)

55. Liu, Y., Fan, H., Ni, F., Xiang, J.: ClsGAN: selective attribute editing model based on classification adversarial network. Neural Netw. **133**, 220–228 (2017)

56. Liu, Z., Luo, P., Wang, X., Tang, X.: Deep learning face attributes in the wild. In: Proceedings of the IEEE International Conference on Computer Vision, pp. 3730–3738 (2015)

57. Mathiasen, A., Hvilshøj, F.: Fast fr\'echet inception distance. arXiv preprint arXiv:2009.14075 (2020)

58. Mirza, M., Osindero, S.: Conditional generative adversarial nets. arXiv preprint arXiv:1411.1784 (2014)

59. Natsume, R., Yatagawa, T., Morishima, S.: FsNet: an identity-aware generative model for image-based face swapping. In: Jawahar, C., Li, H., Mori, G., Schindler, K. (eds.) ACCV 2018. LNCS, vol. 11366, pp. 117–132. Springer, Cham (2018). https://doi.org/10.1007/978-3-030-20876-9_8

60. Natsume, R., Yatagawa, T., Morishima, S.: RsGAN: face swapping and editing using face and hair representation in latent spaces. arXiv preprint arXiv:1804.03447 (2018)

61. Neves, J.C., Tolosana, R., Vera-Rodriguez, R., Lopes, V., Proença, H., Fierrez, J.: GANPrintr: improved fakes and evaluation of the state of the art in face manipulation detection. arXiv preprint arXiv:1911.05351 (2019)

62. Nirkin, Y., Masi, I., Tuan, A.T., Hassner, T., Medioni, G.: On face segmentation, face swapping, and face perception. In: 2018 13th IEEE International Conference on Automatic Face & Gesture Recognition (FG 2018), pp. 98–105. IEEE (2018)

63. Paysan, P., Knothe, R., Amberg, B., Romdhani, S., Vetter, T.: A 3D face model for pose and illumination invariant face recognition. In: 2009 Sixth IEEE International Conference on Advanced Video and Signal Based Surveillance, pp. 296–301. IEEE (2009)

64. Perarnau, G., Van De Weijer, J., Raducanu, B., Álvarez, J.M.: Invertible conditional GANs for image editing. arXiv preprint arXiv:1611.06355 (2016)

65. Pérez, P., Gangnet, M., Blake, A.: Poisson image editing. In: ACM SIGGRAPH 2003 Papers, pp. 313–318 (2003)

66. Prajwal, K., Mukhopadhyay, R., Namboodiri, V.P., Jawahar, C.: A lip sync expert is all you need for speech to lip generation in the wild. In: Proceedings of the 28th ACM International Conference on Multimedia, pp. 484–492 (2020)

67. Reinhard, E., Adhikhmin, M., Gooch, B., Shirley, P.: Color transfer between images. IEEE Comput. Graph. Appl. **21**(5), 34–41 (2001)

68. Rössler, A., Cozzolino, D., Verdoliva, L., Riess, C., Thies, J., Nießner, M.: Faceforensics: a large-scale video dataset for forgery detection in human faces. arXiv preprint arXiv:1803.09179 (2018)

69. Rossler, A., Cozzolino, D., Verdoliva, L., Riess, C., Thies, J., Nießner, M.: Face-forensics++: learning to detect manipulated facial images. In: Proceedings of the IEEE International Conference on Computer Vision, pp. 1–11 (2019)

70. Simonyan, K., Zisserman, A.: Very deep convolutional networks for large-scale image recognition. arXiv preprint arXiv:1409.1556 (2014)

71. Solon, O.: Facial recognition's 'dirty little secret': millions of online photos scraped without consent. NBC News (2019)

72. Stehouwer, J., Dang, H., Liu, F., Liu, X., Jain, A.: On the detection of digital face manipulation. arXiv preprint arXiv:1910.01717 (2019)

73. Tao, R., Li, Z., Tao, R., Li, B.: Resattr-GAN: unpaired deep residual attributes learning for multi-domain face image translation. IEEE Access 7, 132594–132608 (2019)

74. Thies, J., Zollhöfer, M., Nießner, M.: Deferred neural rendering: image synthesis using neural textures. ACM Trans. Graph. (TOG) 38(4), 1–12 (2019)

75. Thies, J., Zollhofer, M., Stamminger, M., Theobalt, C., Nießner, M.: Face2face: real-time face capture and reenactment of RGB videos. In: Proceedings of the IEEE Conference on Computer Vision and Pattern Recognition, pp. 2387–2395 (2016)

76. Tuan Tran, A., Hassner, T., Masi, I., Medioni, G.: Regressing robust and discriminative 3D morphable models with a very deep neural network. In: Proceedings of the IEEE Conference on Computer Vision and Pattern Recognition, pp. 5163–5172 (2017)

77. Wang, X., Yu, K., Dong, C., Loy, C.C.: Recovering realistic texture in image super-resolution by deep spatial feature transform. In: Proceedings of the IEEE Conference on Computer Vision and Pattern Recognition (CVPR), June 2018

78. Wang, Z., Bovik, A.C., Sheikh, H.R., Simoncelli, E.P.: Image quality assessment: from error visibility to structural similarity. IEEE Trans. Image Process. 13(4), 600–612 (2004)

79. Welch, G., Bishop, G., et al.: An introduction to the Kalman filter (1995)

80. Wu, P.W., Lin, Y.J., Chang, C.H., Chang, E.Y., Liao, S.W.: RelGAN: multi-domain image-to-image translation via relative attributes. In: Proceedings of the IEEE International Conference on Computer Vision, pp. 5914–5922 (2019)

81. Zhang, K., Zhang, Z., Li, Z., Qiao, Y.: Joint face detection and alignment using multitask cascaded convolutional networks. IEEE Sig. Process. Lett. 23(10), 1499–1503 (2016)

82. Zhu, J.Y., Park, T., Isola, P., Efros, A.A.: Unpaired image-to-image translation using cycle-consistent adversarial networks. In: Proceedings of the IEEE International Conference on Computer Vision, pp. 2223–2232 (2017)

83. Zhu, P., Abdal, R., Qin, Y., Wonka, P.: Sean: image synthesis with semantic region-adaptive normalization. In: Proceedings of the IEEE/CVF Conference on Computer Vision and Pattern Recognition, pp. 5104–5113 (2020)

84. Zhu, X., Lei, Z., Liu, X., Shi, H., Li, S.Z.: Face alignment across large poses: a 3D solution. In: Proceedings of the IEEE Conference on Computer Vision and Pattern Recognition, pp. 146–155 (2016)

85. Zi, B., Chang, M., Chen, J., Ma, X., Jiang, Y.G.: Wilddeepfake: a challenging real-world dataset for deepfake detection. In: Proceedings of the 28th ACM International Conference on Multimedia, pp. 2382–2390 (2020)

Study on Image Processing of Capillaries Using Microscope: Initial Considerations

Hang Nguyen Thi Phuong[1], Hieyong Jeong[1(✉)] [iD], and Choonsung Shin[2(✉)]

[1] Department of Artificial Intelligence Convergence, Chonnam National University, 77 Yongbongro, Bukgu, Gwangju, Republic of Korea
h.jeong@jnu.ac.kr
[2] Graduate School of Culture, Chonnam National University, 77 Yongbongro, Bukgu, Gwangju, Republic of Korea
cshin@jnu.ac.kr

Abstract. Routine nailfold capillaroscopy is essential for early diagnosis of rheumatic disease, but clinicians struggle to evaluate the same capillaries in every examination because the capillaries are similar in shape; therefore, difficult to differentiate. Here, we propose a method that will enable us to compare previous and real-time images captured by a microscope with low- and high-power objective lenses. Particularly, we would like to look into the method for feature extraction such as template matching, SIFT (Scale Invariant Feature Transform), and so on. After selecting a target nailfold capillary using the low-power objective lens, we assessed the capillary with a high-power objective lens. The captured image of the target capillary was compared in real-time with the previously captured image, irrespective of magnification, using template matching. Our proposed algorithm detected allowable similarity for assessing the same capillary, which was helpful in evaluating the structural abnormalities of the entire area in addition to just the magnified area.

Keywords: Continuous observation · Image processing · Nailfold capillary · Microscopy

1 Introduction

Nailfold capillaroscopy is a simple, safe, and noninvasive imaging technique for the evaluation of microcirculation in vivo [1]. Diseases such as rheumatic disease, diabetes, and hypertension can lead to morphological changes of nailfold capillaries [2,3]. Detecting specific changes in capillary patterns may assist in early detection of these diseases. For example, nailfold capillary is the most reliable tool for the early diagnosis of systemic sclerosis (SSc), an autoimmune rheumatic disease that is difficult to diagnose in its early stages [4]. Nailfold capillary diagnosis may also be useful for monitoring the progression of SSc, and it has predictive value for early detection of clinical complications and outcomes [5]. Thus, routine assessments of nailfold capillary morphology are essential in a clinical setting.

© Springer Nature Switzerland AG 2021
H. Jeong and K. Sumi (Eds.): IW-FCV 2021, CCIS 1405, pp. 157–167, 2021.
https://doi.org/10.1007/978-3-030-81638-4_12

The quality and resolution of capillary imaging is important for accurate diagnosis and evaluation. Ideally, the same capillaries should be evaluated during follow-up examinations of patients. However, finding the same capillaries in each routine assessment is challenging because all nailfold capillaries are similar in shape and they occur at high average densities of as many as nine capillaries per 1 mm [6], making it difficult to identify individual capillaries in successive examinations. Therefore, for the diagnosis of SSc, clinicians often calculate mean values from the analysis of multiple images [7].

Mark et al. [8] developed a hardware system that produced an image of an entire nailfold at the low magnification by merging a series of images covering the whole nailfold, similar to a panorama image. This system may be more efficient than the conventional method for identifying individual nailfold capillaries, but clinicians often require a high-power objective lens to examine capillaries in sufficient detail and high resolution, depending on the purpose of the examination. It is often more important to capture an image of the same capillary, regardless of the magnification, than to capture high-quality images of different capillaries.

Therefore, we propose an algorithm to compare a current image of a nailfold capillary with a previously captured image in real-time by using microscopy with low- and high-power objective lenses. At that time, we would like to make sure which method for the feature extraction from image data are useful among one such as the template matching to find the similar area between two images, or others such as SIFT (Scale Invariant Feature Transform) to find similar edged points between two images. Here, we show that this algorithm enabled us to identify the same capillaries and area. This is a promising tool for routine assessment of nailfold capillary morphology.

2   Experimental Setting

2.1   Experimental System

A human subject placed his or her finger on the stand unit under the capillary microscopy for nailfold capillaroscopy (Fig. 1). An operator viewed the image on a computer monitor in real-time, captured the real-time images for future viewing, and compared two captured images where one was a previously captured image and the other was the real-time image.

The microscope used was a GOKO Bscan-Z (GOKO Imaging Devices, Kanagawa, Japan) with a vertical, cylindrical body and compact size (diameter × length = $\phi 45 \times 106$ mm). The microscope weighs of 150 g total when the focus cap is attached (size of focus cap is diameter × length = $\phi 45$ mm × 10 mm, and the body weight is 10 g). The diameter of the stand unit base is $\phi 120$ mm, the camera holder is $\phi 58$ mm, and the height of the stand unit is 72.5 mm (Fig. 1). The stand unit weights 250 g, the range of the x-directional movement for the stand unit is 10 mm from the left to the right side, and the range of the y-directional movement of the camera holder is 10 mm from the upper to the lower positions. There is no range of the z-directional movement, but a human subject can regulate his or her finger position under the microscope.

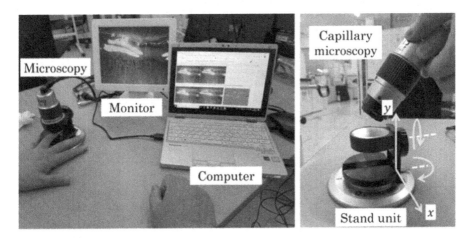

Fig. 1. An overview of the experimental environment and a description of the experimental system.

The real-time image was projected onto a 14-in. monitor under a range of magnification from ×100 to ×410. The ring dial was rotated from low to high magnification without any lens change using the regulation for powerful zoom. The NTSC-USB 2.0 Converter was used to display real-time images on the computer, at a maximum of 30 uncompressed frames per second. This converter enabled saving of the images at an aspect ratio of 4:3.

2.2 Flow Chart

An initial image should be captured and saved for regular assessment (Fig. 2 left side). The low-power objective lens should be used when selecting a particular target capillary, and the optical image-stabilization microscope function should be used to reduce disturbances from hand vibrations while capturing the image. At that time, the low-power objective lens (100×) of microscopy enables us to decide which capillary is necessary to be observed continuously, and then helps increase the probability of similarity between two captured images. The function for optical image stabilization is needed to compensate the vibration reduction according to the health condition of human subjects such as senior citizens before capturing the image.

After selecting a target capillary, the high-power objective lens (×410) should be used to compare the previous vs. real-time similarity. High similarity indicates that the images are of the same capillaries, while lower similarity suggests that different capillaries have been photographed and that a new image should be captured (Fig. 2).

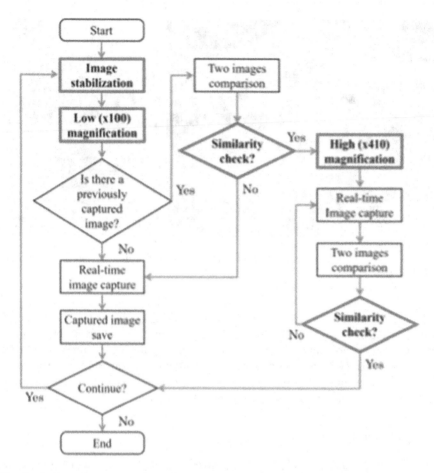

Fig. 2. A flow chart to explain the proposed image quality assessment for capillary microscopy.

3 Methods

3.1 Vibration Reduction Using Optical Flow

The image-stabilization algorithm estimates the global motion between consecutive frames in a video sequence and then compensates for detected jiggling. This algorithm consists of a motion vector module, which detects input image movement and extracts the image fluctuation component. A compensated video signal is generated so that the image's undesirable shake can be counterbalanced.

Denote the image brightness at point (x, y) in the image plane at time t by $E(x, y, t)$. In notation, let $u = \frac{dx}{dt}$, $v = \frac{dy}{dt}$, $E_x = \frac{\delta E}{\delta x}$, $E_y = \frac{\delta E}{\delta y}$, $E_t = \frac{\delta E}{\delta t}$.

The zero-order optical flow computation minimizes a weighted sum of errors of the pixel-to-pixel variation in the velocity field. Thus, the total error to be minimized is [9–11]

$$\epsilon^2 = \int\int (\alpha^2 \epsilon_c^2 + \epsilon_b^2) dx dy, \tag{1}$$

where ϵ_b $(= E_x u + E_y v + E_t)$ denotes the sum of the errors for the rate of change of image brightness, ϵ_c^2 $(= (\frac{\delta u}{\delta x})^2 + (\frac{\delta u}{\delta y})^2 + (\frac{\delta v}{\delta x})^2 + (\frac{\delta v}{\delta y})^2)$ represents the measure of the departure from smoothness in the velocity flow, and α^2 is a weighting factor. The Gauss-Seidel method is commonly applied to solve the equations and yields the following iterative algorithm:

$$u^{n+1} = \bar{u}^n - E_x \frac{[E_x \bar{u}^n + E_y \bar{v}^n + E_t]}{(\alpha^2 + E_x^2 + E_y^2)}, \tag{2}$$

$$v^{n+1} = \bar{v}^n - E_y \frac{[E_x \bar{u}^n + E_y \bar{v}^n + E_t]}{(\alpha^2 + E_x^2 + E_y^2)}.$$

The velocity field $V(x, y) = (u(x, y), v(x, y))$ of each pixel at (x, y) is calculated by the optical flow estimation method.

Next, it is necessary to compensate for the vibration. First, the angular frequency ω of rotational disturbance motion is estimated. Let the motion consist of the general case of containing both translational and rotational motion. For two points (x_{k1}, y_{k1}) and (x_{k2}, y_{k2}) in the image frame, those should satisfy [9, 10]

$$u(x, y) = u' - \omega(y - y_0), \tag{3}$$

$$v(x, y) = v' + \omega(x - x_0),$$

and the velocity difference $\Delta u = u(x_{k1}, y_{k1}) - u(x_{k2}, y_{k2})$ and $\Delta v = v(x_{k1}, y_{k1}) - v(x_{k2}, y_{k2})$ take the $\Delta u = -\omega \Delta y$ and $\Delta v = \omega \Delta x$,

$$\begin{bmatrix} \Delta u \\ \Delta v \end{bmatrix} = \begin{bmatrix} -\Delta y \\ \Delta x \end{bmatrix} \omega, \tag{4}$$

where $\Delta x = x_{k1} - x_{k2}$ and $\Delta y = y_{k1} - y_{k2}$. Any pair of pixels satisfies Eq. 4, which is in the form of $A\omega = b$. A least squares solution is usually adopted to minimize the discrepancy between the pixel pairs in the image. The least squares estimate of ω can be obtained by $\hat{\omega} = (A^T A)^{-1} A^T b$.

Next, the translational and rotational velocities are obtained. From Eq. 4, the translational velocity components in the x-direction, u', and y-direction, v', are obtained by $u' = u(x_0, y_0)$ and $v' = v(x_0, y_0)$ if the rotational center (x_0, y_0) is known. For a given rotational center (x_0, y_0), the velocity components, $u(x_i, y_i)$ and $v(x_i, y_i)$ at point (x_i, y_i) is estimated by [9, 11]

$$\hat{u}(x_i, y_i) = u(x_0, y_0) - \hat{\omega}(y_i - y_0), \tag{5}$$

$$\hat{v}(x_i, y_i) = v(x_0, y_0) + \hat{\omega}(x_i - x_0).$$

It is possible to define the error function e as

$$e = \sum_{(x_0 - p \leq x_i \leq x_0 + p)} \sum_{(y_0 - p \leq y_i \leq y_0 + p)} [\hat{u}(x_i, y_i) - u(x_i, y_i)]^2 + [\hat{v}(x_i, y_i) - v(x_i, y_i)]^2, \tag{6}$$

where $\hat{u}(x_i, y_i)$ and $\hat{v}(x_i, y_i)$ are calculated from Eq. 6, p is related to the window size, and $u(x_i, y_i)$ and $v(x_i, y_i)$ are obtained from the results of optical flow computation.

The rotational center is identified by Eq. 6, and the translational velocities u' and v' can be obtained from $u' = u(x_0, y_0)$ and $v' = v(x_0, y_0)$. Using the estimated rotational center (x_0, y_0) and the translational velocities u' and v', together with $\hat{\omega}$ estimated previously, it is possible to generate a counterbalance signal to stabilize the fluctuation in the current image frame.

3.2   Image Comparison

The goal of image comparison is to find similar pixels or featured points in two images. High similarity of two images insures data reliability of the nailfold capillary.

Template Matching. Template matching is a technique for finding areas of an image that match a template image. Two primary components are used for template matching: a source image in which we expect to find a match to the template image, and the patch image, which will be compared to the template image. The goal for template matching is to detect the highest matching area. During the matching process, the template image moves to all possible positions in the source image and calculates the similarity of each match [12].

For each location of T over I, the metric is stored in the result matrix R. Each location (x, y) in R contains the match metric. In practice, the minMaxLoc function of OpenCV is used to locate the highest value in the R matrix. Although OpenCV implements template matching in the matchTemplate function, cross-correlation is used among six types of template-matching methods [13–15],

$$CC(x, y) = \frac{\sum_{x', y'} T(x', y') I(x + x', y + y')}{\sqrt{\sum_{x', y'} T(x', y')^2 \sum_{x', y'} I(x + x', y + y')^2}}, \tag{7}$$

where T is the template image and I is the input source image. A cross-correlation of 0 is the poorest match, while 1 is the best in the range of [0, 1]. The pixel value in each location (x, y) characterizes the similarity between the template and the input image with the top-left corner at (x, y). Although the matching result may be slightly different depending on the matching algorithm, there was no significant difference in this study.

SIFT. The SIFT algorithm is composed of four stages of computation:

1. Scale-space extrema detection.

   To detect blob structures in an image, a scale space is constructed where the interest points, which are called keypoints in the SIFT framework, are detected. The scale space function is produced from the convolution of a variable-scale Gaussian, $G(x, y, \sigma)$, with an input image, $I(x, y)$.

$$L(x, y, \sigma) = G(x, y, \sigma) * I(x, y). \tag{8}$$

where,

$$G(x, y, \sigma) = \frac{1}{2\pi\sigma^2} e^{-\frac{(x^2+y^2)}{2\sigma^2}}. \tag{9}$$

The normalization of the Laplacian, $\sigma^2 \nabla^2 G$, with the factor σ^2 is required fro true scale invariance. Automatic scale selection is performed in the image after convolution with the normalized Laplacian function:

$$O(x, y, \sigma) = \sigma^2 \nabla^2 G * I(x, y). \tag{10}$$

Difference-of-Gaussian (DoG) function is used to approximate the normalized Laplacian for automatic scale selection. If the scale of the image structure is close to the σ value of the normalized Laplacian function, the output $O(x, y, \sigma)$ calculated from convolution the image with $\sigma^2 \nabla^2 G$ will be extrema.

2. Unreliable keypoints removal.

   This stage is to remove unrealizable keypoints, because scale-space extrema detection produces a lot of keypoint candidates. In this stage the value of $|O(x, y, \sigma)|$ at each candidate keypoint is evaluated. If this value is below some threshold which means that the structure has low contrast, the keypoint will be removed.

3. Orientation assignment.

   In this stage, each keypoint is assigned one or more orientations based on local image gradient directions.

4. Keypoint descriptor.

   The local image gradients are measured at the selected scale in the region around each keypoint.

4 Results and Discussion

4.1 Vibration Reduction

Figure 3 (a) represents vibration reduction through the optical flow without an intentional hand movements, while Fig. 3 (b) represents vibration reduction through the optical flow with intentional hand movements. The image-stabilization function helped compensate for even intentional hand movement, which will be useful for compensation of unavoidable hand movements by the elderly.

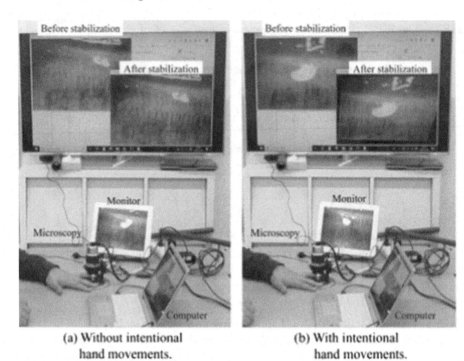

(a) Without intentional
hand movements.

(b) With intentional
hand movements.

Fig. 3. Results of vibration reduction through the optical flow.

4.2   Image Comparison

Figure 3 (a) represents the real-time processing, and Fig. 3 (b) represents the image of similarity check. In the low-power objective lens microscopy, we observed an entire large area (Fig. 4). To ensure imaging of the same nailfold capillaries under high magnification, the targeted capillary was positioned on the stand unit in the center of the monitor before changing to the high-power objective lens. Previously captured and real-time images were 85% similar in this experiment (Fig. 4).

For the low-power objective lens, the entire large area is observed. When the regular observational nailfold capillary was decided, the targeted capillary was positioned on the center of monitor with the stand unit before changing the high-power objective lens. Due to this procedure, it was always easy enough to observe the same area including the targeted capillary. Through the proposed method, it was found that there was the 73% similarity at this time.

Figure 5 shows the results of the real-time image processing and the similarity check for monitor and computer under the high magnification. Under the high-power objective lens microscopy, the targeted capillary was observed in more detail in an enlarged image (Fig. 5). This high-resolution image was used to confirm whether featured points differed from those captured in a previous image. Real-time and previously captured images were 98% similar in this experiment (Fig. 5).

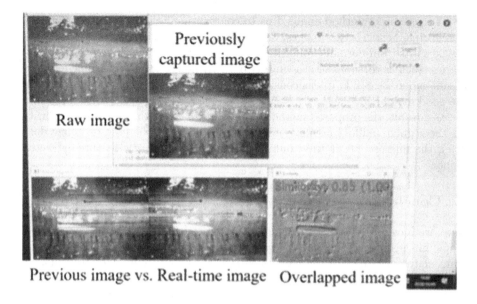

Fig. 4. Output of the low-power objective lens (×100).

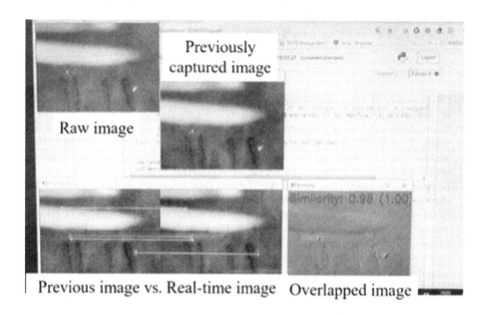

Fig. 5. Output of the high-power objective lens (×410).

The proposed method enabled us to compare nailfold capillary morphology in real-time between two images. Our system help clinicians recognize morphological shifts from normal capillaries (such as hairpin shapes) to nonspecific capillaries (such as tortuous or crossing shapes). Although there were some featured points under the SIFT, it was considered that detected featured points were not the good matching.

As a result, the proposed method enabled us to check the real-time similarity for the regular nailfold capillary observation. Then, in the case of image data using the microscope, it was confirmed that there was little feature-extracted points.

5 Conclusion

Here, we have presented a novel algorithmic method to compare two capillaroscopic images in real time using low- and high-power objective lenses and template matching. Image stabilization enabled us to identify individual capillaries while reducing the vibrational noise in the image. This method can be used for routine assessment of nailfold capillary morphology in future [16].

Acknowledgment. This work was financially supported by the Design Innovation Program (AHA Platform and Personalized Services for the Elderly Using Universal UX Design, No 20012692) funded By the Ministry of Trade, industry & Energy (MOTIE, Republic of Korea), and Chonnam National University (Grant number 2020-2020).

References

1. Chojnowski, M.M., Felis-Giemza, A., Olesinska, M.: Capillaroscopy - a role in modern rheumatology. Reumatologia **54**, 67–72 (2016)
2. Triantafyllou, A., et al.: Accumulation of microvascular target organ damage in newly diagnosed hypertensive patients. J. Am. Soc. Hypertens. **8**, 542–549 (2014)
3. Maldonado, G., Guerrero, R., Paredes, C., Rios, C.: Nailfold capillaroscopy in diabetes mellitus. Microvasc. Res. **112**, 41–46 (2017)
4. Rajaei, A., Dehghan, P., Amiri, A.: Nailfold capillaroscopy in 430 patients with rheumatoid arthritis. Caspian J. Intern. Med. **8**, 269–274 (2017)
5. Rossi, D., et al.: The role of nail-videocapillaroscopy in early diagnosis of scleroderma. Autoimmun. Rev. **12**, 821–825 (2013)
6. Cutolo, M., Sulli, A., Pizzorni, C., Accardo, S.: Nailfold videocapillaroscopy assessment of microvascular damage in systemic sclerosis. J. Rheumatol. **27**, 155–160 (2000)
7. Smith, V., et al.: Reliability of the qualitative and semiquantitative nailfold videocapillaroscopy assessment in a systemic sclerosis cohort: a two-centre study. Ann. Rheum. Dis. **69**, 1092–1096 (2010)
8. Anderson, M.E., Allen, P.D., Moore, T., Hillier, V., Taylor, C.J., Herrick, A.L.: Computerized nailfold video capillaroscopy-a new tool for assessment of Raynaud's phenomenon. J. Rheumatol. **32**, 841–848 (2005)
9. Chang, J., Hu, W., Cheng, M., Chang, B.: Digital image translational and rotational motion stabilization using optical flow technique. IEEE Trans. Consum. Electron. **48**(1), 108–115 (2002)

10. Lim, A., Ramesh, B., Yang, Y., Xiang, C., Gao, Z.: Real-time optical flow-based video stabilization for unmanned aerial vehicles. J. Real-Time Image Process. 1–11 (2017)
11. Li, W., Hu, J., Li, Z., Tang, L., Li, C.: Image stabilization based on Harris corners and optical flow. In: International Conference on Knowledge Science, Engineering and Management, pp. 387–394 (2011)
12. Duan, H., Xu, C., Liu, S., Shao, S.: Template matching using chaotic imperialist competitive algorithm. Pattern Recogn. Lett. **31**, 1868–1875 (2010)
13. Swaroop, P., Sharma, N.: An overview of various template matching methodologies in image processing. Int. J. Comput. Appl. **153**(10), 8–14 (2016)
14. Wang, Z., Bovik, A.C., Sheikh, H.R., Simoncelli, E.P.: Image quality assessment: from error visibility to structural similarity. IEEE Trans. Image Process. **13**(4), 600–612 (2004)
15. Jurie, F., Dhome, M.: Real time robust template matching. In: Proceedings of British Machine Vision Conference 2002, pp. 123–132 (2002)
16. Suga, S., Otomo, A., Jeong, H., Ohno, Y.: Image similarity check of nailfold capillary by template matching. In: 2019 IEEE 8th Global Conference on Consumer Electronics (GCCE), Osaka, 15–18 October 2019

Stair-Step Feature Pyramid Networks for Object Detection

Xuan-Thuy Vo, Tien-Dat Tran, Duy-Linh Nguyen, and Kang-Hyun Jo[✉]

School of Electrical Engineering, University of Ulsan, Ulsan, Korea
{xthuy,tdat}@islab.ulsan.ac.kr, ndlinh301@mail.ulsan.ac.kr,
acejo@ulsan.ac.kr

Abstract. Feature Pyramid Networks have solved scale variation problems in object detection by developing multi-level features with different scales from backbone networks. Although this network achieved promising performance without affecting model complexity, they still suffer feature-level imbalance between multi-level features, i.e., low-level features and high-level features in each stage of the backbone. Moreover, the detection head predicts classification scores and offset regression independently on each feature of multi-level features, which leads to inconsistency among the detection branch. Hence, this paper releases this problem by introducing simple but effective Stair-step Feature Pyramid Networks (SFPN) to harmonize information between multi-level features. Further, the Offset Adaption Module (OA Module) is proposed to improve feature representation by adapting the feature of the classification branch with regressed offsets of the regression branch. On the MS-COCO dataset, the proposed method increases by 1.2% Average Precision when comparing with baseline FCOS without bells and whistles.

Keywords: Stair-step FPN · Offset Adaption · Object detection

1 Introduction

Object detection is one of the challenging tasks in computer vision research. This problem is decomposed into two tasks: classification task and regression task. The classification task classifies each object belonging to a specific class. The regression task identifies where each object locates. Two types of detectors are one-stage and two-stage detector, which are based on the number of networks on each detection head. The two-stage pipeline first obtains a set of region proposals and then the second stage classifies each proposal to a specific class and regresses the coordinates of each proposal by learning offsets. The one-stage object detection directly places dense anchor-boxes on each location and performs classification and regression tasks on each anchor-boxes. Although one-stage detection achieves high efficiency, the accuracy of it is far lower than two-stage detection. The structure of detection architecture includes a backbone

© Springer Nature Switzerland AG 2021
H. Jeong and K. Sumi (Eds.): IW-FCV 2021, CCIS 1405, pp. 168–175, 2021.
https://doi.org/10.1007/978-3-030-81638-4_13

network to extract feature of images, neck network which connects the back-bone and head part to create multi-level features and detection head to predict classification scores and offsets.

One of the most popular necks is Feature Pyramid Networks - FPN [9] selecting multi-level features from backbone network by utilizing top-down pathway and lateral connection to gather neighborhood features. Even though FPN has figured out the scale imbalance problem in which the size of objects changes in large ranges, this method still suffers feature-level imbalance among multi-level features. Since the detection head predicts scores, offsets independently on each feature, it leads to inconsistency between each head branch. To overcome this problem, EFPN [16] introduced a feature aggregation module and refinement module to obtain a uniform feature for all feature pyramid. Inspired by [16], this paper proposes Stair-step Feature Pyramid Networks (SFPN) which employs bi-linear interpolation and summation operation on adjacent features to form a uniform feature, i.e., the top-down pathway. Generally speaking, the multi-level features are converted to a single feature that contains information of all features. Without losing the novelty of FPN, SFPN also creates multi-level features by down-sampling a uniform feature, i.e., bottom-top pathway. Finally, the residual connection between the top-down pathway and down-top pathway is applied to ease hard optimization.

The detection head consists of the classification and regression branch. These two branches are trained independently to predict the class probability and offset values. Hence they ignore the correlation of class prediction and bounding box prediction. To improve feature representation, the Offset Adaption Module (OA Module) is performed by adding four offset values to the rectangular grid sampling locations in 3×3 convolution.

2   Related Work

Feature Pyramid Networks - FPN [9] presented multi-level features to solve scale variation problems in object detection. EFPN [16] enhanced multi-scale features by introducing feature aggregation module and refinement module to improve feature representation.

The popular two-stage object detection is Faster R-CNN [13] which achieves great performance. Inspired by [13], many methods are proposed such as Libra R-CNN [12], TridentNet [8], Mask R-CNN [4]. The one-stage object detection brings a trade-off between accuracy and speed. One of the most popular one-stage detection is RetinaNet [10] which densely places anchor-boxes on each location. After that, the network classifies each anchor-box and predict four offset value, e.g., coordinates of object center, width, and height. Recently, the anchor-free method - FCOS [15] balances both accuracy and speed, which avoids drawbacks of the anchor-based method. The proposed method considers FCOS as a baseline.

Many methods aims to improve object detection accuracy by inserting attention module to backbone network, such as GCNet [1], Non-local Network [18], BNLNet [17]. Different from this strategy, this paper proposes the Offset Adaption Module which correlates class prediction with bounding box prediction. This module is light-weight but boosting the accuracy of detectors.

3   The Proposed Method

The overall architecture is shown in Fig. 1. The backbone network extracts features from the image. Five feature maps with different scales from each stage of the backbone are selected as the input of Stair-step FPN. This architecture will describe in Sect. 3.1.

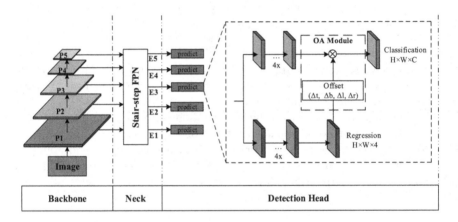

Fig. 1. The overall architecture of the proposed method includes the backbone, neck, and detection head. Stair-step FPN takes five feature maps (P_1, P_2, P_3, P_4, P_5) as input and then obtains balanced features (E_1, E_2, E_3, E_4, E_5). Offset Adaption OA Module takes four offset values and classification features as input. $\otimes$ denotes 3×3 deformable convolution.

The detection head consists of the classification branch and regression branch. The OA module considers the correlation of classification scores and bounding box prediction, described in Sect. 3.2.

3.1   Stair-Step Feature Pyramid Networks

Inspired by FPN [9], Stair-step FPN employs lateral connection using 1×1 conv and bi-linear interpolation to gather low-level and high-level features. Specifically, Stair-step FPN takes (P_1, P_2, P_3, P_4, P_5) as input. Because the number of channels and spatial resolution of each P_i is different. Therefore, 1×1 conv reduces the number of channels of the down feature suitable for summation operation with the top feature. Bi-linear interpolation up-samples the top feature to

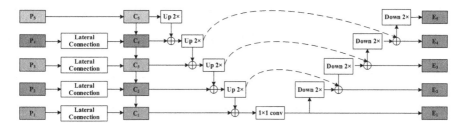

Fig. 2. The detailed architecture of the Stair-step FPN includes a top-down pathway and a down-top pathway. Up 2× denotes Up-sampling operation with scale 2. Down 2× denotes Down-sampling operation with scale 2. $\oplus$ denotes summation operation.

the same size as the down feature. The output of this process produces a feature pyramid $(C_1, C_2, C_3, C_4, C_5)$. The detailed network is shown in Fig. 2.

To model a uniform feature, the Stair-step FPN utilizes a top-down pathway to sum the up-sampled feature C_{i+1} with C_i steadily. Hence, multi-level features with different scales are fused to form a single feature. Then, 1×1 convolution enhances a uniform feature across all channels.

Similar to the top-down pathway, the Stair-step FPN uses the down-top pathway to create multi-level features. The enhanced feature is down-sampling two times by max-pooling operation. The residual connection is applied to improve feature representation by adding a feature in the top-down pathway with a feature in the down-top pathway correspondingly with the same spatial resolution and number of channels. Additionally, the short-cut connection is able to solve hard optimization when propagating gradient to the top-down pathway. Finally, the stair-step FPN outputs balanced multi-level features with different scales $(E_1, E_2, E_3, E_4, E_5)$ to solve scale imbalance in object detection.

3.2   Offset Adaption

The standard convolution layers perform on fixed rectangular grid sampling. Therefore, the receptive field is not adaptive with scales or shapes of objects. Also, the feature of the classification branch can lose to adapt with the feature of the regression branch. To overcome this problem, the Offset Adaption (OA) Module is proposed to adapt the classification feature with regressed offset values, which enhances feature representation. The detailed information is shown in Fig. 1.

Different from standard convolution, deformable convolution [3] adds offset to rectangular grid sampling location. Hence, this strategy can change the receptive field adaptive with scales or shapes of objects. The OA module applies this operation for adapting classification features with four regressed offset values, i.e., four distances $(\Delta t, \Delta b, \Delta l, \Delta r)$. The input of the OA module is the feature of the classification branch and distance offsets of the regression branch. The distance offsets estimate the filter offset $\Delta p_l \in \{\Delta t, \Delta b, \Delta l, \Delta r\}$ which changes rectangular grid sampling location L in deformable convolution operation. The adapted feature $y(p_0)$ at location p_0 is calculated as follows:

$$y(p_0) = \sum_{p_l \in L} w(p_l) * x(p_0 + p_l + \Delta p_l) \tag{1}$$

where x is the feature map of classification, p_l is the original location kernel weight $w(p_l)$ in grid L.

4   Experiment Setup

The Stair-step FPN and OA module are measured on challenging benchmark MS-COCO 2017 [11] for the object detection task. MS-COCO dataset consists of 115k images for training, 5k validation images for selecting the best hyperparameters, and 20k images for testing. Because the annotation of the test set did not provide, the result is measured by the CodaLab system. To evaluate the performance, Average Precision (AP) and Average Recall (AR) are applied.

All experiments are conducted with the deep learning Pytorch framework. The parameters of the baseline FCOS [15] is set by following the standard configuration of the mmdetection [2] with 12 epochs. The integrated model is trained with a batch size of 8 on an NVIDIA Titan GPU, CUDA 10.2, and CuDNN 7.6.5. The initial learning rate is 0.00251 from 1st epochs to 8th epochs. It will decay by a factor of 10 at 9th epochs and 10th epochs. The input image is resized to 1333×800.

Table 1. Results on the validation set 2017.

Method	Backbone	Image size	Schedule	AP	AP^{50}	AP^{75}	AP^S	AP^M	AP^L
Faster R-CNN [13]	ResNet-50	1333×800	1×	37.4	58.1	40.4	21.1	41	48.1
Mask R-CNN [4]	ResNet-50	1333×800	1×	38.2	58.8	41.4	21.9	40.9	49.5
GC-Net [1]	ResNet-50	1333×800	1×	39.9	61.3	43.5	24.3	43.7	51.5
RetinaNet [10]	ResNet-50	1333×800	1×	36.5	55.4	39.1	20.4	40.3	48.1
FoveaBox [6]	ResNet-50	1333×800	1×	36.5	56.0	38.6	20.5	39.9	47.7
Free-Anchor [19]	ResNet-50	1333×800	1×	38.7	57.3	41.5	21.0	42.0	51.3
GHM [7]	ResNet-50	1333×800	1×	37.0	55.5	39.2	20.4	40.3	49.1
FCOS [15]	ResNet-50	1333×800	1×	36.6	55.7	38.8	20.7	40.1	47.4
Ours	**ResNet-50**	1333×800	1×	**37.8**	**55.9**	**38.8**	**21.0**	**40.3**	**50.1**

5   Results

Comparison with State-of-the-Art. The FPN in baseline FCOS is replaced by the proposed Stair-step FPN. The pre-trained backbone ResNet [5] is trained on ImageNet [14]. The results are evaluated on MS-COCO validation set with 5k images and compared with the state-of-the-art object detectors in Table 1. All experiments use backbone ResNet-50 and the learning schedule is 1× denoting 12 epochs.

Fig. 3. The qualitative results of the proposed method on MS-COCO validation set.

The proposed method achieves 37.8 AP, which increases 1.2% higher AP than FCOS [15] with the same backbone and learning schedule without bells and whistles. Furthermore, the proposed method has surpassed most object detectors, e.g., AP of Faster R-CNN [13] with ResNet-50 is 37.4, AP of RetinaNet [10] is 36.5, AP of FoveaBox [6] is 36.5, AP of GHM [7] is 37.0. The performance on the validation set pointed out that the Stair-step FPN and OA module are boosted the accuracy of detectors by a large margin. These results demonstrate the efficiency of the proposed method. Figure 3 visualizes the qualitative results of the proposed method on the MS-COCO validation set with different classes.

Ablation Study. This work individually investigates the importance of each component, i.e., the Stair-step FPN and OA module. When the detector uses the Stair-step FPN in the neck part, the proposed method achieves 37.2 AP that obtains an absolute gain of 0.6% AP comparing with baseline. The OA module is able to improve the feature representation by adapting classification prediction with regressed offsets. Hence, the results demonstrate the effectiveness of the OA module, shown in Table 2. Specifically, the OA module boosts the accuracy

Table 2. The effect of each component in the detector. Results are measured on the validation set.

Stair-step FPN	OA Module	AP	AP^{50}	AP^{75}	AP^S	AP^M	AP^L
		36.6	55.7	38.8	20.7	40.1	47.4
✓		37.2	55.6	38.6	20.9	40.3	48.3
	✓	37.4	55.7	38.9	21.2	40.1	49.6
✓	✓	37.8	55.9	38.8	21.0	40.3	50.1

by 0.8% AP comparing with baseline. Finally, the detector utilizing all proposed methods increases the accuracy by 1.2% AP, compared to the baseline.

6   Conclusion

This paper proposes the simple but effective Stair-step Feature Pyramid Networks solving feature-level imbalance and scale variation problem in object detection. The Stair-step FPN employs the top-down pathway to harmonize feature-levels of multi-level features with different scales from outputs of the backbone network into a uniform feature and down-top pathway to create multi-level features. To better correlate classification prediction with regression branch, the novel Offset Adaption module is introduced to align classification features with four distance offsets by using deformable convolution. The experiments on the MS-COCO dataset confirm the improvement of the proposed methods, achieving state-of-the-art object detection.

Acknowledgment. This work was supported by the National Research Foundation of Korea (NRF) grant funded by the government (MSIT) (No. 2020R1A2C2008972).

References

1. Cao, Y., Xu, J., Lin, S., Wei, F., Hu, H.: GCNet: non-local networks meet squeeze-excitation networks and beyond. In: Proceedings of the IEEE International Conference on Computer Vision Workshops (2019)
2. Chen, K., et al.: MMDetection: open MMLab detection toolbox and benchmark. arXiv preprint arXiv:1906.07155 (2019)
3. Dai, J., et al.: Deformable convolutional networks. In: Proceedings of the IEEE International Conference on Computer Vision, pp. 764–773 (2017)
4. He, K., Gkioxari, G., Dollár, P., Girshick, R.: Mask R-CNN. In: Proceedings of the IEEE International Conference on Computer Vision, pp. 2961–2969 (2017)
5. He, K., Zhang, X., Ren, S., Sun, J.: Deep residual learning for image recognition. In: Proceedings of the IEEE Conference on Computer Vision and Pattern Recognition, pp. 770–778 (2016)
6. Kong, T., Sun, F., Liu, H., Jiang, Y., Li, L., Shi, J.: FoveaBox: beyound anchor-based object detection. IEEE Trans. Image Process. **29**, 7389–7398 (2020)

7. Li, B., Liu, Y., Wang, X.: Gradient harmonized single-stage detector. In: Proceedings of the AAAI Conference on Artificial Intelligence, vol. 33, pp. 8577–8584 (2019)
8. Li, Y., Chen, Y., Wang, N., Zhang, Z.: Scale-aware trident networks for object detection. In: Proceedings of the IEEE International Conference on Computer Vision, pp. 6054–6063 (2019)
9. Lin, T.Y., Dollár, P., Girshick, R., He, K., Hariharan, B., Belongie, S.: Feature pyramid networks for object detection. In: Proceedings of the IEEE Conference on Computer Vision and Pattern Recognition, pp. 2117–2125 (2017)
10. Lin, T.Y., Goyal, P., Girshick, R., He, K., Dollár, P.: Focal loss for dense object detection. In: Proceedings of the IEEE International Conference on Computer Vision, pp. 2980–2988 (2017)
11. Lin, T.Y., et al.: Microsoft COCO: common objects in context. In: Fleet, D., Pajdla, T., Schiele, B., Tuytelaars, T. (eds.) ECCV 2014. LNCS, vol. 8693, pp. 740–755. Springer, Cham (2014). https://doi.org/10.1007/978-3-319-10602-1_48
12. Pang, J., Chen, K., Shi, J., Feng, H., Ouyang, W., Lin, D.: Libra R-CNN: towards balanced learning for object detection. In: Proceedings of the IEEE Conference on Computer Vision and Pattern Recognition, pp. 821–830 (2019)
13. Ren, S., He, K., Girshick, R., Sun, J.: Faster R-CNN: towards real-time object detection with region proposal networks. In: Advances in Neural Information Processing Systems, pp. 91–99 (2015)
14. Russakovsky, O., et al.: ImageNet large scale visual recognition challenge. Int. J. Comput. Vision 115(3), 211–252 (2015)
15. Tian, Z., Shen, C., Chen, H., He, T.: Fcos: a simple and strong anchor-free object detector. IEEE Trans. Pattern Anal. Mach. Intell. (2020)
16. Vo, X.T., Jo, K.H.: Enhanced feature pyramid networks by feature aggregation module and refinement module. In: 2020 13th International Conference on Human System Interaction (HSI), pp. 63–67. IEEE (2020)
17. Vo, X.T., Wen, L., Tran, T.D., Jo, K.H.: Bidirectional non-local networks for object detection. In: International Conference on Computational Collective Intelligence, pp. 491–501. Springer (2020)
18. Wang, X., Girshick, R., Gupta, A., He, K.: Non-local neural networks. In: Proceedings of the IEEE Conference on Computer Vision and Pattern Recognition, pp. 7794–7803 (2018)
19. Zhang, X., Wan, F., Liu, C., Ji, R., Ye, Q.: FreeAnchor: learning to match anchors for visual object detection. In: Advances in Neural Information Processing Systems, pp. 147–155 (2019)

The 2nd Korean Emotion Recognition Challenge: Methods and Results

Songa Kim, Van Thong Huynh[✉], Dung Tran Thi, Aran Oh, Guee-Sang Lee, Hyung-Jeong Yang, and Soo-Hyung Kim[✉]

Department of Artificial Intelligence Convergence, Chonnam National University, Gwangju, South Korea
shkim@jnu.ac.kr

Abstract. The 2nd Korean Emotion Recognition Challenge (KERC-2020) is a global challenge to promote the emotion recognition technologies by using audio-visual data analysis, especially for the emotion of Korean people. KERC2020 comprise of 1236 videos with each length from two to four seconds based on Korean movies are dramas. Around 68 participating teams compete to achieve state-of-the-art in recognizing stress, arousal, valence from Korean video in the wild. This paper provides a summary of dataset, methods and results in the challenge.

Keywords: Korean emotion recognition · Arousal · Valence · Stress · Multimodal · Affective computing

1 Introduction

Artificial intelligence is a computer program or a computer system that artificially implements human learning, reasoning, and understanding of natural languages. Simply, it is an artificial implementation of human intelligence on machines. The original purpose of various artificial intelligence researches was an experimental approach to psychology. However, the world is focusing on artificial intelligence, IoT, cloud computing, and big data in line with the fourth industrial revolution. The KERC aims to develop human emotion recognition technology in line with the original intentions of artificial intelligence research, especially by focusing on Korean emotion recognition to contribute to Korean emotion recognition research.

The KERC2020 decided stress on many emotional states as a topic. Stress means adaptation as a psychological and physical response that causes mental and physical stimulation. As many people in today's society are suffering from stress, we are trying to improve the quality of life and help people well-being by developing the technology to recognize people's stress. Furthermore, through KERC, we aim to increase the interest of Koreans in stress and emotion recognition technology.

© Springer Nature Switzerland AG 2021
H. Jeong and K. Sumi (Eds.): IW-FCV 2021, CCIS 1405, pp. 176–183, 2021.
https://doi.org/10.1007/978-3-030-81638-4_14

2 Dataset

KERC2020 dataset contain 1236 video clips with only one subject in each video. The collection process consists of cropping and remove low-quality videos. First, semi-automatic tool [7] was used to extract clips with a length of 2 to 4 s from 41 different Korean movies and dramas with various contexts. Then, we removed the low-quality clips such as obstructed face or the subject's back facing the camera. Each sample in the dataset is guaranteed that they focus on a clearly visible face, compose of facial expression of a subject in different activities. Table 1 describe some metadata information of our dataset.

Table 1. KERC2020 dataset metadata.

Attribute	Description
Scenario	In the wild
Source	Movie
Lengh of each sample	2–4 s
Frame resolution	$(720 \times 400) \sim (1920 \sim 1080)$ pixels
Number of samples	1236 (Training 636, Validation 300, Test 300)
Emotion categories	Stress, Valence, Arousal
Format	Video (mp4)

The label was annotated by 27 right-handed college students. They have no history of brain damage or psychiatric history, and currently do not take any medication. They were guided by the instructions that every reaction to a facial expression needs to be judged immediately and quickly as they feels it without need to worry or make a conscious effort to respond. The label annotation was performed in 2 days with 3 h each in the morning and afternoon. The students were divided into 2 groups of 14 and 13 people respectively. The first group annotated data on the first day's morning and second day's afternoon. The other group annotated on the remain time. The annotator were asked to rate each video clip on a 9-point scale from 1 to 9, which represent the low and high intensity of emotion. Each samples were annotated with 3 categories as in Table 2. Totally, ew have 33372 labels in each category for 1236 videos. The final score for each video (g) was obtained based on mean (μ) and standard deviation (σ) of scores from 27 annotators for that video as the following equation

$$g_c = \frac{\sum_{i=1}^{27} \alpha_{i,c} r_{i,c}}{\sum_{i=1}^{27} \alpha_{i,c}}, \tag{1}$$

where $r_{i,c}$ is the score for emotion c which is rated by annotator i^{th}, and $\alpha_{i,c} \in \{0, 1\}$ indicate the using or elimination of the score from annotator i^{th} to reduce the dispersion of the data which is formulated as following

$$\alpha_{i,c} = \begin{cases} 1 & \text{if } \mu - 2\sigma \leq r_{i,c} \leq \mu + 2\sigma, \\ 0 & \text{otherwise.} \end{cases} \qquad (2)$$

Table 2. The description of categories and its range in KERC2020 dataset.

Category	Description
Stress (1–9)	How stressed does a person feel? (Non-stressed ~ stressed)
Valence (1–9)	How positive or negative an emotion is? (Negative ~ Positive)
Arousal (1–9)	What is the agitation level of the person? (Inactive ~ Active)

Figure 1 illustrated some examples of a frame in video clips of our dataset.

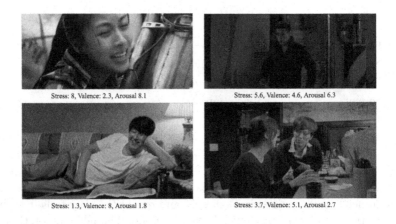

Stress: 8, Valence: 2.3, Arousal 8.1   Stress: 5.6, Valence: 4.6, Arousal 6.3

Stress: 1.3, Valence: 8, Arousal 1.8   Stress: 3.7, Valence: 5.1, Arousal 2.7

Fig. 1. Frame examples with video labels in KERC2020 dataset.

3   Baseline Approach

In this section, we describe our baseline method which is provided as a starting model for participants in KERC2020 challenge. Our approach consists of 3 stages: face detection, feature extraction, and score regression. In the first stage, we used Tiny Face Detector [6] to extract face region from any frames of each video, which produced $43328, 20314$, and 20924 faces in training, validation, and test set, respectively. Each face is cropped and resized to $224 \times 224 \times 3$ image in order to use as the input in second stage. We also resample each video to get 20 face image for each video before feeding to ResNet50 We deployed ResNet50 [5] architecture with pre-trained on VGGFace2, a large scale dataset for face recognition [2], as our feature extractor. We used the last average pooling layer of ResNet50 to obtain a feature vector of 20 × 2048 elements. In regression module, we deployed two LSTM layers followed by four fully connected layers. We built our baseline model on Keras and used Adam algorithm as optimizer with mean square error as objective function and learning rate of 0.001. A visualization of our approach can be seen in Fig. 2.

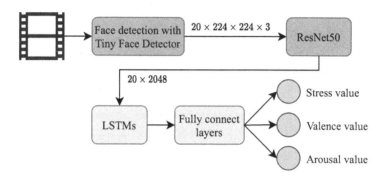

Fig. 2. The visualization of baseline architecture in KERC2020.

4   Challenge Methods and Results

The 2nd Korean Emotion Recognition Challenge was hosted between August 20, 2020 and November 7, 2020 on Kaggle platform[1] which is used for downloading dataset and result submissions. The final ranking is based on private leader board which evaluated on test set and do not public to any participants until the end of challenge. Around 68 teams participated, with about 15 teams publicized result submissions. Submission were evaluated on the weighted average of three emotion categories, M, as following equations

$$M = \frac{\mathrm{MSE}_{arousal} + \mathrm{MSE}_{valence} + 2 \times \mathrm{MSE}_{stress}}{4}, \tag{3}$$

where MSE indicate mean square errors. Table 3 shows the results of 2nd KERC challenge. In this section, we review top 3 winner submission.

---

[1] https://www.kaggle.com/c/2020kerc/overview.

Table 3. Challenge results ranked by weighted average metric M.

Rank	Team name	Affiliation	Score (M)
1	Maybe Next Time	Chonnam Natl. Univ.	0.64838
2	pthmd	Chonnam Natl. Univ.	0.80898
3	scalable	Korea Univ.	0.81167
4	Han Soheon	Sungkyunkwan Univ.	0.93346
5	HouKM	Hallym Univ.	0.96578
6	iPsych	Korea Univ.(Empathy Research Institute)	1.47796
7	King Kong Intelligence	Korea Aerospace Univ.	1.58330
8	sswolf	–	1.58422
9	VI	Chosun Univ.	1.71953
10	sinu	–	1.73596
11	ISPL_emo	–	1.92627
–	**Baseline model**	–	**1.9283**
12	TT	–	1.92834
13	eep_learning	–	1.92834
14	emo	–	1.98704
15	Taeyoung Park	–	2.10328

4.1 Team Maybe Next Time

Their approach focus on the faces and leverage the emotion information from another facial expression datasets which included 3 stages: pre-processing, deep network regression, post-processing. In the first stage, the face region is detected and alignment with Multi-task Cascaded Convolution Networks (MTCNN) [13], then, a mask is used to remove forehead, hair, and anything outside the face. In the second stage, they used AffectNet dataset [10] and AFEW-VA dataset [8] to train the ImageNet pretrained model again. At this point, they fine-tune on 10 epochs with KERC2019 which is contained 7 discrete emotions KERC2020 dataset together in a multi-task scenario to leverage the relationship between continuous and discrete emotions. After that, in the last 5 epochs, they fine-tuned only on the KERC2020 dataset. Their predictions are in frame-level, then they averaged the results to obtain the final prediction for each video in the post-processing step. An illustration of their approach can be seen in Fig. 3.

4.2 Team Pthmd

They deployed an architecture which consists of two streams for audio and visual information. Each stream includes 2 stages: feature extraction, regression module. They leveraged pre-trained models on VGGFace2 [2] for visual information, and AudioSet [4] for audio datato extract the deep representation. Due to the varies in length of each sample, they performed average pooling to downsampling the same time-dimension for all samples. At this point, PCA is used

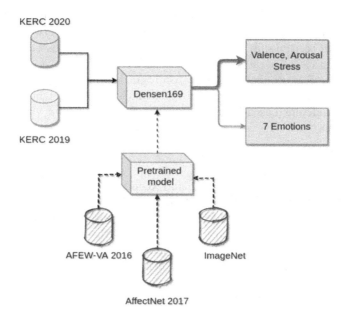

Fig. 3. Overview architecture of team Maybe Next Time.

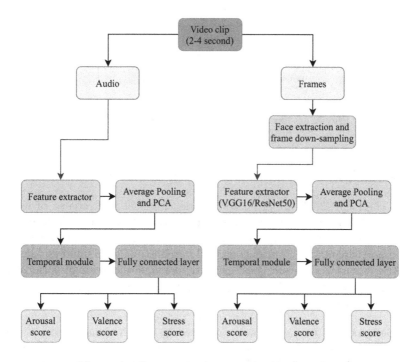

Fig. 4. An illustration of team pthmd's approach.

to select most emphasize features and used as the input to the next stage. In regression module, they deployed Temporal Convolutional Networks [1,11] to learn temporal relationship between frames instead of RNN based architecture to take advantage of parallelism, low memory training, and stable gradients. Then they use fully connected layers to obtain the final score for each emotion categories. Their best performance is achieved by the weighted average of results from different based feature extractor. Figure 4 show a visualization of their approach.

4.3   Team Scalable

They utilized Inception-ResNet-v2 [12] and Xception [3] as feature extractor. For visual information, they deployed both sequential model which involves LSTM layers, and frame-level model which average the results from each frame. They converted audio signals to logspectrogram, then fed them to the deep networks. They used Adam algorithm as optimizer and the learning rate is follow SGDR, a warm restart technique [9] to optimize their architecture. They achieved best performance with the ensemble of both audio and visual signals. Figure 4 show an illustration of their approach (Fig. 5).

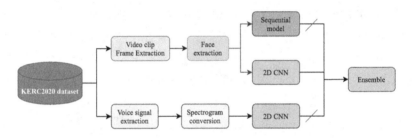

Fig. 5. An illustration of team scalable's approach.

5   Conclusion

Through the KERC2020, we promoted the development and interest of Korean emotion recognition technologies, and make a success. In particular, this competition focused on the topic of stress, especially for Korean people's stress. We provided participants with our dataset and baseline model to build and develop their own systems. As a result, various participants developed high performance methods. We will host the 3rd KERC competition in this year of 2021 again to make a grater growth in the field of Korean emotion recognition.

Acknowledgments. This work was supported by the National Research Foundation of Korea (NRF) grant funded by the Korea government (MSIT) (NRF-2020R1A4A1019191) and by the Korea Sanhak Foundation and the University Industrial Technology Force (UNITEF) Support Group.

References

1. Bai, S., Kolter, J.Z., Koltun, V.: An empirical evaluation of generic convolutional and recurrent networks for sequence modeling, March 2018
2. Cao, Q., Shen, L., Xie, W., Parkhi, O.M., Zisserman, A.: VGGFace2: a dataset for recognising faces across pose and age. In: 2018 13th IEEE International Conference on Automatic Face & Gesture Recognition (FG 2018). IEEE, May 2018. https://doi.org/10.1109/fg.2018.00020
3. Chollet, F.: Xception: deep learning with depthwise separable convolutions. In: 2017 IEEE Conference on Computer Vision and Pattern Recognition (CVPR). IEEE, July 2017. https://doi.org/10.1109/cvpr.2017.195
4. Gemmeke, J.F., et al.: Audio set: an ontology and human-labeled dataset for audio events. In: 2017 IEEE International Conference on Acoustics, Speech and Signal Processing (ICASSP). IEEE, March 2017. https://doi.org/10.1109/icassp.2017.7952261
5. He, K., Zhang, X., Ren, S., Sun, J.: Deep residual learning for image recognition. In: 2016 IEEE Conference on Computer Vision and Pattern Recognition (CVPR). IEEE, June 2016. https://doi.org/10.1109/cvpr.2016.90
6. Hu, P., Ramanan, D.: Finding tiny faces. In: 2017 IEEE Conference on Computer Vision and Pattern Recognition (CVPR). IEEE, July 2017. https://doi.org/10.1109/cvpr.2017.166
7. Khanh, T.L.B., Kim, S.H., Lee, G., Yang, H.J., Baek, E.T.: Korean video dataset for emotion recognition in the wild. Multimed. Tools Appl. (2020). https://doi.org/10.1007/s11042-020-10106-1
8. Kossaifi, J., Tzimiropoulos, G., Todorovic, S., Pantic, M.: AFEW-VA database for valence and arousal estimation in-the-wild. Image Vis. Comput. **65**, 23–36 (2017). https://doi.org/10.1016/j.imavis.2017.02.001
9. Loshchilov, I., Hutter, F.: SGDR: stochastic gradient descent with warm restarts, August 2016
10. Mollahosseini, A., Hasani, B., Mahoor, M.H.: AffectNet: a database for facial expression, valence, and arousal computing in the wild. IEEE Trans. Affect. Comput. **10**(1), 18–31 (2019). https://doi.org/10.1109/taffc.2017.2740923
11. van den Oord, A., et al.: WaveNet: a generative model for raw audio, September 2016
12. Szegedy, C., Ioffe, S., Vanhoucke, V., Alemi, A.: Inception-v4, inception-ResNet and the impact of residual connections on learning, February 2016
13. Zhang, K., Zhang, Z., Li, Z., Qiao, Y.: Joint face detection and alignment using multitask cascaded convolutional networks. IEEE Signal Process. Lett. **23**(10), 1499–1503 (2016). https://doi.org/10.1109/lsp.2016.2603342

Crack Detection and Location Estimation Using a Convolutional Neural Network

Mengling Ding and Kwanghee Won[✉]

South Dakota State University, Brookings, SD 57006, USA
{mengling.ding,kwanghee.won}@sdstate.edu

Abstract. In this paper, we present a CNN-based crack detection approach. Instead of classifying each pixel or an entire image patch, the proposed approach evaluates 48 predefined image stripes (in horizontal, vertical, and diagonal directions), and determine whether each area contains a part of crack or not. In the experiment, the CNN trained with about 1200 labeled images showed 75.9% of detection accuracy.

Keywords: Crack detection · Convolutional Neural Network · Deep learning

1 Introduction

Computer vision techniques have been widely used in developing automated infrastructure health monitoring systems. Cracking is one of the important deficiencies and the development of an automated crack mapping system with imaging sensors has been a challenging application of computer vision technique. Due to the recent advances in deep learning techniques, the development of these systems have been successful. Moreover, the technique enables data-driven development of such a system via end-to-end training instead of designing features or setting up threshold values.

Convolutional Neural Networks (CNNs) designed for image classification have been used for crack detection. The approach divides an input image into smaller patches. A CNN classifies small image patches into two categories, patches with and without crack(s) [5]. The approach is straightforward and easy to implement. However, the location of crack is represented as the location of the image patch. It does not provide exact location of cracks within a patch. The smaller patches can give the finer location information, however, in general, the accuracy of classification may become worse because the smaller patch may fail to represent global shape of a crack. Alternatively, a reasonable size patch centered at each pixel can be fed into a deep neural network. This approach classifies each pixel instead of image patch and produces pixel-level crack map. However, more computation is unavoidable because it classifies image patches at every pixel location of an input image.

Deep neural networks designed for the image segmentation or object detection tasks can be alternatives to the patch classification approach [2,4,6]. The

© Springer Nature Switzerland AG 2021
H. Jeong and K. Sumi (Eds.): IW-FCV 2021, CCIS 1405, pp. 184–188, 2021.
https://doi.org/10.1007/978-3-030-81638-4_15

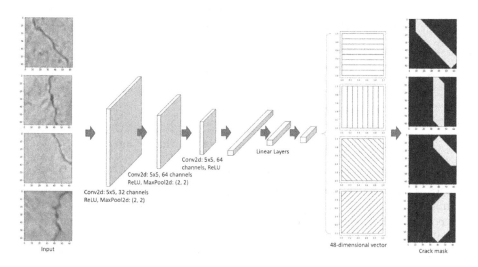

Fig. 1. CNN architecture and illustration of output of the neural network.

CNN architectures, such as fully convolutional neural network [7], U-Net [8], and Mask RCNN [3] can be used for the crack detection task. These networks require pixel-level labeling of the target objects. Also, for instance, the shape of anchors in the Mask RCNN implies that the target objects do not have crack-like shapes, which are irregular and thin.

In this paper, a simple CNN-based crack-detection approach has been proposed. It processes an image patch with a CNN and produces a bit-string that represents existence of cracks in each sub-region of the patch. The regions are stripes of multiple directions and are designed to be able to capture cracks. The classification of regions is combined and used as rough estimation of crack location. The proposed approach provides the finer resolution of location information than that of patch classifiers, and it does not require deconvolution layers nor pixel-level labeling of training data.

2   CNN Architecture for Classification of Image Regions

The input and output of the CNN are an image patch and an n-dimensional vector, respectively. Each element in the output vector represents whether a part(s) of cracks is in the regions or not. The concrete crack images in the SDNET2018 dataset has been used for training of the CNN model. About 1200 images of 256 by 256 pixels have been labeled using an online labeling platform, Labelbox [1]. In the labeling process, cracks are represented by line segments. In training of the CNN model, patches of 64 by 64 pixels have been generated from the labeled

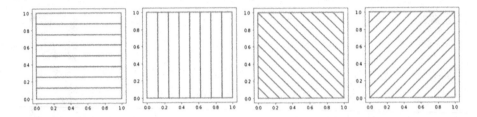

Fig. 2. Horizontal, vertical, and diagonal stripes of interests.

images. The data augmentation techniques have been applied to populate more training data (flipped and rotated image patches). The line segments are converted to 48-dimensional vectors depending on whether a corresponding region contains a part of line segments (1) or not (0). The areas represented by the 48-dimensional vectors are 8 stripes for each vertical, horizontal directions, and 16 stripes for each of 45° and 135° as depicted in Fig. 2. The stripes in various locations and orientations are well suited for representing cracks. The vector can be converted to a mask (crack map) by filling out 1's for all the regions of value 1, and then filling out 0's for all the regions of value 0. Figure 1 illustrates an example of labeled cracks and the corresponding generated mask.

3   Experimental Results

The proposed approach and data preprocessing steps have been implemented using Python language and Pytorch. The annotation of cracks are lists of line segments in the image coordinate. The bit strings were obtained by computing the intersection of line segments and the regions. About 400K image patches and corresponding vectors were collected and used for training the CNN model, and 20% of the data was used as testing data. The MSE loss function and the stochastic gradient descent method were used in training the CNN. Each mini-batch was 64 image patches. Parameters such as the learning rate and the momentum value were set to 0.001 and 0.9, respectively. Figure 2 shows example outputs of the trained CNN. The values in the output vector are converted to 1 if they are greater than 0.5, otherwise, they are 0.

The detection accuracy of the CNN was measured for the test data (20% of the entire data). The Intersection over Union (IoU) was measured for each image by comparing the detection result and the true mask. For the IoU value, 0.9 and greater, the accuracy was 75.9 %, and for the IoU value, 0.8 and greater, the accuracy was 77.3 % (Figs. 3 and 4).

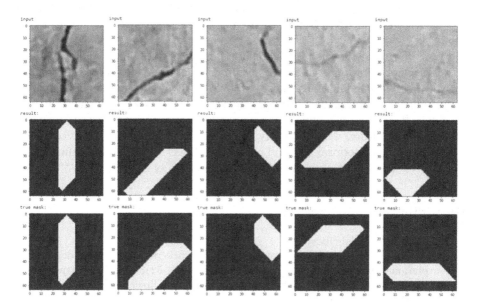

Fig. 3. Crack detection results: input images (top), output mask (middle), true mask (bottom).

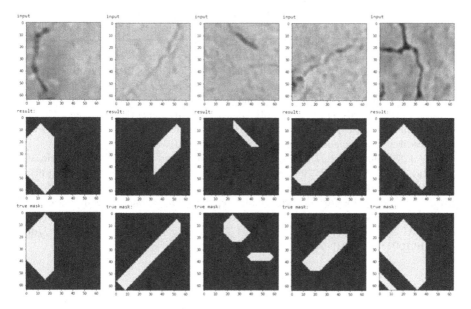

Fig. 4. Additional crack detection results: input images (top), output mask (middle), true mask (bottom).

4   Conclusion and Future Work

In this study, an off-the-shelf CNN architecture has been modified and trained to estimate rough location of cracks in an input image. The location of cracks are represented by a combination of horizontal, vertical, and diagonal image regions. In experiments, the trained CNN was able to detect cracks with the accuracy of 75.9%. The proposed approach was not able to represent curved, concave shapes. In the future, we will modify the 48 regions to represent more complex cracks and we will perform a neural network architecture search to optimize the parameters such as the number of layers and the size of kernels.

References

1. Labelbox. https://labelbox.com/
2. Dung, C.V., Anh, L.D.: Autonomous concrete crack detection using deep fully convolutional neural network. Autom. Constr. **99**, 52–58 (2019). https://doi.org/10.1016/j.autcon.2018.11.028.   http://www.sciencedirect.com/science/article/pii/S0926580518306745
3. He, K., Gkioxari, G., Dollár, P., Girshick, R.: Mask R-CNN. In: 2017 IEEE International Conference on Computer Vision (ICCV), pp. 2980–2988 (2017). https://doi.org/10.1109/ICCV.2017.322
4. Islam, M.M.M., Kim, J.M.: Vision-based autonomous crack detection of concrete structures using a fully convolutional encoder-decoder network. Sensors **19**(2019). https://doi.org/10.3390/s19194251
5. Li, S., Zhao, X.: Image-based concrete crack detection using convolutional neural network and exhaustive search technique. Adv. Civil Eng. **2019** (2019). https://doi.org/10.1155/2019/6520620
6. Liu, Z., Cao, Y., Wang, Y., Wang, W.: Computer vision-based concrete crack detection using U-net fully convolutional networks. Autom. Constr. **104**, 129–139 (2019). https://doi.org/10.1016/j.autcon.2019.04.005. http://www.sciencedirect.com/science/article/pii/S0926580519301244
7. Long, J., Shelhamer, E., Darrell, T.: Fully convolutional networks for semantic segmentation. In: 2015 IEEE Conference on Computer Vision and Pattern Recognition (CVPR), pp. 3431–3440 (2015). https://doi.org/10.1109/CVPR.2015.7298965
8. Ronneberger, O., Fischer, P., Brox, T.: U-Net: convolutional networks for biomedical image segmentation. In: Navab, N., Hornegger, J., Wells, W.M., Frangi, A.F. (eds.) MICCAI 2015. LNCS, vol. 9351, pp. 234–241. Springer, Cham (2015). https://doi.org/10.1007/978-3-319-24574-4_28

Rice Leaf Diseases Recognition Based on Deep Learning and Hyperparameters Customization

Van-Dung Hoang[(✉)]

Faculty of Information Technology, HCMC University of Technology and Education,
Ho Chi Minh City 700000, Vietnam
dunghv@hcmute.edu.vn

Abstract. Rice disease prediction plays important task for automated rice disease recognition systems. Feature extraction and classification based on deep learning play important tasks in vision-based diseases recognition. The advancement of deep convolutional neural network using mage data illustrates the approach for identification of rice diseases using deep features with the expectation of high returns. Instead of fine-tuning task which concerns estimation of internal parameters of a model to adjust precisely with certain observations. This paper focuses on extrinsic parameters for model training, which utilities for improving precise of recognition system. Some pretrain models AlexNet, ResNet101 were implemented as mainstream of the convolutional neural network (CNN) architecture. Our approach directly estimates locations of features based on deep learning classification for of rice leaf diseases recognition. There are four kinds of the rice diseases investigated, such as rice blast, bacterial leaf blight, alum poisoning, and leaf folder. A large dataset resolution images from real scenes in the farm were collected for training and evaluation. In this study, the augmentation of image also applied for evaluation input images. The output prediction results of set samples are used for voting final decision. The experimental results show that the proposed approach with hyperparameters customization and data augmentation outperforms.

Keywords: Deep learning · Smart agricultural · Rice leaf diseases

1 Introduction

In the rice cultivation, there are many difficulties such as preventing insects and diseases of rice plants. Rice disease prediction is key task in automated rice disease recognition systems. Many kinds of insects and diseases still do not have special treatment drugs, diagnose, and classify diseases for proper disease control. Early prediction of insects and diseases is very important task that allow to be zoned and sprayed more effective in private zone. This issue is concerned by many individuals and research organizations. Technology is constantly developing with new ideas about artificial intelligence and has created new products with practical value in daily life. Numerous studies have been concretized in the fields of robotics, automation, intelligent assistance systems, smart

© Springer Nature Switzerland AG 2021
H. Jeong and K. Sumi (Eds.): IW-FCV 2021, CCIS 1405, pp. 189–200, 2021.
https://doi.org/10.1007/978-3-030-81638-4_16

farm application and so on. Developing artificial neural networks capable of intelligent and asymptotic values similar to the human brain has become a major research trend. Thus, CNN models have become a relevant topic due to their capacity for automatically adjusting to diverse specific circumstances.

In this study, we focus on the problem of identifying specific insects and diseases, based on extracting the target area of interest by application AI techniques for classifying and predicting some kinds of insects and diseases in rice plants. The solution uses AI based on the deep CNN model to extract image features and detection of disease manifestation for treatment, which supports to prevent spreading out of rice insects and diseases. The study presents an approach based on combination of image processing and deep learning technique that improves the accuracy of the recognition system. The paper proposes a network architecture and an approach for optimizing parameters support for improving the efficiency of the recognition model. In this study, we have experimentally studied the effect of data augmentation on machine learning classifiers and tried to answer the question of whether data augmentation should be used to improve disease classification performance.

2 Related Works

Recent studies have resulted in recognition solutions with high accuracy and fast training and processing speeds, especially the Deep neural network (DNN) model. Deep DNN was generally considered the state-of-the-art solution in image recognition. Popular CNN recognition models are considered as the research foundation. They include GoogleNet [1], Microsoft ResNet [2], Fast R-CNN [3], Faster R-CNN [4], and so on. Based on these models, several new developments to improve the accuracy and enhance the processing speed of the system are now available. Select detection models: These solutions focus on the automatic selection of recognition model types without using a specific default model. The selection of training models will make it possible to solve each specific case of the data and provide greater accuracy. In addition, these solutions also allow assessment of data types, data models, and so on for automatic selection of an appropriate model [5, 6]. For improving prediction capacity of the system, some potential research based on the CNN approach learn and customize models so that they resemble the behavior model of the human mind. There are many studies regarding online tracking that adjust data to track objects or extract features of these objects [5, 7]. The paper [8] presents a method using adaptive learning based an object tracking process, collecting appropriate data, and automatically retraining the recognition model as a solution to enhance automatic recognition quality of objects. In another approach in [9], we proposed a hybrid machines of CNN for feature extraction and SVM for classification task.

Solving problem with algorithms and parameters is solution focusing on algorithms and parameters of CNN models, which creates architecture changes in CNN layers and then training the model with optimal parameters. Specifically, some proposals centralize building frames that are embedded in different layer positions to change weights in the training and recognition process of the CNN model. Some other contribution on changing features local depth features to achieve model simplification or changing features between convolutional layers and customizing layers [10, 11]. General speaking, the research aims to optimize the structure of the CNN model. The changes in layer customization have resulted in positive changes for training. Recently, several proposals have focused on the automatic selection of training process parameters [12]. Among them, one solution initially used a small dataset to evaluate the parameters' effectiveness before selecting the appropriate parameters and conducting training evaluation on the entire data [7]. A different solution used the random search method of parameters before conducting cross-validation on a given number of times to choose parameters matching the recognition model [13]. Furthermore, a combination of evolutionary algorithms to automatically optimize CNN structure by hyperparameters was used in one study [14]. Regarding the configuration hyperparameter selection of a CNN model, methods using the random search [15], the grid search, Bayer algorithms [16, 17] are the most notable.

Some of the recent researchers related to the recognition and classification of rice plant diseases are presented as follow: Deep feature-based rice leaf disease identification using support vector machine [18]. Authors presented and evaluated on 5.932 on-field images with four types of rice leaf diseases, which are bacterial blight, blast, brown spot and Tungro. For evaluated disease prediction, the performance on 11 CNN models in transfer learning approach and deep feature extraction + SVM was processed. The recognition and classification of paddy leaf diseases using optimized DNN work with Jaya algorithm was investigated in [19]. The image dataset of rice plant leaves was directly captured and collected from the farm field for normal, which included some kinds of disease such as bacterial blight, brown spot, sheath rot and blast diseases. The preprocessing was applied for background removal. HSV images were used based on the hue and saturation parts binary images are extracted to split the diseased and non-diseased part. The diseased portion segmentation for normal portion and background based on some clustering methods. Finally, they classifier diseases based on using optimized DNN with Jaya optimization algorithm. A feedback loop was generated in the post processing step for improving precise the stability of the proposed approach. For the evaluation of ROI, there are many approaches. A segmentation technique based on neutrosophic logic extended from the fuzzy set was introduced in [20]. Three membership functions for the segmentation were applied, supports to detect the plant leaf diseased and subsets feature were considered on the segmented regions. Various classifiers were investigated and studied for the demonstration and the random forest method overcome the other approaches. For experiment, a dataset with 400 leaf images which included 200 positive sample and 200 negative samples were collected.

Another approach also investigated for a novel rice plant disease detection approach based on the basis of DNN, which presented in [21]. The dataset for experiment contains 500 images include diseased and non-diseased paddy stems and leaves, with ten common rice diseases. Experimental evaluation showed that their approach attained higher accuracy than the conventional machine learning method. Meanwhile, a group of researchers in [22] studied the results of the effeteness of four different transfer learning models for DNN-based plant classification on four public datasets. The experimental evaluation demonstrated that transfer learning provided important benefits for automated plant recognition and it can be improved low performance plant recognition models. In the field of rice blast disease, the group in [23] presented an approach using a DCNN. The results illustrated that the method reach higher accuracy rate. Zhang et al. in [24] presented an approach for improving the identification accuracy of maize leaf diseases and reducing the number of network parameters. There are two improved models were used to train and test to nine kinds of maize leaf images. The goal of approach is adjusting the parameters, changing the pooling combinations, adding dropout operations and rectified linear unit functions, and reducing the number of classifiers. The key task of their contribution is DNN architecture with the number of parameters is significantly smaller than that of the VGG and AlexNet architecture.

3   Proposed Disease Recognition

In this study, we propose an insect and disease classification system, which consisting of three main components: data enhancement, the feature extraction module, and disease identification stage. The overall architecture is shown in the following (Fig. 1):

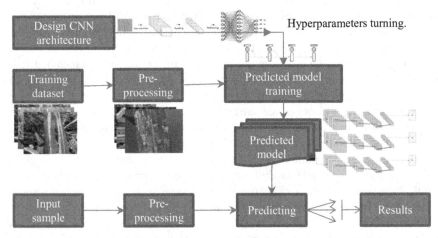

Fig. 1. Overview of rice disease recognition system

In this study, the DNN learner consists of 27 layers, which include some kinds of layers image input layer, convolutional layer, rectified linear unit layer, cross normalization, pooling layer, fully connection layer, classification output layer. They transform the input image into a serial hierarchical feature descriptor. The input data are a set of pixel intensities of an image, which is fed into deep network. The image input data consist of $400 \times 400 \times 3$ resolution. In this model, the filters at the first layer are corresponding to three color channels. Filters are independent connecting to each other, which related to three channels of the input image.

In classification task, there are some approaches, such as using DNN for fully feature extraction and classification, and another approach using DNN and SVM. In the second approach, the output of a full connection network layer is used as vector features to SVM. The SVM method is significant perform in image classification task. The main advantage of the SVM technique is its ability to extract highly discriminative profits.

The problem underfitting of recognition model related training dataset, which does not cover all situations of real application. In the real application, experts may have a dataset of images taken in a limited set of conditions, but our target application may exist in a variety of conditions, such as different orientation, location, scale, brightness etc. To deal with this problem, data augmentation is a good option. Data is augmented with expected to overcome the real-world scenario in practical application. This essentially is the premise of data augmentation. We account for these situations by training recognition model with additional synthetically modified data.

In general speaking, the DNN method requires a large amount of data for training to be effective recognition model. However, in this problem there is little and imbalance training dataset. Therefore, to improve the quality of identification effectively we propose a solution for enhancement image set based on data augmentation technique.

There are widely approaches which are used by not only natural image classification but also specific domain application such as [25, 26]. This is the easiest and most common method to mitigate overfitting problem of scarcity of labeled dataset. The most importance concept of image augmentation is that the deformations applied to the annotated data do not change the semantic meaning of the labels. In this study, three types of data augmentation are implemented. Color normalization and correction: the rice leaf images were collected from in the natural scene with different light resources and they were created by different types of device such cellphone, camera. Therefore, color normalization and correction are very important for improving performance of prediction system. Geometric transformation approach is applied to scale and transform position within the image still maintains the semantic meaning of the character of the leaf diseases and the signal of the insects. Therefore, input images were transformed to generate new samples with the same label of original one by random combination of cropping and horizontal, vertical flips. In current research, the data augmentation module combines these three types of augmentation in two steps. Firstly, the authors normalize input image by adding multiples a converting all pixels into [−1.0, 1.0] range to create normalized data. Secondly, the authors combine cropping, scaling, distorting and horizontal, vertical flips processes in one step to augment the normalized data. In this step, the authors apply random parameters of each function to generate samples from original one. In machine learning, affine transformations such as shearing, distorting, and scaling randomly warp stroke data for image classification [27, 28]. Thus, warping is very well suited to augment data for improving performance and mitigating overfitting of disease classification. Data warping based on the knowledge of agriculture specialists. In this approach, the fact that the agriculture specialist's recognition is performed over the observation of the patterns around the ROI.

4 Hyperparameters Optimization and Data Imbalance

Hyperparameters optimization is concerning the task of estimation appropriate hyperparameters for training deep learning models to extract the last juice out of recognition models. In the task of machine training its model, it requires some different constraints, weights or learning rates, lose function formulation, the method for evaluation convergence and their formula and so on to generalize different data patterns [29]. These hyperparameters need to be tuned so that the model reaches optimally solution of the recognition machine. These hyperparameters determined the quality, time, and more of the training process of a CNN model. These hyperparameters were the important ones that could change and adapting to new datasets, directly affecting the accuracy of the post-trained CNN model. Bayesian approach focuses the task of tuning and finding the best hyperparameters for optimal prediction. In this situation, minimizing the loss function of the model based on turning model parameters. Bayesian optimization method helps us find the minimal point in the minimum number of steps. Bayesian optimization approach also uses an acquisition function which sampling to areas where an improvement over the current best observation is likely. In the case of data imbalance, the majority class loss decreases rapidly in the first iterations, while the minority error increases, which ended up making networks very difficult to converge. Therefore, deep learning approaches to solve an unbalanced dataset have been applied, such as data-level methods, algorithm-level methods, and hybrid methods.

The approach based on oversampling, which randomly increases the samples of the minority classes until their proportions are equal to those of the majority class. The increasing training dataset is repeated until no class has samples smaller than the largest one. This is where the balance is reached. The impact of imbalanced training dataset to recognition system performance in image classification has been investigated by [27]. In their study, the CNN trained on the imbalanced dataset, which created from CIFAR-10 dataset and suggested that oversampling is an effective approach to deal with the impact of imbalances in the training data.

Another approach based on subsampling, which randomly removes samples from the majority classes until they weigh equally to the minority class. The removal task is repeated to until all majority classes is equal to the smallest lass. The repeated is sopped when the dataset to become the balance. The random subsampling of large-sized classes method is used to reduce class imbalance for pre-training a Deep CNN [30]. The method proposed by them demonstrated significant improvement in classification accuracy compared to CNN with and without data augmentation techniques. Algorithm level methods modify deep learning algorithms for handling class imbalance. These methods consist of new loss functions [31, 32]. As they do not make changes to the training data and do not require much data pre-processing, algorithm-level methods make less impact to the data compared to the data level methods, and therefore become better suggestions for big data problems. Except for the misclassification cost definition, these methods require almost no tuning.

5   Experimental Results

Data for experiment for this research: Acquisition of images were captured in natural scene of agriculture farms. The rice plant leaf images were captured by using high resolution digital camera, cellphone in the farm field in real circumstances. Diseases of all the captured images are moved to the computer where the implementation process will be carried out. The dataset contains the images having the leaves with various degree of disease spread. The images are captured, prepared totally with 2.289 images which include 255 blast images, 715 bacterial leaf blight images, 1.042 rice alum poisoning images and 277 leaf-folder images. Some of the sample images are given in Fig. 2. To avoid duplicates and ensure label quality, each image in our dataset is examined and confirmed by rice experts. All the rice images are processed and unified to the same size of 400 × 400 pixels, which extracted from original larger images. In addition to scale, rotation, illumination and viewpoint changes, the dataset also has the following characteristics. The background of rice canopy texture, water body, and soil can cause great difficulty to recognition, as do dead leaf and other plant lesion. Overall, the combination of above factors poses significant challenges for rice disease recognition.

In this experiment, image dataset was divided to training set and testing set, with 60% of samples for training and 40% of samples for testing, as shown in Table 1 and Table 2. For the training dataset, to create balance and universality of the data, we performed a maximum data boost of up to 8 times and created a balance between disease types after zero differences more than 1/3 in pairs of diseases.

(a) Rice blast   (b) Bacterial leaf blight

(c) leaf-folder   (d) Alum poisoning

Fig. 2. Some example datasets of rice leaf diseases

Table 1. Training dataset

	Rice blast	Bacterial leaf blight	Alum poisoning	Leaf folder
Original images	153	429	625	166
Augmentation	1.377	1.716	1.876	1.498

Table 2. Evaluation dataset

Rice blast	Bacterial leaf blight	Alum poisoning	Leaf folder
102	286	417	111

In the training part, there are many approaches for construction a deep network for rice disease recognition. Some pretrain models can be applied in the special situation of application by retrained the model. In this study, we design a small CNN architecture, which is faster than the bigger one, such as Restnet101, VGG19. In our approach, there model architecture is not suitable due to flowing reasons.

Our method processes on both original image and augmented proposal that results different input samples. For visualization parameter results of training, 32 filters of the first convolution layer are illustrated in Fig. 3. The outputs of some layers are shown in Fig. 4, which responds to input image sample.

Fig. 3. Parameter weighting of 7×7 size of 32 filters of the first convolution layer.

(a) weights of kernel filters of the first convolutional layer (layer 2nd).

(b) weights of 32 kernel filters of the second convolutional layer (layer 6nd).

Fig. 4. Activations results of some special layers using the proposed model.

To evaluate the effectiveness of a classification model, we have many evaluation parameters, depending on each problem and the purpose of use, there are different evaluation criteria. Another way to describe a relationship between sensitivity and specificity is a receiver operating characteristic (ROC) chart. The ROC plot has the y-axis which is the positive-true ratio, and the x-axis is the false positive ratio, such as false positive identification. Both these scale values range from 0 to 100 or 0 to 1 in the probability value.

AP (Average Precision): Average accuracy. SEN criterion (Sensitivity): This is the criterion referring to the ability to test to accurately detect the disease assessment sample. The sensitivity of the test is the proportion of those tested positive for the disease in infected plants. This criterion can be calculated using the following formula:

$$\text{Sensitivity} = \frac{\text{True positive}}{\text{positive}} \tag{1}$$

Specificity criteria (SPC): The SPC criterion involves the ability to check the accuracy of samples without real illness without any additional conditions. The specificity of the assessment of the one sample rate of an uninfected plant that is determined to be free of the disease, this plant will be assessed as negative with the current disease. The criterion can be calculated using the following formula:

$$\text{Specificity} = \frac{\text{True negative}}{\text{negative}} \tag{2}$$

The positive predictive value (PPV) criterion is used to indicate the probability that a sample evaluates the positive sample of that tree is positive. PPV depends on 3 indicators: prevalence, sensitivity, and specificity. The formula for PPV is as follows:

$$\text{PPV} = \frac{\text{True positive}}{\text{True positive} + \text{False positive}} \tag{3}$$

Kappa value criterion concerns a measure of how well the classifier performed as compared to it would have performed simply by chance. That means a model reaches high Kappa score if there is a big difference between the accuracy and the error rate. Some comparison results of recognition system when use and not use the stage of hyperparameters customization are shown in (Fig. 5 and Table 3).

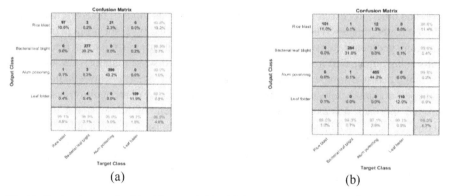

Fig. 5. Evaluation results (a) without and (b) with hyperparameters customization for training

Table 3. Comparision of recognition system without and with hyperparameters customization

	Non customizing	Customizing
Accuracy	95.96%	98.25%
Sensitivity	96.28%	98.64%
Specificity	98.77%	99.48%
Precision	93.07%	96.77%
False positive rate	1.23%	0.52%
F1_score	94.50%	97.63%
Kappa score	89.23%	95.34%

6 Conclusion

Rice disease and insect recognition are challenging due to containing more categories of diseases and variety of noises. This paper introduced an approach for rice leaf disease and insect recognition based on DNN with hyperparameters customization and data augmentation. The designed DNN architecture consists of 27 layers, $400 \times 400 \times x3$ neutrals of input layer, 5 convolution layers with 7×7 kernel size and three full connected layers and other processed layers. The DNN works well on input of both original image and augmented images. The training data were augmented by color normalization and correction, geometric transformation such as rotation, shearing, stretching. Recognition results using augmented images are used for voting for disease diagnosis decision. The fine-tuning task to estimate of external parameters of training task is investigated for the best hyperparameters selection utilities for improving precise of recognition system. The proposed approach was experimented on the natural scene of dataset rice leaf diseases and insects such as rice blast, bacterial leaf blight, alum poisoning, and leaf folder, which collected from real scenes of farms. The experimental results show that our approach by construction of DNN, fine tuning hyperparameters and augmenting data for improving effective and efficiency of the recognition system.

References

1. Szegedy, C., Liu, W., Jia, Y., et al.: Going deeper with convolutions. In: Proceedings of the IEEE Conference on Computer Vision and Pattern Recognition, pp. 1–9 (2015)
2. He, K., Zhang, X., Ren, S., Sun, J.: Deep residual learning for image recognition. In: Proceedings of IEEE Conference on Computer Vision and Pattern Recognition, pp. 770–778 (2016)
3. Girshick, R.: Fast R-CNN, arXiv Prepr arXiv:150408083 (2015)
4. Ren, S., He, K., Girshick, R., Sun, J.: Faster R-CNN: towards real-time object detection with region proposal networks. IEEE Trans. Pattern Anal. Mach. Intell. **39**, 1137–1149 (2017)
5. Li, L., Talwalkar, A.: Random search and reproducibility for neural architecture search. In: Uncertainty in Artificial Intelligence. PMLR, pp. 367–377 (2020)

6. Bertrand, H., Ardon, R., Perrot, M., Bloch, I.: Hyperparameter optimization of deep neural networks: combining hyperband with Bayesian model selection. In: Conférence sur l'Apprentissage Automatique (2017)

7. Domhan, T., Springenberg, J.T., Hutter, F.: Speeding up automatic hyperparameter optimization of deep neural networks by extrapolation of learning curves. In: Twenty-Fourth International Joint Conference on Artificial Intelligence (2015)

8. Tran, D.-P., Hoang, V.-D.: Adaptive learning based on tracking and reidentifying objects using convolutional neural network. Neural Process. Lett. **50**(1), 263–282 (2019). https://doi.org/10.1007/s11063-019-10040-w

9. Hoang, V.-D., Le, M.-H., Tran, T.T., Pham, V.-H.: Improving traffic signs recognition based region proposal and deep neural networks. In: Nguyen, N.T., Hoang, D.H., Hong, T.-P., Pham, H., Trawiński, B. (eds.) Intelligent Information and Database Systems, pp. 604–613. Springer International Publishing, Cham (2018). https://doi.org/10.1007/978-3-319-75420-8_57

10. Huang, C., Lucey, S., Ramanan, D.: Learning policies for adaptive tracking with deep feature cascades, pp. 105–114 (2017)

11. Long, M., Cao, Y., Cao, Z., Wang, J., Jordan, M.I.: Transferable representation learning with deep adaptation networks. IEEE Trans. Pattern Anal. Mach. Intell. **41**(12), 3071–3085 (2019). https://doi.org/10.1109/TPAMI.2018.2868685

12. Snoek, J., Rippel, O., Swersky, K., et al.: Scalable Bayesian optimization using deep neural networks. In: International Conference on Machine Learning. PMLR, pp. 2171–2180 (2015)

13. Le, N.Q.K., Huynh, T.-T., Yapp, E.K.Y., Yeh, H.-Y.: Identification of clathrin proteins by incorporating hyperparameter optimization in deep learning and PSSM profiles. Comput. Methods Programs Biomed. **177**, 81–88 (2019)

14. Bochinski, E., Senst, T., Sikora, T.: Hyper-parameter optimization for convolutional neural network committees based on evolutionary algorithms. In: 2017 IEEE International Conference on Image Processing (ICIP), pp. 3924–3928. IEEE (2017)

15. Florea, A.-C., Andonie, R.: Weighted random search for hyperparameter optimization. arXiv Prepr arXiv:200401628 (2020)

16. Kotthoff, L., Thornton, C., Hoos, H.H., Hutter, F., Leyton-Brown, K.: Auto-WEKA: automatic model selection and hyperparameter optimization in WEKA. In: Hutter, F., Kotthoff, L., Vanschoren, J. (eds.) Automated Machine Learning: Methods, Systems, Challenges, pp. 81–95. Springer International Publishing, Cham (2019). https://doi.org/10.1007/978-3-030-053 18-5_4

17. Dikov, G., Bayer, J.: Bayesian learning of neural network architectures. In: The 22nd International Conference on Artificial Intelligence and Statistics, PMLR, pp. 730–738 (2019)

18. Sethy, P.K., Barpanda, N.K., Rath, A.K., Behera, S.K.: Deep feature based rice leaf disease identification using support vector machine. Comput. Electron. Agric. **175**, 105527 (2020)

19. Ramesh, S., Vydeki, D.: Recognition and classification of paddy leaf diseases using optimized deep neural network with Jaya algorithm. Inf. Process. Agric. **7**, 249–260 (2020)

20. Dhingra, G., Kumar, V., Joshi, H.D.: A novel computer vision based neutrosophic approach for leaf disease identification and classification. Measurement **135**, 782–794 (2019)

21. Lu, Y., Yi, S., Zeng, N., et al.: Identification of rice diseases using deep convolutional neural networks. Neurocomputing **267**, 378–384 (2017)

22. Kaya, A., Keceli, A.S., Catal, C., et al.: Analysis of transfer learning for deep neural network based plant classification models. Comput. Electron. Agric. **158**, 20–29 (2019)

23. Liang, W., Zhang, H., Zhang, G., Cao, H.: Rice blast disease recognition using a deep convolutional neural network. Sci. Rep. **9**, 1–10 (2019)

24. Zhang, X., Qiao, Y., Meng, F., et al.: Identification of maize leaf diseases using improved deep convolutional neural networks. IEEE Access **6**, 30370–30377 (2018)

25. Pham, T.-C., Doucet, A., Luong, C.-M., et al.: Improving skin-disease classification based on customized loss function combined with balanced mini-batch logic and real-time image augmentation. IEEE Access **8**, 150725–150737 (2020)
26. Hoang, V.-D., Jo, K.-H.: Path planning for autonomous vehicle based on heuristic searching using online images. Vietnam J. Comput. Sci. **2**(2), 109–120 (2014). https://doi.org/10.1007/s40595-014-0035-4
27. Wong, S.C., Gatt, A., Stamatescu, V., McDonnell, M.D.: Understanding data augmentation for classification: when to warp? In: 2016 International Conference on Digital Image Computing: Techniques and Applications (DICTA), pp. 1–6. IEEE (2016)
28. Hoang, V.-D., Hoang, V.-T., Jo, K.-H.: Hybrid deep learning and data augmentation for disease candidate extraction. In: Ohyama, W., Jung, S.K. (eds.) IW-FCV 2020. CCIS, vol. 1212, pp. 274–286. Springer, Singapore (2020). https://doi.org/10.1007/978-981-15-4818-5_21
29. Tran, D.-P., Nguyen, G.-N., Hoang, V.-D.: Hyperparameter optimization for improving recognition efficiency of an adaptive learning system. IEEE Access **8**, 160569–160580 (2020)
30. Lee, H., Park, M., Kim, J.: Plankton classification on imbalanced large scale database via convolutional neural networks with transfer learning. In: 2016 IEEE International Conference on Image Processing (ICIP), pp. 3713–3717. IEEE (2016)
31. Wang, S., Liu, W., Wu, J., et al.: Training deep neural networks on imbalanced data sets. In: 2016 International Joint Conference on Neural Networks (IJCNN), pp. 4368–4374. IEEE (2016)
32. Wang, X., Cheng, P., Liu, X., Uzochukwu, B.: Focal loss dense detector for vehicle surveillance. In: 2018 International Conference on Intelligent Systems and Computer Vision (ISCV), pp. 1–5. IEEE (2018)

Human Behaviour

ST-GCN Based Human Action Recognition with Abstracted Three Features of Optical Flow and Image Gradient

Han-Byul Jang⬡ and Chil-Woo Lee$^{(\boxtimes)}$ ⬡

Chonnam National University, Yongbong-ro 77, Buk-gu, Gwangju, Republic of Korea
leecw@chonnam.ac.kr

Abstract. ST-GCN (Spatial temporal graph convolutional network) [1], which uses skeleton data as an input, enables efficient motion recognition because it can express the structural motion of the human body with neural network. However, if the correct skeleton data is not accurate, the network operation becomes unstable, and the recognition rate eventually drops. In this paper, we describe a new ST-GCN algorithm that can precisely recognize action using optical flow and image gradient, which can be obtained simply and stably from input image. Therefore, it has high robustness since it does not use skeleton data that can only be obtained by special devices or complex calculations. In the algorithm, firstly human body region is extracted from the continuous input image. And then optical flow and image gradient, namely the motion and posture information of the body, is obtained from partial regions (this is called Region of Motion: RoM) of the body region. The both data are described with a 16-dimensional HoG (Histogram of gradient) descriptor and it is converted into three features for being used for learning of the network. At this time, to express the scale change of the input information and the structural characteristics of the human body, the three features are combined into a graph structure that mimics the connection structure of the human body. In order to verify the performance of the proposed algorithm, an experiment was performed on 20 actions selected from the NTU RGB + D data set. As the result of the experiment, it was possible to obtain a Top-1 accuracy of 84.19%, equivalent to the existing method.

Keywords: Human action recognition · ST-GCN · Optical flow · Image gradient

1 Introduction

If we can automatically recognize people's daily actions by using computers, it can be used for application services in various fields. For example, it can be importantly used in fields such as intelligent surveillance systems, autonomous vehicles, service robots, smart hospitals, video content analysis, and so on. To take a more specific example, if the intelligent surveillance system can automatically recognize the scenes of beating a person, it will be possible to respond quickly and thus prevent serious violence.

© Springer Nature Switzerland AG 2021
H. Jeong and K. Sumi (Eds.): IW-FCV 2021, CCIS 1405, pp. 203–217, 2021.
https://doi.org/10.1007/978-3-030-81638-4_17

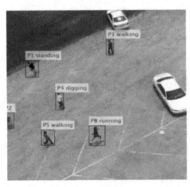

Spatial temporal graph

A) Example of human action recognition

B) Graph of Yan's ST-GCN[1]

Fig. 1. Example of human action recognition and Yan's ST-GCN [1]

In the previous human action recognition research using image, feature with good motion discrimination was extracted from training images and it has been used for the recognition. For the recognition, firstly a feature space was constructed by using the feature as basis vectors. Then, several methods which can perform recognition by comparing a distance between a feature vector of an input image and the vector of a predefined action model in the feature space have been used. However, the problem is that the methods have produced different recognition results depending on the used features which were artificially and intuitively defined by researchers. So, robust recognition result could not be obtained due to unstable features caused by changes in subject person, background, and illumination. In recent years, deep learning techniques based on artificial neural networks can be used to learn the multi-variability of images, so the performance of action recognition has improved. The deep learning technique does not artificially define features and realizes action recognition through artificial neural network learning using a large amount of data. So more natural and improved results can be obtained.

The study of Yan et al.' [1] is the first case of introducing ST-GCN to human action recognition. ST-GCN has the advantage of being able to express the meaning of the context of a problem in a graph structure since the path of information transmission in the learning process is defined by the connection structure of the graph. In action recognition research, it is possible to learn the structural changes of the human body with a neural network by expressing the coordinates of the skeleton joints of the human body that change spatio-temporally by using a graph structure which can mimic the posture of the human body as shown in the Fig. 1 (B).

As in Yan's research, human action recognition generally uses skeleton joint coordinate as input data. Skeleton data is information that records changes over time in three dimensional coordinate of skeleton joints and has the advantage of intuitively reflecting characteristics of actions but it has a problem of obtaining stable and accurate data. A common method of acquiring skeleton data is to use 3D camera equipment such as Kinect or specific software such as OPENPOSE [10]. However, it is difficult to obtain accurate skeleton's coordinate data for these methods because the environment conditions are sensitive so it is easy to produce errors. In particular, it is almost impossible to build systems which might be used in dynamic environment such as outdoor surveillance system.

In this paper, we propose a human action recognition algorithm based on ST-GCN using the optical flow and the image gradient data that can be acquired more stably and easily from input image instead of skeleton coordinate. The proposed algorithm is based on an assumption that actions can be easily recognized by capturing motions and posture of human body that have a special meaning in continuous motion. Consequently optical flow which is suitable for expressing the motion and image gradient which is useful for expressing posture, are selected as input data. In addition, it was hypothesized that if the input data could be acquired through various RoMs (Region of Motion) distributed in the person area (region of entire human body) and the information could be transformed into graph structure, the final result would be enough for a useful recognition result. And the connections in the graph of ST-GCN was designed to reflect the context of the action well to support such hypothesis. This graph has a connection structure that can effectively recognize various actions by structurally combining movement and the posture information acquired from RoM. The optical flow and image gradient information are extracted in 16-dimensional HoG descriptor format and from the HoG description three features are obtained. Through this conversion, the data dimension can be reduced and the resource consumption of neural network training can be saved largely. In this study as the three features, the histogram itself, mean, and standard deviation of the histogram are obtained, and it is used to the input channels.

The proposed algorithm was tested on 20 actions selected from the NTU-RGB + D data set [9], and as a result, it showed a Top-1 accuracy of 84.19%. This result is equal level to 84.39%, which is the result of Yan's algorithm [1] using skeleton data.

The structure of this paper is as follows. In the Sect. 2, brief introduction for related research is described, and the input data generation process is explained in Sect. 3 in detail. And in the Sect. 4, graph composition for the structure of human body is described. After explaining the experimental results in Sect. 5, the thesis is closed with conclusion in Sect. 6.

2 Related Studies

In the conventional research, after analyzing the training image mathematically to find a feature suitable for representing actions, the feature was converted into a basis vector, and the result was obtained by comparing the distance between the reference model of actions and the input action in the feature space. For example, [2] defined the human action as curve in a mathematical space called 'Lie group', and [3] compared the action using the covariance matrix of the skeleton information over time. And [4] selected the nearest neighbor of the "Naïve Bayes model" in spatio-temporal space as the recognition result.

In recent years, with the development of artificial neural network technology, the use of popular deep learning techniques has become the mainstream of human action recognition research. For example, in study [5], the skeleton data was processed into a map form and CNN and LSTM were used for learning. [6] used RNN learning method, and [7] used spatio-temporal LSTM for recognition. These studies were able to obtain more improved results by reflecting the structural characteristics of the human body in the learning theory. In 2018, Yan [1] and Li [8] used ST-GCN for human action recognition for the first time. Yan [1]'s ST-GCN has a graph structure of a human body shape connected in spatio-temporal space, and uses skeleton coordinate information as input data. GCN has the characteristic that information is transmitted in the learning process only through the connection path defined in the graph, so the context of the problem can be reflected through the structure of the graph. Yan's ST-GCN was able to intuitively and easily reflect the context of action through the graph structure of the human body shape and showed significantly improved results compared to previous studies.

It is very difficult to acquire skeleton data accurately and stably. Therefore, the problem of ST-GCN based methods using skeleton coordinate information is that the recognition rate is largely influenced by the quality of the skeleton data. To improve this, [11] reprocessed the skeleton data to obtain a more stable value, and [12] tried to reduce the effect of data errors by grouping the data in units of a large part of the human body. On the other hand, [13] proposed an algorithm that improved the connection structure of the graph to compensate for the loss of information that occurred while passing through the connections in the graph structure of [1].

In this study, after defining that human action can be described as a specific motion and posture of a 2D human image, we propose an algorithm that replaces the skeletal data with optical flow containing motion information and image gradient including posture information. An example of using optical flow data in the existing human action recognition research is DeepMind's i3d [14]. I3d is a CNN based recognition algorithm that uses both an RGB image and an optical flow image as inputs. On the other hand, [15] combines silhouette images and skeleton information. The use of silhouette information suitable for representing shape is similar with this study to use posture information extracted from image gradients. In addition, [16] used the technique of classifying the movement of the skeleton into patterns.

3   Generation of Input Data

3.1   Overall Algorithm Configuration and Input Data Acquisition from RoM

Figure 2 shows the overall sequence of the algorithm proposed in this study. The algorithm first finds the 'person area' from the preprocessed 2D image. After creating the input data in the 'person area', it is used as the input of ST-GCN. After passing through the ST-GCN, the input information is converted into feature information, and finally, the recognition result is output through the action classifier.

As explained in the previous section, we assume that 'human action' can be expressed as a combination of two meaningful information: movement and posture. As shown in the Fig. 3, both actors playing the action-'eat meal' show movement and posture that have common characteristics. These is the movement that moves the hand toward the mouth and the posture that straightens the upper body. Optical flow and image gradient not only contain motion information and posture information generated in the movie frame, but

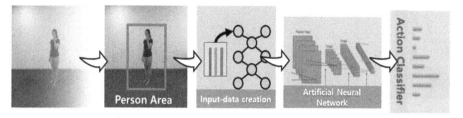

Fig. 2. Overall sequence of the algorithm (with image from [9])

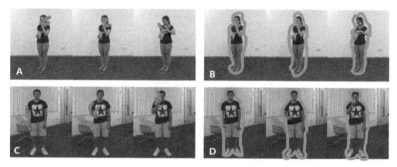

Fig. 3. 2-example of meaningful movement and posture (action: 'eat meal' in NTU RGB + D data set [9]) A) first actor's hand movement B) first actor's body posture C) second actor's hand movement D) second actor's body posture

also can be stably acquired from 2D images, so they are suitable for describing human actions and are applied as input data.

On the other hand, even though it is difficult to accurately and stably acquire skeleton data, it has the advantage of being able to intuitively and easily express human action. In the Yan's research [1], they were able to implement a human action recognition algorithm with ST-GCN that was intuitively easy to understand learning process by adopting a graph of human body shape based on skeleton data. Optical flow and image gradients do not show the clue of human actions as easily and intuitively as skeleton data, so we must consider a method that can express the characteristics from the structural connection of the human body. In other words, the range of acquiring optical flow and image gradient input information is limited by using the input RoM (region of motion) that is appropriately defined for each node of the graph, and the properties similar to the human body skeleton are reflected by hierarchically combining the information obtained from various RoMs.

The generation flow of input data is as follows as shown in the Fig. 4. First, after finding the head of the person in the 2D image as shown in the Fig. 5, based on the size of the head, the 'person area' that contains the entire body of the person is estimated. RoMs are arranged so as to have different position and size properties within the 'person area' as shown in the Fig. 5. Optical flow and image gradient information acquired from one RoM are first expressed in HoG format, and then normalized. Then normalized 16 dimensional data is converted into 3 features and used as input data for ST-GCN.

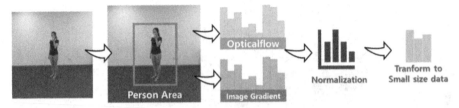

Fig. 4. Generation of input data (with image from [9])

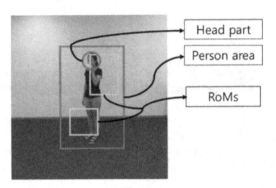

Fig. 5. Person area found at the input image [9]

3.2 Acquisition of Input Date in HoG Format from RoM

In RoM, first, HoG (histogram of gradient) descriptor format data is acquired through the following two step processes. In the first step, the input image is converted into a gray image of the a suitable size, and then the optical flow and image gradient of the RoM area are calculated. At this time, in order to reduce the influence of noise, as shown in Fig. 6 (A), the optical flow uses only the data obtained from the location where the curvature change is large, that is, the corner characteristic is strong. On the other hand, the image gradient uses data obtained from every pixel of the image, as shown in Fig. 6 (B).

In the second step, the obtained optical flow and image gradient data are expressed in HoG format. Since the optical flow and image gradient are expressed in polar coordinates (m, θ), it is suitable to be expressed as HoG, a histogram obtained by accumulating the magnitude of the gradient in the bin of the direction. In this study, bins of 16 direction are used, so the magnitude of the directional angle is 22.5. And the angle is changeable depend on the application. Also, the histogram value is used after dividing by the number of sampling times as shown in Eq. (1) for normalization. In Eq. (1), i is the ID of the histogram and N is the total number of sampling times. The data of 16 bins is obtained for each optical flow and image gradient, and combining the two data, finally a histogram of 32 bins is obtained.

$$\text{Normalized Histogram}_i = \frac{\text{Histogram}_i}{N \text{ Samples}} \tag{1}$$

A) Opticalflow -> sample only strong edge points in RoM

B) Image gradient -> sample all pixels in RoM

Fig. 6. Two types of data [9] acquisition

3.3 Conversion to 3-Feature Data

HoG formatted data can be directly used for learning of the neural-network, however total 32 dimensions of data per each RoM require too large computing resources since we use many combination of the RoMs. Therefore, for each optical flow and image gradient, 16 dimensional HoG-type data is converted into 3 features for simple calculation.

The first feature data is histogram code. The histogram code data can be obtained through a simple calculation process and it express the approximate distribution of histogram. In order to calculate the histogram code, first, in the histogram of 16 bins for each data type, a bins having larger value than neighboring bin, namely the bin is a peak, are searched and n bins are obtained in the order of the larger magnitude. Among these histogram bins, the i-th largest histogram value is defined as 'PeakHistogram$_i$'. Next, calculate the 'Position value$_i$' of 'PeakHistogram$_i$' as shown in Eq. (2). If the 'Peak histogram' is not found in the i-th bin, 'Position value$_i$' becomes 0. Conversely, if the peak histogram is found, 'the position index value of the histogram bin of 16 dimension + 1' is used as 'Position value$_i$'. As a result, 'Position value$_i$' has 17 types of values between 0 and 16. Next, the histogram code is calculated through the conversion process as shown in Eq. (3). In the equation, C can be used as a number greater than 17, which is the number of cases that 'Position value$_i$' can have. In this paper, 20 was used as C for convenience.

$$\text{If i-th Peak-Histogram is found, Position value}_i = \text{Histogram index} + 1$$
$$\text{If i-th Peak-Histogram is not found, Position value}_i = 0 \tag{2}$$

$$HistogramCode = \sum\nolimits_{i=1}^{N} \text{Position value}_i * C^{N-i} \tag{3}$$

The second feature of the converted data is the average value of 16 histogram values, and the third feature is the standard deviation value of 16 histogram values. Therefore, three feature data of (HistogramCode, Mean of Histogram, Standard deviation of Histogram) are finally generated for each optical flow and image gradient.

4 Graph of ST-GCN

4.1 Principle of Graph Design

Since the previous study [1] used 3D skeleton data as input data, it was possible to easily implement an effective neural network by spatially connecting the nodes of the graph with similar structure of the human body. This design follows the simple principle that if the 3D coordinate of the joint is connected so that it flows the shape of a person, a network for human action recognition will be naturally implemented. However, this study uses two raw features; optical flow and gradient, obtained from RoMs that have different positions and areas in 2D images, so a new principle of graph design suitable for these characteristics is necessary.

In order to recognize the other's actions, a person effectively combines various information of modalities. For example, the action of 'eat meal' can be analyzed as a combination of the overall body posture and fine hand movements (ie, straightening the body + the movement of bringing a hand to the mouth). Likewise, effective human action recognition can be realized by combining and using information observed in various large-area RoMs and small-area RoMs. In other words, if it is insufficient to recognize the action through the information obtained through one RoM, the problem can be solved by synthesizing the information obtained through various RoMs. Therefore, in the graph of ST-GCN, a form in which the nodes of the large area RoMs and the nodes of the small area RoMs are connected to each other should be applied. In addition, various RoMs must exist so that sufficient information can be obtained from images to recognize various actions, and the nodes need to be systematically connected. This is because if the graphs are not systematically connected, information cannot be processed fairly, and there is a high possibility that the recognition rate will show a large gap according to actions. In conclusion, the design of the graph in ST-GCN is implemented through the principle of having a structure in which information in a large area and information in a small area can be systematically exchanged.

4.2 Structure of the Graph

As explained in the previous section, an important principle of graph design is to have a systematic structure. In this study, the nodes of the graph are arranged in three layers as shown in the Fig. 7 for systematic composition. At this time, the three layers are called the top layer, the mid layer, and the bottom layer from the top as shown in the Fig. 8. However, if this arrangement is described in terms of the nodes of the graph, there is a problem that it is too complicated for a person to understand the graph design. Therefore, by using the definition of two graph-units, it is easier to describe the graph design by the arrangement of graph nodes.

The first graph-unit is a single-graph-unit as shown in the Fig. 9. The single-graph-unit corresponds to one graph node. In other words, it has one RoM. The second graph-unit is the multi-graph-unit. The multi-graph-unit is a group of 5 graph nodes connected as shown in the following Fig. 9. In other words, a multi-graph-unit is like five connected single-graph-units. Single-graph-units in the multi-graph-unit have RoMs that

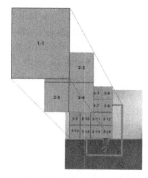

Fig. 7. 3 layers arranged on 'person area' (with image from [9])

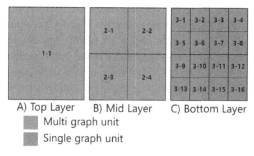

A) Top Layer   B) Mid Layer   C) Bottom Layer

       Multi graph unit

       Single graph unit

Fig. 8. 3 types of layers ('A-B' in each graph unit area indicate id of graph unit)

are partially divided into local regions. As shown in the Fig. 9, RoMs of these single-graph-units occupy the entire (A), left (B), right (C), top (D), and lower (E) areas of whole region. And the single-graph-unit of the entire region (A) and the remaining 4 single-graph-units (B ~ E) are connected to each other. Therefore, the Multi-graph-unit allows the information collected from entire area and partial area to be exchanged with each other.

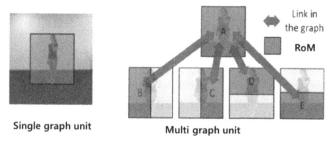

Single graph unit   Multi graph unit

Fig. 9. Two types of graph unit (with image from [9])

Arrange these graph-units in 3 layers as shown in the Fig. 8. Multi-graph-units are placed in the top-layer and mid-layer, and single-graph-units are placed in the bottom-layer. Deployed multi-graph-units already have graph node connections defined internally. Also, the single-graph-unit of the partial region (B ~ E) in the multi-graph-unit at the upper layer is connected to the single-graph-unit of the entire region (A) in the multi-graph-unit at the lower layer if their RoMs are overlapped each other as shown in the Fig. 10. In the case of the bottom layer, only single-graph-units are arranged, so the single-graph-unit of the partial region (B ~ E) in the multi-graph-unit at the mid layer and the single-graph-unit of the bottom layer are connected if their RoMs are overlapped each other.

These connections are summarized in the following Table 1. Table 1 shows what other nodes each node is connected to in the spatial domain of the graph. Here, one node is described in the form of 'A-B-C'. 'A-B' is same as the definition of the graph-unit arranged in the layer shown in Fig. 8. The last C indicates five types of single-graph-units belonging to the multi-graph-unit. As shown in the Fig. 9, A is a unit of the whole area, B is a left partial area unit, C is a right partial area unit, D is an upper partial area unit, and E is a lower partial area unit. Also, each node in the graph are connected in temporal domain. When the ST-GCN uses n frames of video data as input, the nodes of each frame are sequentially connected to the same node of the immediately preceding and following frames. That is, $node_i$ of the i-th frame is connected to $node_{i-1}$ and $node_{i+1}$.

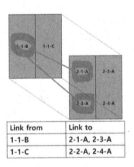

Link from	Link to
1-1-B	2-1-A, 2-3-A
1-1-C	2-2-A, 2-4-A

Fig. 10. Example of connection between layers

Table 1. All links of the nodes in the graph

Link from	Link to
1-1-A	1-1-B, 1-1-C, 1-1-D, 1-1-E
1-1-B	2-1-A, 2-3-A
1-1-C	2-2-A, 2-4-A

(continued)

Table 1. (*continued*)

Link from	Link to
1-1-D	2-1-A, 2-2-A
1-1-E	2-3-A, 2-4-A
2-1-A	2-1-B, 2-1-C, 2-1-D, 2-1-E
2-1-B	3-1-A, 3-5-A
2-1-C	3-2-A, 3-6-A
2-1-D	3-1-A, 3-2-A
2-1-E	3-5-A, 3-6-A
2-2-A	2-2-B, 2-2-C, 2-2-D, 2-2-E
2-2-B	3-3-A, 3-7-A
2-2-C	3-4-A, 3-8-A
2-2-D	3-3-A, 3-4-A
2-2-E	3-7-A, 3-8-A
2-3-A	2-3-B, 2-3-C, 2-3-D, 2-3-E
2-3-B	3-9-A, 3-13-A
2-3-C	3-10-A, 3-14-A
2-3-D	3-9-A, 3-10-A
2-3-E	3-13-A, 3-14-A
2-4-A	2-4-B, 2-4-C, 2-4-D, 2-4-E
2-4-B	3-11-A, 3-15-A
2-4-C	3-12-A, 3-16-A
2-4-D	3-11-A, 3-12-A
2-4-E	3-15-A, 3-16-A

5 Experiment Result

In the study of [1], an experiment was conducted on 60 actions of NTU RGB + D data set, and as a result, a high Top-1 accuracy of 81.5% was obtained. The NTU RGB + D data set is records of acting performances that can occur in a variety of daily lives through a Kinect camera, and provides skeleton coordinate information of the action and RGB and depth video. In this study, as shown in Table 2, 10 distinct actions and 10 indistinct actions were selected from the NTU RGB + D data set, and an experiment was conducted for these 20 actions, and the recognition rate and degree of confusion were evaluated. In addition, Yan's algorithm [1] was tested on the same data set and the results were compared.

The ST-GCN used in this experiment differs from Yan's ST-GCN in its input data and graph structure. However, for comparison of experiments, the network structure and parameters of ST-GCN is set same as those used in Yan's. That is, the ST-GCN has a

Table 2. Selected 20 actions for experiment

Distinct 10 actions	Indistinct 10 actions
2: eat meal	1: drink water
5: drop	3: brush teeth
6: pick up	4: brush hair
7: throw	10: clapping
8: sit down	11: reading
9: stand up	12: writing
17: hand waving	13: tear up paper
18: kicking	14: put on jacket
something	15: take off jacket
19: jump up	16: cheer up
20: staggering	

structure in which it goes through 4 layers of the network with 64 outs, then 3 layers of the network with 128 outs, 3 layers of the network with 256 outs, and finally generates an output by using a class classifier.

As a result of the experiment, the algorithm proposed in this study was able to obtain the optimal result when 55 epochs were learned. On the other hand, Yan's algorithm yielded optimal results at 80 epochs. The results of the two algorithms are as shown in Table 3, and the algorithm of this study achieved 84.19% Top1 accuracy, and Yan's obtained 84.39%. Meanwhile, in the F1 score, both algorithms recorded the same 0.85. From these results, it can be obtained that the recognition performance of this study's algorithms is similar with the Yan's ST-GCN algorithm using skeleton data. In addition, the recognition error of the algorithm was analyzed through the confusion matrix. Figure 11 shows the confusion matrix of the proposed algorithm and Yan's algorithm as an image map, respectively. Dark blue in the image map means higher recognition score. In common between the two algorithms, the false positive recognition rate of 10 distinct actions was lower and that of 10 indistinct actions was higher. And there were differences in the types of actions showing more errors according to the algorithm. For example, the algorithm of this study distinguishes between 'reading' and 'writing' better than [1], but it does not distinguish 'staggering' well, which [1] recognizes very well. This difference seems to be the influence of the characteristics of the input data and graph design. Although the overall capabilities are similar, the detailed capabilities differ depending on the algorithm.

In addition, in order to verify the effectiveness of the data compressed with 3 features, 16 dimensions of uncompressed HoG descriptor format data for each optical flow and image gradient were compared with the compressed 3 feature data. The recognition rates of the algorithm of Yan's [1] using skeleton data and the algorithm of this study using 16 dimensions of HoG data and 3 feature of data were compared for 10 clearly distinct actions in Table 2. As a result, as shown in Table 4, the 16 dimensional data showed the same level of recognition rate as 93.88% compared to the skeleton data used in algorithm of [1]. In addition, the compressed 3-feature data was also 88.61%, showing that there was no significant difference, showing that this data-dimensional compression was effective.

Table 3. Experiment result of this study

	Yan [1]'s ST-GCN	This study's algorithm
Top1 accuracy	84.39%	84.19%
Top5 accuracy	98.47%	98.93%
Precision	0.84	0.84
Recall	0.85	0.85
F1-score	0.85	0.85

Table 4. Experiment result for effectiveness of the data compressed

	Yan [1]'s ST-GCN with skeleton data	This study's 16 dimensional HoG data	This study's 3 feature data
Top1 accuracy	93.56%	93.88%	88.61%
Top5 accuracy	99.67%	99.78%	99.82%

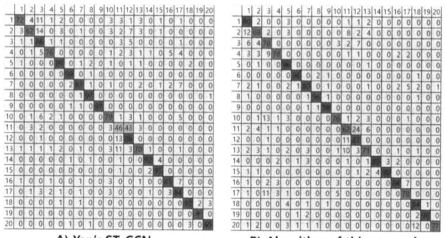

A) Yan's ST-GCN   **B) Algorithm of this research**

Fig. 11. Confusion matrix of two algorithm (The darker blue color means the higher value) (Color figure online)

6 Conclusion

This study have aimed to implement ST-GCN based human action recognition by using the research of Yan [1] as a basis to find contextual features of human action with the new definition of a graph. Skeleton data, which has been generally used in the previous researches, is replaced with optical flow and image gradient information that can be obtained more stably with 2D image processing, and the design of the graph is redefined so that the context of action can be found well from the replaced input data.

The new input data, optical flow and image gradient, contain movement and posture information suitable to express actions. In order to find the clue of action recognition from input data, the principle of graph design was established that information acquired from a large area of RoM and information acquired from a small area of RoM are exchanged with each other. According to this principle, input data were generated using RoMs that were systematically defined appropriately for each node of the graph and connected them in a neural network. In addition, the acquired optical flow and image gradient are individually processed in a 16 dimensional HoG format, and then converted into three features (histogram code, average of the histogram, and standard deviation of the histogram). Through this conversion, it was possible to greatly reduce the consuming of the learning resources for the neural network. Data input to the nodes of the graph was processed through systematically connected graphs using a layered structure.

An experiment was conducted on 20 actions of NTU RGB + D, and a Top-1 accuracy of 84.19% was obtained. This is similar to 84.39% of Yan [1]'s algorithm, showing that the newly defined input data and the structure of the graph were suitable and efficient neural network training was possible. Through these results, it is expected that the algorithm proposed in this study will be particularly useful in surveillance systems using camera of CCTV, where it is difficult to reliably acquire skeleton data. However, human action recognition studies, including this study, are mainly verified by experiments using specially prepared data sets, so there is a question about whether good recognition results can be obtained even with natural actions that occur in real world. Common actions have boundaries that are difficult to distinguish, and characteristics of continuous occurrence. The most important thing in action recognition using ST-GCN is the definition of the graph structure that can grasp the contextual characteristics of the action well. To implement this, it is necessary to analyze the action and establish a principle that can encompass the information. In other words, finding a principle that can better grasp the characteristics of generally occurring actions and implementing an improved ST-GCN algorithm based on it will be an important future task of this study.

Acknowledgement. This research is supported by Ministry of Culture, Sports, and Tourism (MCST) and Korea Creative Content Agency (KOCCA) in the Culture Technology (CT) Research & Development Program (R2020060002) 2020.

References

1. Yan, S., Xiong, Y., Lin, D.: Spatial temporal graph convolutional networks for skeleton-based action recognition. In: Thirty-Second AAAI Conference on Artificial Intelligence (2018)

2. Vemulapalli, R., Arrate, F., Chellappa, R.: Human action recognition by representing 3D skeletons as points in a lie group. In: Proceedings of the IEEE Conference on Computer Vision and Pattern Recognition, pp. 588–595 (2014)
3. Hussein, M.E., Torki, M., Gowayyed, M.A., El-Saban, M.: Human action recognition using a temporal hierarchy of covariance descriptors on 3D joint locations. In: International Joint Conference on Artificial Intelligence (IJCAI), vol. 13, pp. 2466–2472 (2013)
4. Weng, J., Weng, C., Yuan, J.: Spatio-temporal naive-bayes nearest-neighbor (ST-NBNN) for skeleton-based action recognition. In: IEEE Conference on Computer Vision and Pattern Recognition, CVPR, pp. 4171–4180 (2017)
5. Li, C., Wang, P., Wang, S., Hou, Y., Li, W.: Skeleton-based action recognition using LSTM and CNN. In: 2017 IEEE International Conference on Multimedia & Expo Workshops (ICMEW), pp. 585–590. IEEE, July 2017
6. Du, Y., Wang, W., Wang, L.: Hierarchical recurrent neural network for skeleton based action recognition. In: IEEE Conference on Computer Vision and Pattern Recognition, CVPR, pp. 1110–1118 (2015)
7. Liu, J., Shahroudy, A., Xu, D., Wang, G.: Spatio-temporal LSTM with trust gates for 3D human action recognition. In: Leibe, B., Matas, J., Sebe, N., Welling, M. (eds.) ECCV 2016. LNCS, vol. 9907, pp. 816–833. Springer, Cham (2016). https://doi.org/10.1007/978-3-319-46487-9_50
8. Li, C., Cui, Z., Zheng, W., Xu, C., Yang, J.: Spatio-temporal graph convolution for skeleton based action recognition. In: Proceedings of AAAI, pp. 3482–3489, February 2018
9. Shahroudy, A., Liu, J., Ng, T.T., Wang, G: NTU RGB+ D: a large scale dataset for 3D human activity analysis. In: Proceedings of the IEEE Conference on Computer Vision and Pattern Recognition, pp. 1010–1019 (2016)
10. Cao, Z., Hidalgo, G., Simon, T., Wei, S.E., Sheikh, Y.: OpenPose: realtime multi-person 2D pose estimation using Part Affinity Fields, arXiv preprint arXiv:1812.08008 (2018)
11. Gao, X., et al.: Optimized skeleton-based action recognition via sparsified graph regression. In: Proceedings of the 27th ACM International Conference on Multimedia (2019)
12. Thakkar, K., Narayanan, P.J.: Part-based graph convolutional network for action recognition, arXiv preprint arXiv:1809.04983 (2018)
13. Li, M., Chen, S., Chen, X., Zhang, Y., Wang, Y., Tian, Q.: Actional-structural graph convolutional networks for skeleton-based action recognition. In: Proceedings of the IEEE Conference on Computer Vision and Pattern Recognition, pp. 3595–3603 (2019)
14. Carreira, J., Zisserman, A.: Quo vadis, action recognition? A new model and the kinetics dataset. In: Proceedings of the IEEE Conference on Computer Vision and Pattern Recognition (2017)
15. Chaaraoui, A., Padilla-Lopez, J., Flórez-Revuelta, F.: Fusion of skeletal and silhouette-based features for human action recognition with RGB-D devices. In: Proceedings of the IEEE International Conference on Computer Vision Workshops, pp. 91–97 (2013)
16. Devanne, M., Wannous, H., Berretti, S., Pala, P., Daoudi, M., Del Bimbo, A.:3-D human action recognition by shape analysis of motion trajectories on riemannian manifold. IEEE Trans. Cybern. 45(7), 1340–1352 (2014)

Deep Visual Anomaly Detection with Negative Learning

Jin-Ha Lee[1,2], Marcella Astrid[1,2], Muhammad Zaigham Zaheer[1,2], and Seung-Ik Lee[1,2(✉)]

[1] University of Science and Technology (UST), 217, Gajeong-ro, Yuseong-gu, Daejeon, Republic of Korea
{jhlee,marcella.astrid,mzz}@ust.ac.kr
[2] Electronics and Telecommunications Research Institute (ETRI), 218, Gajeong-ro, Yuseong-gu, Daejeon, Republic of Korea
the_silee@etri.re.kr

Abstract. With the increase in the learning capability of deep convolution-based architectures, various applications of such models have been proposed over time. In the field of anomaly detection, improvements in deep learning opened new prospects of exploration for the researchers whom tried to automate the labor-intensive features of data collection. First, in terms of data collection, it is impossible to anticipate all the anomalies that might exist in a given environment. Second, assuming we limit the possibilities of anomalies, it will still be hard to record all these scenarios for the sake of training a model Third, even if we manage to record a significant amount of abnormal data, it's laborious to annotate this data on pixel or even frame level. Various approaches address the problem by proposing one-class classification using generative models trained on only normal data. In such methods, only the normal data is used, which is abundantly available and doesn't require significant human input. However, such approaches have two drawbacks. First, these are trained with only normal data and at the test time, given abnormal data as input, still generate normal-looking output. This happens due to the hallucination characteristic of generative models, which is not desirable in anomaly detection systems because of their need to be accurate and reliable. Next, these systems are not capable of utilizing abnormal examples, however small in number, during the training. In this paper, we propose anomaly detection with negative learning (ADNL), which employs the negative learning concept for the enhancement of anomaly detection by utilizing a very small number of labeled anomaly data as compared with the normal data during training. The idea, which is fairly simple yet effective, is to limit the reconstruction capability of a generative model using the given anomaly examples. During the training, normal data is learned as would have been in a conventional method, but the abnormal data is utilized to maximize loss of the network on abnormality distribution. With this simple tweaking, the network not only learns to reconstruct normal data but also encloses the normal distribution far from the possible distribution of anomalies. In order to evaluate the efficiency of our proposed method, we defined the baseline using Adversarial

© Springer Nature Switzerland AG 2021
H. Jeong and K. Sumi (Eds.): IW-FCV 2021, CCIS 1405, pp. 218–232, 2021.
https://doi.org/10.1007/978-3-030-81638-4_18

Auto-Encoder (AAE). Our experiments show significant improvement in area under the curve (AUC) over conventional AAE. An extensive evaluation, which has been carried out on the MNIST dataset as well as a locally recorded pedestrian dataset, is reported in this paper.

Keywords: Anomaly detection · Auto encoder · Limiting reconstruction capability

1 Introduction

Anomaly Detection is one of the most challenging tasks in the field of machine-learning which naturally makes it particularly interesting for researchers [1,2]. Various variants of anomaly detection algorithms are being used in the field of signal processing [3,4], medical diagnosis [5], network intrusion detection [6–8], and video surveillance [9,10]. Anomaly detection systems, although difficult to train, are expected to have high efficiency as such models are expected to reduce human labor for their corresponding domains. Specifically, in video surveillance for the purpose of safety and security, autonomous anomaly detection systems contribute significantly by analysing hundreds of concurrent video streams which otherwise would take a lot of human resources as well as attention. With the recent development in deep-learning algorithms it is becoming handy to apply these low computational yet highly efficient algorithms for the learning problems. 2D and 3d convolutions, auto-encoders, object detectors, aaaaa are few among many other algorithms which are being used for anomaly detection.

These techniques can be widely divided into two categories. The first type is where the network is learnt based on normal as well as abnormal examples. During the test time, each scenario is compared against the train model to identify anomalies. In contrary, the other type is the one in which learning is done using only normal data to define a corresponding distribution. In order to check whether the test data is anomalous or not, it is compared against the learned normal distribution and checked if it is an outlier. However, each of these categories have its own limits or drawbacks. For the formal category, one common problem is the absolute necessity of defining abnormality. However, in real world scenarios anomalies cannot be anticipated. There is always a possibility of something new happening and, if it is not learnt as abnormal during the training time, it might get overlooked during the test time. Moreover, another problem that such system face is the lack of data. It is mostly due to the limiting factor of defining the abnormalities. Even if the actors are used to generate anomalous scenes, it is phisicaly impossible to create all possible scenarios. In addition, this category of anomaly detection solutions require huge amount of labeled data for training which is laborious to obtain.

The rapid development in recent deep learning filed seems to meet those expectations, but still, some problems have remained. One is, how to define Abnormal. The definition of abnormal can be made by the definition of normal, which can be everything that is not normal. The definition of normal is also difficult. For example, when a car in on the highway, it is normal. However, if the car is on the pedestrian road, that is abnormal. Considering the situations, how to find out the context of a scene is the problem (Fig. 1).

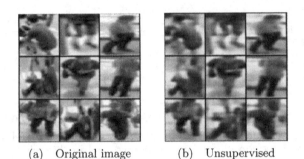

(a)   Original image   (b)   Unsupervised   (c)   Negative learning

Fig. 1. Reconstruction of images (3 × 3) with unsupervised and negative learning methods. Colored line under each images shows the label of image. Orange is abnormal, green is normal data. (Color figure online)

For abnormal detection, two types of model can be used, a discriminative model and a generative model. Discriminative models are a class of models used in statistical classification, especially in supervised machine learning, which requires labeled data for training. On the other hand, the generative model doesn't need any labeled data for training, it can easily obtain desired data. For the training of the discriminative model, which requires labeled data, it is impossible to include all normal or abnormal events into the training data. Because of its limitation to make a dictionary of normal and abnormal events or to define a standard for abnormal events, generating capability of the generative model is more preferred for abnormal detection. With the generative model, by defining 'what is normal', the model can distinguish things far from normal as abnormal, which called novelty detection in other word.

The generative model is trained only with ordinary situations, to learn a generalized feature of normal data. Therefore, the model learns about distribution or a general feature of normal data to detect abnormals as outliers., However, there is another problem in this approach, which is the generalization capability of the generative model, that model can generate the anomalies too, which is not learned during the training and not desireable for our intension.

To solve this problem, limitation of reconstruction capability is suggested, which is called negative learning, in [11]. Negative learning limits the reconstruction capability (LRC) of the generative model, and hinder the reconstruction of abnormal data by using labeled data. Therefore, the network will only to generative learned data, and fails to generate unwanted feature.

In this work, we applied LRC for anomaly detection application. For normal data, reconstruction is performed using the encoder-decoder structure as in the conventional generative model case. But, for the abnormal data, negative learning [11] is applied. The negative learning is supervised learning, which is learning a general distribution of normal data but also using labeled abnormal data during the training. Negative learning can leverage the benefit of labeled abnormal data. Because it's impossible to make a dictionary of every event, most anomaly detection methods use an unsupervised approach with generative models. However, even if labeled data is expensive and very scares, it a waste if we don't use. We can use abnormal data during the conventional training process, to leverage benefits from every data we got. With negative learning, even a small amount of abnormal data can be used efficiently.

Conclusively this paper, we purpose an application for anomaly detection using the generative model with negative learning, which benefits from both labeled and unlabeled data, Showing limited reconstruction capability, only restrained to normal data.

2 Related Works

Labeless approach becomes a recent trend due to the nature of abnormal data, which is expensive to collect. Clustering [12–15], SVM network [16] and isolation forest [6] are ways to perform anomaly detection without labels. Because normal data is relatively easy and inexpensive to collect, training only with normal data become one branch, which called novelty detection. Adversarially Learned One-Class Classifier [17] and Old is Gold (OGNet) [18] are GAN (Generative Adversarial Net) [19] based architectures, which use discriminator for anomaly detection. During the training, the adversarial model trained on one-class, and inference time, generator and discriminator co-work for anomalous-classification. Deep-cascade net [20] is also trained with normal data to learn the Gaussian model during the training and use this model for anomaly detection in each step of the deep network. These labeless, unsupervised learning approaches are more robust to an unknown anomaly compared to supervised learning. However, they have an opposite problem of supervised learning approaches, which is hard to tell anomaly data near to the normal data, not as accurate as supervised learning in detecting known anomalies. OGNet attempts to specifically handle this issue by generating psuedo anomalies using an old state of the generator however, the overall training still utilizes only normal data.

Advance from labeless training, one intuition is to use weak-label for training. The idea proposed by Sultani [21], and further extended in [13–15], used a video-level label, which only informs there is an anomaly in somewhere of video. With this weak video-level label, separate the anomaly video into small segments, assume at least one of those segments contain anomalous-scene for sure. Another study, Yang [22] used implicit human support, from Youtube videos. They used user-edited short videos from youtube, assume that short videos(less than 4min) searched by specific keyword have a high chance to be consist of dominant scene correlated to the keyword.

Even if labeled anomaly data is expensive to collect, there is no reason not to use if we can have it. LRC [11] tried to leverage advantages from labeled anomaly data. By using labeled anomaly data, they limit the reconstruction capability of the generative model, which also capable of reconstructing anomaly data too. Similar to LRC, Bian [23] also used negative learning stage to limit the reconstruction of GAN. They trained on normal data, but also get advantage from the labels.

3   Method

In this section, methodology and objective are defined. First, assume that two data distributions X and Y are in the same signal space. And x, y be the instances that represent each distribution, so that X and Y can be expressed as $X = \{x_1, x_2, x_3, ..., x_k\}$, $Y = \{y_1, y_2, y_3, ..., y_j\}$. Our goal is to make the network regenerate X effectively while failing for Y. Here X and Y represent the normal and abnormal data. Let the distribution of regenerated X be $\hat{X}$ and the distribution of regenerated Y be $\hat{Y}$. Then the goal is to maximize the following equation:

$$p_\theta(\hat{X}|X) - p_\theta(\hat{Y}|Y) = \sum_i^k \log_\theta(\hat{X}|X) - \sum_i^j \log_\theta(\hat{Y}|Y) \tag{1}$$

that network will reconstruct very well the from the X, but fail to reconstruct from Y.

For simplicity, the mean square error is used for loss function. Network parameter $\theta = \{\alpha, \beta\}$ is being trained, which α is parameter of encoder and β is parameter for decoder. For the X, the normal data, the objective is to minimize the loss to find optimal θ^*:

$$\theta^* = \underset{\theta}{argmin} \sum_{i=1}^k \{\hat{x}_i - x_i\}^2 \tag{2}$$

the theta that can well reconstruct from normal distribution. On the other hand for the Y, the abnormal data, the objective is the opposite of that, to maximize the loss to hinder the reconstruction of the network:

$$\theta^* = \underset{\theta}{argmax} \sum_{i=1}^k \{\hat{y}_i - y_i\}^2 \tag{3}$$

Negative-learning is the opposite concept of normal(positive) learning, which makes network hard to reconstruct undesired data. Both equations are trying to optimize the same parameter, θ simultaneously.

The Algorithm 1 shows the process of training with negative learning. For negative learning, everything is identical to the conventional training sequence, only the loss for the abnormal data is changing. For normal data represented as X, Eq. (2) is used. However, for the abnormal data Y, Eq. (3) is used, which mean negative learning. Two loss functions are working with the same parameter, to

---

Algorithm 1

Require: X: Normal dataset Y: Abnormal dataset $TRAINING\_START$
 1: **while** NOT TERMINATION CONDITION **do**
 2:     **if** $DATA \in X$ **then**
            DO POSITIVE LEARNING
 3:     **else if** $DATA \in Y$ **then**
            DO NEGATIVE LEARNING
 4:     **end if**
 5: **end while**
    $TRAINING\_END$

---

achieve different goal respectively, generate good normal reconstruction and fail to do the same thing for anomaly data. And because there are unbalance in the data quantity, in LRC [11] used multiple iterations for negative learning to keep the balance between normal and abnormal data. For our case, because the ratio of normal and abnormal data was 10:1, we tried an experiment for the weighted loss. Instead of multiple iterations, extra 10-time weight is given for the abnormal data during the negative learning in the experiment. However, there was no significant difference between weighting and without-weighting in the test results, so we decide to use the same equation with only the opposite sign for positive and negative learning.

4   Experiments

4.1   Data Set

The experiment is separated into two phases. First train and test on a new dataset, which is our own, and next test on the public MNIST dataset. The first dataset, which named 'lobby dataset', is consist of records from a surveillance camera installed on the entrance of the building. The video contains people entering and leaving the building through the main gate. We collected 20 normal videos and each of them is 24 h long. Abnormal video is 2 h long and made of actors playing certain situations, like sudden fall or running, an unusual gathering or running of people. With the videos, we detect the bounding box of appearing human in the scenes and extract the cropped human-size images. We collected 55,247 normal image patches and 3,569 abnormal image patches. Then divide them into $7 : 1 : 2 = train : validation : test$ for experiment. By including the same sequence to the same data group, a similar scene doesn't appear in train and test dataset at the same time during the training. That is mot all the anomaly scene contained in train dataset, so the network will face an unknown anomaly in the test step.

4.2   Network Structure

We use the Adversarial Auto-Encoder [24] as a basic structure and for some part of the network refer to the DCGAN [25] for better performance. However, any Auto-encoder structure can be used instead. Images are transformed into 64×64 size RGB 3 channel and fed to network as input. Every training was done with 1000 epoch with batch size 1024. Adam is used for an optimizer and we used the same parameter as paper [26]. Batch normalization [27] is applied after convolution layer and we used ReLU as an activation function for both encoder and decoder. However, only the last layer of the decoder, we used tanh exceptionally [25]. With adversarial part of AAE, we simply impose gaussian distribution to the latent code [24] for simplicity.

4.3 Comparison Methods

With the same structure and dataset, only the loss function is changed for comparison. First, the unsupervised setting has experimented as a baseline. During the training, only normal train set was used, which is identical to the train set used for the negative learning phase. The unsupervised network was trained to learn only normal situations and tested on the dataset, that contains both normal and abnormal scene, to distinguish them. For the supervised negative learning approach, the network learned normal data in same manners of the unsupervised model. However, after training with normal data, the supervised model trained with extra abnormal data set by negative learning. Both unsupervised and supervised approach used the same data set (train & test), but extra abnormal data was used for negative learning. This extra abnormal train data set was excluded during the unsupervised phase. This separation is to show the effect of leveraging the advantage of existing anomaly data.

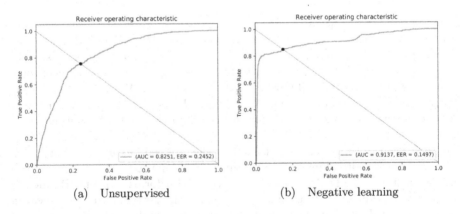

(a)   Unsupervised   (b)   Negative learning

Fig. 2. ROC comparision of unsupervised and negative learning.

Receiver Operating Characteristic (ROC) and Area Under Curve (AUC) are calculated for evaluation, during the training (Fig. 3) and after (Fig. 2) training with validation set and test set respectively. The result during the training shows that AUC of the negative learning exceeded that of unsupervised learning for all

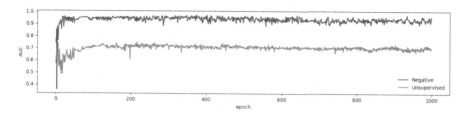

Fig. 3. Negative learning AUC change during the training.

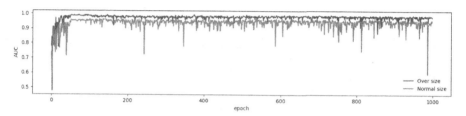

Fig. 4. Oversize learning AUC change during the training.

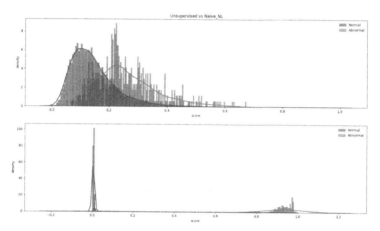

Fig. 5. Score distribution after unsupervised and negative learning

times (Fig. 3). Negative learning method's AUC value get close to around 0.95, which outperformed the AUC value of unsupervised learning, stays around 0.73. Overall performance and discriminating capability of negative learning model were much better than the unsupervised model, which is only trained with normal data.

At the test time, the AUC value of Unsupervised model rises to 0.82. Despite the AUC value of negative learning model slightly decreased, compared to that result during training, but still very high compared to the unsupervised model, around 0.91. The training was done eight times each for both methods and we selected the best model for evaluation. The result of all training is shown in Table 2. Negative learning performs better given average AUC value, 0.89 compared to 0.76 of unsupervised learning. Also, the standard deviation of AUC value shows that negative learning is more stable in training.

The Fig. 5 shows the Score distribution of the dataset The score calculation is based on reconstruction error, which bigger the reconstruction error leads to higher the score. After computing the score, scores are scaled to 0–1. Upper one in the Fig. 5 is the unsupervised method and the other is the negative learning method. In each distribution, blue represents normal data and red represents abnormal data. The upper distribution in Fig. 5 is the unsupervised method. There is a large overlap between normal and abnormal data. That means it's hard to tell normal from abnormal with this model. On the other hand, in the below distribution in Fig. 5, two data sets(normal and abnormal) have a large gap between them, so the network can easily detect anomalies.

Table 1. AUC comparison with MNIST dataset. Anomaly numbers were used as anomaly input in each test.

Method ‖ Anomaly Number	0	1	2	3	4	5	6	7	8	9	Avg.
Unsupervised (Baseline)	73.57	17.06	62.54	55.48	43.33	45.16	56.41	41.81	58.63	42.91	49.69
Negative learning	99.64	99.59	98.99	99.40	99.34	99.11	99.14	98.82	98.86	98.17	99.11

Table 2. AUC comparison between negative learning and unsupervised learning. Test was done 8 times with 1000 epoch each.

Method ‖ Test seed	1	2	3	4	5	6	7	8	Avg.	STDEV
Unsupervised (Baseline)	82.70	82.51	66.45	80.39	63.86	80.08	81.28	70.70	75.99	0.077
Negative learning	92.66	91.37	87.45	83.24	89.47	88.66	90.68	88.61	89.01	0.028

4.4   Test on MNIST Dataset

In the second phase of experiment, network tested on MNIST, public dataset. For the training, first set one digit from 0–9 as anomaly number. Then train network with the other numbers. The MNIST dataset was separated into 8 : 2 = Train : Test. After training 100 epoch with 256 batch size, the test is done by ten times with all numbers (0–9) as anomaly number at each test case. The Table 1 show the experimental result. With unsupervised learning, few numbers were barely discriminated, compared to average 99 of negative learning result.

The Fig. 6 show outputs of the MNIST experiment. Four experiment results are shown in Fig. 6. Unsupervised learning reconstructs abnormal number very

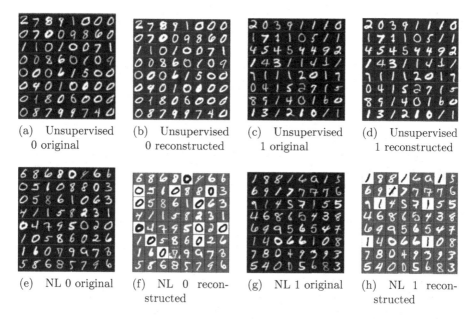

| (a) Unsupervised 0 original | (b) Unsupervised 0 reconstructed | (c) Unsupervised 1 original | (d) Unsupervised 1 reconstructed |

| (e) NL 0 original | (f) NL 0 reconstructed | (g) NL 1 original | (h) NL 1 reconstructed |

Fig. 6. Result of MNIST reconstruction Comparison between unsupervised and negative learning (NL) methods. Digit 0 and 1 are used as anomaly data. The network was trained with MNIST data but without anomaly number (0 & 1). Unsupervised network well generalized the data and reconstructed anomaly very good. NL method also reconstructed well but anomaly is distinguishable from others.

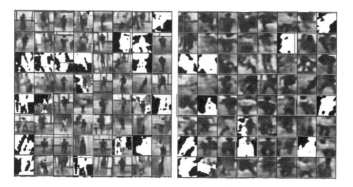

Fig. 7. Comparison between over crop size test and normal crop size test. Green or orange line under each image show data is normal (green) or abnormal (orange). Red box indicates abnormal images discriminated correctly in oversize, but not in normal size. Blue box indicates normal images predicted as abnormal in normal size training, but discriminated properly as normal in oversize test. Finally green box is normal images which is properly discriminated in normal size test but failed to predict in oversize test. (Color figure online)

well, even they never trained with them, because of their generalization capability. Negative learning also reconstructed well, but in an inverted pixel, which makes network easily separate them. The average AUC of negative learning was 0.99, outperformed unsupervised learning 0.49 (Table 1), which shows the effect of negative learning in anomaly detection.

4.5 Oversize Test

After verification in public dataset, an extra experiment was performed, with an oversized crop image, assuming that bigger image will contain more information to help the prediction of the network. The Oversize crop image size is 2.5 times bigger in width and 1.5 time in the height of the object bounding box. However, before fed to the network, also resized into 64×64, same like normal crop images used in the previous experiment. Other things (architecture, loss function, dataset) are all the same condition. Only the initial crop size is bigger between them. AUC during the training is shown in Fig. 4. Oversize training converges faster and higher than normal size training. Table 3 shows the comparison of the test result for oversize between normal negative learning. The average AUC of oversize training is 0.04 higher compared to normal negative training result. The Fig. 7 show more detailed output of test. Oversize training reduced true negative (normal predicted as abnormal) and false positive (abnormal predicted as normal) cases. With this test, we confirm the effect of bigger crop size, which contains more appearance information of the image, does help network.

Table 3. Test AUC result on oversize crop image.

#	1	2	3	4	5	6	Avg
Oversize	0.9850	0.9808	0.9759	0.9775	0.9757	0.9804	0.9792
Normal size	0.9379	0.9164	0.9352	0.9317	0.9227	0.9367	0.9301

4.6 Scaling Negative Loss

There is some work called Auto-encoding Binary Classifier (ABC) [28], archived but yet published, which also utilize LRC for their work. The interesting point of this work is limiting the boundary of negative loss. Without limitation, the negative loss can be really huge so that can may overwhelm the positive loss. Similar to this work, We used a different loss to scale negative loss during the training:

$$loss = \sum_{i}^{j} \exp^{-(\hat{y}_i - y_i)^2} \qquad (4)$$

This will scale the range of negative loss between 0 to 1, which is maximum reconstruction negative loss will be 1, and become smaller as reconstruction loss gets bigger, that network will aim to minimize this loss. With this loss, we compare the result to the result of naive loss, which is Eq. 3. Detail of comparison is shown in Table 4. Average AUC of both tests was very similar, or we can say limitation doesn't affect the result. Further, we analyze the output of both tests in detail, which is explained in the next section.

Table 4. Test AUC result on scaled negative loss test.

Methods	1	2	3	4	5	6	7	8	Avg
Scale	0.8621	0.8869	0.8954	0.8752	0.9056	0.9049	0.8830	0.9221	0.8919
Naive	0.9266	0.9137	0.8745	0.8324	0.8947	0.8866	0.9068	0.8861	0.8901

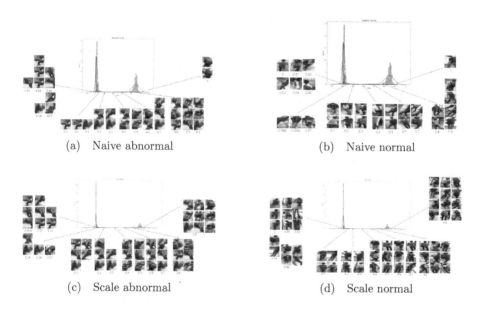

(a)   Naive abnormal   (b)   Naive normal

(c)   Scale abnormal   (d)   Scale normal

Fig. 8. Result of score tracking.

4.7   Score Tracking

In this section, we track the score distribution of naive and ABC network, to see the effect of each approach. Figure 8 show the distribution of images in detail. The score is determined by the loss, scaled into 0–1. (a), (b) shows the distribution of abnormal and normal images of naive training and (c), (d) shows the distribution of Scaled training. Looking at the (b), (d) we can find out how the network gives the score. In general, someone wears a colored shirt or bag gets a high score. Also, when they show a big angle in their leg, which mean walking horizontally against the camera got the high score. This phenomenon reflects the feature of the lobby. On the other hand, looking at the abnormal image score distribution, there are some peculiar parts in their appearance. The general part follows the rule like normal distribution (color, angle), but some images are shown in every point of the score distribution. We figured out that with only 2d appearance without temporal information, it is difficult to tell whether you are standing or lying. Even if we consider it, it is difficult to understand the causes seen in all sections. This seems to be the limit of this network that uses only instantaneous images as input.

5   Conclusion

We proposed an application of anomaly detection utilizing negative learning to limit the reconstruction capability of the generative model. Supervised learning with negative loss help network gets advantage from labeled anomaly data. The effect of using labeled data, along with conventional unsupervised manner, was confirmed with outperforming result of experiments. Still, there are few more work to do, like the current network only receives frame as input which doesn't contain any temporal information. With only the appearance information, it is hard to tell some situations shown in Sect. 4-G. Better performance is expected with adding temporal information, which is left for future work.

Acknowledgements. This work was supported by the ICT R&D program of MSIT/IITP. [2019-0-01309, Development of AI Technology for Guidance of a Mobile Robot to its Goal with Uncertain Maps in Indoor/Outdoor Environments].

References

1. Chandola, V., Banerjee, A., Kumar, V.: Anomaly detection: a survey. ACM Comput. Surv. (CSUR) **41**(3), 15 (2009)
2. Chalapathy, R., Chawla, S.: Deep learning for anomaly detection: a survey. arXiv preprint arXiv:1901.03407 (2019)
3. Lu, W., Ghorbani, A.A.: Network anomaly detection based on wavelet analysis. EURASIP J. Adv. Sig. Process. **4** (2009)
4. Ranney, K.I., Soumekh, M.: Hyperspectral anomaly detection within the signal subspace. IEEE Geosci. Remote Sens. Lett. **3**(3), 312–316 (2006)
5. Stafford, R.G., Beutel, J., et al.: Application of neural networks as an aid in medical diagnosis and general anomaly detection, 19 July 1994. US Patent 5,331,550
6. Liu, F.T., Ting, K.M., Zhou, Z.-H.: Isolation forest. In: 2008 Eighth IEEE International Conference on Data Mining, pp. 413–422. IEEE (2008)
7. Mukkamala, S., Janoski, G., Sung, A.: Intrusion detection using neural networks and support vector machines. In: Proceedings of the 2002 International Joint Conference on Neural Networks, IJCNN 2002 (Cat. No. 02CH37290), vol. 2, pp. 1702–1707. IEEE (2002)

8. Ryan, J., Lin, M.-J., Miikkulainen, R.: Intrusion detection with neural networks. In: Advances in Neural Information Processing Systems, pp. 943–949 (1998)
9. Mahadevan, V., Li, W., Bhalodia, V., Vasconcelos, N.: Anomaly detection in crowded scenes. In: 2010 IEEE Computer Society Conference on Computer Vision and Pattern Recognition, pp. 1975–1981. IEEE (2010)
10. Kratz, L., Nishino, K.: Anomaly detection in extremely crowded scenes using spatio-temporal motion pattern models. In: 2009 IEEE Conference on Computer Vision and Pattern Recognition, pp. 1446–1453. IEEE (2009)
11. Munawar, A., Vinayavekhin, P., De Magistris, G.: Limiting the reconstruction capability of generative neural network using negative learning. In: 2017 IEEE 27th International Workshop on Machine Learning for Signal Processing (MLSP), pp. 1–6. IEEE (2017)
12. Leung, K., Leckie, C.: Unsupervised anomaly detection in network intrusion detection using clusters. In: Proceedings of the Twenty-eighth Australasian conference on Computer Science, vol. 38, pp. 333–342. Australian Computer Society Inc. (2005)
13. Zaheer, M.Z., Mahmood, A., Astrid, M., Lee, S.-I.: CLAWS: clustering assisted weakly supervised learning with normalcy suppression for anomalous event detection. In: Vedaldi, A., Bischof, H., Brox, T., Frahm, J.-M. (eds.) ECCV 2020. LNCS, vol. 12367, pp. 358–376. Springer, Cham (2020). https://doi.org/10.1007/978-3-030-58542-6_22
14. Zaheer, M.Z., Mahmood, A., Shin, H., Lee, S.-I.: A self-reasoning framework for anomaly detection using video-level labels. IEEE Sig. Process. Lett. **27**, 1705–1709 (2020)
15. Zaheer, M.Z., Lee, J.-H., Astrid, M., Mahmood, A., Lee, S.-I.: Cleaning label noise with clusters for minimally supervised anomaly detection. In: Proceedings of the IEEE Conference on Computer Vision and Pattern Recognition Workshops, June 2020
16. Cortes, C., Vapnik, V.: Support-vector networks. Mach. Learn. **20**(3), 273–297 (1995)
17. Sabokrou, M., Khalooei, M., Fathy, M., Adeli, E.: Adversarially learned one-class classifier for novelty detection. In: Proceedings of the IEEE Conference on Computer Vision and Pattern Recognition, pp. 3379–3388 (2018)
18. Zaheer, M.Z., Lee, J.-H., Astrid, M., Lee, S.-I.: Old is gold: redefining the adversarially learned one-class classifier training paradigm. In: Proceedings of the IEEE/CVF Conference on Computer Vision and Pattern Recognition, pp. 14183–14193 (2020)
19. Goodfellow, I., et al.: Generative adversarial nets. In: Advances in Neural Information Processing Systems, pp. 2672–2680 (2014)
20. Sabokrou, M., Fayyaz, M., Fathy, M., Klette, R.: Deep-cascade: cascading 3D deep neural networks for fast anomaly detection and localization in crowded scenes. IEEE Trans. Image Process. **26**(4), 1992–2004 (2017)
21. Sultani, W., Chen, C., Shah, M.: Real-world anomaly detection in surveillance videos. In: Proceedings of the IEEE Conference on Computer Vision and Pattern Recognition, pp. 6479–6488 (2018)
22. Yang, H., Wang, B., Lin, S., Wipf, D., Guo, M., Guo, B.: Unsupervised extraction of video highlights via robust recurrent auto-encoders. In: Proceedings of the IEEE International Conference on Computer Vision, pp. 4633–4641 (2015)
23. Bian, J., Hui, X., Sun, S., Zhao, X., Tan, M.: A novel and efficient CVAE-GAN-based approach with informative manifold for semi-supervised anomaly detection. IEEE Access **7**, 88903–88916 (2019)

24. Makhzani, A., Shlens, J., Jaitly, N., Goodfellow, I., Frey, B.: Adversarial autoencoders. arXiv preprint arXiv:1511.05644 (2015)
25. Radford, A., Metz, L., Chintala, S.: Unsupervised representation learning with deep convolutional generative adversarial networks. arXiv preprint arXiv:1511.06434 (2015)
26. Kingma, D.P., Adam, J.B.: A method for stochastic optimization. arXiv preprint arXiv:1412.6980 (2014)
27. Ioffe, S., Szegedy, C.: Batch normalization: accelerating deep network training by reducing internal covariate shift. arXiv preprint arXiv:1502.03167 (2015)
28. Yamanaka, Y., Iwata, T., Takahashi, H., Yamada, M., Kanai, S.: Autoencoding binary classifiers for supervised anomaly detection. In: Nayak, A.C., Sharma, A. (eds.) PRICAI 2019. LNCS (LNAI), vol. 11671, pp. 647–659. Springer, Cham (2019). https://doi.org/10.1007/978-3-030-29911-8_50

Video Analysis of Wheel Pushing Actions for Wheelchair Basketball Players

Keita Fukue[1], Hisato Fukuda[1], Yoshinori Kobayashi[1(✉)], Yoshinori Kuno[1],
Nami Shida[2], Mari Sugiyama[3], Takashi Handa[4], and Tomoyuki Morita[5]

[1] Saitama University, Saitama, Japan
yosinori@hci.ics.saltama-u.ac.jp
[2] Tokyo Metropolitan University, Tokyo, Japan
[3] Tokyo Professional University of Health Sciences, Tokyo, Japan
[4] Saitama Industrial Technology Center, Saitama, Japan
[5] Kanagawa Rehabilitation Hospital, Kanagawa, Japan

Abstract. In wheelchair basketball, the performance of a player is not only determined by his/her physical ability but also depending on the settings of the wheelchair such as the height and/or angle of its seat and the size and/or position of its wheels. However, these wheelchair settings are based on the rules of thumb of players and instructors, and there are no specific guidelines or rules regarding the settings of wheelchair according to the physical characteristics and/or types of disabilities of the athletes. This study, therefore, aims to provide the suggestions to improve the performance of the athletes by analyzing the wheelchair starting actions in comparison to the top players with the highest ability of wheelchair operation. We propose the method to measure the detailed behaviors of players during starting actions from video footages. Through the experimental verification, we successfully retrieved the detailed behaviors of players and wheelchairs. We also confirmed it is possible to measure the difference in the behaviors among multiple participants and different wheelchair settings, respectively.

Keywords: Wheelchair basketball · Video analysis · Wheel pushing action

1 Introduction

In recent years, in order to improve physical and mental health, the national government has taken the initiative in increasing the value of sports and spreading them widely to the people. The sports for people with disabilities are also focused and promoted. In this study we focus on wheelchair basketball, which is one of the sports competitions for the disabled. In wheelchair competition, the performance of an athlete is not simply determined by the physical ability of the athlete but produced by the interaction between the athlete and the wheelchair. It is also known that it also depends on the wheelchair settings such as the height and/or angle of its seat and the size and/or position of its wheels. According to the instructor who is involved in coaching wheelchair basketball athletes, the ability for operating a wheelchair can be significantly improved by changing the

© Springer Nature Switzerland AG 2021
H. Jeong and K. Sumi (Eds.): IW-FCV 2021, CCIS 1405, pp. 233–241, 2021.
https://doi.org/10.1007/978-3-030-81638-4_19

setting of wheelchair appropriately based on the physical characteristics and disabilities of the athlete. However, these wheelchairs are currently set based on the rules of thumb of players and instructors, and there are no specific guidelines or rules regarding the setting of wheelchairs based on the physical characteristics of the athlete and the type of disability.

In the previous studies, researchers have been conducted to measure the performance by using sensors attached on a wheelchair, and to clarify the difference of performance due to different settings of the wheelchair. However, since these studies use sensors attached on wheelchairs, they do not consider how the athlete behaves during the actions. In addition, there is a problem that the measurement method cannot be adapted in actual wheelchair basketball game.

In this study, we, therefore, propose a method for analyzing the pushing action of athletes in wheelchair basketball by employing image analysis. The future purpose of this study is to analyze the behaviors of top players from the video during the game and to provide suggestion that might help the athletes. In this paper, as the first step of this research, we focus on the pushing action of a wheelchair from a video and examined whether it can be used for analysis of performance in wheelchair competition.

2 Related Work

In studies to analyze human motions from images, there are many studies such as research on general action recognition and sports for healthy people, and research on wheelchair sports and rehabilitation. In motion analysis for sports, a wide range of research has been conducted, including methods for performing analysis using depth cameras and machine learning, and methods for performing detailed analysis by using motion sensors and images. On the other hand, in analysis of wheelchair motion, many studies have used methods that use sensors and markers because of its easiness to attach sensors to wheelchairs.

References [1–3] are studies that perform exercise analysis using images for healthy person sports. [1, 2] use Openpose [4] to detect the human skeleton of a person and perform motion analysis. Reference [1] verifies the effectiveness of the method by applying Openpose to the squat motion and comparing the obtained indirect angle data with the method using markers. Reference [2] proposes a system that predicts the shooting probability of basketball by generating a logistic regression model using the joint coordinates obtained from Openpose as an explanatory variable. Reference [3] proposes a motion analysis method using a Kinect sensor. The authors propose a system that quantitatively evaluates the performance of handball based on image, depth, and skeletal data, and compare the difference in performance between beginners and advanced users using the system.

References [5, 6] are studies that analyze the movement of wheelchair sports using sensors. Reference [5] proposes a method for analyzing movements assuming a wheelchair basketball game using three IMU sensors attached to a wheelchair and verify its effectiveness by comparing the method with an accurate method using 24 cameras and markers. Reference [6] proposes a method to classify wheelchair operations into PUSH, STOP, and NONE by using the rotation of the wheels obtained from the angular velocity of the IMU sensor attached to the axle of the wheelchair.

Reference [7] analyzes the motion of paraplegic wheelchair users by combining sensors and images. By applying Openpose to camera images from multiple viewpoints, the authors measured changes of a wheelchair trajectory. In addition, they measured the degree of shoulder fatigue using an EMG sensor and investigate the relationship between the wheelchair trajectory and the degree of fatigue.

3 Analysis of Pushing Action

In studies on exercise analysis in wheelchair sports, to analyze wheelchair movement and competitiveness, most of studies use motion sensors attached on wheelchairs. However, since the motions sensors just measure movement of a wheelchair, they cannot measure actual motion of the athlete during actions. In addition, it is difficult to acquire and analyze the data during the actual game because the sensors are attached on the wheelchairs.

In order to measure the performance of wheelchair basketball from the video of actual games, we, therefore, propose a method to measure the movement of the wheelchair and the behavior of the pushing action of the wheelchair user from the video footages. In this paper, we developed a system that can measure the speed of the wheelchair and the rotation of the wheel as information of the motion of the wheelchair, and the changes in the gripping angle (angle between the axle and the wrist) as the information of how to push the wheelchair. In this paper, as a first stage of research, we used a general wheelchair for long-term care (Fig. 1). For wheelchair pushing motion analysis, we developed marker-less method which use skeleton detection instead of markers. For wheelchair motion analysis, we used a simple marker to understand rotation of a wheel. In data measurement, the camera was placed in the direction perpendicular to the moving direction of the wheelchair, and we measured that the wheelchair passed in front of the camera from right to left.

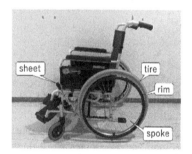   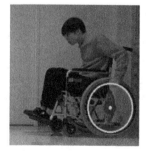

Fig. 1. A wheelchair used in experiments.   **Fig. 2.** Axle detection by Hough transformation.

3.1 Analysis of Wheelchair Motion

In order to analyze the behavior of the wheelchair, the center of the wheelchair's axle and the rotation angle of the wheel were measured using circle detection and markers.

Wheels and hand rims of a wheelchair are usually black and characteristic, so the axle coordinates were detected using those characteristics. The acquired image is converted into a grayscale image, and the circle detection by Hough transform is applied to the image to detect the wheels. We assumed the coordinates of the axle were the coordinates of the center of the detected circle. At this step, since the circle detection by the Hough transform often causes a deviation, a red marker was installed on the axle part this time for purpose the of data correction by manually. In addition, to reduce the noise of the detected coordinate values, we used averaged coordinate values using detected coordinates values for 3 frames (previous frame, current frame and next frame). Figure 2 shows the axle center detection by the Hough transformation.

For the measurement of speed of the wheelchair, which is one of the information on wheelchair motion, the distance between the axle coordinates of two consecutive frame images is calculated. Here, the speed on the image (how many pixels were moved during one frame) was measured instead of the actual speed. Figure 3 shows a graph of speed measured using our developed system. The participant's pushing motion in which the motion of pushing and stopping was repeated four times is recorded. In Fig. 3, the situation can be confirmed as the number of peaks in the graph. The value of the stop motion scene also contains noise due to the deviation of the axle coordinates, but it is considered that the measurement can be performed appropriately.

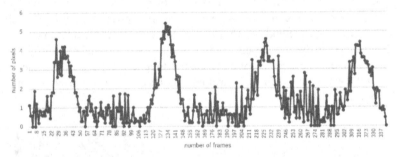

Fig. 3. Changes in speed of wheelchair.

In addition, to investigate the relationship between the pushing motion of a user and the speed of the wheelchair, we measured the wheel rotation angle. The wheel rotation angle is the change in the angle between the green marker coordinates installed on the spokes of the wheel and the axle coordinates. Figure 4 shows the green marker and how to calculate the wheel rotation angel. The marker coordinates were detected by extracting the green area near the center of the axle and calculating the coordinates of the center of gravity of the green marker area. The wheel rotation angle was measured from the difference between the vector angle θ formed by the axle coordinates and the marker coordinates and the vector angle θ' formed by the axle coordinates and the marker coordinates in previous frame.

Figure 5 shows a graph of wheel rotation angles measured from the video of the same scene as in Fig. 3 using our developed system. As in Fig. 3, the number of pushing movements can be seen as the number of peaks in the graph.

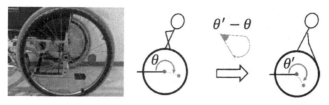

Fig. 4. The green marker and how to calculate the wheel rotation angel. (Color figure online)

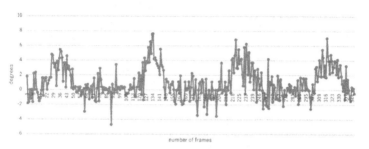

Fig. 5. Change in wheel rotation.

3.2 Analysis of Wheelchair Pushing Action

As a wheelchair pushing motion, we focused on the changes in the angle between the axle and the wrist. The changes in the angle between the axle and the wrist are calculated based on the changes in the vector angle between the vector connecting form the wrist coordinates to the axis center coordinates and the vector in the direction horizontal to the ground (Fig. 6). Hereafter, this angle will be referred to as the gripping angle. It would be effective to analyze the change of the gripping angle for understanding of interaction between a wheelchair user and the wheelchair.

First, the coordinates of each joint of the wheelchair user were detected by using Openpose. Openpose is a DNN framework for skeleton detection, which can estimate joint coordinates in an image such as "right wrist" and "left ankle" and calculate related vectors between each joint. In this method, first, the joint angle, which is information of how to push, is measured from the detected coordinates of each joint. As for the measurement of the gripping angle, the angle is obtained by calculating the frame difference of the angle between the vector from the axle to the wrist and the horizontal vector.

Figure 7 shows the graph of change in gripping angles measured from the video of the same scene as in Fig. 3 using the developed system. Assuming that the forward direction of the participant's body is the positive direction, the value of the angle change is positive when pushing forward, and the value of the angle change is negative when the hand is returned to the pushing position. The orange line shows the wheel rotation angle shown in Fig. 5, and it can be confirmed that the value of the gripping angle in the scene where the participant is pushing a wheelchair, similar to the wheel rotation angle.

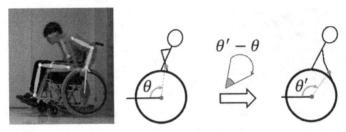

Fig. 6. Detected skeleton and how to calculate the gripping angle.

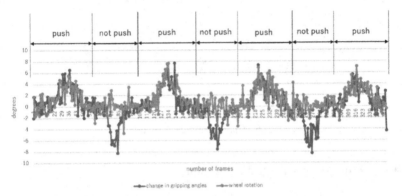

Fig. 7. Change in gripping angles and wheel rotation.

4   Experiment in a Laboratory Setting

We examined whether this method can properly deal with the difference in pushing action when different participants push the same wheelchair and the change in pushing action when the same participant pushed a wheelchair with different settings. The experiment was conducted indoors at the university to which the authors belong. The actual experimental environment is shown in Fig. 8.

Fig. 8. Experimental environment.

4.1   Experiment 1: Pushing Action Analysis Between Participants

In an experiment to analyze pushing actions among individuals, three participants (all three were male university students, all three were 22 years old and did not normally use a wheelchair). The participants were instructed to push the wheelchair 5 m forwards of the participant as fast as possible and stop suddenly at the destination. As a result of the experiment 1, participant 1 pushed a wheelchair 7 times, participant 2 pushed a wheelchair 5 times, and participant 3 pushed a wheelchair 4 times. In addition, the time to finish pushing the same distance was shorter in the order of participant 3, participant 2, and participant 1.

Figure 9 shows the changes in the gripping angles of the 3 participants. The number of pushing motion of each participants was different, and the difference can be confirmed in Fig. 9 as the difference in the number of peaks of each waveform. Comparing the graph of changes in the gripping angles of participant 3 with the graphs of participant 1 and 2, the amplitude of the waveform is the largest and the interval distance between the peaks is short. From the characteristics of these graphs, the pushing action by participant 3 has the fastest instantaneous speed and the shortest time for one pushing action. In addition, since participant 3 had the fastest actual pushing speed, it was confirmed that the characteristics of the pushing action of the participants could be expressed by the data obtained from this system.

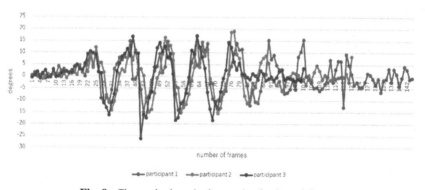

Fig. 9. Change in the gripping angles for 3 participants.

4.2   Experiment 2: Pushing Action Analysis with Different Wheelchair Settings

In the experiment of pushing action analysis with different wheelchair settings, we asked participant 3 of experiment 1 to use 2 type of wheelchair. The first setting was for the seating surface of a normal wheelchair, and the second setting was for the seating surface to be 9 cm higher than normal one. The instructions were the same as in Experiment 1. As a result of the experiment, the time required for the wheelchair in setting 1 was shorter than the time required for the wheelchair in setting 2, and the number of times of pushing was the same.

Figure 10 shows the change in the gripping angles of each setting. In Fig. 10, the amplitude of the waveform in setting 1(+0cm) is large and the interval between peaks is short. Since these results are also plausible from the data obtained from actual observations, it was confirmed that the characteristics of the pushing action of the participants could be expressed by the data obtained from this system.

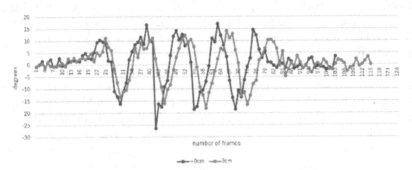

Fig. 10. Change in gripping angles with 2 type of wheelchairs.

5   Conclusion

In this research, we examined an image analysis method to acquire information of how to push a wheelchair and information on wheelchair motion for wheelchair basketball players and instructors. The differences in the pushing motion of different participants and the differences in the pushing action when the same participant pushed a wheelchair with different settings can be measured by our proposed method.

Since the participants in this experiment are not actual athletes and wheelchairs are also not for competitive use, it has not been possible to examine how effective they are for actual competition scenes. In future work, we will apply our proposed method to the videos of the actual pushing motion of a wheelchair basketball player taken with the same settings and verify whether the data can be measured appropriately. In addition, since the gripping angle can be measured only from the images taken from the side, and the marker is used to measure the wheel rotation, we, therefore, plan to modify our method to deal with actual videos of wheelchair basketball game.

References

1. Ota, M., et al.: Verification of reliability and validity of motion analysis systems during bilateral squat using human pose tracking algorithm. Gait Posture **80**, 62–67 (2020)
2. Nakai, M., Tsunoda, Y., Hayashi, H., Murakoshi, H.: Prediction of basketball free throw shooting by Openpose. In: Kojima, K., Sakamoto, M., Mineshima, K., Satoh, K. (eds.) JSAI-isAI 2018. LNCS (LNAI), vol. 11717, pp. 435–446. Springer, Cham (2019). https://doi.org/10.1007/978-3-030-31605-1_31

3. Elaoud, A., Barhoumi, W., Zagrouba, E., Agrebi, B.: Skeleton-based comparison of throwing motion for handball players. J. Ambient. Intell. Humaniz. Comput. **11**(1), 419–431 (2019). https://doi.org/10.1007/s12652-019-01301-6
4. Cao, Z., et al.: Realtime multi-person 2D pose estimation using part affinity fields. In: Proceedings IEEE Conference on Computer Vision and Pattern Recognition (CVPR) (2017)
5. van der Slikke, R.M.A., et al.: Opportunities for measuring wheelchair kinematics in match settings; reliability of a three inertial sensor configuration. J. Biomech. **38**, 3398–3405 (2015)
6. Hasegawa, R., et al.: Maneuver classification in wheelchair basketball using inertial sensors. In: Proceedings IEEE International Conference on Mobile Computing and Ubiquitous Network (ICMU), pp. 1–6 (2019)
7. Sebastiani, M., et al.: Joint trajectory and fatigue analysis in wheelchair users. In: Proceedings IEEE International Conference on Computer Vision Workshops (ICCVW) (2019)

Efficient Spatial-Attention Module
for Human Pose Estimation

Tien-Dat Tran, Xuan-Thuy Vo, Duy-Linh Nguyen, and Kang-Hyun Jo[✉]

School of Electrical Engineering, University of Ulsan, Ulsan 44610, South Korea
{tdat,xthuy}@islab.ulsan.ac.kr, ndlinh301@mail.ulsan.ac.kr,
acejo@ulsan.ac.kr

Abstract. Not only for human pose estimation but also other machine vision tasks (e.g. object recognition, semantic segmentation, image classification), convolution neural networks (CNNs) have obtained the highest performance today. Besides, their performance over other traditional networks is shown by the Attention Module (AM). Hence, this paper focuses on a valuable feed-forward AM for CNNs. First, feed the feature map into the attention module after a stage in the backbone network, divided into two different dimensions, channel and spatial. After that, by multiplication, the AM combines these two feature maps and gives them to the next stage in the backbone. In long-range dependencies (channel) and spatial data, the network can capture more information, which can gain better precision efficiency. Our experimental findings would also demonstrate the disparity between the use of the attention module and current methods. As a result, with the change to make the spatial better, the expected joint heatmap retains the accuracy while decreasing the number of parameters. In comparison, the proposed architecture benefits more than the baseline by 1.3 points in AP. In addition, the proposed network was trained on the benchmarks of COCO 2017, which is now an open dataset.

Keywords: Deep learning · Attention module · Spatial-attention module · Human pose estimation

1 Introduction

In today's modern world, 2D human pose estimation performs a critical but difficult role in computer vision, which can support multiple purposes such as human pose estimation [2,24], activity recognition [7,11], human re-identification [13,27] or 3D human pose estimation [1]. The key aim of human pose is to identify body parts for human body joints. Spatial and channel data play an important role in making the regression of key points more precise. As a result, this paper will focus on how to make the network learn more about the attention information.

Important developments in human pose have now been archived by deep convolution of neural networks [8,17]. However, these networks still have a lot

© Springer Nature Switzerland AG 2021
H. Jeong and K. Sumi (Eds.): IW-FCV 2021, CCIS 1405, pp. 242–250, 2021.
https://doi.org/10.1007/978-3-030-81638-4_20

of issues to discuss. First of all, how to boost accuracy in different forms of networks (e.g., real-time network, accuracy network). Second, there is often a need to consider the speed of the network while changing or modifying it. Last but not least, the current network has to achieve better accuracy while maintaining speed as fast as possible. This paper describes a novel network and the reliability of the attention module for speed and accuracy. The proposed experiment shows a comparison between the focus module used and not used. The experiment also contrasts with the Simple Baseline [26] which did not use the attention mechanism and used the transpose convolution [3] for upsampling. Our experiment would concentrate on how efficient and cost-effective each case for the network.

In paricular, our approach was implement based on simple fine-tune attention module [22] which shows significant improve in mean Average Precision (mAP). Inspired by VGG16 [19], the proposed network try to improve the spatial attention module (SAM) by using two 3×3 convolution layer instead of 7×7 convolution layer. By used 3×3 kernel, the network still maintain the mAP while decrease the implementation cost. In addition, the number of parameter decrease so the speed of our network was upgraded. To make clear about modify SAM, our network increase 0.2 point in AP for accuracy and reduces around 1.6% of parameters compared with the Attention mechanism baseline [22] when used ResNet-50 [5] as a backbone network. This paper introduces a new SAM module for the network, which can easily respond to a range of problems in many applications, such as object recognition, image classification and human pose estimation. The suggested approach calculates joint human pose estimates based on the recovery of feature maps using the up-sampling network.

2   Related Work

Human Pose Estimation. The leading part of human pose estimation lies in joint detection and their relationship with spatial space, which illustrates in Fig. 1. Deeppose [21], Simple baseline utilizes joints prediction thought an end to end network with higher parameter. Later, Newell with Stacked hourglass network [18] decreases the number of the setting while still keep high accuracy. All of the methods used Gaussian distribution to represent local joints. Then used a convolution neural network to estimate human pose estimation. To decrease the employment cost, they need to reduce the number of parameters, and applying suitable up-sampling methods will lower the network's parameter. So, the proposed method used interpolation as up-sampling module.

On the other hand, to enhance the speed of the network, interpolation shows a lot of benefits than the transpose convolution. However, in some complex and higher cost architecture, the transpose convolution gives better accuracy. In comparison, our up-sampling module provides an adequate view for designing the network, with a small number in parameter and high speed or higher parameter and lower speed. Then this paper shows how up-sampling will work in each method and each result.

Attention Mechanism: Human visualization plays an important role in computer vision, and there are a variety of focus processing attempts to enhance the efficiency of CNNs. Wang et al. [23] also suggested a non-local network to collect long-range dependencies. Inspired by SENet [6] and Inception [20], then SKNet [14] merged the SENet Channel Focus Module with the Inception Multi-Branch Convolution. In addition, the Module for Spatial Focus comes from the STN [10] suggested by Google, which aggregates the background details of the feature maps. In addition, the attention module shows a lot of advantages for the detection of saliency, the multi-label classification for the recognition of the individual.

In this paper, the proposed method was inspired by CBAM network [25] to make the effective between both channel and spatial module by using element-wise multiplication. After that, the feature map takes an addition to the last feature map to combine the original information and new information from the AT module.

3   Methodology

3.1   Network Architecture

Backbone Network. There are ResNet-101 and ResNet-50[5] in the backbone network, as can be seen in Fig. 1 for complete architecture. Every ResNet has four blocks, including convolution layers and shortcut connections. The input RGB picture reduces the size to 256×192 (ResNet-50, ResNet-101), the feature maps pass across each column block, and the resolution of $W \times H$ decreases twice for each block. Finally, after passing along the spine, the size of the function map is reduced to $\frac{W}{16} \times \frac{H}{16}$ with 2048 channels at the end of the spine. In addition, the size of the channels also would be doubled for each block. It's coming from 256 after the first block to 2048 in the last layer. The mission of the backbone network is to collect information and feature maps from the input image and feed it to the Up-Sampling Training System.

After extracting the information by utilized the backbone network, the upsampling network takes the feature map from the last layer of the backbone network and upsampling to recover the information. Next, the feature map will then practice with the Ground-truth Heat Maps, as is seen in Fig. 1. The default heat map size is 64×48 for 256×192 photos and 96×72 for 384×288. This heat maps need to understand the scale of the image in order to match the size of the feature maps in the training process. The network will use these heat maps and the ground truth heatmap for regression to calculate the predicting main point. For the up-sampling network, this paper uses the up-sampling module, which contains one bilinear [16] layer and one convolution layer (in Fig. 2). And there's an alternative to this two-layer. Batch normalization and ReLU [9] are both within the up-sampling block.

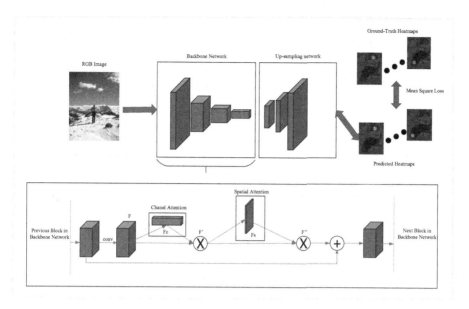

Fig. 1. Illustrating the design of the proposed human-pose estimation network. The suggested approach split the system into two sub-networks, Backbone, and Up-sampling. Backbone extracts a feature map while Up-sampling retrieves a feature map for regression. In comparison, this figure indicates the description of the attention module, which included the channel and the spatial module at the bottom of the list.

Attention Module. The Attention Mechanism contains two major modules seen in Fig. 2. First, after block one in the backbone network, the feature map was fed to the channel attention module (CAM). In CAM, the feature map takes global average pooling to squeeze the feature map from $H \times W \times C$ to $1 \times 1 \times C$. First, it goes into the convolution layer, which transforms the feature map to $1 \times 1 \times \frac{C}{r}$, which r is the reduction ratio, and r is set to 16. The CAM then used the ReLU to trigger the weight. The final step in CAM is to use 1×1 convolution layer again to restore the channel to $1 \times 1 \times C$ and use the sigmoid to normalize the feature map. After that, the element-wise multiplication was used to merge the details for CAM.

When the feature map goes through the CAM, it will be fed into the Spatial Attention Module (SAM). In SAM, the feature map takes the average channel pooling from $H \times W \times C$ to $H \times W \times 1$. After pooling, two 3×3 convolution layers were used to extract the spatial information attribute diagram, and the final stage in SAM is identical to the CAM that can be seen in Fig. 2. Finally, the planned approach used the element-wise extension to the initial feature map and the feature map after AT to be merged and a new feature map for the next block in the backbone network.

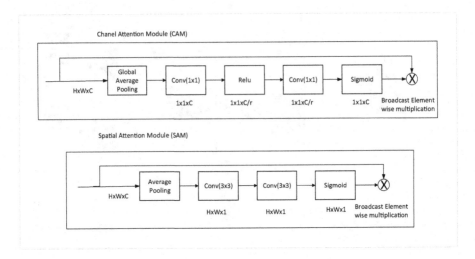

Fig. 2. Architecture of Channel Attention Module (CAM) and Spatial attention Module (SAM)

3.2 Loss Function

This paper uses heat maps to represent body joint positions for the loss function. As the position of the ground-truth in Fig. 1 by $a = \{ak\}\, k = 1^K$, where $xk = (xk, yk)$ is the spatial coordinate of the kth body joint in the picture. Then the ground-truth heat map value Hk is generated from the Gaussian distribution with the mean ak and the variance $\sum$ as follows.

$$H_k(p) \sim N(a_k, \textstyle\sum) \tag{1}$$

where $\mathbf{p} \in \mathbb{R}^2$ denotes the coordinate, and $\sum$ is empirically set as an identity matrix $\mathbf{I}$. Final layer of neural network predicts K heat maps, $i.e.,$ $\hat{S} = \left\{ \hat{S}_k \right\}_{k=1}^{K}$ for K body joints. A loss function is defined by the mean square error, measured as::

$$L = \frac{1}{NK} \sum_{n=1}^{N} \sum_{k=1}^{K} \left\| S_k - \hat{S}_k \right\|^2 \tag{2}$$

where N is the number of samples in the training session. The network developed predictive heat maps from ground-truth heat maps using information from the last layer of the backbone network.

4   Experiments

4.1   Experiment Setup

Dataset. During the tests, the suggested approach used the Microsoft COCO 2017 dataset [15]. This dataset contains about 200K images and 250K human samples, which have 17 keypoint labels for one person. The data collection of the study included three folder train set, validation set, test-dev set, respectively, with training, validation and testing images. In addition, the validation and training annotations are public and accompanied by the original.

Evaluation Metrics. This paper used Object Keypoint Similarity (OKS) for COCO [15] with $OKS = \frac{\sum_i exp(-d_i^2/2s^2 k_i^2)\delta(v_i>0)}{\sum_i \delta(v_i>0)}$. Here d_i is the Euclidean distance between the predicted keypoint and the groundtruth while v_i is the visibility flag of the target, s is the object scale and k_i is a keypoint for each joints. Then calculate the standart average precision and recall score. In table I, AP and AR is the average from OKS = 0.5 to OKS = 0.95, while AP^M for medium object and AP^L for large object.

Implementation Details. In model training, the proposed approach used data raise, such as flip, rotation at 40 degrees by design, and scale, which set the factor at 0.3. Set the batch size to 4 and use the shuffle for training photos. The total of the epoch is 270, while the based learning-rate at 0.001 and multiple by 0.1 (learning rate factor) at the 170-th and 200-th epoch in our experiment. The momentum is 0.9, and the Adam optimizer [12] was used.

All experiments are implemented with Pytorch framework and testing in two datasets. The input resolution of images resized to 256×192. The model was trained on one NVIDIA GTX 1080Ti GPUs with CUDA 10.2 and CuDNN 7.3.

4.2 Experiment Result

Table 1. The result of using the different kernel of convolution layer in the SAM module. $3 \times 3 + 3 \times 3$ means using continuously two 3×3 kernel and $3 \times 3 // 3 \times 3$ means using two parallel 3×3 kernel

Backbone	Convolution layer	#Param	mAP
ResNet-50	7×7	31.2M	71.4
ResNet-50	$3 \times 3 + 3 \times 3$	30.7M	71.6
ResNet-50	$3 \times 3 // 3 \times 3$	30.7M	71.5
ResNet-101	7×7	51.3M	72.3

To show clearly about performance of SAM in AT, The proposed method compares each situation when used different convolution kernel, which show in Table 1. The Average Precision (AP) shows that used two 3×3 convolution kernel gain 0.2 in mAP than used 7×7 while the number of parameter decrease 1.6% in ResNet50 (Table 2).

COCO Datasets Result. The AP in the suggested approach is greater than the Basic benchmark in all situations of 1.3 AP, 1.1 AP in ResNet-50, ResNet-101, respectively. The number of parameters also reduces relative to the standard due to the variation in the up-sampling network. Although the benchmark

Table 2. Comparison on COCO TEST-DEV Dataset. AM is mean attention module, new AM is new attention module proposed in this paper

Method	Backbone	Input size	#Params	AP	AP^{50}	AP^{75}	AP^M	AP^L	AR
8-Stage Hourglass [18]	8-Stage Hourglass	256 × 192	25.1M	66.9	–	–	–	–	–
Mask-RCNN [4]	ResNet-50-FPN	256 × 192	–		63.1	87.3	68.7	57.8	71.4	–
SimpleBaseline [26]	ResNet-50	256 × 192	34.0M	70.4	88.6	78.3	67.1	77.2	76.3
SimpleBaseline [26]	ResNet-101	256 × 192	53.0M	71.4	89.3	79.3	68.1	78.1	77.1
SimpleBaseline [26]	ResNet-152	256 × 192	68.6M	73.7	91.9	81.1	70.3	80.0	79.0
Fine-tuning AM [22]	ResNet-50	256 × 192	31.2M	71.4	91.6	78.6	68.2	75.7	76.3
Fine-tuning AM [22]	ResNet-101	256 × 192	50.2M	72.3	92.0	79.4	68.3	77.1	77.1
Our + new AM	ResNet-50	256 × 192	30.7M	71.7	91.8	80.3	69.0	78.2	76.9
Our + new AM	ResNet101	256 × 192	49.7M	72.5	92.2	80.9	69.9	79.5	78.1

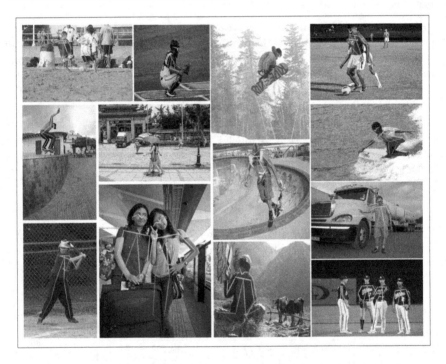

Fig. 3. Qualitative result for human pose estimation in COCO2017 test-dev set

used transposes convolution costs a number of parameters, the proposed approach uses bi-linear interpolation at no cost for settings. Our solution adds a new module (AT) but changes the up-sampling module such that the number of parameters are different. In this experiment the number of parameter was smaller 9.7% and 6.2% in case or ResNet-50, ResNet-101, respectively. Besides, the average recall (AR) gain better result in case of ResNet-101 with 1.0 points higher. In all cases of Fine-tuning AM, our network gain 0.3 in mAP for both ResNet-50 and Resnet-101 (Table 2).

However, as with many architectures today, human pose estimation also has many problems that need to be tackled. The first problem being that the pictures included unseen joints that were impossible to train and predict. Second, low-resolution photographs of humans need to be properly extracted for human body joints. Next, there are photos of crowd scenes, which are often hard to establish all the locations of the joints for all participants. Finally, there is a lack of details on photographs containing partial sections for estimating human poses (Fig. 3).

5   Conclusion

This paper demonstrates the influence of the attention module on CNNs, and reveals that the attention module used has a stronger effect by not changing the number of parameters. In comparison, the Attention Module highlighted the essential function maps instead of the other component. The network will therefore boost efficiency, particularly for several tasks in the field of computer vision. Future analysis is to define certain applications or environments to be added to our study, such as the surveillance system. Another task is due to the difficulties of human exposure assessment, which limits the precision of the network.

Acknowledgement. This work was supported by the National Research Foundation of Korea (NRF) grant funded by the Korea government. (MSIT) (No. 2020R1A2C2008972).

References

1. Chen, C., Ramanan, D.: 3D human pose estimation = 2d pose estimation + matching. In: 2017 IEEE Conference on Computer Vision and Pattern Recognition (CVPR), pp. 5759–5767, July 2017. https://doi.org/10.1109/CVPR.2017.610
2. Chou, C.J., Chien, J.T., Chen, H.T.: Self adversarial training for human pose estimation (2017)
3. Dumoulin, V., Visin, F.: A guide to convolution arithmetic for deep learning (2016)
4. He, K., Gkioxari, G., Dollár, P., Girshick, R.: Mask R-CNN (2017)
5. He, K., Zhang, X., Ren, S., Sun, J.: Deep residual learning for image recognition (2015)
6. Hu, J., Shen, L., Albanie, S., Sun, G., Wu, E.: Squeeze-and-excitation networks (2017)
7. Hussain, Z., Sheng, M., Zhang, W.E.: Different approaches for human activity recognition: a survey (2019)
8. Insafutdinov, E., Pishchulin, L., Andres, B., Andriluka, M., Schiele, B.: DeeperCut: a deeper, stronger, and faster multi-person pose estimation model (2016)
9. Ioffe, S., Szegedy, C.: Batch normalization: accelerating deep network training by reducing internal covariate shift (2015)
10. Jaderberg, M., Simonyan, K., Zisserman, A., Kavukcuoglu, K.: Spatial transformer networks (2015)

11. Kim, E., Helal, S., Cook, D.: Human activity recognition and pattern discovery. IEEE Pervasive Comput. **9**(1), 48–53 (2010). https://doi.org/10.1109/MPRV.2010.7
12. Kingma, D., Ba, J.: Adam: a method for stochastic optimization. In: International Conference on Learning Representations (2014)
13. Li, W., Zhao, R., Wang, X.: Human reidentification with transferred metric learning. In: Lee, K.M., Matsushita, Y., Rehg, J.M., Hu, Z. (eds.) ACCV 2012. LNCS, vol. 7724, pp. 31–44. Springer, Heidelberg (2013). https://doi.org/10.1007/978-3-642-37331-2_3
14. Li, X., Wang, W., Hu, X., Yang, J.: Selective kernel networks (2019)
15. Lin, T., et al.: Microsoft COCO: common objects in context. CoRR abs/1405.0312 (2014). http://arxiv.org/abs/1405.0312
16. Mastyło, M.: Bilinear interpolation theorems and applications. J. Funct. Anal. **265**, 185–207 (2013). https://doi.org/10.1016/j.jfa.2013.05.001
17. Moon, G., Chang, J.Y., Lee, K.M.: PoseFix: model-agnostic general human pose refinement network (2018)
18. Newell, A., Yang, K., Deng, J.: Stacked hourglass networks for human pose estimation. CoRR abs/1603.06937 (2016). http://arxiv.org/abs/1603.06937
19. Simonyan, K., Zisserman, A.: Very deep convolutional networks for large-scale image recognition (2015)
20. Szegedy, C., Ioffe, S., Vanhoucke, V., Alemi, A.: Inception-v4, inception-ResNet and the impact of residual connections on learning (2016)
21. Toshev, A., Szegedy, C.: DeepPose: human pose estimation via deep neural networks. CoRR abs/1312.4659 (2013). http://arxiv.org/abs/1312.4659
22. Tran, T.-D., Vo, X.-T., Russo, M.-A., Jo, K.-H.: Simple fine-tuning attention modules for human pose estimation. In: Hernes, M., Wojtkiewicz, K., Szczerbicki, E. (eds.) ICCCI 2020. CCIS, vol. 1287, pp. 175–185. Springer, Cham (2020). https://doi.org/10.1007/978-3-030-63119-2_15
23. Wang, X., Girshick, R.B., Gupta, A., He, K.: Non-local neural networks. CoRR abs/1711.07971 (2017). http://arxiv.org/abs/1711.07971
24. Wei, S.E., Ramakrishna, V., Kanade, T., Sheikh, Y.: Convolutional pose machines (2016)
25. Woo, S., Park, J., Lee, J.-Y., Kweon, I.S.: CBAM: convolutional block attention module. In: Ferrari, V., Hebert, M., Sminchisescu, C., Weiss, Y. (eds.) ECCV 2018. LNCS, vol. 11211, pp. 3–19. Springer, Cham (2018). https://doi.org/10.1007/978-3-030-01234-2_1
26. Xiao, B., Wu, H., Wei, Y.: Simple baselines for human pose estimation and tracking. CoRR abs/1804.06208 (2018). http://arxiv.org/abs/1804.06208
27. Yang, X., Wang, M., Tao, D.: Person re-identification with metric learning using privileged information. CoRR abs/1904.05005 (2019). http://arxiv.org/abs/1904.05005

Algorithm/Application

GCN-Calculated Graph-Feature Embedding for 3D Endoscopic System Based on Active Stereo

Michihiro Mikamo[1][(✉)], Hiroshi Kawasaki[2], Ryusuke Sagawa[3], and Ryo Furukawa[1]

[1] Hiroshima City University, 3-4-1, Oozuka-higashi, Asaminami-ku, Hiroshima-shi, Hiroshima, Japan
mikamo@hiroshima-cu.ac.jp
[2] Kyushu University, 744, Motooka, Nishi-ku, Fukuoka-shi, Fukuoka, Japan
[3] National Institute of Advanced Industrial Science and Technology (AIST), 1-1-1, Umezono, Tsukuba-shi, Ibaraki, Japan

Abstract. One of the promising fields for active-stereo sensors is medical applications such as 3D endoscope systems. For such systems, robust correspondence estimation between the detected patterns and the projected pattern is the most crucial. In this paper, we propose an auto-calibrating 3D endoscopic system using a 2D grid-graph pattern, where codes are embedded into each grid point. Since the pattern is a grid graph, we use a graph convolutional network (GCN) to calculate node-wise embedding accumulating code information of nearby grid points in the graph. The correspondence estimation using the GCN-calculated feature embedding is shown to be stable, even without using epipolar constraints. Using the correspondence estimation, we show that the auto-calibrating 3D measurement system can be realized. In the experiment, we confirmed that the proposed system achieved high accuracy and robust estimation comparing to the previous methods.

Keywords: Deep learning · Graph convolutional network · Auto-calibration · Active stereo · 3D endoscope system

1 Introduction

Active stereo using structured-light illumination has been a major approach for practical depth estimation methods [9,18,25,26]. One of the promising fields for one-shot active-stereo systems is that of medical application; *e.g.*, active stereo systems for endoscope or laparoscopic systems [5,8,14,19]. Active stereo systems can be build simply by adding a static pattern projector to endoscopic or laparoscopic cameras, thus it is easier than building endoscopes or laparoscopes with stereo cameras [15,21]. For example, Furukawa *et al.* proposed to use a micro-sized projector that can be inserted into instrument channels of flexible endoscopes [3–5].

© Springer Nature Switzerland AG 2021
H. Jeong and K. Sumi (Eds.): IW-FCV 2021, CCIS 1405, pp. 253–266, 2021.
https://doi.org/10.1007/978-3-030-81638-4_21

Some researchers have proposed to use SfM approach [11], however, many organ surfaces are not texture-rich, and the scale ambiguity of SfM is a difficult problem. On the contrary, active stereo systems can be used for surfaces with no textures, and the scale ambiguity can be solved not only for known extrinsic parameters, but also for auto-calibrated systems using appropriate projector-pose modeling [4].

For designing active stereo systems, coding strategies for the correspondence problem have been critical [18]. Many existing systems embed codes into the pattern and use them for identification of pattern features such as points or lines. One problem is that information obtained from a single code is limited. Especially, for severe environments, *i.e.*, measuring organ surfaces from endoscopic images, information that can be obtained from a single code stably may be just a few [6]. In such cases, combinations of multiple codes should be used for identifications of pattern features.

Another aspect of coding strategies is using 1D-aligned lines or 2D-aligned grid points. For 1D-aligned line features, lines are identified with codes and the 3D shapes are constructed with light sectioning method [25]. For 2D-aligned grid features, grid points are identified [9,20,26]. One problem for 1D codification is that we cannot obtain information for calibration; thus, the system should be precisely pre-calibrated. In 2D codification, epipolar constraints may be used for calibration purposes or calibration-error detection.

In this paper, we propose a 3D endoscopic system using a 2D grid pattern, where codes are embedded into each grid point. A code of a grid point can be just one of three alphabets that can be stably detected even from organ surfaces with strong subsurface scattering. To enrich the code information so that each grid-point can be uniquely identified, We use a deep-learning framework. Since the pattern is a grid graph, we use graph convolutional network (GCN) [1] to learn to calculate node-wise embedding accumulating code information of nearby grid points in the graph.

Also, since we use 2D-aligned grid points, we can use epipolar constraints. We use epipolar constraints for two purposes; one for calibrating the active-stereo system, and the other for improving the accuracy of identifying 2D grid points. Using this technique, we can auto-calibrate extrinsic parameters in the process of measurement. After auto-calibration, we can use the parameters both for increasing correspondence accuracy and for 3D reconstruction This greatly improves the practicability of the 3D endoscope system, because we can add a pattern projector to an endoscope in operations and then calibrate on-the-fly as Furukawa *et al.* [4].

Our contributions are as follows: (1) GCN-calculated feature embedding for matching graph patterns attributed with structured-light codes for active stereo is proposed. (2) An active-stereo 3D endoscope system that can be auto-calibrated is proposed. For auto-calibration, correspondence estimation without epipolar constraints can be used. After auto-calibration, epipolar constraints can be taken into account to solve the correspondence problem.

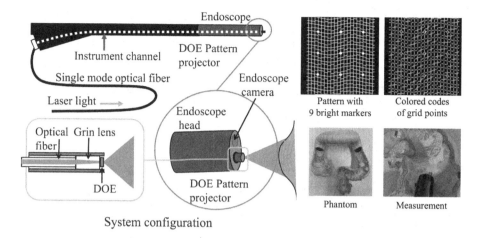

System configuration

Fig. 1. System configurations, projected patterns, and the appearances of the phantom model that was used for experiments of this paper.

2 Related Works

For endoscopic diagnosis and treatment, 3D information is desired for many purposes. Recently, deep-learning-based 3D shape reconstruction for endoscopic images. These methods use photometric information [10,12,13,16,22], or texture information based on shape-from-motion (SfM) techniques [11]. Photometric information heavily rely on source light intensity and characteristics and surface albedo; thus, absolute distance accuracy is limited. SfM-based approaches have problems with texture requirements and scale ambiguity.

The structured light technique has been used for practical applications for 3D scanning purposes [18]. For endoscope systems, since the endoscope head always moves, the system should be realtime, and a typical solution is using one-shot scanning techniques [9,26]. One severe problem for one-shot scan approaches is that they encode positional information into small regions, patterns tend to be complicated and easily affected and degraded by environmental conditions, such as noise, specularity, blur, etc. Recently learning-based techniques are proposed [5].

U-Net [17] is a standard architecture of fully convolutional neural network (FCNN), which can receive an image and produces a labeled image.

Song et al. [20] proposed to decode active-stereo patterns using a CNN. They use conventional methods for grid detection, and a CNN is used for classifying specifically designed 256 characters embedded into the grid pattern. We also use U-Net for pattern detection in our method.

Recently, deep-learning-based approaches to efficiently find correspondences are proposed [23,24].

Deep neural networks have the potential for outperforming existing correspondence estimation criteria. In this paper, we use a structured-light

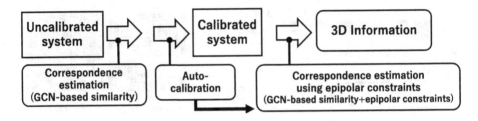

Fig. 2. 3D reconstruction process with auto-calibration.

pattern represented as a grid graph. Since detection errors for the grid graphs are inevitable, the graphs tend to be have erroneous or missing edges. Thus, 2D CNN is cannot be applied simply. Recently, graph convolutional networks (GCN) have been proposed for aggregating node-wise features of graphs [1]. GCN can be applied to graphs that have erroneous or missing edges; thus, it can be applied to matching for active stereo with graph-based coded patterns.

For matching graphs with codes, loopy belief propagation (LBP) [2] can also be a solution. One disadvantage of LBP is that the cost function of LBP should be defined manually by users. How to define the cost function for a specific task is an open problem. On the contrary, GCN can be trained for the target tasks based on training data.

3   System Configuration

For this study, a projector-camera system was constructed by inserting a fiber-shaped, micro pattern projector into the instrument channel of a standard endoscope. We used a Fujifilm EG-590WR endoscope and a pattern projector with a diffractive optical element (DOE) to generate structured-light illumination. The pattern projector can be inserted into the endoscope's instrument channel and patterns are projected from the projector to surfaces in front of the head of the endoscope (Fig. 1). As shown in Fig. 1, we used a grid pattern that is robust against subsurface scattering [6]. All vertical edges are connected; horizontal edges have small gaps, representing code letters S, L and R as shown as colored codes in Fig. 1, where red dots mean that the right and the left edges of the grid point have the same height (code letter S) blue means the left side is higher (code letter L), and green means the right is higher (code R).

As previously described, we can auto-calibrate extrinsic parameters in the process of measurement. First, after the projector is inserted into the instrument channel, the system is uncalibrated. In this situation, the correspondence estimation is done purely by GCN-calculated embedding. The auto-calibration is done by RANSAC to cope with correspondence outliers. After auto-calibration, we use the estimated extrinsic parameters both for increasing correspondence accuracies as shown in Fig. 2.

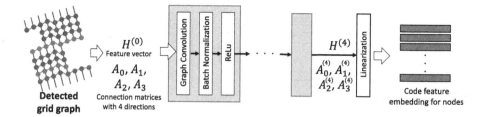

Fig. 3. Network architecture of GCN for calculating node-wise code-feature embedding.

4 Building Code-Attributed Graphs of Detected Features

As described previously, the projected pattern is a grid structure with code letters $(S/L/R)$ associated with the grid points.

We extract the grid-structure and gap-code information by using U-Nets in the same method as [17].

In the paper, to add extra information to the feature vector of each node, we also add 9 bright markers into the projected pattern as shown in Fig. 1 (top right) white dots. To utilize these markers in our method, we train CNNs to classify each of the markers into 5 classes (up to rotational symmetry, 9 markers can be classified into 5 classes). By applying the trained CNNs, every pixel of the captured frames is classified into 6 classes (5 plus one for non-marker).

In the output image from U-Net, the lines of the grid can be extracted as the boundaries between the regions to two labels. By performing the 8-neighbor labeling process on extracted boundary curves, different labels are assigned for each curve. Then, intersections between vertical and horizontal curves are extracted as grid points. By sorting the set of grid points on one vertical curve by y coordinates, the adjacency relationships between these grid points along the vertical curve are determined. By applying this process for all of the vertical and horizontal curves, the grid structure of the extracted curves can be represented as a graph.

For each grid point, a feature vector is assigned using outputs of U-Net, such as 2D coordinates on the image, estimated code, and estimated marker class. Figure 5 (left/middle) show examples of an image and a graph extracted from the image. This attribute is embedded in feature vectors of $2 + 4 + 6$ dimensions (2D coordinates, 4D code classes (three types for codes and one for unknown code), 6D marker classes (five types for markers, and one for non-markers)).

5 GCN-Calculated Embedding of Detected Features

Once the code-attributed grid graph is detected from the image, correspondences between the nodes of the detected graph and those of the original projected graph are estimated.

Each grid point of the detected graph is attributed with a code of three alphabets, $\{S, L, R\}$. Although a single grid point is not enough for estimating

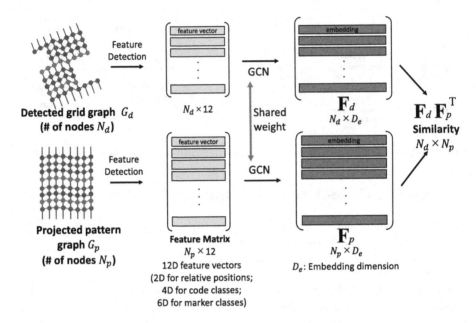

Fig. 4. Node-wise similarity calculation.

correspondence, combinations of the nearby grid points with code attributes can be enough for estimating correspondences.

In this paper, we calculate node-wise feature embedding by using Graph Convolutional Network (GCN) [1]. A feature embedding of a single grid point is a compressed representation of codes, markers, and positional information of nearby grid points. The GCN is trained so that a simple cosine similarity function can be used for matching the detected grid graph and the original projected graph. The architecture of the GCN for calculating feature embedding is shown in Fig. 3, and the matching process of the detected graph and the original graph is shown in Fig. 4.

In [6], the correspondences were estimated using both code information and epipolar constraints. However, if the extrinsic parameters of the projector are unknown or have large errors, the epipolar constraint cannot be used. To deal with this problem, we separated the matching measure into graph similarity measure and epipolar-constraint measure. The graph similarity measure represents the similarities between nodes of two graphs, and the epipolar-constraint measure represents the fulfillment of epipolar constraints between the nodes. Correspondences of the nodes are estimated by the weighted sum of those two measures. This strategy can be applied both with unknown or known extrinsic parameters. For a system with unknown extrinsic parameters, the weight of the epipolar-constraint measure can be set to zero. Once the correspondences are estimated, auto-calibration can be processed. Then, the correspondences can be re-estimated using the calibrated extrinsic parameters as shown in Fig. 2.

As shown in Fig. 3, The layer operation of a GCN is applied to a data matrix $H^{(l)}$, where l-th layer feature vectors of all the grid points are stacked to one matrix of $N \times 12$, where N is the number of the grid points and 12 is the dimension of feature vectors (2D for relative positional information, 4D for code information including unknown, and 6D for marker information including unknown). The operation produces $H^{(l+1)}$, which is $(l+1)$-th layer data matrix.

It can be represented as

$$H^{(l+1)} = f(H^{(l)}, A, W^{(l)}) = \sigma(\hat{D}^{-1/2}\hat{A}\hat{D}^{-1/2}H^{(l)}W^{(l)}), \tag{1}$$

where $\hat{A} = A+I$ is the adjacency matrix of graph G with added self-connections, I is the identity matrix, $\hat{D}$ is the degree matrix of $\hat{A}$, $W^{(l)}$ is the Weight matrix of this layer, and σ is an activation function (ReLU).

In [1], the network is an undirected graph, but in the case of this research, the information of a grid point can be obtained from adjacent nodes of 4 directions of top, bottom, right and left, and information from different directions has different meanings. Thus, for treating the 4 directions differently, we set A_0, A_1, A_2, A_3 as the adjacency matrix of the directed graph that includes only the connections of top, bottom, right, and left directions, respectively. Calculation of $H^{(l+1)}$ is performed by the following formula.

$$H^{(l+1)} = \sum_{d=0}^{3} f(H^{(l)}, A_d, W_d^{(l)}), \tag{2}$$

where $W_d^{(l)}$ is the weight matrix of layer l specific to direction $d \in \{0, 1, 2, 3\}$.

After repeating Eq. (2) and batch normalization by 5 times, D_e dimensional feature embeddings are calculated from $H^{(5)}$ by a fully connected linear transformation.

As shown in Fig. 4, both the detected grid graph $\mathbf{G}_d$ and the projected grid graph $\mathbf{G}_p$ are processed with the same GCN, producing feature embedding matrix of $\mathbf{F}_d$ with size $N_d \times D_e$, and $\mathbf{F}_p$ with size $N_p \times D_e$, where N_d and N_p are the numbers of grid points of $\mathbf{G}_d$ and $\mathbf{G}_p$. Then $\mathbf{F}_d\mathbf{F}_p^\top$ becomes the matrix with cosine similarities of the feature embeddings between the nodes of these graphs. By taking argmax $(\text{softmax}(\mathbf{F}_d\mathbf{F}_p^\top))$ where argmax and softmax are row-wise, we can estimate the mapping from nodes of the detected grid graph to nodes of the projected pattern graph.

Training of the GCN is done in a supervised manner. First, a graph structure is extracted from an actual endoscopic image using U-Net. Separately, for the same endoscopic image, the class IDs of both vertical and horizontal lines are manually annotated as shown in Fig. 5 (right), which are used as teacher data. The GCN is trained by using the cost function of cross-entropy between softmax $(\mathbf{F}_d\mathbf{F}_p^\top)$ and the teacher data labels.

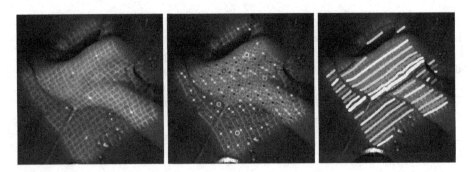

Fig. 5. Training data for GCN: (left) a sample image; (middle) a grid detection result; (right) annotated column ID.

6   Correspondence Estimation Using Epipoloar Constraints

In the proposed system, the correspondence estimation can be done both with and without epipolar constraints. If the extrinsic parameters are known, epipolar constraints are taken into account.

The approach is simple. The similarity measure matrix $\mathbf{M}_s$ is defined to be softmax $(\mathbf{F}_d\mathbf{F}_p^\top)$. It includes similarities for all the node pairs between $\mathbf{G}_d$ and $\mathbf{G}_p$. For each of the pairs, epipolar constraint can be calculated. Let the distance between the epipolar line of j-th node of $\mathbf{G}_p$ and the 2D position of i-th node of $\mathbf{G}_d$ be $Dist(i,j)$, then the epipolar constraint measure matrix M_e is defined by

$$(\mathbf{M}_e)_{i,j} \equiv -\{max(Dist(i,j) - T_e, 0)\}^2 \tag{3}$$

where T_e is the margin of epipolar constraints so that epipoloar-constraint errors that are smaller than T_e do not affect the measure.

Then the total measure $\mathbf{M}_t$ is

$$\mathbf{M}_t \equiv \mathbf{M}_s + w_e\mathbf{M}_e \tag{4}$$

where w_e is the weight for the epipolar constraints. The correspondences are estimated by row-wise argmax of $\mathbf{M}_t$. Epipolar constraints can be switched on and off by setting w_e to a plus value and zero.

7   Auto-calibration of the Projector and 3D Reconstruction

In the proposed system, we assume that the extrinsic parameters are not known, because medical doctors can freely insert the projector to the endoscope and capture the image. Thus, we auto-calibrate the extrinsic parameters as shown in Fig. 2.

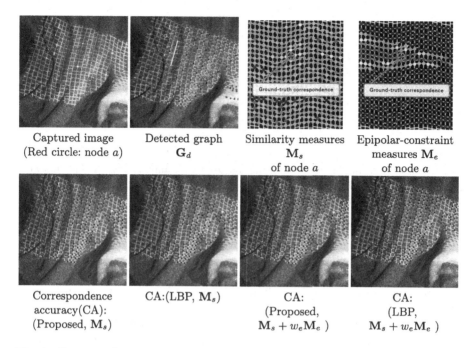

Fig. 6. Correspondence estimation results of sample image A, using the proposed method and LBP [2]. Blue/red dots in correspondence accuracy images mean correct (blue)/incorrect (red) correspondence estimations. (Color figure online)

First, correspondences are estimated with $w_e = 0$. Then, the extrinsic parameters are estimated so that the epipolar constraints are fulfilled. To deal with outlier correspondences, the RANSAC algorithm is used.

In this process, we use a model of projector pose proposed in [4], where most of the projector pose is explained as one-dimensional translation along the instrument channel and rotation about the center-line of the channel. Such restriction also allows the scale to be determined, which is normally impossible for auto-calibration, and leads to stabilization of the auto-calibration.

After extrinsic parameters are estimated, correspondences are estimated with w_e to be a plus value so that the epipolar constraints are taken into account. These correspondences are used for 3D reconstruction.

8   Experiments

We implemented the proposed method, and trained the GCN using 49 images of real bio-tissues and a phantom model that is not the phantom in Fig. 1. $D_e = 96$ and $N_p = 21 \times 21$. The intermediate dimensions between the GCN layers were all 96. Then, we captured images of the colon phantom shown in Fig. 1 and processed the correspondence estimation. For evaluation, we manually annotated ground-truth correspondences, similarly to making the training data for the GCN.

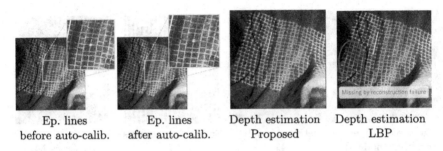

| Ep. lines | Ep. lines | Depth estimation | Depth estimation |
| before auto-calib. | after auto-calib. | Proposed | LBP |

Fig. 7. Auto-calibration and depth estimation results of sample image A. The first and second images show epipolar lines of bright markers. The bright markers should be on the epipolar lines. Depth estimation is visualized with heat map colors.

We compared the proposed method with LBP [2]. LBP is processed on graph $\mathbf{G}_d$. Data cost was defined by using the node-wise match of codes between $\mathbf{G}_d$ and $\mathbf{G}_p$, and regularization cost was defined by using the adjacencies of $\mathbf{G}_p$. In this experiment, we applied three iterations for the LBP-based correspondence estimation.

Figure 6 shows the correspondence estimation results for sample image A. Figure 7 shows the result of auto-calibration and the depth estimation. Figure 8 shows results for other sample images, B and C, and the accuracy rates of correspondence estimation are shown in Table 1. The execution times in CPU implementation for the correspondence estimation was about 0.09 s for the proposed method, and about 0.6 s for LBP.

The results show that the proposed method is comparable or outperform LBP, while the execution time was significantly smaller. Since LBP explicitly models the continuity of matching nodes of graphs, LBP tends to perform better for continuous graphs. On the other hand, GCN-calculated embedding tends to be more robust against discontinuity of the graphs. LBP sometimes makes mistakes for multiple adjacent nodes in a certain area at the same time, as can be seen in Fig. 6. Both results of the proposed method and LBP were improved by the additional epipolar constraints after auto-calibration (Fig. 6 and Table 1: $\mathbf{M}_s$ vs. $\mathbf{M}_s + w_e \mathbf{M}_e$).

In Table 1, the correspondence accuracies obtained by using the method of Furukawa et al. [7] is also compared with the proposed method. This method does not use the similarity calculation instead, directly predicts the node IDs using a GCN. Specifically, the method iterates 21 classification problems of the node ID estimation for each column and row, respectively. The result of Sample A shows that, without the epipolar constraint, the accuracy rate of the proposed method (0.909) is slightly lower than the method [7] (0.917). The epipolar constraint improves correspondence accuracy in the proposed method (0.986). In addition, the proposed method outperforms in Sample B and Sample C, which shows that the similarity calculations is more stable than the direct estimation method [7].

Using the proposed method, the total performance of the 3D endoscope was about 7 frames per second, which was semi-realtime.

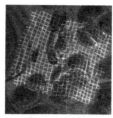

Sample B: Captured image

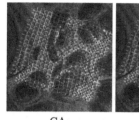  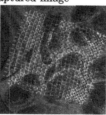 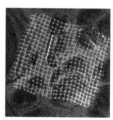

CA:	CA:	CA:	Estimated depth:
Proposed,	LBP,	Direct ID prediction,	Proposed,
$\mathbf{M}_s + w_e\mathbf{M}_e$	$\mathbf{M}_s + w_e\mathbf{M}_e$	[7]	$\mathbf{M}_s + w_e\mathbf{M}_e$

Sample C: Captured image

CA:	CA:	CA:	Estimated depth:
Proposed,	LBP,	Direct ID prediction,	Proposed,
$\mathbf{M}_s + w_e\mathbf{M}_e$	$\mathbf{M}_s + w_e\mathbf{M}_e$	[7]	$\mathbf{M}_s + w_e\mathbf{M}_e$

Fig. 8. 3D measurement results of sample B (top) and C (bottom): Visualization of correspondence accuracies (CA) and depth estimation. Blue/red dots in correspondence accuracy images mean correct (blue)/incorrect (red) correspondence estimations. (Color figure online)

Table 1. Accuracy rates of correspondence estimation

	Proposed, $\mathbf{M}_s$	LBP, $\mathbf{M}_s$	Proposed, $\mathbf{M}_s + w_e\mathbf{M}_e$	LBP, $\mathbf{M}_s + w_e\mathbf{M}_e$	Direct ID prediction [7]
Sample A	0.909	0.760	**0.986**	0.819	0.917
Sample B	0.857	0.904	**0.981**	0.948	0.817
Sample C	0.634	0.641	**0.777**	0.741	0.607

9 Conclusion

In this paper, we propose an efficient correspondence estimation method using GCN-calculated node-wise code-feature embedding for an active-stereo-based 3D endoscope. The proposed correspondence estimation works well without epipolar constraints. Using the characteristics, self-calibrating, semi-realtime 3D endoscope was realized. The proposed correspondence estimation method was compared with the loopy belief propagation and the direct ID prediction method, and shown to be comparable or to outperform in accuracy, and outperform significantly in computational cost.

References

1. Defferrard, M., Bresson, X., Vandergheynst, P.: Convolutional neural networks on graphs with fast localized spectral filtering. In: Advances in Neural Information Processing Systems, pp. 3844–3852 (2016)
2. Felzenszwalb, P.F., Huttenlocher, D.P.: Efficient belief propagation for early vision. Int. J. Comput. Vision **70**(1), 41–54 (2006)
3. Furukawa, R., et al.: Simultaneous shape and camera-projector parameter estimation for 3D endoscopic system using CNN-based grid-oneshot scan. Healthcare Technol. Lett. **6**(6), 249–254 (2019)
4. Furukawa, R., et al.: 2-DOF auto-calibration for a 3d endoscope system based on active stereo. In: 2015 37th Annual International Conference of the IEEE Engineering in Medicine and Biology Society (EMBC), pp. 7937–7941. IEEE (2015)
5. Furukawa, R., Mizomori, M., Hiura, S., Oka, S., Tanaka, S., Kawasaki, H.: Wide-area shape reconstruction by 3D endoscopic system based on CNN decoding, shape registration and fusion. In: Stoyanov, D., et al. (eds.) CARE/CLIP/OR 2.0/ISIC -2018. LNCS, vol. 11041, pp. 139–150. Springer, Cham (2018). https://doi.org/10.1007/978-3-030-01201-4_16
6. Furukawa, R., Morinaga, H., Sanomura, Y., Tanaka, S., Yoshida, S., Kawasaki, H.: Shape acquisition and registration for 3d endoscope based on grid pattern projection. In: Leibe, B., Matas, J., Sebe, N., Welling, M. (eds.) ECCV 2016. LNCS, vol. 9910, pp. 399–415. Springer, Cham (2016). https://doi.org/10.1007/978-3-319-46466-4_24
7. Furukawa, R., et al.: Fully auto-calibrated active-stereo-based 3d endoscopic system using correspondence estimation with graph convolutional network, vol. 2020, pp. 4357–4360 (2020). https://doi.org/10.1109/EMBC44109.2020.9176417

8. Geurten, J., Xia, W., Jayarathne, U., Peters, T.M., Chen, E.C.S.: Endoscopic laser surface scanner for minimally invasive abdominal surgeries. In: Frangi, A.F., Schnabel, J.A., Davatzikos, C., Alberola-López, C., Fichtinger, G. (eds.) MICCAI 2018. LNCS, vol. 11073, pp. 143–150. Springer, Cham (2018). https://doi.org/10.1007/978-3-030-00937-3_17

9. Kawasaki, H., Furukawa, R., Sagawa, R., Yagi, Y.: Dynamic scene shape reconstruction using a single structured light pattern. In: 2008 IEEE Conference on Computer Vision and Pattern Recognition, pp. 1–8. IEEE (2008)

10. Liu, X., et al.: Self-supervised learning for dense depth estimation in monocular endoscopy. In: Stoyanov, D., et al. (eds.) CARE/CLIP/OR 2.0/ISIC -2018. LNCS, vol. 11041, pp. 128–138. Springer, Cham (2018). https://doi.org/10.1007/978-3-030-01201-4_15

11. Ma, R., Wang, R., Pizer, S., Rosenman, J., McGill, S.K., Frahm, J.-M.: Real-time 3D reconstruction of Colonoscopic surfaces for determining missing regions. In: Shen, D., et al. (eds.) MICCAI 2019. LNCS, vol. 11768, pp. 573–582. Springer, Cham (2019). https://doi.org/10.1007/978-3-030-32254-0_64

12. Mahmood, F., Chen, R., Durr, N.J.: Unsupervised reverse domain adaptation for synthetic medical images via adversarial training. IEEE Trans. Med. Imaging 37(12), 2572–2581 (2018)

13. Mahmood, F., Durr, N.J.: Deep learning and conditional random fields-based depth estimation and topographical reconstruction from conventional endoscopy. Med. Image Anal. 48, 230–243 (2018)

14. Maurice, X., Albitar, C., Doignon, C., de Mathelin, M.: A structured light-based laparoscope with real-time organs' surface reconstruction for minimally invasive surgery. In: 2012 Annual International Conference of the IEEE Engineering in Medicine and Biology Society, pp. 5769–5772. IEEE (2012)

15. Nagakura, T., Michida, T., Hirao, M., Kawahara, K., Yamada, K.: The study of three-dimensional measurement from an endoscopic images with stereo matching method. In: 2006 World Automation Congress, pp. 1–4. IEEE (2006)

16. Rau, A., et al.: Implicit domain adaptation with conditional generative adversarial networks for depth prediction in endoscopy. Int. J. Comput. Assist. Radiol. Surg. 14(7), 1167–1176 (2019). https://doi.org/10.1007/s11548-019-01962-w

17. Ronneberger, O., Fischer, P., Brox, T.: U-net: convolutional networks for biomedical image segmentation. In: Navab, N., Hornegger, J., Wells, W.M., Frangi, A.F. (eds.) MICCAI 2015. LNCS, vol. 9351, pp. 234–241. Springer, Cham (2015). https://doi.org/10.1007/978-3-319-24574-4_28

18. Salvi, J., Pages, J., Batlle, J.: Pattern codification strategies in structured light systems. Pattern Recogn. 37(4), 827–849 (2004)

19. Schmalz, C., Forster, F., Schick, A., Angelopoulou, E.: An endoscopic 3D scanner based on structured light. Med. Image Anal. 16(5), 1063–1072 (2012)

20. Song, L., Tang, S., Song, Z.: A robust structured light pattern decoding method for single-shot 3D reconstruction. In: 2017 IEEE International Conference on Real-time Computing and Robotics (RCAR), pp. 668–672. IEEE (2017)

21. Stoyanov, D., Scarzanella, M.V., Pratt, P., Yang, G.-Z.: Real-time stereo reconstruction in robotically assisted minimally invasive surgery. In: Jiang, T., Navab, N., Pluim, J.P.W., Viergever, M.A. (eds.) MICCAI 2010. LNCS, vol. 6361, pp. 275–282. Springer, Heidelberg (2010). https://doi.org/10.1007/978-3-642-15705-9_34

22. Visentini-Scarzanella, M., Sugiura, T., Kaneko, T., Koto, S.: Deep monocular 3D reconstruction for assisted navigation in bronchoscopy. Int. J. Comput. Assist. Radiol. Surg. 12(7), 1089–1099 (2017)

23. Zagoruyko, S., Komodakis, N.: Learning to compare image patches via convolutional neural networks. In: Proceedings of the IEEE Conference on Computer Vision and Pattern Recognition, pp. 4353–4361 (2015)
24. Žbontar, J., LeCun, Y.: Stereo matching by training a convolutional neural network to compare image patches. J. Mach. Learn. Res. **17**(1), 2287–2318 (2016)
25. Zhang, L., Curless, B., Seitz, S.M.: Rapid shape acquisition using color structured light and multi-pass dynamic programming. In: Proceedings. First International Symposium on 3D Data Processing Visualization and Transmission, pp. 24–36. IEEE (2002)
26. Zhang, Z.: Microsoft Kinect sensor and its effect. IEEE MultiMedia **19**, 4–12 (2012). https://www.microsoft.com/en-us/research/publication/microsoft-kinect-sensor-and-its-effect/

Uncalibrated Photometric Stereo Using Superquadrics with Cast Shadow

Takumi Nasu, Tsuyoshi Migita$^{(\boxtimes)}$, and Norikazu Takahashi

Okayama University, Okayama, Japan
migita@cs.okayama-u.ac.jp

Abstract. Formulated as an inverse problem of computer graphics, inverse rendering (or photometric stereo) can estimate parameters, such as the shapes and configurations of objects and light sources in the scene, from a set of images. Such results can be useful for applications including recognition, inspection, and/or VR. In the present paper, we extend previous studies in such a way as to incorporate more complex image formation models, specifically superquadrics with cast shadows, that are implemented on a standard graphics API and verify the framework on synthetic and real-world data.

Keywords: Inverse rendering · Uncalibrated photometric stereo · Superquadrics · Levenberg-Marquardt method · Cubic equation · Cast shadow · Computer graphics

1 Introduction

Inverse rendering [1–6] is a method for obtaining information from a set of images and is formulated as an inverse problem of computer graphics, i.e., inverse rendering estimates scene parameters, such as object shapes and/or the positions of light sources. If the parameters of both the objects and the lighting condition are estimated simultaneously, inverse rendering is referred to as an uncalibrated photometric stereo method [1,3–5]. Such methods can separate the characteristics of the objects from environment-related effects and have various applications, such as object recognition/inspection, photogrammetry, autonomous vehicles, and realization of VR space. An inverse problem is usually expensive in terms of computation, involving iterated application of corresponding forward calculation, which, in this case, is image generation of computer graphics. In the present paper, we implement and verify a framework of inverse rendering that has the potential to make use of GPU-accelerated graphics APIs, possibly with some of a vast variety of complicated graphics algorithms, instead of depending on CPU- or GPGPU-based image generation as was the case previously [1,4]. Specifically, in the present paper, we proposed the use of superquadrics [7] of some limited parameters, with cast shadows taken into account, in order to address the problems reported in a previous study [1] that the estimation is deteriorated by cast shadows and that quadratic surfaces are not sufficient for approximating a wide variety of shapes observed in the real world.

Supported by JSPS KAKENHI Grant Number 20K11866.

© Springer Nature Switzerland AG 2021
H. Jeong and K. Sumi (Eds.): IW-FCV 2021, CCIS 1405, pp. 267–280, 2021.
https://doi.org/10.1007/978-3-030-81638-4_22

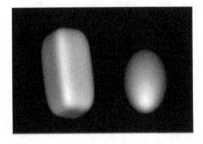

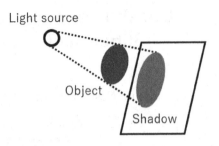

Light source

Object

Shadow

Fig. 1. Examples of superquadrics   **Fig. 2.** Example of cast shadow

2   Basic Formulation of Uncalibrated Photometric Stereo

First, the basic formulation of inverse rendering [1,4] is introduced. Let p be a vector consisting of parameters to be estimated, such as the shape of the object and the position of the light source. The vector p is estimated by searching for parameters that best approximate the input images, and the quality of the approximation is evaluated by a cost function $E(p)$:

$$E(p) = \sum_{f,i} |r_{fi}|^2 = |r|^2, \tag{1}$$

where r is a residual vector consisting of the residual vectors for each pixel for each image (with pixel index i and image index f) and is given as

$$r^T = (\cdots, r_{0,i}^T, r_{1,i}^T, \cdots, r_{fi}^T, \cdots, r_{F-1,i}^T, r_{0,i+1}^T, \cdots), \tag{2}$$

and

$$r_{fi} = e_{fi} - e'_{fi}, \tag{3}$$

which is the difference between the intensity calculated from the estimated parameters e_{fi} and that of the input image e'_{fi}. Here, f is an integer in $0 \leq f \leq F - 1$, where F is the number of input images, and i is an integer in $0 \leq i \leq I - 1$, where I is the number of effective pixels. In the present paper, we extend/modify the method described in [1] in several ways. (a) Dealing with superquadric surfaces. Despite the basic formulation, the differences of intensity values alone are not sufficient for uncalibrated photometric stereo estimation, in which the contours of the object do not match between the input and estimated images. In such cases, we cannot even define a meaningful difference. Therefore, instead of using intensity differences, an alternative function was introduced for pixels near the object contours, and the function was basically the signed distance from the contour of a conic (quadratic surface). We extend this to a quartic (fourth-order) superquadric. Figure 1 shows examples of superquadrics. (b) The synthesized image intensities e_{fi} are computed using a standard computer graphics library [8] to make use of a GPU, rather than using a CPU-based implementation as was previously the case. The drawback is that the intensity values can be stored in at most single-precision accuracies, which may be inadequate for several numerical algorithms. Therefore, the sufficiency of this method for uncalibrated photometric stereo estimation should be verified. In the experiments, various linear algebra operations are calculated in double precision, whereas their inputs, i.e., image intensities, are calculated in single precision. (c) Using a graphics library, there is a possibility that inverse rendering can be applied to very complicated image generation models. In the present paper, cast shadows are taken into account. Figure 2 shows an example of a cast shadow. In fact, the shadow computation requires the same type of ray tracing as the aforementioned alternative function, and hence their source codes have a lot in common.

2.1   Superquadric Surfaces and Coordinate Systems

We use the superquadric surface equation as follows:

$$\Phi = \left|\frac{x}{a}\right|^r + \left|\frac{y}{b}\right|^s + \left|\frac{z}{c}\right|^t - 1 = 0, \tag{4}$$

where $(x, y, z)^T$ represents the coordinates of the point of interest in the object coordinate system (object coordinates), and the set of parameters (a, b, c) satisfies $a > 0$, $b > 0$, and $c > 0$. In the present paper, the parameters (r, s, t) all take identical values of either 2 or 4 only. The left-hand side of Fig. 1 shows the case in which $r = s = t = 4$, and the right-hand side of the figure shows the case in which $r = s = t = 2$.

Using an orthographic camera at the coordinate origin, assuming that the image coordinates are denoted by (u, v) and the depth of the pixel is denoted by w, the object coordinates $(x, y, z)^T$ are expressed as follows using a rotation matrix $\boldsymbol{R}$ and the position $\boldsymbol{c} = (c_x, c_y, c_z)^T$:

$$\begin{pmatrix} x \\ y \\ z \end{pmatrix} = \boldsymbol{R} \begin{pmatrix} u - c_x \\ v - c_y \\ w - c_z \end{pmatrix}. \tag{5}$$

2.2   Rendering Superquadric Surfaces

In standard graphics libraries, an object is usually approximated as a set of triangles. Care must be taken in our estimation scenario, i.e., how to treat the shape of a superquadric, because the parameters are not fixed, but rather change with time. Therefore, instead of using a pre-calculated superquadrics, a unit sphere is given as the graphics pipeline input, and a vertex shader [8] transforms the sphere into designated superquadrics, which are then projected onto the image plane. In the transformation, each vertex should be scaled so that the vertex satisfies (4) or

$$(\sigma\xi)^r + (\sigma\eta)^s + (\sigma\zeta)^t = 1, \tag{6}$$

where (ξ, η, ζ) is a vertex on the unit sphere and σ is the vertex-wise scale, which is easy to obtain when $r = s = t = 2$ or 4. At the same time, the surface normal is calculated by normalizing the following vector:

$$
N = \begin{pmatrix} \frac{\partial}{\partial u} \\ \frac{\partial}{\partial v} \\ \frac{\partial}{\partial w} \end{pmatrix} \varPhi \left(R^T \begin{pmatrix} u - c_u \\ v - c_v \\ w - c_w \end{pmatrix} \right). \tag{7}
$$

3   Image Generation Model

3.1   Shading Model

Based on the Lambertian reflection model [9], the intensity of each pixel is expressed as

$$
e = \begin{cases} L^T N \cdot C \cdot S & \text{if } L^T N > 0 \\ 0 & \text{otherwise,} \end{cases} \tag{8}
$$

where e is the intensity (a vector with three elements (r, g, b) ranging from 0 to 1), L is a three-dimensional unit vector pointing to the light source from the point of interest (hereinafter referred to as the light source vector), N is a unit normal vector at the point, and C is the intrinsic color of the point. When the inner product of L and N is negative, the pixel is black ($e = 0$) because the point is not lit by the light.

In addition, S describes whether the pixel is in a cast shadow, i.e., $S = 1$ if there are no objects between the point and the light source, otherwise S is smaller than 1, say 0.5. A specific method is described later in Sect. 3.2 to determine whether a superquadric exists between a point and a light source.

3.2   Contour of the Superquadric Surface and Its Cast Shadow

We describe how to check whether a ray intersects with a superquadric. Consider a straight line $x = x_1 + w x_0$ or a semi-straight line with $w \geq 0$, where $x_1 = (x_1, y_1, z_1)^T$ is the starting point and $x_0 = (x_0, y_0, z_0)^T$ is the direction, both are described in the object coordinate system of the superquadric of interest. Then, consider a function

$$
\varPhi(w) = \left| \frac{x_1 + x_0 w}{a} \right|^r + \left| \frac{y_1 + y_0 w}{b} \right|^s + \left| \frac{z_1 + z_0 w}{c} \right|^t - 1 = 0, \tag{9}
$$

which is quadratic or quartic in w. The former case is rather trivial, and so we focus on the latter case.

There are at most two real solutions w to (9) for a convex surface, i.e., when $\min(r, s, t) \geq 1$. If there is no real solution to (9), then the straight line does not intersect with the object, and if $w \geq 0$, then the object is on the semi-straight line. However, rather than checking the number of real solutions of (9), it is easier to calculate

$$
\min_w \varPhi(w), \tag{10}
$$

because this involves a cubic (third-order) equation $(d/dw)\Phi = 0$, not quartic (fourth-order) equation. In addition, the cubic equation has only one real solution, because it is monotonically increasing, because Φ has only one minimum. Let w^* be the w that gives the minimum value of Φ and is obtained by, for example, a method described in the next subsection. The ray intersects the superquadric if $w^* \geq 0$ and $\Phi(w^*) \leq 0$. This condition is used for two purposes in the present paper and is implemented in fragment shaders.

i. Signed Distance from the Contour

Using a semi-straight line passing through a pixel (u, v) on the image plane from the camera, where $w \geq 0$ represents the area in front of the camera, the value $\Phi(w^*)$ is 0 if the pixel (u, v) is on the 2d contour of the superquadrics, whereas the value approximates the signed distance from the contour if the pixel is sufficiently near the contour. This value will be referred to later herein as $D(u, v)$.

ii. Cast Shadow

In order to determine whether a point on the object surface is a cast shadow, the semi-straight line should start at the point of interest towards the light source (at infinity, in the present paper). In this case, if $w^* \geq 0$ and $\Phi(w^*) \leq 0$, then the point is shadowed by the superquadric, because the superquadric is between the point and the light source.

3.3 Solving a Monotonically Increasing Cubic Equation

Consider solving a cubic equation (coefficients in this subsection should not be confused with superquadratic parameters (a, b, c))

$$f(x) = ax^3 + bx^2 + cx + d = 0. \tag{11}$$

Although it is well known [10] that there are analytic solutions to a general cubic equation, also known as Cardano's Method, it may be very complicated or numerically unstable, especially in the case of single-precision operations. Fortunately, since we are only interested in solving monotonically increasing cubic equations, which have only one real solution, the analytic solution does not involve any trigonometric functions nor complex numbers, as described below.

The equation is translated and scaled as

$$f_2(y) = y^3 + 3py - 2q = 0, \tag{12}$$

where

$$y = x + b/(3a), \tag{13}$$
$$3p = 3(3ac - b^2)/(9a^2), \tag{14}$$
$$2q = 2(9abc - 2b^3 - 27a^d)/(54a^3). \tag{15}$$

Since $f(x)$ is monotonically increasing, so is $f_2(y)$, and therefore $p \geq 0$ because $f_2'(y) = 3y^2 + 3p \geq 0$.

If $q = 0$, then the real solution is $y = 0$.

Otherwise, the solution takes the form $y = s - p/s$ because it is straightforward to show that

$$f_2(s - p/s) = (s^3 - p^3/s^3) - 2q = 0, \tag{16}$$

which is essentially a quadratic equation in s^3, and thus

$$s^3 = q \pm \sqrt{q^2 + p^3}. \tag{17}$$

In addition, the s^3 is always a real number, because $p \geq 0$. The sign should be chosen in order to avoid cancellation. Hence, the solution of (11) is

$$x = -b/(3a) + s - p/s \quad \text{where} \quad s = \text{sign}(q)\left(|q| + \sqrt{q^2 + p^3}\right)^{1/3}, \tag{18}$$

which is optimized for implementation on a vertex shader, where the power function does not accept a negative argument.

4   Minimization Method

4.1   Levenberg-Marquardt Method

The Levenberg-Marquardt method [11,12] (hereinafter referred to as the LM method) is used to solve the nonlinear minimization problem of (1). In this method, the estimated parameter p is updated by a correction amount Δp, as follows:

$$p \leftarrow p - \Delta p, \tag{19}$$

where

$$\Delta p = (J^T J + M)^{-1}(J^T r), \tag{20}$$

and M is a diagonal matrix that is used as a regularization term in order to prevent the LM method from diverging. The details of the M are described in Sect. 4.6.

The matrix J is a Jacobian matrix:

$$J = \left(\frac{\partial r}{\partial p_0}, \frac{\partial r}{\partial p_1}, \cdots\right), \tag{21}$$

with $p = (p_0, p_1, \cdots)^T$.

4.2   Elements of p

The vector p contains parameters of multiple objects and positions of a moving light source. All of these parameters are estimated simultaneously by iterations of (19). More precisely, the vector p consists of (a_m, b_m, c_m) in (4), parameters of the rotation matrix R_m and translation vector $(c_{mx}, c_{my}, c_{mz})^T$ for each object (m^{th} object), and the light source vector for each input image $(L_0, L_1, \cdots, L_{F-1})$.

A rotation matrix R is parametrized by a quaternion [13] as

$$R = \frac{1}{|q|^2} \begin{pmatrix} q_0^2 + q_1^2 - q_2^2 - q_3^2 & 2(q_1 q_2 - q_0 q_3) & 2(q_1 q_3 + q_0 q_2) \\ 2(q_1 q_2 + q_0 q_3) & q_0^2 - q_1^2 + q_2^2 - q_3^2 & 2(q_2 q_3 - q_0 q_1) \\ 2(q_1 q_3 - q_0 q_2) & 2(q_2 q_3 + q_0 q_1) & q_0^2 - q_1^2 - q_2^2 + q_3^2 \end{pmatrix}, \tag{22}$$

where $|q|^2 = q_0^2 + q_1^2 + q_2^2 + q_3^2$.

4.3   Finite Difference for Jacobian

Each column of J is approximated as a finite difference as

$$\frac{\partial r}{\partial p_k} = \frac{r(p + \varepsilon b_k) - r(p - \varepsilon b_k)}{2\varepsilon}, \tag{23}$$

where b_k is a vector with the same dimension as p, where the value of the kth row is 1, and the other values are 0. A single fixed value of ε may not be appropriate, when there are huge differences among magnitudes of parameters, namely shape parameters (a, b, c), rotation matrix R, translation vector c (the object index m is omitted here for simplicity), and light source vector L_f. Hence, as shown in (24), (a, b, c) and c are multiplied by different factors, s_1 or s_2, respectively, so that these scaled quantities have values near $[-1 : 1]$, which is the range of (q_0, q_1, q_2, q_3) and unit light source vectors:

$$p = (s_1 a, s_1 b, s_1 c, q_0, q_1, q_2, q_3, s_2 c_x, s_2 c_y, s_2 c_z, l_{00}, l_{01}, l_{02}, \cdots)^T. \tag{24}$$

With such a normalization, $\varepsilon = 2^{-7}$ is appropriate for any element.

4.4   Average Image as a Reflectance Map

Since the target objects are often textured, the reflectance C in (8) is a function $C(u, v)$ and is not known in advance. Instead, the function is approximated by the average of the input images. We denote the intensity of each pixel in the average image by m_i. Then, the reflectance C in (8) is $C(u, v) = m_i$, where (u, v) are the coordinates of the ith pixel, and

$$m_i = \frac{\sum_f e'_{fi}}{F}. \tag{25}$$

Note that, a texture is usually associated with object vertices and changes its appearance according to the pose of the object. In our case, on the other hand, a texture, or the reflectance map, is associated with the image pixels and does not change regardless of the pose the object takes, because associating with image pixels rather than object vertices is simpler and suffices as we assume that the camera and objects are fixed during the acquisition of input images.

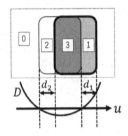

Fig. 3. Pixel distinction based on the contours of the input images and estimated superquadric surfaces

4.5 Dealing with Contour Mismatch

Each pixel is classified into one of four classes, as shown in the Venn diagram in Fig. 3, where areas 1 and 3 represent the target object in the input image, and areas 2 and 3 represent the estimated superquadric surface. Then, the residual r_{fi} is defined differently for each class. For class 3, r_{fi} is defined as (3). For class 0, $r_{fi} = 0$. For classes 1 and 2, r_{fi} is defined as proportional to $D(u, v)$ defined in Sect. 3.2. The multiplicative factors differ as follows in order to balance the magnitude of $D(u, v)$ and the differences given by (3):

$$r_{fi} = \begin{cases} h_1 \cdot D(u, v) \cdot (1, 1, 1)^T & \text{for class-1} \\ h_2 \cdot D(u, v) \cdot (1, 1, 1)^T & \text{for class-2} \end{cases}, \tag{26}$$

where h_1 and h_2 are multiplicative factors. In the present paper, coincidentally $h_1 = h_2 = 1$. The lower part of Fig. 3 illustrates a typical behavior of $D(u, v)$ with respect to coordinate u. The term d_1 represents the width of class-1 pixels, and d_2 represents that of class-2 pixels. The figure shows that, as the width of d_1 or d_2 increases, the value of $|D|$ becomes larger. Therefore, the cost function is minimized when these contours are aligned as closely as possible, i.e., the number of pixels classified as class-1 or -2 should be minimized.

4.6 Diagonal Terms

The diagonal matrix M in (20) is defined as follows:

$$M = \text{diag}(\mu_0, \mu_1, \cdots, \mu_{N-1}), \tag{27}$$

where N is the dimension of p. The matrix M is added to $J^T J$ in (20), so that $J^T J + M$ is not rank deficient and prevents the LM method from diverging. Furthermore, it is known [12] that larger values of the diagonal elements of M result in smaller values of the correction amount Δp in (20). In other words, convergence is slow. Conversely, smaller diagonal element values of M result in larger values of correction Δp. In other words, convergence is fast. In the present paper, the values of the diagonal elements of M are determined manually in advance and gradually decrease during iterations.

Table 1. Initial values of diagonal terms

	a	b	c	q_0	q_1	q_2	q_3	c_x	c_y	c_z	$\boldsymbol{L}$
Simulation	10^7	10^7	10^7	10^9	10^9	10^9	10^9	10^9	10^9	10^9	10^9
Grapes	10^7	10^7	10^7	10^9	10^9	10^9	10^9	10^9	10^9	10^9	10^9
Popsicles	10^8	10^8	10^8	10^{10}	10^{10}	10^{10}	10^{10}	10^9	10^9	10^9	10^8

5 Experimental Results

5.1 Datasets

We evaluated the proposed method using a set of simulated images and two sets of real-world images, as shown in Figs. 4, 10, and 16. These datasets are referred to as the Simulation, Grapes, and Popsicles datasets, respectively. Each of these figures shows four images taken from a fixed viewpoint under different lighting conditions. The target objects in Figs. 4 are superquadric surfaces with a stripe texture. Figure 10 shows images of a bunch of grapes placed on a sheet of black drawing paper, and Fig. 16 shows images of two Popsicles placed on a black foam styrene box. The real-world images were taken by a fixed camera (Grapes) and a fixed smart phone (Popsicles). The sizes of the images are 384×288, 374×250, and 412×226 pixels, for each dataset. The ground truth parameters, including light positions and reflectance map, are only available for the Simulation dataset.

5.2 Initial Values

Figures 7, 13, and 19 are the average images created from Figs. 4, 10, and 16, respectively, and are used as the reflectance maps. The initial values for estimation were manually given so that the superquadric surfaces would be fairly close to the target objects in the input images. Basically, the initial values of light source vectors were uniformly $(0, 0, 1)^T$. However, if there is a cast shadow in the image, the initial values of light source vectors were chosen so as to produce a similar shadow. With this set of parameters, the initial images shown in Figs. 5, 11, and 17 are synthesized. The elements of the diagonal matrix M were determined, as shown in Table 1, according to some preliminary experiments.

5.3 Results

Simulation. Figure 6 shows the estimated images after 100 iterations. We can verify that the approximation accuracy is improved from the initial value, in that the shades, shadows, and contour shapes in Fig. 6 are much closer to the input images in Fig. 4 as compared to the initial estimation in Fig. 5. Moreover, Fig. 9 shows the estimated light sources after 100 iterations. There are four light positions corresponding to four input images, and O is the position of the object $(0, 0, 0)^T$. Figure 9 shows that the light sources moved from the initial

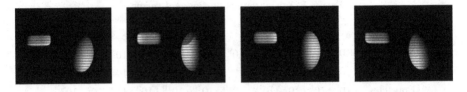

Fig. 4. Input images of the Simulation dataset

Fig. 5. Synthesized images of the Simulation dataset under initial values

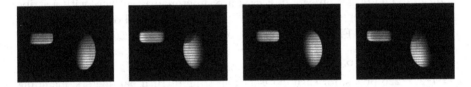

Fig. 6. Synthesized images of the Simulation dataset after 100 iterations

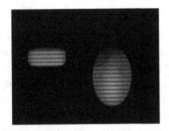

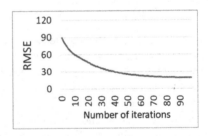

Fig. 7. Average image used in the Simulation dataset

Fig. 8. Root mean square error of the
Simulation dataset

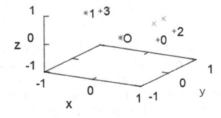

Fig. 9. Estimated light sources with ground truths in the Simulation dataset

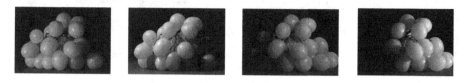

Fig. 10. Input images of the Grapes dataset

Fig. 11. Synthesized images of the Grapes dataset under initial values

Fig. 12. Synthesized images of the Grapes dataset after 100 iterations

Fig. 13. Average image of the Grapes dataset

Fig. 14. Target berries of the Grapes dataset

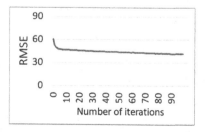

Fig. 15. Root mean square error of the Grapes dataset

Fig. 16. Input images of the Popsicles dataset

Fig. 17. Synthesized images of the Popsicles dataset under initial values

Fig. 18. Synthesized images of the Popsicles dataset after 100 iterations

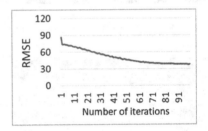

Fig. 19. Average images of the Popsicles dataset

Fig. 20. Root mean square error of the Popsicles dataset

positions, most of which are at $(0, 0, 1)^T$. The +-signs are the estimated light source positions, and the ×-signs are the ground truth positions. We can see that the light sources moved closer to the ground truth positions, but did not perfectly match them. Note that, since a distant light model is used in the present paper, the figure shows only the orientation of the light sources. Figure 8 shows the transition of the root mean square error (RMSE), which is expressed as $||r'||/\sqrt{2F \cdot 3I'}$, where r' and I' are residuals and the number of pixels classified as class-3 only, respectively. Figure 8 shows that the RMSE decreased significantly up until the 50th iteration. After that, the changes in the RMSE and each element of the parameter p were relatively small. We can also see a limitation of the current formulation. Generally speaking, estimation from a simulation dataset is expected to produce a perfect reconstruction of the parameters free from errors. However, although we are conducting such an ideal experiment here, the resulting parameters are not exactly the same as the ground truth. One of the reasons is that the average image is used as the reflectance map. The map should also be estimated, rather than fixed as in the experiments. In fact, we observed that a better result was obtained if the ground truth reflectance map was used.

Grapes. We focus only on two out of several of the individual berries photographed in the images in Fig. 10. Figure 14 shows the berries of interest, and Fig. 12 shows the estimated berries after 100 iterations. Figure 12 is clearly improved from the initial estimation in Fig. 11. In particular, by comparing the right-most images of Fig. 10 and Fig. 12, we can see that the shadow of the result image is similar to that of the input image. The RMSE transition is shown in Fig. 15. The RMSE quickly decreases until the eighth iteration. After that, the changes in the RMSE and each element of the parameter p were relatively small.

Popsicles. A superquadric with $r = s = t = 4$ is a rectangular object with rounded edges. As real-world examples of such shapes, we chose images of Popsicles. In Fig. 16, two Popsicles are placed so that the cast shadow appears in one image. After 100 iterations, parameters are estimated so that the resulting images in Fig. 18 become more similar to the input images in Fig. 16. We can confirm that the cast shadow appears in the right-most image, similar to the input image. Figure 20 shows the RMSE transition for the Popsicles dataset. The RMSE decreased significantly at the first iteration and then gradually up until the 60th iteration. After that, the changes in the RMSE and each element of the parameter p were much smaller. There are several reasons why the RMSE of the Popsicles images is larger than that of the Simulation images. (a) The input images are brighter, and absolute differences tend to be large for such images. (b) The shadow in the right-most input image does not have sharp edges because the light source is too close to the left-hand Popsicle, and such soft shadows require a very complicated rendering model. (c) The Popsicles in the images are more rectangular than the superquadric surfaces we used. Therefore, the method should accept much larger values for r, s, and t.

6 Conclusions

In the present paper, we proposed an uncalibrated photometric stereo method using superquadric surface models with cast shadows taken into account. We verified the proposed method using not only a set of simulated images but also two sets of real images, and the proposed method estimated the parameters of the superquadric surfaces of the target objects, as well as the light source positions. Future areas of research include generalizing superquadrics parameters, estimating the albedo map, and using more complex graphics models/algorithms for reflection, projection, and lighting.

References

1. Nasu, T., Migita, T., Shakunaga, T., Takahashi, N.: Uncalibrated photometric stereo using quadric surfaces with two cameras. In: Ohyama, W., Jung, S.K. (eds.) IW-FCV 2020. CCIS, vol. 1212, pp. 318–332. Springer, Singapore (2020). https://doi.org/10.1007/978-981-15-4818-5_24

2. Ramamoorthi, R., Hanrahan, P.: A signal-processing framework for inverse rendering. SIGGRAPH **2001**, 117–128 (2001)

3. Shi, B., Mo, Z., Wu, Z., Duan, D., Yeung, S.-K., Tan, P.: A benchmark dataset and evaluation for Non-Lambertian and uncalibrated photometric stereo. IEEE Trans. Pattern Anal. Mach. Intell. (TPAMI) **41**(2), 271–284 (2019)

4. Migita, T., Ogino, S., Shakunaga, T.: Direct bundle estimation for recovery of shape, reflectance property and light position. In: Forsyth, D., Torr, P., Zisserman, A. (eds.) ECCV 2008. LNCS, vol. 5304, pp. 412–425. Springer, Heidelberg (2008). https://doi.org/10.1007/978-3-540-88690-7_31

5. Belhumeur, P.N., Kriegman, D.J., Yuille, A.L.: The bas-relief ambiguity. Int. J. Comput. Vision **35**(1), 33–44 (1999)

6. Matusik, W., Pfister, H., Brand. M., McMillan, L.: A data-driven reflectance model. ACM Trans. Graph. **22**(3), 759–769 (2003)

7. Barr, A.H.: Superquadrics and angle-preserving transformations. IEEE Comput. Graphics Appl. **1**(1), 11–23 (1981)

8. https://www.khronos.org/opengl/

9. Koppal, S.J.: Lambertian Reflectance. In: Ikeuchi, K. (ed.) Computer Vision. Springer, Boston (2014). https://doi.org/10.1007/978-0-387-31439-6_534

10. Olver, F.W.J., et al. (eds.): NIST Digital Library of Mathematical Functions. http://dlmf.nist.gov/. Release 1.1.0 of 15 Dec 2020

11. Levenberg, K.: A method for the solution of certain non-linear problems in least squares. Q. Appl. Math. **2**(2), 164–168 (1944)

12. Marquardt, D.: An algorithm for least-squares estimation of nonlinear parameters. SIAM J. Appl. Math. **11**(2), 431–441 (1963)

13. Diebel, J.: Representing attitude: Euler Angles, Unit Quaternions, and Rotation Vectors, Technical report, Stanford University (2006)

Robust Training of Deep Neural Networks with Noisy Labels by Graph Label Propagation

Yuichiro Nomura and Takio Kurita[✉]

Graduate School of Advanced Science and Engineering, Hiroshima University,
Higashi-Hiroshima, Hiroshima 739-8521, Japan
{d202757,tkurita}@hiroshima-u.ac.jp

Abstract. Recent developments in technology, such as crowdsourcing and web crawling, have made it easier to train machine learning models that require big data. However, the data collected by non-experts may contain noisy labels, and training a classification model on the data will result in poor generalization performance. In particular, Deep Neural Networks (DNNs) tend to over-fit to the noisy labels more significantly due to the large number of parameters. In this study, we propose a novel method to train DNNs robustly against the noisy labels by updating the network parameters with the labels corrected by graph label propagation on the similarity graph of training samples. The effectiveness of the proposed method is confirmed by comparing it with baseline MLP and CNNs on the noisy MNIST and CIFAR-10 datasets. Experimental results prove that the proposed method successfully corrects the noisy labels and trains DNNs more robustly than the baseline models.

Keywords: Noisy labels · Deep learning · Graph label propagation

1 Introduction

In recent years, the development of technologies such as crowdsourcing [17] and crawling images and labels from websites [14,16] has made it easier to collect big data. Those techniques have contributed to the development of data-intensive machine learning models such as deep learning [7]. However, those techniques label the data by non-expert labelers when they collect the data, and the labels given may be missing or wrong [14,16,17]. Training a classification model on a dataset with the noisy labels significantly reduces the generalization performance. In particular, Deep Neural Networks (DNNs) has high capability to memorizes the noisy labels due to the large number of parameters. This problem is called the memorization effect [1,9]. Since clean labels in large quantities are not always available in the real world setting, training machine learning models robustly on the noisy labels is an important issue.

Several methods have been proposed in recent research to solve the problem by using DNNs model. Patrini et al. leveraged a noise transition matrix of labels

© Springer Nature Switzerland AG 2021
H. Jeong and K. Sumi (Eds.): IW-FCV 2021, CCIS 1405, pp. 281–293, 2021.
https://doi.org/10.1007/978-3-030-81638-4_23

and incorporate it into the loss function to train the model to estimate the correct labels [10]. Co-teaching [5] prepares two models of DNNs and trains the models by teaching samples without noisy labels to each other. In [11,13,18], the model is robustly trained by updating the noisy labels to reduce the value of loss function during training.

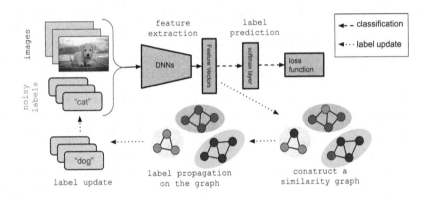

Fig. 1. The illustration of the proposed method.

Our proposed method is a novel approach to train the model robustly by updating the noisy labels during training. The proposed method constructs a similarity graph between the feature vectors output by a hidden layer of DNNs of all samples before the model starts over-fitting to the noisy labels, and performs label noise removal by label propagation on the graph. Then it resumes training the model with the updated label. By repeating these steps during training, the proposed method trains the DNNs robustly and cleans up the noisy labels simultaneously. The illustration of our proposed method is shown in Fig. 1. In this study, we show that the proposed method successfully removes the noisy labels and robustly train the DNNs. We compare the proposed method with the baseline CNN approach on MNIST and CIFAR-10.

2   Related Works

2.1   Deep Neural Networks with Noisy Labels

Several deep learning-based methods have been proposed to solve the image classification with the noisy labels. In addition to co-teaching [5] and pseudo-labeling methods [11,13,18], some methods estimate the transition matrix of the noise to train a robust model. Goldberger et al. proposed a method to model the noise transition matrix by adding a softmax layer to the model, which reduces the effect of label noise while learning [4]. The method proposed by Patrini et al. [10] estimates the noise transition matrix and incorporate it into the loss function so that the model can estimate the correct label.

As well as the proposed method, the following approaches utilize a small set of samples with clean labels. The clean samples are utilized to train a classification model in the framework of semi-supervised learning and remove the noisy labels by the model [2]. The method proposed by Li et al. [8] distills the knowledge from clean labels to learn better model with the noisy labels. The method proposed by Ren et al. [12] reduces the classification loss of the clean samples by reweighting the importance of the training samples with noisy labels.

2.2 Label Propagation for Image Classification

One of the representative methods of machine learning with label propagation based on the similarity between samples is Zhou et al. [19]. The label propagation was used for the semi-supervised learning problem with labeled and unlabeled samples. There are several derivatives of Zhou et al. [19] that use label propagation on graphs in image classification problem with noisy labels [3,15]. These methods differ from the proposed method in that they are trained using hand-made feature extraction methods such as Bag-of-Visual-Words, rather than deep learning features during the training process. A semi-supervised learning method for label propagation on the feature space of deep learning is proposed in [6], but this method does not consider the noisy labels.

3   Robust Training of Deep Neural Networks with Noisy Labels by Graph Label Propagation

3.1   Problem Setting: Classification with Noisy Labels

Here we will introduce the problem setting and the notation of symbols used in the following explanation. Column vectors and matrices are denoted in bold font (e.g. x) and capitals (e.g. X), respectively. Specifically, let 1 be a vector whose elements are all 1. In supervised image classification problem with k classes, we denote a set of n training samples with clean labels as $\mathcal{D}^{\mathrm{GT}} = \{(x_i, y_i^{GT})\}_{i=1}^n = (X, Y^{GT})$ where x_i is a training image and y_i^{GT} is a one-hot vector representation of the ground truth label for the image x_i. We define the set of hard-labels as $\{y_i : y_i \in \{0,1\}^k, 1^\top y_i = 1\}_{i=1}^n$ and the set of soft-labels as $\{y_i : y_i \in [0,1]^k, 1^\top y_i = 1\}_{i=1}^n$. The objective function to be minimized with the true labels is the cross-entropy loss defined as:

$$\mathcal{L} = \frac{1}{n} \sum_{i=1}^n \sum_{j=1}^k y_{ij}^{GT} \log s_j(\theta, x_i), \tag{1}$$

where θ denotes the parameters of DNNs and s is the output vector from the k-class softmax layer of the model.

In this study, we denote a set of n training samples with noisy labels as $\mathcal{D} = \{(x_i, y_i)\}_{i=1}^n = (X, Y)$. Training a classification model by minimizing the objective function Eq. (1) with $\mathcal{D}$ deteriorates its generalization performance and classification accuracy. Also we assume that a small set of clean samples are always available with a minimum effort by experts. We denote a small set of clean samples as $\mathcal{D}^c = \{(\boldsymbol{x}_i^c, \boldsymbol{y}_i^c)\}_{i=1}^{n^c} = \{X^c, Y^c\}$, where n_c is the number of clean samples and $n \gg n^c$.

3.2   Iterative Label Correcting Algorithm

In this subsection, we describe how to train the parameters of the DNNs model robustly against the noisy labels. The noisy labels are corrected by using graph label propagation on the feature space. To make the model more robust to noisy labels, we add a small subset of clean samples to each mini-batch during training of the model with the stochastic gradient descent (SGD) on the loss function. The overall procedure of the proposed method is summarized in Algorithm 1.

Algorithm 1 Training DNNs by iteratively updating $\boldsymbol{\theta}$ and Y

Input: $\mathcal{D} = \{X, Y\}$, $\mathcal{D}^c = \{X^c, Y^c\}$, network parameter $\boldsymbol{\theta}$, epoch t_{start}, $t_{\max}$;

1: **for** $t = 1, 2, \ldots t_{\max}$ **do**
2:     **Update** $\boldsymbol{\theta}^{(t+1)}$ by SGD on $\mathcal{L}(\boldsymbol{\theta}^{(t)} | X, X^c, Y^{(t)}, Y^c)$;
3:     **if** $t \geq t_{start}$ **then**
4:         **Extract** all feature vectors $\{\boldsymbol{h}_i\}_{i=1}^{n'}$ from X and X^c;
5:         **Construct** the similarity matrix $W^{(t)}$ of the feature vectors;
6:         **Compute** the Graph Laplacian $L = I - D^{-1/2}WD^{-1/2}$ where $D_{ii} = \sum_{j=1}^{n'} W_{ij}$
7:         **Finds** $\phi_1, \phi_2, \ldots, \phi_p$, the p eigenvectors with smallest eigenvalue of $L^{(t)}$;
8:         **Update** $Y^{(t+1)}$ by a linear combination of the eigenvectors.
9:     **end if**
10: **end for**
    Output: $\boldsymbol{\theta}^{(t_{\max})}$, $Y^{(t_{\max})}$

Training DNNs with Noisy Labels for Some Epochs. Usually DNNs model in the early stage of training in classification problem is robust against the noisy labels because it only learns simple patterns before it over-fits to the noisy labels. Therefore our proposed scheme trains DNNs model on training dataset with the noisy labels for some epochs ($t < t_{\text{start}}$), and starts correcting the labels before it over-fits ($t \geq t_{\text{start}}$).

Graph Label Propagation on Feature Space. This graph-based label propagation approach is inspired by the semi-supervised method [3]. After the label update starts ($t \geq t_{\text{start}}$), we extract the feature vectors of all training and clean images from the hidden layer of DNNs, specifically the fully-connected layer. The set of feature vectors is denoted as $H = \{\boldsymbol{h}_i\}_{i=1}^{n'}$ where $\boldsymbol{h}_i$ is the extracted feature of i-th image and $n' = n + n^c$.

Then we compute a sparse affinity graph $A \in \mathbb{R}^{n' \times n'}$ whose elements A_{ij} are non-negative pairwise similarities between $\boldsymbol{h}_i$ and $\boldsymbol{h}_j$ as follows:

$$A_{ij} = \begin{cases} \exp\left(-\|\boldsymbol{h}_i - \boldsymbol{h}_j\|/\sigma^2\right) & \text{if } i \neq j \wedge \boldsymbol{h}_j \in \text{NN}_m(i) \\ 0, & \text{otherwise} \end{cases} \tag{2}$$

where NN_m denotes a set of m nearest neighbors in H, and σ is the hyperparameter of RBF kernel. Then we define $W = A^T + A$ as a sparse symmetric adjacency matrix with zero diagonal. The normalized graph Laplacian L is defined as $L = I - D^{\frac{1}{2}} W D^{\frac{1}{2}}$ with diagonal matrix D whose diagonal elements are $D_{ii} = \sum_j W_{ij}$.

Let $\boldsymbol{f} \in \mathbb{R}^{n'}$ be any real valued function on the graph defined above. The smoothness of the function is measured by the following loss function:

$$\boldsymbol{f}^T L \boldsymbol{f} = \frac{1}{2} \sum_{i,j} W_{ij} \left(\frac{1}{\sqrt{D_{ii}}} f_i - \frac{1}{\sqrt{D_{jj}}} f_j \right)^2. \tag{3}$$

Let $\boldsymbol{\psi} \in \mathbb{R}^{n'}$ be any real valued target function on the graph. Then we minimize the following criterion to get $\boldsymbol{f}$ which is a smooth function with respect to graph and agrees with the target signal $\boldsymbol{\psi}$:

$$J(\boldsymbol{f}) = \boldsymbol{f}^T L \boldsymbol{f} + \left(\sum_{i=1}^{n'} \mu_i (f_i - \psi_i)^2 \right) = \boldsymbol{f} L \boldsymbol{f} + (\boldsymbol{f} - \boldsymbol{\psi})^T M (\boldsymbol{f} - \boldsymbol{\psi}) \tag{4}$$

where M is a diagonal matrix whose diagonal elements $M_{ii} = \mu_i$ assign the importance of i-th sample. In the experiment, we assign larger value to the μ of clean sample.

Solving the above problem (Eq. 4) requires expensive computational costs for large n. We can reduce the computational costs by working with a small number of eigenvectors of the graph Laplacian. We denote the sets of p eigenvectors and eigenvalues of the graph Laplacian as $\{\phi_i, \lambda_i\}_{i=1}^p$. Note that the smoothness of the eigenvector ϕ_i on the graph is measured by $\phi_i^T L \phi_i = \lambda_i$. Therefore the eigenvector with smaller eigenvalue is smoother function on the graph. Since any function $\boldsymbol{f} \in \mathbb{R}^{n'}$ can be written as $\boldsymbol{f} = \sum_i \alpha_i \phi_i$, the function will be a linear combinations of the eigenvectors and with smallest eigenvalue.

Therefore we can reduce the dimension of the function by a linear combination of the eigenvectors $\boldsymbol{f} = U\boldsymbol{\alpha}$ where U is a $n' \times p$ matrix whose columns are p eigenvectors with smallest eigenvalues. Then we substitute the reduced function into Eq. (4):

$$J(\boldsymbol{\alpha}) = \boldsymbol{\alpha}^T \Lambda \boldsymbol{\alpha} + (U\boldsymbol{\alpha} - \boldsymbol{\psi})^T M (U\boldsymbol{\alpha} - \boldsymbol{\psi}) \tag{5}$$

where $\Lambda_{ii} = \lambda_i$. The optimal $\boldsymbol{\alpha}$ solves the following $p \times p$ system of equations:

$$(\Lambda + U^T M U)^T \boldsymbol{\alpha} = U^T M \boldsymbol{\psi} \tag{6}$$

Then the prediction signals are computed by $f = U\alpha$.

In our experimental setting, we denote the concatenated matrix of the training and clean one-hot labels as $(Y')^T = (Y^T|(Y^c)^T)$. Each column of Y' is a real valued vector whose elements are in $[0, 1]$. Then we solve the following criterion for matrix A to obtain the smooth functions on the graph for each class j:

$$(\Sigma + U^T M U)^T A = U^T M Y' \tag{7}$$

After we obtain the k smooth functions $F \in \mathbb{R}^{n' \times k}$ on the graph by $F = UA$, each row of training labels Y is updated as follows:

$$\boldsymbol{y}_i = \begin{cases} 1, & \text{if } j = \arg\max_{j'} F_{ij'} \\ 0, & \text{otherwise} \end{cases} \tag{8}$$

While updating the noisy label $\boldsymbol{y}_i$, we used the average predicted labels of the past some epochs as the final updated labels $\boldsymbol{y}_i$ to stabilize the variability of the update labels. The averaged labels are soft-labels and capture the degree of confidence of each sample belongs to a certain class.

Loss Function. The proposed method trains the DNNs model with the following loss function constructed by three terms:

$$\mathcal{L} = \mathcal{L}_n(\boldsymbol{\theta}|X, Y) + \alpha \mathcal{L}_c(\boldsymbol{\theta}|X^c, Y^c) + \beta \mathcal{L}_e(\boldsymbol{\theta}|X) \tag{9}$$

where $\mathcal{L}_n$, $\mathcal{L}_c$, $\mathcal{L}_e$ denote the two classification losses and regularization loss respectively, and α and β are hyper-parameters. In this study, we use the Kullbuck-Leibler(KL) divergence for $\mathcal{L}_n$ and $\mathcal{L}_c$ as follows:

$$\mathcal{L}_n(\boldsymbol{\theta}|X, Y) = \frac{1}{n}\sum_{i=1}^{n} D_{KL}(\boldsymbol{y}_i \| \boldsymbol{s}(\boldsymbol{x}_i, \boldsymbol{\theta})) = \frac{1}{n}\sum_{i=1}^{n}\sum_{j=1}^{k} y_{ij} \log\left(\frac{y_{ij}}{s_j(\boldsymbol{\theta}, \boldsymbol{x}_i)}\right) \tag{10}$$

$$\mathcal{L}_c(\boldsymbol{\theta}|X^c, Y^c) = \frac{1}{n^c}\sum_{i=1}^{n^c} D_{KL}(\boldsymbol{y}_i^c \| \boldsymbol{s}(\boldsymbol{x}_i^c, \boldsymbol{\theta})) = \frac{1}{n^c}\sum_{i=1}^{n^c}\sum_{j=1}^{k} y_{ij}^c \log\left(\frac{y_{ij}^c}{s_j(\boldsymbol{\theta}, \boldsymbol{x}_i^c)}\right) \tag{11}$$

$\mathcal{L}_e$ is the regularization term that concentrates the probability distribution of each soft-label to a single class as follows:

$$\mathcal{L}_e(\boldsymbol{\theta}|X) = -\frac{1}{n}\sum_{i=1}^{n}\sum_{j=1}^{k} s_j(\boldsymbol{\theta}, \boldsymbol{x}_i) \log s_j(\boldsymbol{\theta}, \boldsymbol{x}_i) \tag{12}$$

Because the regularization enforces the soft-label of each image to belong to a single class, each feature vector also tends to belong to a single class and increases the similarity between samples belonging to the same class.

4 Experiments

4.1 Datasets and Settings

Table 1. Summary of datasets used in the experiments.

	# of training	# of clean	# of validation	# of test	# of class
Two-Moon	1000	10	200	200	2
MNIST	20000	100	900	10000	10
CIFAR10	45000	1000	4000	10000	10

We use Two-moon dataset, MNIST and CIFAR10 with noisy labels to evaluate
the proposed method. The sizes of training, clean, validation, and test set for
each dataset are shown in Table 1.

We added artificial label noise to these datasets for evaluation. To add 40%
label noise to the Two-Moon dataset, we randomly select 40% training samples
of the dataset and flip their labels to another class. The left and middle images
in Fig. 2 are the original Two-Moon and the noisy version of Two-Moon, respectively. For MNIST and CIFAR10 dataset, we select r% training samples from
each dataset and randomly assign their labels to one of the ten classes. We added
40% and 80% label noise to each dataset and the label accuracies before label
update are summarized in Table 4.

4.2 Experiments with Two-Moon Dataset

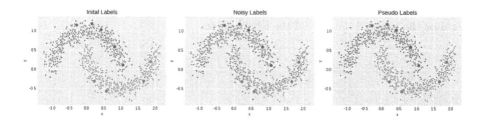

Fig. 2. Images of Two-Moon experiments. **Left**: Original Two-Moon without noisy
labels. The large dot point indicate where the cleans samples are present. **middle**:
Two-Moon dataset with noisy labels. **right**: The pseudo labels after label update at
the end of training.

In the experiment with Two-Moon, we used a 4-layers MLP with 100 units in
each hidden layer. To prevent the over-fitting, weight decay is introduced and
dropout with rate of 0.2 is applied to each hidden layer. The objective function
(Eq. 9) is optimized by SGD with the learning rate 0.01 for 50 epochs. The hyperparameters of the label propagation and the loss function are set as follows:

$\{\sigma^2 = 0.02, m = 10, p = 10, \alpha = 1.0, \beta = 0.4, t_{\text{start}} = 15\}$. As a comparison method, we used the 4-layers MLP trained on the loss function (Eq. 9) without the label update. Our proposed method and the baseline method achieved 99.5% and 95.5% accuracy on the test set, respectively. The pseudo labels output by our proposed method at the end of training are shown in the right image of Fig. 2 and we can verify that our method successfully clean the noisy labels in the noisy version of Two-Moon dataset.

Visualizing Eigenvectors on the Input. In this experiment, we have visualized the eigenvectors $\phi_i \in \mathbb{R}^{n'}$ output during the process of our method to understand how their linear combination cleans up the noisy labels. The eigenvectors in Fig. 3 and Fig. 4 were obtained at the beginning of the label update and end of training, respectively. Each figure shows the first 5 eigenvectors with smallest eigenvalue and the second eigenvector from the left divides the dataset into two classes in the input space. Comparing the two figures, we see that the second eigenvector in Fig. 3 ambiguously classifies the two classes at the boundary of the two clusters, while the second eigenvector in Fig. 4 clearly separates the two clusters. This suggests that the two clusters are clearly separated in the feature space of the MLP at the end of training.

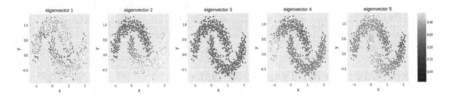

Fig. 3. The first 5 eigenvectors with smallest eigenvalues of the graph laplacian visualized on the input at the start of the label update.

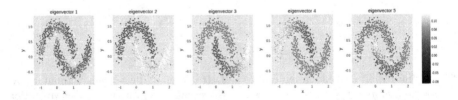

Fig. 4. The first 5 eigenvectors with smallest eigenvalues of the graph laplacian visualized on the input at the end of training.

4.3 Experiments with MNIST and CIFAR10

The MNIST digit dataset consists of 28×28 gray-scale images and the CIFAR-10 dataset consists of 32×32 color images. We randomly split training set of each dataset into training, clean, and validation set as shown in Table 1.

We implement the 4-layers MLP for MNIST and the 9-layers CNN for CIFAR-10. We compare our proposed method (Ours) with the following approaches that have the same architecture as the proposed method and do not update the labels: a model trained on $\mathcal{L}_n$ only (Baseline), a model trained on $\mathcal{L}_n + \mathcal{L}_c$ (Baseline+clean), and a model trained on $\mathcal{L}_n + \mathcal{L}_c + \mathcal{L}_e$ (Baseline+clean+reg).

In the both datasets, all images are normalized to in range of $[-1, 1]$ and data augmentation by vertical and horizontal random flip and random crops after padding 4 pixels. The size of random crop is 28×28 for MNIST and 32×32 for CIFAR-10.

The loss function for DNNs is optimized by SGD with a momentum of 0.9, a weight decay of 10^{-4}, a learning rate of 0.01. In the both datasets, the batch size of the training samples with noisy labels was 100, and the batch size of clean samples were set to 5 and 30 for MNIST and CIFAR-10, respectively. The models were trained for 100 epochs for MNIST, and 400 for CIFAR-10. In the both datasets, we set 0.2 for σ^2, 100 for m, 50 for p. The values of α, β, t_{start} are given by the grid search over the following hyper-parameter spaces: $\alpha = \{0.0, 0.1, 1.0, 10.0\}$, $\beta = \{0.0, 0.1, 1.0, 10.0\}$, $t_{\text{start}} = \{\text{no update}, 20, 40, 60\}$ for MNIST, $t_{\text{start}} = \{\text{no update}, 100, 200, 300\}$ for CIFAR-10. The obtained values are summarized in Table 2.

Table 3 shows the classification accuracy of the proposed method and the other methods for the test set. These results are calculated from the average of five trials of the experiment. It was confirmed that the proposed method achieves better accuracy than the other methods for any noisy rate in all datasets. Table 4 reports the label accuracy before and after updating the labels. It shows that the proposed method succeeds in removing the label noise in the both datasets. Therefore the proposed method is trained on the more accurate labels after the label update and achieves higher classification accuracy on the test set.

Table 2. The hyperparameters for experiments.

Dataset	MNIST		CIFAR-10	
Noise rate (%)	40%	80%	40%	80%
α	0.0	1.0	0.1	0.1
β	1.0	1.0	1.0	1.0
t_{start}	20	20	300	200

Table 3. The classification accuracy on the test set.

#	Method	Test Accuracy (%)					
Dataset		MNIST			CIFAR10		
Noise rate (%)		0	40	80	0	40	80
#1	Baseline	97.61	83.58	44.34	88.95	66.94	29.70
#2	Baseline+clean	97.60	81.53	42.34	89.39	68.39	50.57
#3	Baseline+clean+reg	–	84.67	59.28	–	76.84	64.04
#4	Ours	–	**96.26**	**89.58**	–	**86.05**	**77.78**

Table 4. Label accuracy before and after label update.

#	Noise rate (%)	Label Accuracy (%)			
Dataset		MNIST		CIFAR10	
Label update		Before	After	Before	After
#1	40%	64.05	97.12	64.01	90.03
#2	80%	28.05	89.34	28.02	80.57

Accuracy Curves on the Validation Set. We plot the validation accuracy of the both datasets for each epoch in Fig. 5, 6, 7 and 8. The transparent colored area is the standard deviation of the validation accuracy at each epoch. In the case of MNIST, the Fig. 5 and Fig. 6 plot the validation accuracy with noise rate of 40% and 80%, respectively. While other baseline approaches cause overfitting and gradually reduce the validation accuracy as the training progresses, the validation accuracy of the proposed method remains high after label update.

In the case of CIFAR-10, the Fig. 7 and Fig. 8 plot the validation accuracy with noise rate of 40% and 80%, respectively. The proposed method achieves higher accuracy than the other approaches at the end of training. In the both figures, we can confirm that the validation accuracy spikes immediately after the label update. It was confirmed that the classification accuracy in the validation data was recovered by correcting the label noise.

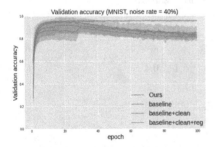

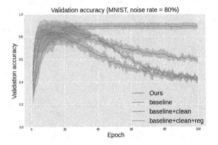

Fig. 5. Validation accuracy on MNIST with noise rate = 40%, $t_{start} = 20$

Fig. 6. Validation accuracy on MNIST with noise rate = 80%, $t_{start} = 20$

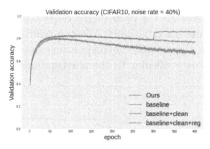

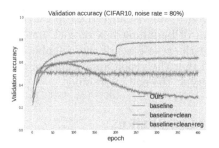

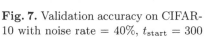

Fig. 7. Validation accuracy on CIFAR-10 with noise rate = 40%, $t_{\text{start}} = 300$

Fig. 8. Validation accuracy on CIFAR-10 with noise rate = 80%, $t_{\text{start}} = 200$

Visualizing the Neighborhoods of Samples in the Feature Space. To see what samples each vertex on the graph has as its neighbors, we visualize the closest neighbors of each sample in the feature space. We used the CIFAR-10 dataset which has the noisy labels with a noisy rate of 80%. At the end of training, we saved the graph W and randomly picked up 6 samples as queries.

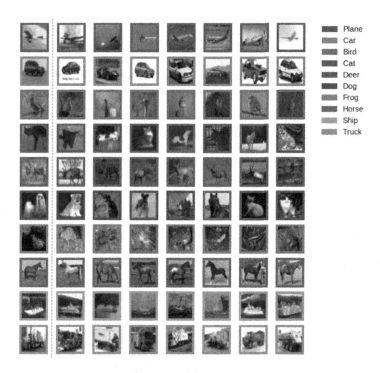

Fig. 9. The leftmost image in each row is the query and the other seven images are neighbors on the feature space of the query. The color of the bounding box of each image represents the true class.

In Fig. 9, we visualize the top 7 neighbors closest to the each query on W. The color of bounding box of each image represents its true label. We can confirm that the true class of the neighbors is almost same as the corresponding query and that the visual appearance of the neighbors is similar to the corresponding query at the end of training.

5   Conclusion

In this work, we proposed a new method to train DNNs robustly against the noisy labels by updating the labels and the network parameters alternately. Our key idea is that we denoise the labels by label propagation on the similarity graph of feature vectors output by the hidden layer of DNNs of training samples. Experimental results proved that the proposed method successfully cleaned the noisy labels and achieved higher test accuracy on the noisy version of MNIST and CIFAR10 than the baseline methods.

References

1. Arpit, D., et al.: A closer look at memorization in deep networks. In: ICML (2017)
2. Ding, Y., Wang, L., Fan, D., Gong, B.: A semi-supervised two-stage approach to learning from noisy labels. In: 2018 IEEE Winter Conference on Applications of Computer Vision (WACV), pp. 1215–1224. IEEE (2018)
3. Fergus, R., Weiss, Y., Torralba, A.: Semi-supervised learning in gigantic image collections. In: Advances in Neural Information Processing Systems, pp. 522–530 (2009)
4. Goldberger, J., Ben-Reuven, E.: Training deep neural-networks using a noise adaptation layer. In: 5th International Conference on Learning Representations, ICLR (2017)
5. Han, B., et al.: Co-teaching: robust training of deep neural networks with extremely noisy labels. In: Advances in Neural Information Processing Systems, pp. 8527–8537 (2018)
6. Iscen, A., Tolias, G., Avrithis, Y., Chum, O.: Label propagation for deep semi-supervised learning. In: Proceedings of the IEEE Conference on Computer Vision and Pattern Recognition, pp. 5070–5079 (2019)
7. LeCun, Y., Bengio, Y., Hinton, G.: Deep learning. Nature **521**(7553), 436–444 (2015)
8. Li, Y., Yang, J., Song, Y., Cao, L., Luo, J., Li, L.J.: Learning from noisy labels with distillation. In: Proceedings of the IEEE International Conference on Computer Vision, pp. 1910–1918 (2017)
9. Ma, X., et al.: Dimensionality-driven learning with noisy labels. In: ICML, pp. 3355–3364 (2018)
10. Patrini, G., Rozza, A., Krishna Menon, A., Nock, R., Qu, L.: Making deep neural networks robust to label noise: a loss correction approach. In: Proceedings of the IEEE Conference on Computer Vision and Pattern Recognition, pp. 1944–1952 (2017)
11. Reed, S., Lee, H., Anguelov, D., Szegedy, C., Erhan, D., Rabinovich, A.: Training deep neural networks on noisy labels with bootstrapping. In: ICLR (2015)

12. Ren, M., Zeng, W., Yang, B., Urtasun, R.: Learning to reweight examples for robust deep learning. In: ICML, pp. 4334–4343 (2018)
13. Tanaka, D., Ikami, D., Yamasaki, T., Aizawa, K.: Joint optimization framework for learning with noisy labels. In: Proceedings of the IEEE Conference on Computer Vision and Pattern Recognition, pp. 5552–5560 (2018)
14. Thomee, B., et al.: YFCC100M: the new data in multimedia research. Commun. ACM **59**(2), 64–73 (2016)
15. Wang, J., Jiang, Y.G., Chang, S.F.: Label diagnosis through self tuning for web image search. In: 2009 IEEE Conference on Computer Vision and Pattern Recognition, pp. 1390–1397. IEEE (2009)
16. Xiao, T., Xia, T., Yang, Y., Huang, C., Wang, X.: Learning from massive noisy labeled data for image classification. In: Proceedings of the IEEE Conference on Computer Vision and Pattern Recognition, pp. 2691–2699 (2015)
17. Yan, Y., Rosales, R., Fung, G., Subramanian, R., Dy, J.: Learning from multiple annotators with varying expertise. Mach. Learn. **95**(3), 291–327 (2014)
18. Yi, K., Wu, J.: Probabilistic end-to-end noise correction for learning with noisy labels. In: Proceedings of the IEEE Conference on Computer Vision and Pattern Recognition, pp. 7017–7025 (2019)
19. Zhou, D., Bousquet, O., Lal, T.N., Weston, J., Schölkopf, B.: Learning with local and global consistency. In: Advances in Neural Information Processing Systems, pp. 321–328 (2004)

Fast Separation of Specular, Diffuse, and Global Components via Polarized Pattern Projection

Yuto Nisaka[1], Ryo Matsuoka[2], Toshiyuki Amano[3], and Takahiro Okabe[1]($\boxtimes$) (ID)

[1] Kyushu Institute of Technology, Iizuka, Japan
okabe@ai.kyutech.ac.jp
[2] The University of Kitakyushu, Kitakyushu, Japan
[3] Wakayama University, Wakayama, Japan

Abstract. In this paper, we propose a method for fast separation of specular, diffuse, and global components of a dynamic scene by using a projector-camera system. Both the direct-global separation using spatially high-frequency patterns and the specular-diffuse separation based on polarization have been studied, but a straightforward combination of those methods has limited temporal resolution. Accordingly, our proposed method rapidly changes not only the spatial patterns but also the polarization states of illumination by using a self-build polarization projector, and captures their effects on a scene by using a high-speed camera. Our method is easy-to-implement, because it does not require projector-camera temporal synchronization and it automatically calibrates the correspondence between the projection pattern and camera pixel. In addition, our method is robust due to the optimized and quickly-shifted projection pattern and the weights for incorporating spatial correlation. We implemented the prototype setup and achieved fast separation with 60 fps.

Keywords: Direct-global separation · Specular-diffuse separation · Projector-camera system · Polarization

1 Introduction

When a scene is illuminated by a light source, the radiance value observed at each point in the scene consists of two components: *direct* and *global* [10]. The direct component such as (direct) *specular* reflection and (direct) *diffuse* reflection is caused by the direct illumination from the light source itself. On the other hand, the global component is caused by the illumination from the other points in the scene due to inter-reflection, subsurface scattering, volumetric scattering, diffusion, and so on. Separating those components of a scene is important for various CV and CG applications such as shape recovery, image-based material editing, and improving image quality [4,9,10,17].

In a *static* scene, we can separate specular and diffuse reflection components on the basis of polarization by using a rotating linear polarizer in front of a

© Springer Nature Switzerland AG 2021
H. Jeong and K. Sumi (Eds.): IW-FCV 2021, CCIS 1405, pp. 294–308, 2021.
https://doi.org/10.1007/978-3-030-81638-4_24

light source and a camera with a fixed linear polarizer [18] or a light source with a fixed linear polarizer and a polarization camera. This is because specular reflection components are polarized but diffuse reflection components are unpolarized. On the other hand, we can separate direct and global components by projecting spatially high-frequency patterns from a projector [10], because the global components are low-frequency in general. Therefore, those techniques can be combined for separating specular, diffuse, and global components of a static scene. Unfortunately, however, a straightforward combination of those techniques is not applicable to dynamic scenes, since the frame rates of off-the-shelf projectors and polarization cameras are not so high in general.

In this paper, we propose a method for fast separation of specular, diffuse, and global components of a *dynamic* scene by using a projector-camera system [1–3,12]. The key idea of our proposed method is to change not only the spatial patterns but also the polarization states of illumination rapidly by using a self-build polarization projector. Our polarization projector is based on a DLP (Digital Light Processing) projector; we replace a rotating color wheel in a DLP projector with a rotating linear polarizer. Then, the image sequence of the scene is captured by using a high-speed camera so that the effects of the rapidly-varying illumination conditions on the scene are observed.

Our proposed method investigates the image sequence of a scene, when the input to our polarization projector is a single high-frequency pattern. Note that the output from the projector rapidly changes in both polarization states and intensities because of the rotating linear polarizer and the temporal dithering [9] due to DMD (Digital Mirror Device) even for a single input pattern. Our method uses a reference object, and then does not require projector-camera temporal synchronization and automatically calibrates the correspondence between the projection pattern and the camera pixel even in a dynamic scene. Furthermore, in order to improve the quality of the separated images, our method optimizes the projection pattern on the basis of noise propagation analysis, makes use of the 3D mode in the side-by-side format of a projector for rapidly shifting the projection pattern, and introduces pixel weights for taking spatial correlation into consideration.

The main contribution of this study is threefold. First, we achieve fast separation of specular, diffuse, and global components with 60 fps by exploiting the rapidly-varying polarization states and the temporal dithering of our self-build polarization projector. Second, our proposed method is easy-to-implement, because it does not require projector-camera temporal synchronization and achieves auto-calibration of the projection pattern-camera pixel correspondence. Third, our method is robust due to the optimized and shifted projection pattern and the incorporated spatial correlation.

The rest of this paper is organized as follows. In Sect. 2, we briefly summarize related work. In Sect. 3, our polarization projector is introduced, and a method for fast separation of specular, diffuse, and global components of a dynamic scene is proposed. We report the experimental results in Sect. 4 and present concluding remarks in Sect. 5.

2   Related Work

2.1   Specular-Diffuse Separation

In general, the reflected light observed on an object surface consists of a diffuse reflection component and a specular reflection component. Shafer [14] proposes a method for specular-diffuse separation based on the difference of their colors. Specifically, the color of a specular reflection component is the same as the color of a light source, but the color of a diffuse reflection component depends on the reflectance of a surface according to the dichromatic reflection model.

We can separate specular and diffuse reflection components on the basis of the low-rank structure of diffuse reflection components under varying light source directions. Specifically, the image of a Lambertian object under an arbitrary directional light source is represented by the linear combination of three basis images of the object [15]. The low-rank structure is used for separating specular and diffuse reflection components of the images taken under a multi-spectral light stage [6].

We can separate specular and diffuse reflection components on the basis of the difference of the polarization states of a specular reflection component and a diffuse reflection component. Specifically, when we observe the reflected light from an object surface illuminated by polarized light, the former is polarized whereas the latter is unpolarized [18]. The polarization-based approach requires a set of images taken by placing linear polarizing filters in front of a light source and a camera, and rotating one of them.

In contrast to the above existing methods, we propose a method for separating specular, diffuse, and global components of a scene by using a projector-camera system. We separate not only specular and diffuse reflection components within direct components but also global components by projecting spatially high-frequency patterns.

2.2   Direct-Global Separation

The direct-global separation reveals how the light radiated from a light source interacts with a scene. Nayar *et al.* [10] propose a method for separating direct and global components in a scene by projecting high-frequency patterns from a projector on the basis of the insight that global components are spatially low-frequency in general.

Gu *et al.* [4] extend the above direct-global separation for a single light source to that for multiple light sources. Specifically, they optimize a set of high-frequency projection patterns in terms of SNR (signal-to-noise ratio) on the basis of illumination multiplexing [13], and then show that it is effective for scene recovery. Mukaigawa *et al.* [8] show that projecting high-frequency patterns is useful also for studying the light transport in scattering media, in particular for decomposing multiple scattering into each bounce component.

In contrast to the above existing methods, we propose a method for separating specular, diffuse, and global components of a scene. In other words, we further separate the direct components into specular and diffuse reflection components on the basis of polarization.

2.3   Active Illumination Using DLP Projector

Narasimhan *et al.* [9] propose a method for separating direct and global components of a dynamic scene by using a DLP projector and a high-speed camera on the basis of the temporal dithering, *i.e.* the rapid changes in intensities due to the DMD in a DLP projector. They show that the temporal dithering is useful also for fast active vision such as structured light-based range finding and photometric stereo.

On the other hand, Han *et al.* [5] propose a method for recovering the spectral reflectance of a moving object by using a DLP projector and a high-speed camera on the basis of the color switch, *i.e.* the rapid changes in colors due to the rotating color wheel in a DLP projector. Maeda and Okabe [7] exploit the rapidly-varying illumination colors due to the color switch of a multi-primary DLP projector, and then propose a method for separating direct and global components of a static scene per primary color of the projector by using an usual camera with a short exposure time. In addition, they propose a method for estimating the SPDs (Spectral Power Distributions) of the primary colors in a non-destructive manner.

Torii *et al.* [17] exploit both the color switch and the temporal dithering of a DLP projector, and achieve the direct-global separation of dynamic scenes per illumination color. Their method is not a straightforward combination of the above existing methods based on the temporal dithering [9] and the color switch [7]. In particular, they realize auto-calibration of the projection pattern-camera pixel correspondence on the basis of the consistency in pixel intensities. Furthermore, they optimize the high-frequency projection pattern on the basis of noise propagation analysis so that it is robust to noises.

In contrast to the above existing methods, in particular to Torii *et al.* [17], we exploit polarization. Specifically, by replacing a rotating color wheel with a rotating linear polarizer, we exploit the rapid changes in not colors but polarization states for fast separation of specular, diffuse, and global components.

3   Proposed Method

3.1   Principle of Direct-Global Separation

Nayar *et al.* [10] propose a method for direct-global separation of a static scene by using a projector-camera system. It exploits the properties of global components, *i.e.* they are spatially low-frequency in general, and studies the images of the scene under high-frequency projection patterns. Specifically, their simplest method uses two images; they are captured when a black-and-white checkered pattern or its negative-positive reversed pattern are projected from a projector to the scene.

Let us denote the two output intensities from a projector corresponding to white and black input intensities of a checkered pattern by a and b, *e.g.* $a = 1$ and $b = 0$. The pixel values observed at a certain point in a scene are given by

$$I^+ = aL_D + \frac{1}{2}(a+b)L_G, \tag{1}$$

$$I^- = bL_D + \frac{1}{2}(a+b)L_G, \tag{2}$$

where L_D and L_G are the direct and global components at the point, and I^+ and I^- are the larger and smaller pixel values observed there, when $a > b$ [9,10]. Therefore, we can obtain the direct component L_D and the global component L_G by solving the simultaneous linear equations in Eq.(1) and Eq.(2), when the pixel values I^+ and I^- and the output intensities from the projector a and b are given.

3.2   Principle of Specular-Diffuse Separation

Wolff and Boult [18] show that specular and diffuse reflection components can be separated on the basis of polarization, since specular reflection components are polarized but diffuse reflection components are unpolarized. Specifically, they propose a method for specular-diffuse separation of a static scene by using a rotating linear polarizer in front of a light source and a camera with a fixed linear polarizer or a light source with a fixed linear polarizer and a rotating linear polarizer in front of a camera. Recently, we can replace the pair of the camera and the rotating linear polarizer with a single polarization camera in the latter setup.

Let us consider the latter case, *i.e.* a light source with a fixed linear polarizer and a rotating linear polarizer in front of a camera. The pixel values observed at a certain point in a scene are given by

$$I_{\max} = L_s + \frac{1}{2}L_d, \tag{3}$$

$$I_{\min} = \frac{1}{2}L_d, \tag{4}$$

where L_s and L_d are the specular and diffuse reflection components at the point, and $I_{\max}$ and $I_{\min}$ are the maximal and minimal pixel values observed there, when the linear polarizer is rotated in front of the camera. Therefore, we can obtain the specular reflection component L_s and the diffuse reflection component L_d by solving the simultaneous linear equations in Eq.(3) and Eq.(4), when the pixel values $I_{\max}$ and $I_{\min}$ are given.

3.3   Self-build Polarization Projector

Both the methods for direct-global separation and specular-diffuse separation require multiple images taken under different spatial patterns and with different polarization states. Note that we still require multiple images taken under

Fig. 1. Our self-build polarization projector based on a DLP projector. The rotating color wheel in the DLP projector is replaced with a rotating linear polarizer.

different spatial patterns, even if we use a polarization camera. Therefore, a straightforward combination of those techniques is not applicable to dynamic scenes, since the frame rates of off-the-shelf projectors and polarization cameras are not so high in general[1].

Accordingly, our proposed method rapidly changes not only the spatial patterns but also the polarization states of illumination by using a self-build polarization projector. Our polarization projector is based on a DLP projector. In a single-chip DLP projector, a color wheel consisting of three (or more) color filters with different spectral transmittances is placed between a white lamp and a DMD. The color wheel rotates at high speed in front of the lamp, and generates various colors by mixing the transmitted lights with different SPDs via time-division multiplexing. Then, the DMD controls the intensity of the light transmitted from the color wheel by temporal dithering; it switches micro mirrors "on" and "off" directions at high speed. We replace the rotating color wheel in a DLP projector with a rotating linear polarizer as shown in Fig. 1; the linear polarizer is installed outside the projector housing in order to prevent heat damage due to the projector lamp.

3.4 Specular-Diffuse-Global Separation

Figure 2(a) shows our setup for separating specular, diffuse, and global components by using a projector-camera system. Specifically, a scene of interest is illuminated by our polarization projector, and its images are captured by using a high-speed camera through a fixed linear polarizer. The input to the projector is a single checkered pattern with two intensities, but the output from the projector rapidly changes in both the polarization states and intensities due to the rotating linear polarizer and DMD respectively.

The propagation of the polarized light is computed by using the Stokes vectors and Mueller matrices. We can derive that the pixel value I_n observed at a certain point in a scene at the n-th frame ($n = 1, 2, 3, ..., N$) is given by

$$I_n = a_n L_s [\cos 2(\chi_n + \phi) + 1] + a_n L_d + \frac{1}{2}(a_n + b_n) L_G \qquad (5)$$

---

[1] See the experimental results and discussion in Sect. 4.3 for more detail.

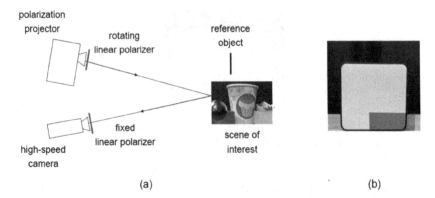

Fig. 2. (a) Our setup for separating specular, diffuse, and global components. A scene of interest is illuminated by our polarization projector, and its images are captured by using a high-speed camera through a linear polarizer. (b) Our reference object; a part of a white diffuse target is covered by a linear polarizer.

or

$$I_n = b_n L_s [\cos 2(\chi_n + \phi) + 1] + b_n L_d + \frac{1}{2}(a_n + b_n)L_G, \qquad (6)$$

when the point is directly illuminated by the checkered pattern with the output intensity of a_n or b_n. Here, L_s, L_d, and L_G are the specular, diffuse, and global components to be estimated, a_n and b_n are the output intensities from the projector, and χ_n and ϕ are the polarization angle of the projected light and the pixel-wise phase of the polarization angle respectively.

Our proposed method assumes that the scene is approximately static while N images are captured by using a high-speed camera, *e.g.* 16 msec in our experiments, and that the output intensities a_n and b_n and the polarization angle χ_n of the projected light are known (see Sect. 3.5 for more detail). Then, our method estimates the specular, diffuse, and global components and the phase of the polarization angle from N images by solving the set of equations in Eq.(5) or Eq.(6). Specifically, we fix the phase ϕ of the polarization angle to a certain value, and then solve the simultaneous linear equations in Eq.(5) or Eq.(6) with respect to L_s, L_d, and L_G by least squares. We change the value of the phase in a coarse-to-fine manner, and find the optimal L_s, L_d, L_G, and ϕ with the minimal least-square errors.

3.5   Auto Spatio-Temporal Calibration

Our proposed method calibrates the output intensities a_n and b_n and the polarization angle χ_n by using a reference object placed in a scene of interest and captured at the same time. It consists of a white diffuse target and a linear polarizer; a part of the white diffuse target is covered by the linear polarizer as shown in Fig. 2(b). Specifically, we calibrate the output intensities a_n and b_n from the pixel values of the white target object and compute the polarization angle χ_n

from the pixel values when the white target object is illuminated and observed through the linear polarizer. Thus, our method calibrates a_n, b_n, and χ_n from the captured images in situ, and therefore it does not require projector-camera temporal synchronization.

In order to solve the set of equations in Eq.(5) or Eq.(6), we need to calibrate the correspondence between the projection pattern and the camera pixel. In other words, we need to known which block, whose output intensity is a_n or b_n, directly illuminates each point in a scene. To this end, we select two images whose polarization angles are almost the same $\chi_n \simeq \chi_m$ and output intensities satisfy $a_n > a_m$, $b_n < b_m$, and $(a_n + b_n) \simeq (a_m + b_m)$, and study the difference between I_n and I_m. Because $(I_n - I_m)$ is proportional to $(a_n - a_m)$ or $(b_n - b_m)$ according to the correspondence between the projection pattern and the camera pixel, we can calibrate the correspondence from the sign of $(I_n - I_m)$.

3.6   Optimizing Projection Pattern

The output intensities from our DLP-based polarization projector, *i.e.* how the output intensities vary due to the temporal dithering depends on the input intensities to the projector. Therefore, we can optimize the two input intensities of the checkered pattern in order to separate specular, diffuse, and global components robustly. We take account of the noises in the observed pixel values, and then optimize those input intensities on the basis of the noise propagation analysis.

Specifically, we study the sum of the condition numbers [11] of the coefficient matrices of the set of equations in Eq.(5):

$$
\begin{pmatrix}
a_1[\cos 2(\chi_1 + \phi) + 1] & a_1 & (a_1 + b_1)/2 \\
a_2[\cos 2(\chi_2 + \phi) + 1] & a_2 & (a_2 + b_2)/2 \\
\vdots & \vdots & \vdots \\
a_N[\cos 2(\chi_N + \phi) + 1] & a_N & (a_N + b_N)/2
\end{pmatrix},
\tag{7}
$$

and in Eq.(6):

$$
\begin{pmatrix}
b_1[\cos 2(\chi_1 + \phi) + 1] & b_1 & (a_1 + b_1)/2 \\
b_2[\cos 2(\chi_2 + \phi) + 1] & b_2 & (a_2 + b_2)/2 \\
\vdots & \vdots & \vdots \\
b_N[\cos 2(\chi_N + \phi) + 1] & b_N & (a_N + b_N)/2
\end{pmatrix},
\tag{8}
$$

where N is the number of the captured images from which we compute the specular, diffuse, and global components of a single frame. The condition number tells how much noises in the observation I_n propagate to the unknowns to be estimated; L_s, L_d, and L_G[2]. We compute the condition numbers for all the pairs of the input intensities in 8 bit (from 0 to 255), and then select the optimal pair of the input intensities from 32,640 $(=\ _{256}C_2)$ pairs. Note that smaller condition number is better.

---

[2] We assume $\phi = 0$ when computing the condition numbers. We tested other values, but the condition numbers were almost constant with respect to ϕ.

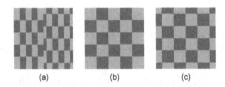

(a)   (b)   (c)

Fig. 3. The 3D mode in the side-by-side format: (a) a single input image, (b) an output image for left eye, and (c) an output image for right eye.

3.7   Use of 3D Mode in Side-by-side Format

The simplest direct-global separation described in Sect. 3.1 uses two projection patterns; one is a black-and-white checkered pattern and the other is its negative-positive reversed pattern. It is known that the simplest method often causes visible artifacts near the boundaries between the blocks of the checkered pattens, because the spatial resolutions of a projector and a camera are limited. Nayar *et al.* [10] show that those artifacts can be reduced by using more than two projection patterns, e.g. spatially shifted patterns from the original checkered patten.

Accordingly, our proposed method makes use of the 3D mode in the side-by-side format, which is relatively common function even for consumer projectors, and then projects two spatially-shifted checkered patterns. When a single image in Fig. 3 (a) is input to the projector, the projector outputs (b) a left-eye image and (c) a right-eye image in turn. Since we can distinguish the two spatially-shifted checkered patterns from the pixel values on the reference object, we can realize the specular, diffuse, and global separation by using spatially-shifted projection patterns in a similar manner to the case without the 3D mode.

3.8   Incorporating Spatial Correlation

In addition to the optimized and quickly-shifted projection pattern in Sect. 3.6 and Sect. 3.7, we further improve the quality of the separated images by taking the spatial correlation into consideration. Specifically, our proposed method solves the set of equations in Eq.(5) or Eq.(6) from not only the pixel values observed at a certain point pixel-wisely but also those at surrounding pixels by weighted least squares.

We introduce a single weight per pixel, *i.e.* per set of equations in Eq.(5) or Eq.(6). The weight is given by the product of three Gaussian weights. The first one depends on the distance between the pixels, and the second one depends on the difference between the pixel values when the output intensities are almost the same, *i.e.* $a_n \simeq b_m$. Therefore, the product of those weights is similar to the weight for the bilateral filter [16]. The third weight has small/large values if the pixel is close to/far from the boundaries between the blocks of the checkered patten. The boundaries are detected from the zero crossing of the difference $(I_n - I_m)$ (see Sect. 3.5 for more detail).

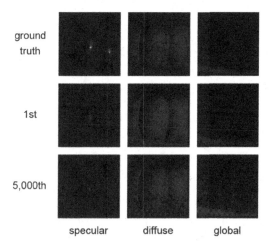

Fig. 4. The ground truth images (top row), our result images using the best (middle row) and the 5,000th best (bottom row) combinations of the input intensities of the checkered pattern.

Table 1. The quantitative comparison of Fig. 4. The numerical values in each cell are the PSNR (upper) and SSIM (lower).

	Specular	Diffuse	Global	Average
Ours:	**30.29**	26.38	**32.85**	**29.84**
1st	0.733	**0.797**	**0.774**	**0.768**
Ours:	30.18	**27.41**	26.82	28.14
5,000th	**0.749**	0.776	0.608	0.711

4   Experiments

4.1   Experimental Setup

In our experiments, we used a self-build polarization projector based on a DLP projector MH534 from BenQ and a high-speed camera Fastcam Mini UX50 from Photron. The 3D mode of the projector quickly switches the left-eye and right-eye images in about 8 msec (about 120 fps), and one revolution of the rotating linear polarizer takes about 14 msec[3]. The frame rate and the exposure time of the high-speed camera were set to 10,000 fps and 0.1 ms respectively. Therefore, our proposed method achieves specular, diffuse, and global separation from about 160 images in about 60 fps. As described in Sect. 3.5, we optimized the pixel intensities of the input checkered pattern, and then set them to 255 and 203 for the left-eye image and 255 and 210 for the right-eye image.

---

[3] The revolving speed is slower than the original color wheel, because our linear polarizer has larger moment.

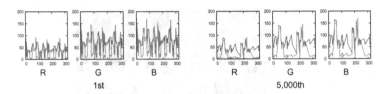

Fig. 5. The output intensities a_n and b_n of each color channel for the 1st and the 5,000th best combinations.

4.2 Experimental Results for Static Scenes

We tested our proposed method on static scenes for quantitative evaluation. In a static scene, we can acquire the ground truth images of specular, diffuse, and global components by using a number of spatially high-frequency patterns. Specifically, we used 50 ($= 2 \times 5 \times 5$) projection patterns; a black-and-white checkered pattern and its reversed pattern were sifted along the horizontal and vertical directions 5 times respectively.

Optimization of Projection Pattern: First, we confirm the effectiveness of the optimized projection pattern. Figure 4 shows the ground truth images (top row), our result images using the best (middle row) and the 5,000th best (bottom row) combinations of the input intensities of the checkered pattern. This scene consists of a plastic pumpkin with specular and diffuse components and cotton with global components. The pixel intensities of the 5,000th best combinations are 169 and 45 for the left-eye image and 215 and 156 for the right-eye image.

We can see that our method using the best combination works better than that using the 5,000th best combination; block artifacts are more visible in the result images using the 5,000th best combination. The PSNR and SSIM of the result images in Table 1 quantitatively show the effectiveness of the optimized projection pattern.

Note that the separation using the 5,000th best combination was not robust; we sometimes could not solve the set of equations in Eq.(5) or Eq.(6) due to ill-conditioned problems, and then some of the result images are collapsed. Figure 5 shows the output intensities a_n and b_n of each color channel for the 1st and the 5,000th best combinations. We can see that the output intensities of the 1st combinations significantly vary and would yield better condition numbers for solving Eq.(5) or Eq.(6).

3D Mode for Shifting Projection Pattern: Second, we confirm the effectiveness of the 3D mode for quickly shifting projection pattern. Figure 6 shows the ground truth images (top row), our result images with (second row) and without (third row) shift. This scene includes a mirror hemisphere with specular components, a paper cup with specular and diffuse components, a ceramic shoe with specular and diffuse components, and a soap with global components.

We can see that line artifacts corresponding to the boundaries between the blocks of the checkered pattern are more visible in the result images without shift.

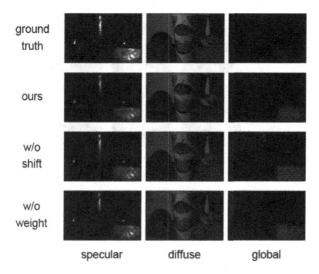

ground truth

ours

w/o shift

w/o weight

specular   diffuse   global

Fig. 6. The ground truth images (top row), our result images (second row) , those without shift (third row) and weight (fourth row).

Table 2. The quantitative comparison of Fig. 6. The numerical values in each cell are the PSNR (upper) and SSIM (lower).

	Specular	Diffuse	Global	Average
Ours	22.44	**24.60**	**25.01**	**24.02**
	0.720	**0.703**	**0.498**	**0.640**
w/o	**22.98**	22.61	21.78	22.46
shift	0.718	0.610	0.358	0.562
w/o	22.81	23.02	22.81	22.88
weight	**0.740**	0.688	0.405	0.611

Comparing the PSNR and SSIM of those results in Table 2, the effectiveness of the 3D mode for shifting projection pattern is clear quantitatively.

Weights for Incorporating Spatial Correlation: Third, we confirm the effectiveness of the weights for incorporating spatial correlation. Figure 6 shows the ground truth images (top row), our result images with (second row) and without (fourth row) the weights for incorporating spatial correlation. We empirically set the standard deviations of the Gaussian weights in Sect. 3.8.

We can see that the result images taking spatial correlation into consideration are smoother than those without spatial correlation, *i.e.* pixel-wise separation. Table 2 quantitatively shows the effectiveness of incorporating spatial correlation into specular, diffuse, and global separation.

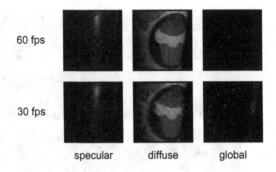

Fig. 7. Our result images with 60 fps (upper) and 30 fps (lower).

4.3   Experimental Results for Dynamic Scenes

Our proposed method achieves fast separation of specular, diffuse, and global components with about 60 fps. Since we capture the effects of the temporal dithering by using a high-speed camera, our method requires only a single projection pattern, *i.e. two* projection patterns in fact: a checkered pattern with gray intensities for the left-eye image and a shifted checkered pattern with gray intensities for the right-eye image.

On the other hand, consumer polarization cameras cannot capture the effects of the temporal dithering, because their frame rates are not so high. Then, separating specular, diffuse, and global components by using a pair of a polarized light source and a polarization camera requires projector-camera temporal synchronization and *four* projection patterns; a black-and-white checkered pattern, its negative-positive reversed pattern, and their shifted patterns. Therefore, the frame rate of the polarization camera-based method is half in theory, if a projector has the same frame rate as ours.

Accordingly, we compared the performance of our proposed method for varying temporal resolution. Figure 7 shows the result images with 60 fps and 30 fps. The latter corresponds to the frame rate of the polarization camera-based method. The object is a paper cup in motion. We can see that the texture on the paper cup is blurred due to motion in the result images with 30 fps. This result demonstrates the advantage of our method over the polarization camera-based method.

4.4   Application to Image-Based Material Editing

As a direct application of our specular, diffuse, and global separation, we conducted image-based material editing. Specifically, we synthesized various image sequences by linearly combining the separated components with different weights; s, d, and g for the specular, diffuse, and global components. Figure 8 shows the original and synthesized images of a single frame; the glossiness and translucency are edited in the images at the upper and lower rows respectively.

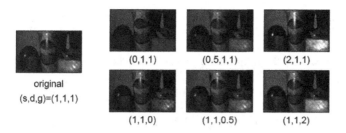

Fig. 8. Application to image-based material editing. The glossiness (upper) and translucency (lower) are edited.

We can see that our proposed method is effective for photorealistic image-based material editing.

5   Conclusion and Future Work

We proposed a fast, robust, and easy-to-implement method for separating specular, diffuse, and global components of a dynamic scene by using a projector-camera system. Specifically, our proposed method exploits the rapidly-varying illumination conditions due to both the rotating linear polarizer and the temporal dithering. We conducted a number of experiments using our prototype setup and showed the effectiveness of our method and its components: the optimization of projection pattern, the use of the 3D mode for quickly shifting projection pattern, and the weights for incorporating spatial correlation. Our future study includes the extension to colored and polarized pattern projection; we can integrate a color wheel and a linear polarizer into a single colored and polarized filter for multispectral and polarimetric scene analysis.

Acknowledgments. This work was supported by JSPS KAKENHI Grant Numbers JP20H00612 and JP17H01766.

References

1. Amano, T.: Shading illusion: a novel way for 3-D representation on the paper media. In: Proceedings PROCAMS2012 (2012)
2. Bimber, O., Iwai, D., Wetzstein, G., Grundhöfer, A.: The visual computing of projector-camera systems. Comput. Graph. Forum **27**(8), 2219–2245 (2008)
3. Grossberg, M., Peri, H., Nayar, S., Belhumeur, P.: Making one object look like another: controlling appearance using a projector-camera system. In: Proceedings IEEE CVPR2004, pp. I-452-459 (2004)
4. Gu, J., Kobayashi, T., Gupta, M., Nayar, S.: Multiplexed illumination for scene recovery in the presence of global illumination. In: Proceedings IEEE ICCV2011, pp. 691–698 (2011)
5. Han, S., Sato, I., Okabe, T., Sato, Y.: Fast spectral reflectance recovery using DLP projector. IJCV **110**(2), 172–184 (2014)

6. Kobayashi, N., Okabe, T.: Separating reflection components in images under mul-tispectral and multidirectional light sources. In: In Proceedings ICPR2016, pp. 3199–3204 (2016)
7. Maeda, K., Okabe, T.: Acquiring multispectral light transport using multi-primary DLP projector. In: Proceedings of IPTA2016, pp. 1–6 (2016)
8. Mukaigawa, Y., Yagi, Y., Raskar, R.: Analysis of light transport in scattering media. In: Proceedings of IEEE CVPR2010, pp. 153–160 (2010)
9. Narasimhan, S.G., Koppal, S.J., Yamazaki, S.: Temporal dithering of illumination for fast active vision. In: Forsyth, D., Torr, P., Zisserman, A. (eds.) ECCV 2008. LNCS, vol. 5305, pp. 830–844. Springer, Heidelberg (2008). https://doi.org/10. 1007/978-3-540-88693-8_61
10. Nayar, S., Krishnan, G., Grossberg, M., Raskar, R.: Fast separation of direct and global components of a scene using high frequency illumination. Proc. ACM SIG-GRAPH **2006**, 935–944 (2006)
11. Press, W., Teukolsky, S., Vetterling, W., Flannery, B.: Numerical Recipes in C 3rd Edition: The Art of Scientific Computing. Cambridge University Press (2007)
12. Raskar, R., Welch, G., Low, K.-L., Bandyopadhyay, D.: Shader lamps: animating real objects with image-based illumination. In: Gortler, S.J., Myszkowski, K. (eds.) EGSR 2001. E, pp. 89–102. Springer, Vienna (2001). https://doi.org/10.1007/978-3-7091-6242-2_9
13. Schechner, Y., Nayar, S., Belhumeur, P.: A theory of multiplexed illumination. In: Proceedings IEEE ICCV2003, pp. 808–815 (2003)
14. Shafer, S.: Using color to separate reflection components. Color Res. Appl. **10**(4), 210–218 (1985)
15. Shashua, A.: On photometric issues in 3D visual recognition from a single 2D image. IJCV **21**(1/2), 99–122 (1997)
16. Tomasi, C., Manduchi, R.: Bilateral Filtering for Gray and Color Images, pp. 839–846 (1998)
17. Torii, M., Okabe, T., Amano, T.: Multispectral direct-global separation of dynamic scenes. In: Proceedings of IEEE WACV2019, pp. 1923–1931 (2019)
18. Wolff, L., Boult, T.: Constraining object features using a polarization reflectance model. IEEE Trans. PAMI **13**(6), 167–189 (1991)

Saliency Prediction with Relation-Aware Global Attention Module

Ge Cao and Kang-Hyun Jo[✉]

School of Electrical Engineering, University of Ulsan, Ulsan, Republic of Korea
caoge@islab.ulsan.ac.kr, acejo@ulsan.ac.kr

Abstract. The deep learning method has achieved great success in saliency prediction task. Like depth and depth, the attention mechanism has been proved to be effective in enhancing the performance of Convolutional Neural Network (CNNs) in many studies. In this paper, we propose a new architecture that combines encoder-decoder architecture, multi-level integration, relation-aware global attention module. The encoder-decoder architecture is the main structure to extract deeper features. The multi-level integration constructs an asymmetric path that avoid information loss. The Relation-aware Global Attention module is used to enhance the network both channel-wise and spatial-wise. The architecture is trained and tested on SALICON 2017 benchmark and obtain competitive results compared with related research.

Keywords: Saliency prediction · Attention mechanisms · Relation-aware global attention

1 Introduction

Saliency prediction is a very basic research field in computer vision but can be used in many other tasks like object recognition [1], tracking regions of interest [2], image retargeting [3] and so on. For human visual attention, we would pick the most interesting region in your mind the first time when we see a scene. Then our attention will be distracted and begin to notice other things that are more subtle and detailed. These operations effectively help humans focus limited attention on key information, save visual resources, and obtain the most significant information quickly.

For the saliency prediction task, it describes the spatial location of an image that attracts the observer most. For traditional saliency prediction, some low-level features such as color, texture, and semantic concepts. Obviously, these kinds of methods cannot achieve satisfactory performance. With the development of CNNs, saliency prediction task can also use deep learning method to train complicated models thanks to generous data-driven methods and large scale annotated datasets [4]. And many works [5] achieved great results in saliency prediction tasks.

© Springer Nature Switzerland AG 2021
H. Jeong and K. Sumi (Eds.): IW-FCV 2021, CCIS 1405, pp. 309–316, 2021.
https://doi.org/10.1007/978-3-030-81638-4_25

To extract deep feature and high-level semantic information, this paper constructs an encoder-decoder architecture to do feature extraction. For enhancing the robustness of the network and avoid information loss by pooling operations in CNNs, and U-Net [6] like architecture, we called multi-level integration is used. Recently, many works resort to attention mechanism and surely obtain better results. In this paper, we propose a new architecture that combines encoder-decoder architecture, multi-level integration, and relation-aware global attention (RGA) module which proposed by [7]. In the paper [7], they proved that both channel-wise relation-aware global attention (RGA-C) module and spatial-wise relation-aware global attention (RGA-S) module improve the performance of the baseline network. As shown in their visualization results we can surely find that the attention mechanism makes the network pay more attention to the discriminative features part. In this paper, we combine the RGA-SC (sequential spatial-channel) module in encoder-decoder architecture and successfully improve the performance of the baseline.

To prove the effectiveness of the architecture proposed by this paper, we compared with [8] which proposed similar architecture with this paper. In [8], the self-attention module is used to enhance the global relation of the final convolutional layer of the encoder. Compared with [8], the experimental results show that using the RGA-SC module could effectively predict the saliency map.

The remaining content is organized as follows. Section 2 summarized the related work. The details of each component in the whole architecture and the loss functions used are introduced in Sect. 3. Section 4 provides the details and results of the experiments. Finally, Sect. 4.4 concludes the paper.

2 Related Work

The traditional methods of saliency prediction task focus on low-level features. Far-reaching work by Itti [9] relied on color, intensity, and orientation maps, and then using Gabor filter to integrate the features to get global saliency feature map. Bruce [10] use low-level local features in combination with information-theoretic ideas. Borji [11] combined low-level features of previous best bottom-up models with top-down cognitive visual features and learn a direct mapping from those features to human eye fixations.

With the continuous development of deep learning techniques and large-scale datasets, the performance of saliency prediction is steadily improving. Most of this success can be attributed to Convolutional architectures. Some work researched to combine CNN with recurrent neural networks [12]. The LSTM architecture makes a great improvement in saliency prediction. And [12] also proposed to use combined evaluation metrics loss to train the model. In attention mechanism fields, Woo [13] use large filter size of 7×7 over the spatial features in their Convolutional Block Attention Module (CBAM) to produce a spatial attention map. Followed by [7,13] proposed Relation-aware Global Attention (RGA) module with spatial-wise and channel-wise sequentially (RGA-SC). Their extensive ablation studies demonstrate that our RGA can significantly enhance the feature representation power.

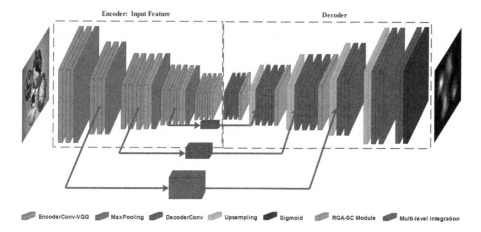

Encoder: Input Feature   Decoder

EncoderConv-VGG   MaxPooling   DecoderConv   Upsampling   Sigmoid   RGA-SC Module   Multi-level Integration

Fig. 1. The overview of the proposed saliency prediction model. The left image is the input image, we use the proposed CNNs architecture to extract feature and process the saliency prediction. The module shown in different color would be introduced in detail in Sect. 3.

3   Proposed Architecture

In this section, we introduce the proposed architecture.

3.1   Overview Structure

The whole architecture of the proposed network is introduced in this subsection. For saliency prediction, the fully convolutional network (FCN) has achieved great performance. To extract the deeper features and high-level semantic information, we need an encoder to decrease the size of the feature map and save computation resources. As shown in Fig. 1, the encoder of the proposed architecture has convolutional layers, max-pooling operations which decrease the size and increase the receptive field, and the RGA-SC module which would introduce in subsection 2. After the process of the encoder, the proposed network obtain a multi-channel tensor which has a smaller size feature map and high-level information. To reduce the size, we use upsampling operations in the decoder and finally get the saliency probability map through the final sigmoid layer.

The size of input images is generally changed to 256 × 256 with initial 3 channels. In the encoder part, except the RGA-SC module, the architecture of the network is identical in architecture to VGG16 [14] except the final max-pooling layer and three fully connected layers. Through the encoder part, the size of the input feature map is changed to 16 × 16, where the RGA-SC module would not change the size of the feature map. For the decoder part, the order of its layer is revered with the encoder with max-pooling operations replaced by upsampling operations to restore the size of the feature map. At the final of the network is a 1 × 1 convolutional layer with sigmoid non-linearity which ultimately produces the predicted saliency map. There also have 3 U-Net like architecture that concatenates the feature maps in the same scale in encoder and decoder, we call multi-level integration (MI) in this paper. Each MI module has 3 convolutional layers followed by ReLU.

3.2 Relation-Aware Global Attention Module

Though the RGA module [7] is proposed to solve problems for other field, we could also draw lessons from it in saliency prediction. In RGA module, spatial-wise Relation-aware Global Attention (RGA-S) and channel-wise Relation-aware Global Attention (RGA-C) are introduced respectively.

Spatial Relation-Aware Global Attention (RGA-S)

Given input tensor $X \in \mathbb{R}^{C \times H \times W}$, where C denotes channel, H denotes height, W denotes width. For learning the spatial attention map of size $H \times W$, RGA-S block is proposed. Taken C-dimensional feature vector at each position as a feature node, so there are $N = H \times W$ nodes. Each feature node of RGA-S can be represented as $\mathbf{x}_i \in \mathbb{R}^C$, where $i = 1, 2, ..., N$.

Then the pairwise relation between i-th node and j-th node can be defined as:

$$r_{i,j} = f_s(\mathbf{x}_i, \mathbf{x}_j) = \theta_s(\mathbf{x}_i)^T \phi_s(\mathbf{x}_j), \tag{1}$$

where θ_s and ϕ_s are both 1×1 convolutional layer followed by bath normalization (BN) and ReLU activation, and BNs are omitted to simplify the equation. Then the pairwise relations for all the nodes can be represented by Affinity Matrix $R_s \in \mathbb{R}^{N \times N}$.

For the i-th feature node, the relation vector can be denoted as:

$$\mathbf{r}_i = [R_s(i,:), R_s(:,i)] \in \mathbb{R}^{2N} \tag{2}$$

To learn the attention of the i-th feature node, they combine the pairwise relations $\mathbf{r}_i$ and the feature node itself to get the spatial relation-aware feature $\tilde{y}_i$:

$$\tilde{y}_i = [pool_c(\psi_s(\mathbf{x}_i)), \varphi_s(\mathbf{r}_i)] \in \mathbb{R}^{1+N/s_1}, \tag{3}$$

where ψ_s and φ_s are both 1×1 convolutional layer followed by BN and ReLU activation, $pool_c$ denotes global average pooling along the channel dimension to reduce the channel of the input tensor to 1.

For mining valuable information from the spatial relation-aware feature $\tilde{y}_i$, two 1×1 convolutional layer W_1 and W_2 followed by BN are implemented to get spatial attention value a_i:

$$a_i = Sigmoid(W_2 ReLU(W_1 \tilde{y}_i)), \tag{4}$$

where W_2 decreases the channel with a ratio and W_2 shrinks the channel to 1 to save computation resources.

Channel Relation-Aware Global Attention (RGA-C)

Similar to RGA-S, when RGA-C get the input tensor $X \in \mathbb{R}^{C \times H \times W}$, they take the $d = H \times W$-dimensional feature map at each channel as a feature node. So each feature node of RGA-C can be represented as $\mathbf{x}_i \in \mathbb{R}^d$, where $i = 1, 2, ..., C$.

Then the pairwise relation between i-th node and j-th node can be defined as:

$$r_{i,j} = f_s(\mathbf{x}_i, \mathbf{x}_j) = \theta_s(\mathbf{x}_i)^T \phi_s(\mathbf{x}_j), \tag{5}$$

where θ_s and ϕ_s are same to RGA-S. Then the pairwise relations for all the nodes can be represented by Affinity Matrix $R_c \in \mathbb{R}^{C \times C}$.

For the i-th feature node, the relation vector can be denoted as:

$$\mathbf{r}_i = [R_c(i, :), R_c(:, i)] \in \mathbb{R}^{2C} \tag{6}$$

Then follow the Eq. (3) and (4), we can get the channel relation-aware feature $\tilde{y}_i$ and channel attention value a_i.

3.3 Multi-level Integration and Loss Function

The proposed architecture employs a U-Net like architecture that symmetrically expands the feature maps after upsampling operations in the decoder. Information vanishing is inevitable Due to the max-pooling operation in the encoder. As shown in Fig. 1, three MI module are combined in the proposed architecture. The input feature map of MI is the feature map before the last three max-pooling operations. Every step of expansion is composed of an upsampling of the feature map and concatenation with the same scale feature map from the encoder. Additionally, three 3×3 convolutional layers with stride 1 padding 1 followed by ReLU are used in each MI.

For the loss function, we follow the paper [8]:

$$L(\hat{\mathbf{I}}, \mathbf{I}) = \alpha KLdiv(\hat{\mathbf{I}}, \mathbf{I}) + \beta CC(\hat{\mathbf{I}}, \mathbf{I}) + \gamma SIM(\hat{\mathbf{I}}, \mathbf{I}), \tag{7}$$

where $\hat{\mathbf{I}}$ and $\mathbf{I}$ are predicted saliency maps and the ground truth, α, β and γ are three coefficients take 10, -1, -1 followed [8].

4   Experiments and Analysis

In this section, we show the details of experiments and comparison results.

4.1   Experimental Setup

We use the largest available dataset SALICON [4] to train and test the proposed model. The dataset consists of 10,000 images for training, 5,000 images for validating and 5,000 images for testing. In this paper, we train the proposed model on SALICON datasets with 10,000 training images and use 5,000 images for validating. All experiments are conducted with the deep learning Pytorch framework. The model trains for 10epochs with the learning rate 1e−4 and reducing after every 3 epochs. The ADAM optimization algorithm is employed to train the whole network. The proposed model is trained with a batch size of 8 on one NVIDIA GeForce GTX 1080Ti GPU with 11 GB memory.

4.2   The Contribution of Each Component

In Table 1, we compare the contribution of each component, where VGGM denotes the original encoder-decoder architecture without multi-level integration and RGA-SC module. VGGM+RGA(1) denotes the original encoder-decoder architecture with only one RGA-SC module which added after the final convolutional layer and symmetrical position. VGG+RGA(1)+MI denotes the previous model plus three multi-level integration. It is obviously that each component effectively enhance the network, we call the model combined with the original encoder-decoder architecture, RGA-SC module and multi-level integration module VGGRGA. Table 2 compare the performance when add different number of RGA-SC module. VGGRGA(n) means there are 2 × n RGA-SC modules in the architecture. VGGRGA(3) is shown as Fig. 1. We don't do the experiments of VGGRGA(4) and (5) is due to the limited computation memory. After all, we can find that even if add more RGA-SC module, the performance would not improve a lot from Table 2.

Table 1. Performance comparison of different version on validation set of Salicon-2017

Model	KLdiv↓	CC↑	SIM↑
VGGM	0.272	0.854	0.745
VGGM+RGA(1)	0.266	0.858	0.748
VGGM+RGA(1)+MI	**0.241**	**0.876**	**0.768**

The results are evaluated by three Evaluation metrics: Kullback-Leibler Divergence (KLdiv), Pearson Cross-Correlation (CC) and Similarity (SIM). Differently from the KLdiv loss which value should be minimized, the CC and the SIM loss is maximized to obtain the higher performance in saliency prediction.

Table 2. Performance comparison of the proposed model with 1, 2, 3 RGA-SC module

Model	KLdiv↓	CC↑	SIM↑
VGGRGA(1)	0.241	0.876	0.768
VGGRGA(2)	0.239	0.876	0.768
VGGRGA(3)	**0.239**	**0.877**	**0.769**

4.3   Comparison with Other Work

VGGSSM [8] is a similar work which using self-attention as enhancing tool to improve the performance of network for saliency prediction task. They use self-attention after the final convolutional layer of encoder to enhance global relation among all the pixels in feature map. We compare the results with them in validation set of Salicon-2017 dataset. And the comparison results show the proposed model obtains competitive performance in saliency prediction. Although RGA module achieved better results in the contest between itself and self-attention module. It is likely that RGA module can stack more in the structure with the same computing source, which leads to better effect. But the advantage of RGA shows that it takes less memory in the calculation (Table 3).

Table 3. Performance comparison with the proposed model and VGGSSM [8]

Model	KLdiv↓	CC↑	SIM↑
VGGSSM	0.251	0.876	0.769
VGGRGA(3)	**0.239**	**0.877**	**0.769**

4.4 Conclusions

In this paper, a saliency prediction model VGGRGA upon encoder-decoder architecture is proposed. The model integrates three important components and the experimental results demonstrate the efficiency of the components. Additionally, this paper also research the results with different numbers of RGA module. Furthermore, we would compare all the attention methods' contribution to saliency prediction task.

Acknowledgement. This work was supported by the National Research Foundation of Korea (NRF) grant funded by the government (MSIT) (No. 2020R1A2C2008972).

References

1. Schauerte, B., Richarz, J., Fink, G.A.: Saliency-based identification and recognition of pointed-at objects. In: 2010 IEEE/RSJ International Conference on Intelligent Robots and Systems, Taipei, pp. 4638–4643 (2010). https://doi.org/10.1109/IROS.2010.5649430
2. Frintrop, S., Kessel, M.: Most salient region tracking. In: 2009 IEEE International Conference on Robotics and Automation, Kobe, pp. 1869–1874 (2009). https://doi.org/10.1109/ROBOT.2009.5152298
3. Saeko, T., Ramesh, R., Michael, G., Bruce, G.: Automatic image retargeting. In: Proceedings of the 4th International Conference on Mobile and Ubiquitous Multimedia, MUM 2005, vol. 154, pp. 59–68 (2005). https://doi.org/10.1145/1149488.1149499
4. Jiang, M., Huang, S., Duan, J., Zhao, Q.: SALICON: saliency in context. In: 2015 IEEE Conference on Computer Vision and Pattern Recognition (CVPR), Boston, MA, pp. 1072–1080 (2015). https://doi.org/10.1109/CVPR.2015.7298710
5. Reddy, N., Jain, S., Yarlagadda, P., Gandhi, V.: Tidying deep saliency prediction architectures (2020). abs/2003.04942
6. Ronneberger, O., Fischer, P., Brox, T.: U-Net: convolutional networks for biomedical image segmentation. arXiv e-prints. arXiv:1505.04597 (2015)

7. Zhang, Z., Lan, C., Zeng, W., Jin, X., Chen, Z.: Relation-aware global attention for person re-identification. In: 2020 IEEE/CVF Conference on Computer Vision and Pattern Recognition (CVPR), Seattle, WA, USA, pp. 3183–3192 (2020). https://doi.org/10.1109/CVPR42600.2020.00325

8. Cao, G., Tang, Q., Jo, K.: Aggregated deep saliency prediction by self-attention network. In: Huang, D.-S., Premaratne, P. (eds.) ICIC 2020. LNCS (LNAI), vol. 12465, pp. 87–97. Springer, Cham (2020). https://doi.org/10.1007/978-3-030-60796-8_8

9. Itti, L., Koch, C., Niebur, E.: A model of saliency-based visual attention for rapid scene analysis. IEEE Trans. Pattern Anal. Mach. Intell. **20**(11), 1254–1259 (1998). https://doi.org/10.1109/34.730558

10. Bruce, N.D.B., Tsotsos, J.K.: Saliency, attention, and visual search: AN information theoretic approach. J. Vis. **9**(3), 5 (2009)

11. Borji, A.: Boosting bottom-up and top-down visual features for saliency estimation. In: 2012 IEEE Conference on Computer Vision and Pattern Recognition, Providence, RI, pp. 438–445 (2012). https://doi.org/10.1109/CVPR.2012.6247706

12. Cornia, M., Baraldi, L., Serra, G., Cucchiara, R.: Predicting human eye fixations via an LSTM-based saliency attentive model. IEEE Trans. Image Process. **27**(10), 5142–5154 (2018). https://doi.org/10.1109/TIP.2018.2851672

13. Woo, S., Park, J., Lee, J.-Y., Kweon, I.S.: CBAM: convolutional block attention module. In: Ferrari, V., Hebert, M., Sminchisescu, C., Weiss, Y. (eds.) ECCV 2018. LNCS, vol. 11211, pp. 3–19. Springer, Cham (2018). https://doi.org/10.1007/978-3-030-01234-2_1

14. Simonyan, K., Zisserman, A.: Very deep convolutional networks for large-scale image recognition. arXiv e-prints. arXiv:1409.1556 (2014)

Author Index

Printed in the United States
by Baker & Taylor Publisher Services